DESIGNING SYSTEMS WITH MICROCOMPUTERS

A Systematic Approach

DESIGNING SYSTEMS WITH MICROCOMPUTERS

A Systematic Approach

M. DAVID FREEDMAN

President
M. David Freedman & Associates, Inc.
and
Adjunct Associate Professor
University of Michigan—Dearborn

LANSING B. EVANS

Senior Project Engineer
Bendix General Aviation Avionics Division

PRENTICE-HALL, INC.
Englewood Cliffs, New Jersey 07632

Library of Congress Cataloging in Publication Data

Freedman, M. David
Designing systems with microcomputers.

Bibliography: p.
Includes index.
1. System design. 2. Microcomputers. 3. PL/M
(Computer program language) I. Evans, Lansing B.
II. Title
QA76.9.S88F73 1983 001.64'25 82-16518
ISBN 0-13-201350-9

The terms *Intel, iSBC,* and *Multibus* are trademarks belonging to the Intel Corporation. They are used in this book to describe Intel products exclusively in accordance with pertinent copyright laws. The Intel *Multibus* is a patented bus structure.

Editorial/production supervision and interior design: Nancy Milnamow
Cover design: Edsal Enterprises
Manufacturing buyer: Gordon Osbourne

Printed in the United States of America

10 9 8 7 6 5 4 3 2 1

ISBN 0-13-201350-9

Prentice-Hall International, Inc., *London*
Prentice-Hall of Australia Pty. Limited, *Sydney*
Editora Prentice-Hall do Brasil, Ltda., *Rio de Janeiro*
Prentice-Hall of Canada Inc., *Toronto*
Prentice-Hall of India Private Limited, *New Delhi*
Prentice-Hall of Japan, Inc., *Tokyo*
Prentice-Hall of Southeast Asia Pte. Ltd., *Singapore*
Whitehall Books Limited, *Wellington, New Zealand*

Contents

Foreword

> *There is a tide in the affairs of men,*
> *Which, taken at the flood, leads on to fortune;*
> *Omitted, all the voyage of their life*
> *Is bound in shallows and in miseries:*
>
> William Shakespeare, *Julius Caesar*, act IV, scene iii, line 217.

At such a moment of opportunity are we, practitioners of systems design, novice or veteran, now poised. That the microprocessor is well afloat, there is no question; that we are prepared in its handling, there may be doubt. Such is the concern of this book: instruction in the systematic design of microprocessor/microcomputer systems.

It is apparent that the rate of growth of computer-based systems has been truly prodigious: Between the late fifties and the early seventies, the number of computer installations doubled and redoubled so often that growth was almost exponential. Subsequently, as microelectronics made a greater impact, emphasis shifted to smaller systems, but to systems in vastly greater quantity. Presently, the market for microprocessors is expanding at a rate which is so rapid that it makes previous growth appear insignificant by comparison. However, such growth has not been without trauma.

A major challenge faced by the computer systems design fraternity has been that of providing an appropriate interface to the rapidly expanding end-user community. The challenge has been in effect to make the computer increasingly transparent to the end user: to provide the required operating function while reducing the need for total computer literacy. Of course, basic to this process have been developments in the process itself: for example, the creation of more powerful and economic tools and techniques for system design.

A major thrust in this recursion has been the rapid growth of microelectronic technology which has rapidly reduced the cost of hardware while, at the same time, has provided enormously enhanced opportunities for programmed customization: larger memories, richer instruction sets, and so on. The difficulty has been that as the cost of hardware has fallen dramatically, the corresponding cost of software customization has not followed at nearly the same rate. The result has been an increasing imbalance in the distribution of costs in a typical microprocessor-based system, the cost of software now far outweighing that of hardware (being estimated at 90% of the total system in 1982).

While economics alone is of concern, representing, as it does, an impediment to the expeditious seizure of the microelectronic opportunity, it is not the most critical factor. Much more critical is the problem of providing people. While the growth of hardware quantity and complexity have each doubled and redoubled at a significant rate, and continue to do so with no insurmountable physical limit apparent, the corresponding growth of system software is limited both at the intellectual and social levels. The difficulty is that each doubling of a hardware opportunity implies a corresponding doubling of the software task. While productivity improvement in the software process remains relatively low, each doubling of demand implies a doubling of person power. Unfortunately, the capacity of our systems of education to provide the appropriate people is sorely limited. Even doubling the number of system/software trainees will not suffice, since the training time is seen to take years and the existing cadre of designers has taken us decades to acquire.

Thus, it is apparent that the solution lies elsewhere, that is, in the enhancement of productivity in the systems/software sector. Such is the topic of this book.

The authors, Freedman and Evans, are designer-educators who have faced the productivity problem at the industrial-academic interface. They provide here a distillation of experience perfected in practice and in pedagogy, a methodology incorporating high-level and structured concepts for the solution of the problem of productivity in microprocessor-based systems design; in short, directions for the productive negotiation of the microelectronics tide.

The course which they have set is an excellent one: This book, their travel planning guide, begins with the important premise that is the user/client who must be served, whose voyage it is, whose goals must be reached. Accordingly, a language natural to the user/client is identified, for establishing early a common language is to avoid ambiguity and the recurrent cost of translation and interpretation, tasks suited more to linguists and lawyers than to creative designers. Subsequently, methodologies are provided for the identification and analysis of client goals and routes by which they can be reached. The continuing emphasis throughout this guide is an overall planning and orderly implementation of these plans within a hardware structure whose functional attributes are emphasized. Modularization is mandated; module integration is insisted. Integration of hardware and software is emphasized. Checkout, test, and maintenance of all aspects of the system are a recurrent theme. As well, recurring examples threaded through the text serve well to integrate all aspects of the plan.

Now that the time is right, and the text is ready, read on! The opportunities for those who make it to microprocessor land are great indeed. Bon voyage!

K. C. Smith

Toronto, Canada

K. C. Smith, B.A.Sc., M.A.Sc., Ph.D, P.Eng., Fellow IEEE. Professor of Electrical Engineering and Department of Computer Science (also Professor of Library and Information Science), University of Toronto.

Preface

In Chapter 1 we provide an introduction to the book. In the *Preface to the Instructor* we discuss the two-semester course based on this book which we teach at The University of Michigan—Dearborn and describe the resources we use to teach the course. We also provide suggestions of different ways to organize and teach both college-level and short courses based on the material in this book. Here, we discuss how we came to write it.

Several years ago M. David Freedman was asked to evaluate and reorganize the minicomputer and microcomputer courses being offered through the Electrical Engineering Department at the University. Bringing both industrial and academic experience to bear on this task, a decision was made to create a new course sequence that would deal with microcomputers from a *systems* viewpoint. Furthermore, many of the so-called *structured programming* and *modular top-down* design concepts were incorporated into the course so that it would address the subject from a *systematic engineering* point of view. We made the course *self-contained* and brought together concepts often taught in different courses so that the students who complete the course would be able to fill a need that exists in industry. We wanted the course to be *both* interesting and practical.

Since a suitable textbook was not available, we embarked on a project to develop text material for the course. By keeping the book self-contained, it becomes suitable, not only as a textbook for a college-level course but also as a professional book for self-study and reference or as a basis for short courses for computer and engineering personnel in industry. It has been used successfully for this latter purpose by the authors. The book can also be used by owners of personal computer systems who do their own programming to help them organize and develop their software systematically.

The book does not treat every subject to its greatest possible depth. To do so would require a volume of encyclopedic proportions. Instead, we have presented the material so that the student develops a reasonable understanding of each concept. This understanding is sufficient to permit a nontrivial microcomputer system to be designed and implemented by the student as a class project. The manuals which are easily obtained from microcomputer vendors can be used to supplement the material in the book. Some of these manuals are listed in the bibliography which lists books and manuals by subject matter to enable the reader to delve further into an interesting topic.

The manuscript for this book was produced on a microcomputer-based word processing system and then transferred to a computer-based phototypesetting system from which the final pages were obtained. Thanks are due to the Bendix Corporation for the use of their word processing systems and to the word processing specialists, Penny Day, Karen Hindy, Virginia Hanadel, and Judy Brown who keyed the manuscript into the word processing systems. We also want to thank the people at Prentice-Hall, especially Bernard M. Goodwin, our editor, whose encouragement for this project never waned, the anonymous reviewers whose criticism was always welcome, Professor Murray H. Miller of The University of Michigan—Dearborn—who provided us with the opportunity to develop the course, and Professor K. C. Smith of the University of Toronto for his critique and for writing the *Foreword* for the book. Finally, we want to acknowledge those closest to us who provided us with support and encouragement: Roberta, Sandra, and Craig on the Freedman side, and Kathy and Lisa on the Evans side.

To our many friends, colleagues, and students who repeatedly ask the question, ''When is the book going to be finished?'' we can now answer, ''It is done!''

M. David Freedman

Southfield, Michigan

Lansing B. Evans

Boca Raton, Florida

Preface to the Instructor

This preface provides the instructor with:

- A description of the two-semester course based on this book which is taught at The University of Michigan—Dearborn.
- A description of the resources which are provided for the students to enable them to design and implement a microcomputer-based system as a class project.
- Recommendations for other resource configurations which can fulfill the needs of the course.
- Suggestions for other college-level and short courses which use the material in the book.

The course taught at The University of Michigan—Dearborn is taught to both seniors and masters-level graduate students. The first semester consists of a three-hour lecture course and covers each topic in the book in order. During the semester, homework exercises are assigned for a microcomputer system class project; by the end of the semester, each student is expected to have completed the *design language* version of the procedures for the project.

The exercises are graded and discussed in class so that each student designs essentially the same system. Thus, after the exercise to develop a modularization for the class project is graded and discussed, each student has a preliminary list of the modules and procedures which comprise the system. The homework exercises to design the procedures are then assigned piecemeal over a period of several weeks so that the procedures in one module are designed, graded, and discussed before the procedures in the next module are assigned as homework. Procedure design during this first semester is done with paper and pencil; no text-editing computer system is used by the students at this point.

Since not all students enroll for the three-hour laboratory course in the second semester, the first-semester part of the course is designed to be self-contained. Concepts such as the conversion of a design into a high-level programming language and the integration of the system are taught, but the student is not required to do the corresponding exercises at this time.

During the second-semester laboratory part of the course, the student enters the text for the design into a computer system, converts it into PL/M, and compiles, integrates, and debugs the software. When completed, the listings, along with the functional specification, modularization, integration plan, et cetera, comprise a complete set of documentation for the system used in the class project. The student retains this documentation as an example of a design project for future reference.

The computerized tools we provide as resources for the student at the University are modest compared to some of the tools we describe in Chapter 7. The preparation of the design language text and its conversion into PL/M are done manually using punched cards. The punched cards are then read into our MTS-based computer system and a simple line-oriented editor is used to correct errors. The MTS-based system is a large-scale central time-shared computer facility which is available to the students at The University of Michigan and at its satellite campuses. A PL/M cross-compiler has been modified so that it emulates the standalone version of PL/M which is provided by the Intel Corporation. The cross-compiler is used to compile the PL/M modules and convert them into Intel 8085 machine language modules. A simple *downloader* is used to transfer these modules into a standalone Digital Group SYSTEM III microcomputer system which contains a Zilog Z-80 microcomputer. The Z-80 microcomputer can execute the Intel 8085 instruction set since the latter is a subset of the Z-80 instruction set. The software is then executed on the Z-80 to integrate it and check it out. Any Intel 8085-compatible system can be used for the latter purpose. Since only one Digital Group microcomputer system is available, the students are divided into small groups and time is scheduled throughout the week for each group of students. The students, each of whom has designed, coded, and compiled his or her own design, then work together as a team and help each other download, integrate, and debug the software. A manual describing how to download software from the MTS-based system and how to operate the Digital Group microcomputer system is provided.

If more sophisticated tools, such as cursor-based editors, were available, a more efficient interface between the student and the computer would be possible. Chapter 7 provides an introduction to the different editors and tools and provides a starting point for a discussion of this topic in the laboratory course.

The book is suitable for use as a textbook for a variety of other college-level and short courses. Chapters 1 through 4 with some material from Chapter 5 and Appendix D can be used for a general course on the *Systematic Design of Software*. One-day workshops, three-day short courses, two-week hands-on short courses, and one-semester college courses have been developed using the material in the book. The workshops and short courses are also suitable for in-house presentation. In the latter case, the authors have combined the short course format with on-the-job *team development* to create *design teams* which learn together and then work together on actual projects.

DESIGNING SYSTEMS WITH MICROCOMPUTERS

A Systematic Approach

Chapter 1

Introduction

Since the first electronic digital computer was built over a quarter of a century ago, computers have become more and more prevalent in our lives. Now, thanks to the widespread availability of inexpensive microcomputers, we can expect them to have an even greater influence in the future. The primary goal of this book is to present methods for the systematic design of electronic systems that contain microcomputers as components. Let us therefore begin by examining this question: *What is a system?*

CONCEPT OF A SYSTEM

A *system* consists of a collection of component parts that performs a useful function with respect to its environment. Thus, a system must be connected to the environment and be able to sense information from and provide information to its environment, that is, it must have both *inputs* and *outputs*. A general representation of a system and its environment is shown in Figure 1-1. INPUT 1 through INPUT *n* are

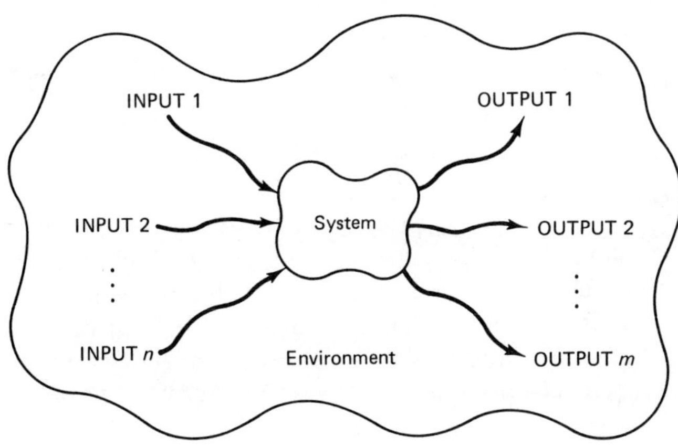

Figure 1-1. General representation of a system.

the inputs to the system from the environment and OUTPUT 1 through OUTPUT *m* are the outputs from the system to the environment.

Our everyday experience provides us with examples of both naturally occurring and manufactured systems. An example of a naturally occurring system is the human being in the environment of society. The *system*, in this case, obtains its inputs through one or more of its senses, that is, by seeing, hearing, feeling, smelling, or tasting. It provides outputs through its ability to talk, write, or move parts of the body. The useful function of the human being varies with each individual and ranges over a very broad spectrum. A teacher, for example, interacts with students by providing them knowledge and then examining how well they have learned.

An example of a manufactured system is a cutting machine in the environment of a factory that processes raw materials into finished products. The inputs to the machine are provided through hand wheels or levers that are actuated by an operator. The outputs consist of the movements of a cutting tool. The useful function of the machine is to modify a piece of raw material by moving the cutting tool so that it cuts the material in response to the inputs provided by the operator. The piece of material then takes on a new size and shape as part of the manufacturing process.

ELECTRONIC SYSTEM

Many manufactured systems use electronic component parts. An example of this type of system is the electronic amplifier. Here the input is an electrical waveform and the output is an amplified replica of the input. Typical component parts of the electronic amplifier are resistors, capacitors, transistors, diodes, and integrated circuits.

More sophisticated electronic systems that are used in complex control applications have also been developed. For many years these systems consisted of standard electronic parts wired together into an inflexible or hardwired configuration in much the same manner as in the amplifier mentioned above. However, the cost and the size of computing devices, such as the *microcomputer*, have decreased greatly in recent years. Therefore, it is now feasible to incorporate microcomputers into electronic systems as if they were *components*. When this is done, system users may be as unaware of the existence of the microcomputers as they are of the existence of specific capacitors, resistors, or transistors. Let us examine the *microcomputer component* in more detail.

MICROCOMPUTER COMPONENT

Designing a capacitor or a resistor into an electronic system consists of determining the value of the component in microfarads or ohms and specifying the voltage or power limit for the component. Its functional characteristics and performance are then completely predictable. In the case of a transistor or a simple integrated circuit, the functional characteristics of the component cannot be specified by the value of one or two parameters. However, the characteristics for such a device can be specified as a transfer function that provides the relationship between the input and output of the device. This permits selecting components to suit the requirements of the electronic system.

The microcomputer, unlike other electronic components, does not possess a fixed set of functional characteristics. Its characteristics are added during the construction of the system by a process called *programming*. The virtually unlimited range of functionality that can be assigned to the microcomputer through programming is what gives this component its unique capability.

In this book we examine the nonprogrammable characteristics of the microcomputer as well as how to design and build the *programs* that give the microcomputer its functional characteristics. The electronic components of the system including the microcomputer are called *hardware* since they are relatively inflexible and difficult to alter once they are selected and the system is built. By comparison, the programs developed during the design of the system are called *software* since they are relatively easy to alter even after the design is completed and the system constructed.

Whether a system consists only of hardware components or whether it contains a microcomputer with its associated software, its design should be cost-effective. The design of both the hardware and the software should be carried out systematically to enable both the design cost and production schedule to be minimized. To better understand these concepts, let us examine the *system design cycle*.

SYSTEM DESIGN CYCLE

The first step in the system design cycle consists of obtaining a set of *user requirements* and developing a *functional specification* for the system from the user requirements. The user requirements specify what the user wants the system to do. A good functional specification specifies the functions that the system will provide for the user when it is completed, thereby indicating how the system will satisfy the user requirements. It includes a description of the formats that both the inputs and outputs take and the environmental conditions under which the system will operate. The functional specification and the user requirements provide a measure by which to gauge the performance of the system after it is completed.

The next step is to design the system so that it meets the functional specification. For a system that contains only hardware, this entails selecting a configuration for the system, determining the values of the component parts, and determining how to interconnect the parts. The hardware is constructed, tested, and integrated into its environment, and then its performance is evaluated. At any step of the system design cycle, it may be necessary to redesign and modify the system to ensure that the functional specification is being met. Note that the sooner a problem is detected during the design cycle, the less expensive it is to correct. The design cycle for a hardware system is illustrated in Figure 1-2.

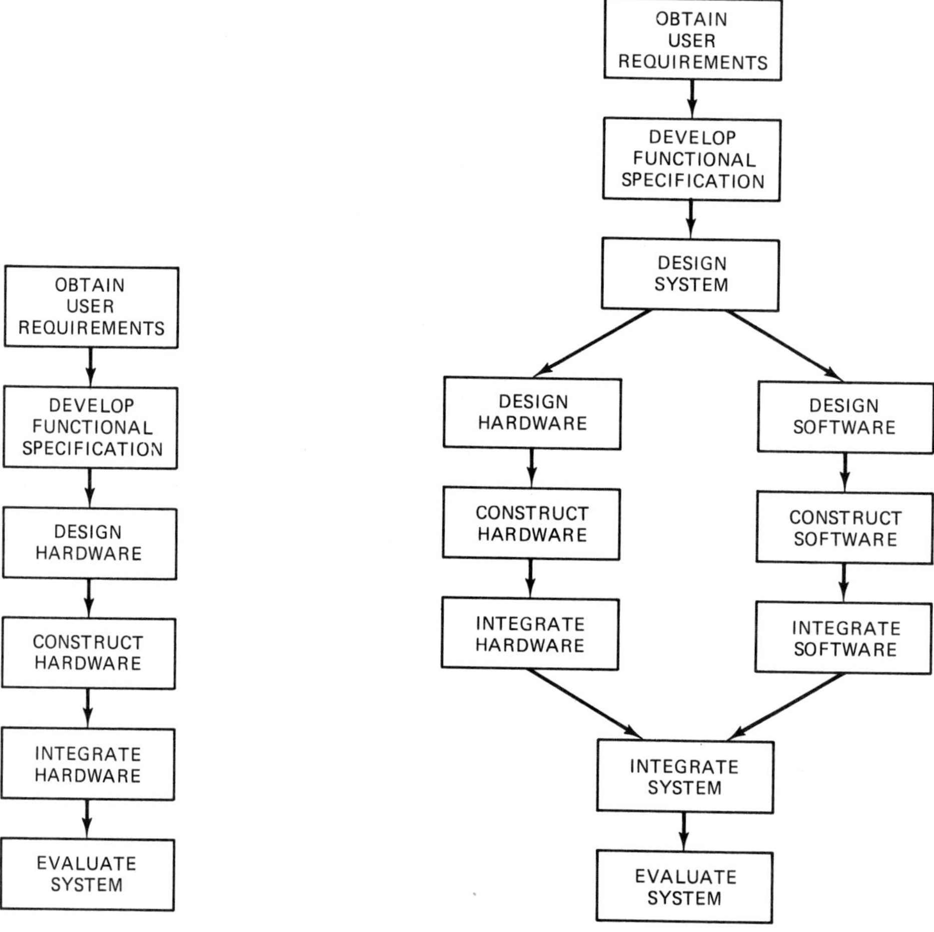

Figure 1-2. The design cycle for a hardware system.

Figure 1-3. The design cycle for a system which contains a microcomputer.

For a system that contains a microcomputer, both hardware and software design are required. It is necessary to specify both the hardware and the software configuration, to determine what *parts* are needed, and to specify how the parts are interconnected. For the hardware, the design can be done using standard hardware design methodology. For the software, the design is best done using a *design language* that is similar to natural language. The software is constructed from the design by converting it into a *microcomputer programming language*. It is tested and integrated with the hardware into its environment, and then the system performance is evaluated. The design cycle for a system consisting of both software and hardware is shown in Figure 1-3. The two parts of the system can often be worked on concurrently and so are shown as separate *paths* in the figure.

Because of the increased capability of the microcomputer component, more flexible designs can be achieved with fewer hardware components than with systems containing only hardware. But since it is very easy for such a system to become overly complex and unwieldy, the software must be designed and constructed in a systematic manner so that the completed system will be cost-effective. One of our major goals is to use systematic design techniques to reduce the software complexity of the system to a manageable level. The systematic techniques that we will describe for this purpose include the use of *top-down* and *modular* techniques in addition to the use of design language. Since the use of design language is central to systematic design, we now introduce the concept.

DESIGN LANGUAGE

We introduce design language by means of a simple example whose functional specification is illustrated by the transfer functions and the block diagram shown in Figure 1-4. INPUT 1 and INPUT 2 are analog inputs and OUTPUT 1 and OUTPUT 2 are analog outputs. The system consists of a microcomputer with two inputs and two outputs; since the microcomputer is a digital device, analog-to-digital converters and digital-to-analog converters are needed to convert the input and output signals appropriately.

Since the system has inputs and outputs, we deduce that the microcomputer must be able to *examine* the *value* of each input; it must also be able to *set* each of

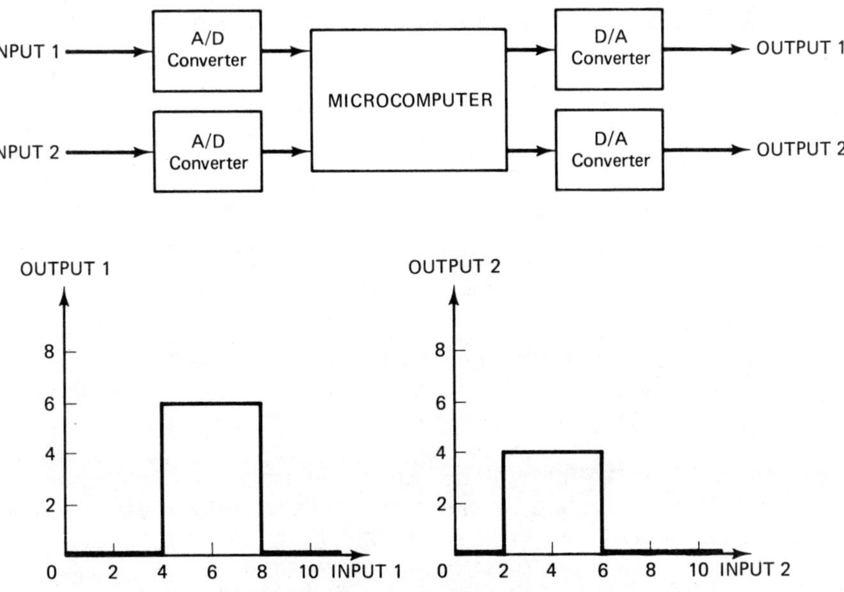

Figure 1-4. Microcomputer system example.

the outputs to an appropriate *value*. At the design language level, we use a single *construct* for each *examine* and *set* operation, as shown in the following examples:

```
EXAMINE INPUT 1 AND SAVE ITS VALUE
SET OUTPUT 1 TO THE VALUE 6
```

We must also be able to test the saved value of each input in order to determine how to set the output values. For this purpose, we use a *test* construct that takes the general form:

```
IF a test condition is true
  THEN  do something
  ELSE  do something different
```

Thus, for our example, the design begins to take shape, as follows:

```
EXAMINE INPUT 1 AND SAVE ITS VALUE
EXAMINE INPUT 2 AND SAVE ITS VALUE
IF THE VALUE OF INPUT 1 IS GREATER THAN 4 AND LESS THAN 8
  THEN  SET OUTPUT 1 TO THE VALUE 6
  ELSE  SET OUTPUT 1 TO THE VALUE 0
IF THE VALUE OF INPUT 2 IS GREATER THAN 2 AND LESS THAN 6
  THEN  SET OUTPUT 2 TO THE VALUE 4
  ELSE  SET OUTPUT 2 TO THE VALUE 0
```

When the system is functioning, the microcomputer performs its programmed operations in a step-by-step manner. Thus, if the program in the microcomputer corresponds to the design shown above, the correct functional behavior is observed. But once the inputs have been examined, there is no provision for reexamining them should one of them change at a later time. An operation is needed to allow the other operations in the software design to be repeated indefinitely. For this purpose, we use the construct:

```
DO FOREVER
  .
  .
  .
END
```

to indicate that the set of operations between the DO FOREVER and the END are to be repeated indefinitely. Thus, our example becomes:

```
DO FOREVER
  EXAMINE INPUT 1 AND SAVE ITS VALUE
  EXAMINE INPUT 2 AND SAVE ITS VALUE
  IF THE VALUE OF INPUT 1 IS GREATER THAN 4 AND LESS THAN 8
    THEN  SET OUTPUT 1 TO THE VALUE 6
    ELSE  SET OUTPUT 1 TO THE VALUE 0
  IF THE VALUE OF INPUT 2 IS GREATER THAN 2 AND LESS THAN 6
    THEN  SET OUTPUT 2 TO THE VALUE 4
    ELSE  SET OUTPUT 2 TO THE VALUE 0
END
```

and, once started, the operations of examining and testing the values of the inputs and setting the values of the outputs are repeated for as long as the system remains in operation.

From the example and the above discussion, we have learned the following facts about the microcomputer:

- The microcomputer is a sequential device and it performs its operations one at a time.
- In many cases, to change the functional behavior of the microcomputer system, only the operations specified in the software design need to be changed.
- Digital data are manipulated by the microcomputer. Thus, if analog signals exist in the system, then analog-to-digital converters are needed to convert input signals into digital form and digital-to-analog converters are needed to convert output signals into analog form.

As indicated earlier, it is necessary to convert the software design into a microcomputer program before the microcomputer can perform the operations. Microcomputer programming languages that have many similarities to our design language have been developed. For example, several microcomputer programming languages contain the IF . . . THEN . . . ELSE . . . construct allowing operations in the program to correspond closely to similar operations in the design language. We discuss how to convert a software design into a program in Chapter 5.

DOCUMENTATION

One of the most important factors contributing to good system design is good documentation. By *good* we mean well-organized, easy to read and understand, easy to update, and concise yet complete. As we move through the design cycle, from the user requirements and functional specification to the integration and evaluation of the operational system, we will show what information should be included at each level of documentation for the system being designed and built. To make it easy to follow the discussion, each segment of the documentation is assigned a documentation level number. Figure 1-5 illustrates the organization of the documentation for the complete design cycle.

The first documentation level contains the written descriptions of the user requirements and the functional specification. The second level contains the system design documentation and the third level contains the software documentation. The latter two levels are maintained together since they are very closely related, as we shall see.

Since we must keep track of our progress through each step of the integration process, we prepare an *integration plan*. This becomes the fourth level of documentation. Finally, the fifth and sixth levels consist of the hardware documentation and the *hardware checkout plan*. Together, these six levels constitute a complete set of system documentation that can be maintained and kept up-to-date in a straightforward manner.

1. User requirements and functional specification
2. System design documentation
3. Software documentation
4. Integration plan
5. Hardware documentation
6. Hardware checkout plan

Figure 1-5. Documentation organization.

ORGANIZATION OF THE BOOK

In Chapter 2 we describe how to obtain a set of user requirements and to develop a meaningful functional specification from the user requirements. We also examine the tradeoffs that are made during the planning and specification phases for every system. Throughout the book we use several examples of computerized systems. Not only do these examples provide the continuity necessary to thoroughly understand each aspect of design, but they also provide us with examples that have been classroom tested and found to be both intuitive and instructive. In Chapter 2 we also examine the topic of *human factors* in design. Since most microcomputer systems interact with people in some manner, it is important to consider this interaction during system design.

Using the functional specification developed in Chapter 2 for a burglar alarm system, we proceed in Chapter 3 to examine how to carry out the system design. System design consists of dividing the system into *modules*, some of which are implemented in hardware and the remainder in software. The concept of top-down design is introduced in Chapter 3. The tradeoffs between implementing a function in hardware as opposed to implementing it in software are also considered in this chapter.

In Chapter 4 we start with the modularization developed during the system design and proceed to design the software. Software design consists primarily of developing a design language version of the software modules. In Chapter 4 we also describe methods for verifying the correctness of the software design before it is converted into a microcomputer programming language.

In Chapter 5 we show how to convert the design into a high-level programming language that can be executed by the microcomputer. Because of the similarities between the design language and several high-level programming languages, programming the microcomputer is a relatively straightforward task.

In Chapter 6 we describe microcomputer architecture, assembly language, and machine language so that the reader will be able to understand the relationship

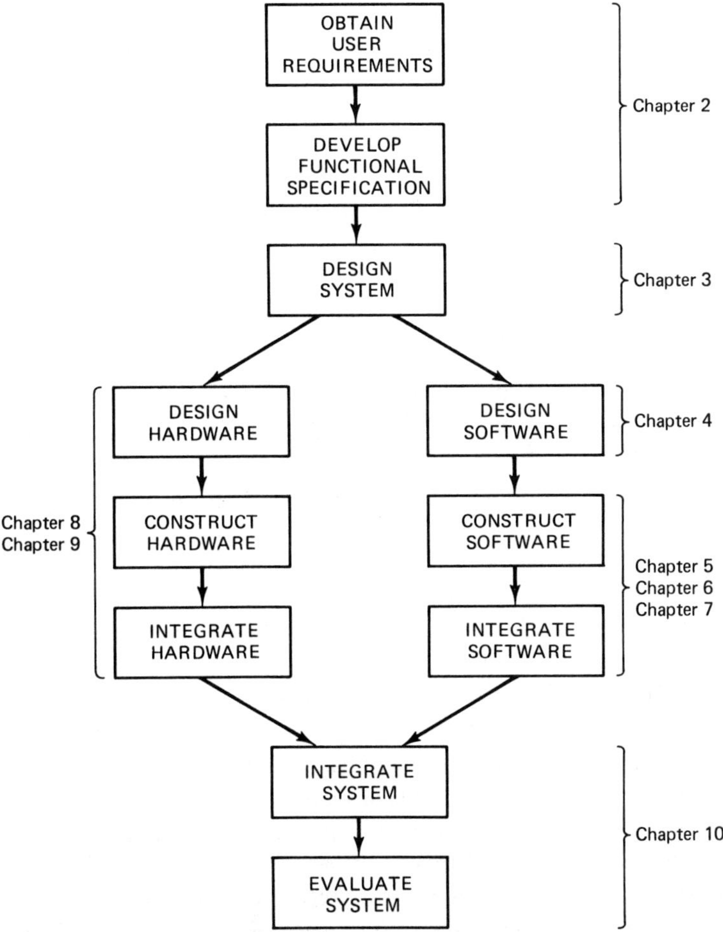

Figure 1-6. The organization of the book and its relationship to the system design cycle.

between the microcomputer hardware and its software. Chapter 6 also introduces the concept of assembly language programming so that the reader will be familiar with it should he or she ever need to use it.

In Chapter 7 we discuss how to integrate the software modules into a software system that can then be integrated into the hardware.

In Chapter 8 we describe the hardware design of a system that contains a microcomputer, and in Chapter 9 we show how to construct and integrate the hardware modules into an operational system ready to receive the software. We also describe how to verify that the hardware is operating correctly before the software is integrated with the hardware.

In Chapter 10 we show how to integrate the software into the hardware and how to verify that the completed system is functioning correctly. As we have already stated, software design can be complex and both design and programming errors are likely to be encountered before the system is completed. Therefore, in Chapters 4, 7, 9, and 10 we describe the tools and techniques that are available to help develop, checkout, and integrate the parts of the system, to detect and eliminate errors, and to ensure that the completed system meets the functional specification and the user requirements.

The relationship of Chapters 2 through 10 to the system design cycle is illustrated in Figure 1-6. This figure is a *road map* of the book; the reader should refer to it as we work our way through each of the sections of the book.

Finally, in Chapter 11 we describe several other systems to illustrate the wide variety of potential applications of microcomputers.

Our goal is to present an efficient method for systematically designing a system containing a microcomputer so that it accurately and cost-effectively meets the desired user requirements and the related functional specification.

EXERCISES

Engineers use the term *black box* to refer to an *inseparable* collection of components that has a well-defined functional relationship.

1-1. What is the relationship between a black box and a system?

1-2. What are some examples of black boxes with which you are familiar?

1-3. Can a microcomputer be a black box? Explain.

1-4. Can a black box contain a microcomputer? Explain.

1-5. We have mentioned several techniques that can be used to reduce complexity in a microcomputer-based system. Can you think of any others? Describe them.

1-6. How is complexity reduced by the techniques you described in Exercise 1-5?

1-7. Using design language, create a design for a microcomputer system to meet the functional specification shown below:

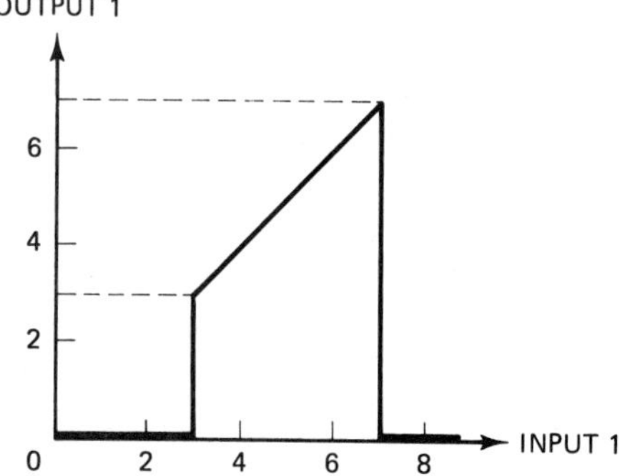

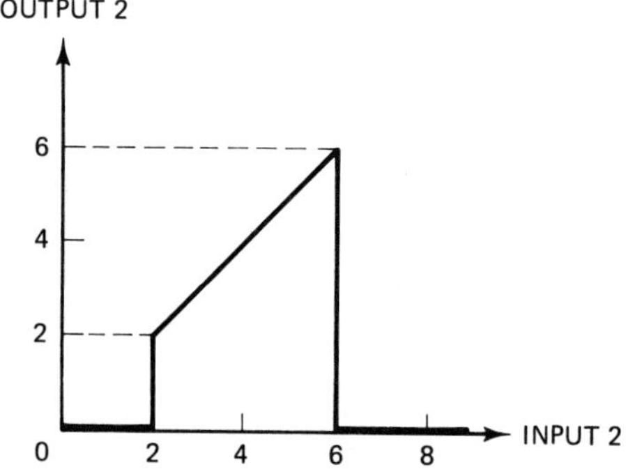

1-8. Using design language, create a design for a microcomputer system to meet the functional specification shown below:

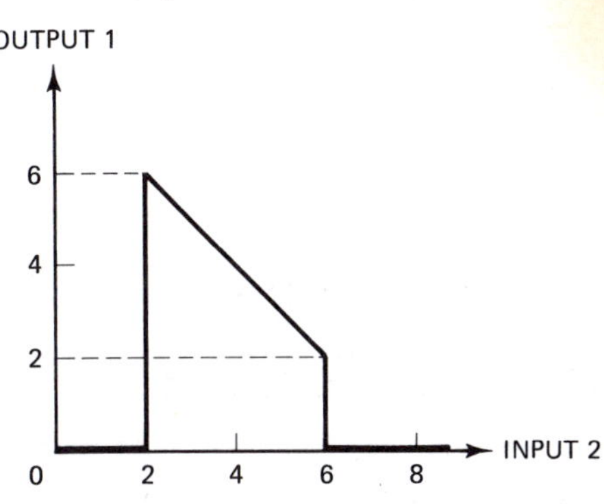

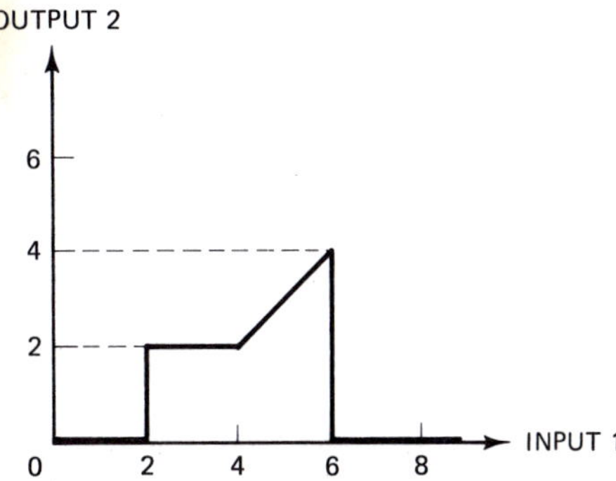

1-9. Why is it important to develop and maintain good documentation for a microcomputer-based system?

Chapter 2

User Requirements and the Functional Specification

We are now ready to start a more detailed description of the system design cycle. In this chapter we discuss how to obtain the user requirements and show how to develop the functional specification for a system from these requirements. User requirements specify what the user or customer wants the system to do; the functional specification documents what the system must do and what its interface with its environment is. Once the functional specification is developed, it is used along with the user requirements as the basis for the design, implementation, and evaluation of the system. For this reason, it is important that both user requirements and the functional specification not only be complete and accurate but also concise and easy to understand.

USER REQUIREMENTS

User requirements specify what the user or customer wants or needs. User requirements can be obtained by meeting with the user or customer to evaluate his or her needs and thereby determine what the user wants. Alternately, for a planned product line, user requirements can be determined by conducting a marketing survey of a broad customer base. Of course, an examination of what the competition is marketing can also provide insight into what will or will not be salable in the marketplace.

Let us assume that a *company* is planning to develop a computerized burglar alarm system in order to expand its product line and let us develop a set of user requirements for the system. The first step in developing the user requirements for a burglar alarm system is to obtain information about what it should do. In this case, we would likely have a large customer base, which means we would work very closely with our marketing department as well as with a few representative customers to obtain the needed information. The questions we ask at this point should be concerned only with what the burglar alarm system should do. Specifically, the questions that should be answered include:

- What kind of intruder detection is required?
- What action is desired if an intruder is detected?
- What other features are considered desirable?

From the answers to these questions we can deduce what a suitable set of user requirements would be. For the burglar alarm system, a suitable set of user requirements is shown below. A functional specification can be developed from these requirements. The burglar alarm system should:

- Detect when a door or window is opened.
- Detect when someone is moving inside the protected area.
- Have the ability to frighten off an intruder and summon aid.
- Provide allowance for the operator's forgetting to reset the alarm.
- Be easy to arm and reset.
- Minimize false alarms.

FUNCTIONAL SPECIFICATION

A functional specification must specify what functions are needed to satisfy the user requirements, as well as the interface between the system and its environment. Thus, a functional specification consists of two major components:

1. A list of functions to be performed by the system.
2. A description of the interface between the system and the user.

Because the system is designed and built based on information contained in both user requirements and the functional specification, it is important that the functions be described in enough detail to reflect the desired system behavior. Referring to the user requirements, we see that for the burglar alarm system, the functional specification should answer the following questions:

- What mechanisms should be provided to detect the unauthorized opening of a door or window?
- What mechanisms should be provided to detect motion?
- What mechanisms should be provided to frighten off an intruder and to summon aid?
- What mechanism should be provided to allow for the operator's forgetting to reset the alarm?
- What mechanism should be provided to arm and reset the system?
- What mechanism should be provided to prevent false alarms?

As we answer these questions, we begin to develop the functional specification for the burglar alarm system. In our system,

- Switches will be used to detect the unauthorized opening of a door or a window.
- An ultrasonic motion detector will be used to detect motion. To prevent false alarms, motion will be monitored and must be continuous for at least five seconds before an intruder will be considered to be present.
- The operator will be warned that he or she has forgotten to reset the system by a visual alarm that will be turned on for sixty seconds before an audible alarm is sounded. If the system is not reset within the sixty seconds, the audible alarm will be sounded to frighten the intruder and summon aid.
- A keyswitch will be used to arm and reset the system.

These answers provide us with the information needed to develop the functional specification. Let us put it into a format that is easy to use and easy to reference during the remaining steps of the design cycle. If we organize the information into the categories of INPUTS, OUTPUTS, and FUNCTIONS, we can document the functional specification for the burglar alarm system as shown in Figure 2-1. In many systems, a good functional specification would include sketches of parts of the system. For example, in a system that contains a panel of push buttons, a sketch of the push-button layout can be incorporated into the functional specification. An example of a push button layout for a simple point-of-sale system (computerized cash register) is shown in Figure 2-2.

A. INPUTS
   1. Switches.
   2. Motion detector.
   3. Keyswitch.

B. OUTPUTS
   1. Visual alarm.
   2. Audible alarm.

C. FUNCTIONS
   1. System is armed and reset by keyswitch.
   2. Visual alarm is actuated by either
      (a) Tripping the switches, or
      (b) Continuous activation of the motion detector for at least five seconds.
   3. Audible alarm is actuated sixty seconds after the visual alarm is actuated if the system is not reset by the keyswitch during this interval.

Figure 2-1. Functional specification for the burglar alarm system.

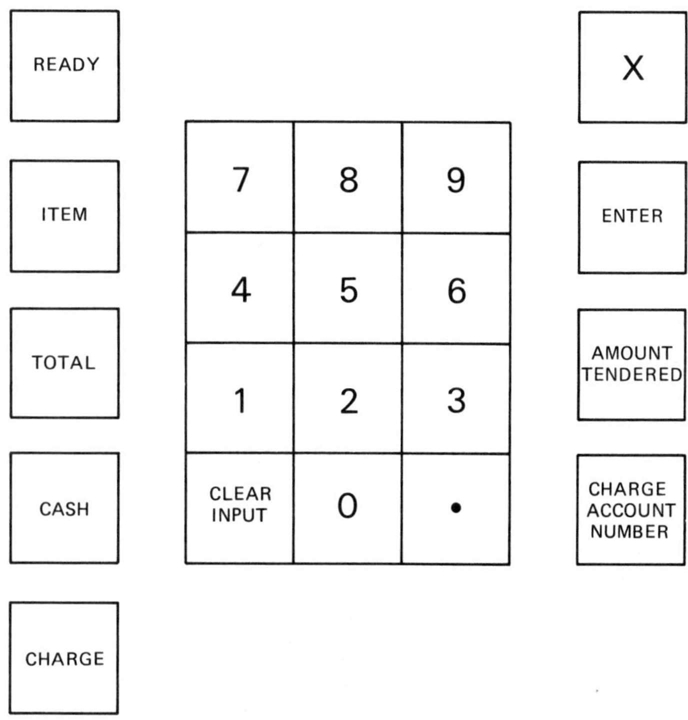

Figure 2-2. Push button layout for a simple point-of-sale terminal.

Now that we have completed the documentation for the functional specification of the burglar alarm system, let us make several observations about functional specifications in general. The specific system for which we have generated a functional specification is extremely simple and has therefore resulted in a relatively short functional specification. In more complex systems the functional specification, even though it is a high-level description, is longer. In these cases, it may be better to decompose the system into several smaller *subsystems* and prepare a separate functional specification for each subsystem. In some instances, the functional specification may contain a description of an implementation instead of a function. Such a description is permissible if it is important to describe how the system operates. An example would be to describe the input switches in the burglar alarm system as being normally closed and series wired in the functional specification. In the case of a burglar alarm system, these are important characteristics of inputs and could legitimately be added to the functional specification although we have chosen not to do so. Implementation information usually belongs in the *design specification* instead of in the functional specification. Let us briefly examine the differences between the functional specification and the design specification.

FUNCTIONAL SPECIFICATION VS. DESIGN SPECIFICATION

A functional specification usually describes *what* the system does. It does not present the specific details that describe *how* the system is implemented. During the system design cycle, as we move from general details to more specific details, it is often tempting to include too many specific details at the more general or higher levels of design; this temptation should be avoided.

To illustrate, let us use an inventory control system as an example. The functional specification for the inventory control system includes information on how many different items the system should be able to keep track of, whether maximum and minimum levels of inventory should be maintained for each item, and whether the system should require the entry of a valid password before a change is permitted. The latter function, if implemented, prevents an unauthorized person from gaining access to and changing the information stored in the system. The design specification contains specific information about the implementation of the inventory control system, including how inventory data are organized, how the data are accessed, and where the data are stored.

We have now seen the steps involved in the development of a set of user requirements and a functional specification. Several iterations consisting of reviewing user requirements and the functional specification with the customer or marketing department and making appropriate updates to the requirements and the specification are most likely required and are encouraged. *Remember, the completed system should do what the customer wants it to do and it should not do anything that the customer does not want it to do.*

Because the interaction between the system and the user is very important, let us next look at the *human factors* involved in the design of microcomputer-based systems.

HUMAN FACTORS

In the burglar alarm system the interaction between the system and the user is predominately through the keyswitch. In general, however, many different types of interfaces exist between an operator and a system. These interfaces include:

- *Tactile inputs.* The user may push buttons, twist knobs, manipulate levers, et cetera.
- *Visual outputs.* The visual alarm of the burglar alarm system is an example of a visual output. Other systems display information on digital readouts, TV screens, printers, and so forth.
- *Indirect inputs.* In the burglar alarm system, indirect inputs are provided by the intruder through the switches and the motion detector. In other systems, an operator may provide indirect input to the system. For example, if the operator of a point-of-sale system that has an automatic weigh scale attached places a

commodity on the scale, the price is transmitted directly to the point-of-sale system. Bar code and magnetic stripe readers that read commodity information directly into a point-of-sale system provide other examples of commonly used indirect inputs.

- *Audible outputs*. The audible alarm in the burglar alarm system is an example of an audible output. In a point-of-sale system a beeper is often used to inform the operator that a particular input sequence has been completed or that an error has been made.

Human factors deal with making a system easy and natural to use. These goals are accomplished by designing the system interface to provide an economical flow of information between the operator and the machine. This enables the operator to interact with the system with little effort and with minimal training. The point-of-sale system is an example of a system in which speed and accuracy are essential. An error in typing the price of an item can cause a business establishment either to lose money or to inadvertently overcharge a customer. In many self-serve or fast-service businesses, customers can select products more rapidly than the cashiers are able to handle them. Two alternatives to long checkout lines are possible. More cashiers can be hired or the efficiency of the cashiers can be improved. A well-designed point-of-sale system can help improve cashier efficiency. Let us look at specific examples.

In a point-of-sale system designed for a fast-food business we can provide a key for each item and allow the manager to *program* each key with the current price of the item. This permits the cashier to *ring up* a hamburger by pressing the *hamburger key* instead of a series of three or four numeric keys followed by an ENTER key as in the standard system whose keyboard is shown in Figure 2-2. In the fast-food point-of-sale system hamburger buyers are always charged the same price and errors are virtually eliminated. Information flow from the cashier to the point-of-sale system is highly economical since a single keystroke replaces several individual keystrokes. Accuracy is improved since the cashier is working with *function keys* instead of with numeric keys.

In the standard point-of-sale system designed for general retail use the system can be designed to *lead* the cashier through each sequence needed to correctly operate the system. Whenever information is needed by the system, a suitable light is turned on to indicate what type of information is needed. For example, if the information needed is the customer's charge account number, the *charge account number* light is turned on. Only after a number is typed by the cashier and verified to be a valid charge account number by the system is the light turned off and the cashier permitted to continue with the transaction.

The microcomputer has also found a place in many systems that heretofore consisted exclusively of hardware components. An example of such a system is the computerized oscilloscope. The presence of a microcomputer in the oscilloscope permits a digital display of a measurement to be superimposed on the analog display on the CRT screen. It also permits the operator to accurately measure parameters, such as a waveform average, which are either difficult or impossible to measure with an analog oscilloscope. The human factors aspect of the design of a computerized oscilloscope is heavily influenced by existing analog oscilloscopes. For example, the engineer who uses an oscilloscope is accustomed to twisting knobs to set the horizontal time base and the vertical gain. Thus, even though these functions are now under the control of a microcomputer, the designer should retain the knobs; the user should not have to relearn how to use functions with which he or she is familiar, especially if they are already well designed from a human factors standpoint. Assume that the user will have his or her hands full learning how to take advantage of the new digital functions without also having to relearn how to make the old analog functions work.

This completes our introduction to human factors in the design of microcomputer-based systems.

FIRST DOCUMENTATION LEVEL

As we indicated in Chapter 1, the user requirements and functional specification constitute the first level of documentation for the system. This level contains the information needed to evaluate the performance of the system and is therefore an important part of the system documentation.

In some systems a *user's manual* or *operator's manual* is needed to describe the operation of the system for the customer. Historically, the user's manual is prepared at the completion of the design cycle and is often looked upon as a *necessary evil*. However, it is often feasible and usually best to prepare the functional specification in the form of a user's manual. Then, even though revision may be required, there is no need for separate documents for the functional specification and the user's manual. In fact, there are many advantages to being able to show the user's manual to a customer for his or her evaluation even before the system design is begun. Thus, for such a system, the user's manual doubles as a functional specification and becomes a part of the first level of documentation.

EXERCISES

When working each of the following exercises, consider:

1. How information is fed into the system by the operator.
2. How the system provides feedback to the operator.
3. What internal functions the system should provide.

Be sure that each functional specification you develop takes into account that a system should be convenient, simple to operate, cost-effective, and have features that appeal to different customers. Note that the microcomputer allows a system to be *customized* so that different models can be built from similar hardware and yet perform different functions for different customers.

2-1. Assume we are going to build a television set containing a microcomputer. List a set of suitable functions that can be performed by the microcomputer.

2-2. Develop a set of user requirements for the computerized television set.

2-3. From the user requirements in Exercise 2-2, develop a functional specification for the television set.

2-4. What human factors considerations should be taken into account when designing a computerized traffic light controller? (Keep in mind what the primary objective for a traffic light controller is!)

2-5. Develop a set of user requirements for the computerized traffic light controller.

2-6. From the user requirements in Exercise 2-5, develop a functional specification for the traffic light controller.

2-7. What are suitable questions to be asked of the customers for a computerized sports scoreboard to obtain a suitable set of user requirements?

2-8. Develop a set of user requirements for the computerized sports scoreboard by answering the questions in Exercise 2-7.

2-9. From the user requirements in Exercise 2-8, develop a functional specification for the computerized sports scoreboard.

2-10. What are suitable questions that can be used to obtain a suitable set of user requirements for a computerized point-of-sale (POS) system (computerized cash register)?

2-11. By answering the questions in Exercise 2-10, develop a set of user requirements for the computerized POS system.

2-12. From the user requirements in Exercise 2-11, develop a functional specification for the computerized POS system.

Chapter 3

System Design

We have shown how to obtain a set of user requirements and how to develop a functional specification for a system. We know what the system must do and how it interfaces with its environment. In this chapter we show how to work from the functional specification to develop a set of *modules* that constitutes the first level of system design. Once the system has been modularized, the modules must then be divided into hardware modules and software modules. The hardware modules are then designed and implemented using standard or custom-built integrated circuits.

The software modules are divided into a set of *procedures* each of which corresponds as closely to a single function as possible. Software design entails writing a description of what each procedure does using the design language introduced in Chapter 1. This method of developing a software design starting from the functional specification, then breaking the system into modules, and finally breaking the software modules into procedures is known as *top-down design*.

In this chapter we examine the system design process; we examine the software design process in Chapter 4.

PRELIMINARY SYSTEM DESIGN AND HARDWARE/SOFTWARE TRADEOFFS

Before the detailed software and hardware design can be carried out, it is necessary to determine which functions are best performed by the microcomputer software and which are best performed by the hardware. All unassigned functions should then be subjected to a tradeoff study and assigned to either the software or the hardware on a preliminary basis. Although it is desirable at this point to freeze the design, it should be noted that this can rarely be done in practice. During the detailed design of the hardware and the software, it may become obvious that a hardware function is better done in the software, or vice versa. Thus, modifications of the preliminary design can take place during the later stages in the design process.

A general hardware modularization scheme for a microcomputer-based system is shown in Figure 3-1. The system is broken into modules that are related to the INPUT, OUTPUT, SIGNAL CONDITIONING, MICROCOMPUTER, and MISCELLANEOUS HARDWARE functions needed by the system. The INPUT SIGNAL CONDITIONING module and the OUTPUT SIGNAL CONDITIONING module contain the components needed to obtain input signals from and provide output signals to the environment of the system. The analog-to-digital and digital-to-analog converters that are needed to allow analog signals to be processed by the microcomputer are examples of the type of components found in the latter two modules. The INPUT INTERFACE module, the MICROCOMPUTER module, and the OUTPUT INTERFACE module contain the microcomputer and its associated components as well as the components needed for the microcomputer to interface with the other system modules. The MISCELLANEOUS HARDWARE module contains the components needed to implement other system functions. It is with respect to the latter functions that many tradeoff decisions must be made as to whether a function is better implemented in the hardware or in the software.

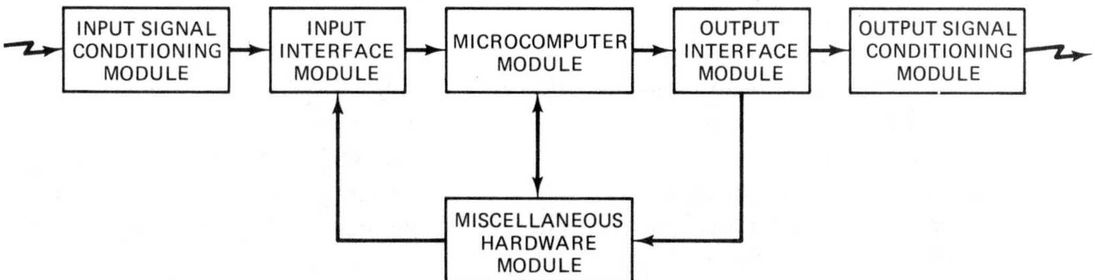

Figure 3-1. General hardware modularization for a microcomputer-based system.

As an example of the type of tradeoff decisions that need to be made, we again draw on the burglar alarm system. For differentiating between valid motion and false alarms and for determining when to actuate the audible alarm, it is necessary to provide a time delay function. The time delay function can be implemented in one of several ways such as: completely in the software using a program that simply *counts* to five or to sixty seconds; completely in the MISCELLANEOUS HARDWARE module using a set of integrated circuit logic elements configured as a counter that can be set to time out after either five seconds or sixty seconds; or in a combination of hardware and software using an *intelligent* programmable timer integrated circuit that is contained in the MISCELLANEOUS HARDWARE module. The alternative that is chosen affects both the software and the hardware design of the timing function. After we have discussed software modularization, we will reexamine these tradeoffs. Top-down design is applicable to both hardware design and to software design and it helps illustrate where the interface between the hardware and the software lies. Therefore, let us next discuss the philosophy of top-down design which then leads us to the *functional modularization* of the software.

TOP-DOWN DESIGN

The design of a system can be partitioned into a number of functional levels. In general, the top functional level of a design is the most general and the bottom functional level is the most detailed. For hardware, the top level of the design consists of a block diagram showing a fairly coarse subdivision. This top-level subdivision may show the subsystem level for large systems or the module level for smaller systems. Subsequent levels of the hardware design consist of further subdivisions until, finally, detailed interconnection charts or wiring lists comprise the lowest level. In the top-level hardware design shown in Figure 3-1 the next level of modularization of the SIGNAL CONDITIONING modules would show the analog-to-digital and digital-to-analog converters and other signal conversion devices needed to implement these top-level modules.

For software, the top level of the design documentation consists of a module diagram of the system. At the top of the modularization as shown in the module diagram, there are modules containing the most general software functions; at the bottom of the modularization, there are modules containing the most detailed software functions. Each module contains a set of procedures that implement the specific functions for that module. Thus, for the burglar alarm system, the fact that a visual alarm is actuated immediately when a switch is tripped is a description of a general function and belongs near the top level. The details of how the switches are sensed and how the alarm is physically actuated are low-level details and therefore belong near the bottom level. The software modules at these lower levels of modularization interface most closely with the hardware modules of the system. It is often tempting to design these detailed bottom levels first since they appear to be easy to understand. But there are good reasons for resisting this temptation:

- It may be unclear initially how these low-level software functions interact with the higher-level ones. Thus, if they are developed first, it may be necessary to revise them extensively later. Waiting until the higher-level functions are designed often permits the low-level functions to be designed not only more quickly but also more accurately so that they need minimal revision later.
- Let us assume that, after a design is partially completed, either a time or cost overrun appears likely. If top-down design is being employed, it may be possible to temporarily eliminate some of the software functions that are not yet complete. Although the resulting system is not able to completely meet user requirements and the functional specification, it will nevertheless operate and be able to demonstrate feasibility. If a *bottom-up* design approach is used, there is little choice but to complete the design of the top level functions before being able to demonstrate any functionality at all.

Let us assume that the top-level hardware modularization for the burglar alarm system is represented by the block diagram shown in Figure 3-1 and proceed with the next step of the design, namely, the *functional modularization* of the software.

FUNCTIONAL MODULARIZATION

In Chapter 1 we noted that the microcomputer is a sequential device that performs its operations one at a time. Therefore, at the highest level of software modularization, a control function is needed to ensure that the system performs the required functions in a sequential manner. We call this control function the EXECUTIVE procedure and designate that a module called the EXECUTIVE module contain the software needed to implement the EXECUTIVE procedure.

To determine how to divide the remainder of the burglar alarm system software into functional modules, let us examine the functional specification that was developed in Chapter 2 and is reproduced in Figure 3-2. From the functional specification we can divide the system into three parts: INPUT, OUTPUT, and FUNCTION. In this case, the INPUT and OUTPUT parts can each be implemented by a single module since each is relatively simple and straightforward. In more complex systems, it may be necessary to divide these two modules further and design several INPUT modules and several OUTPUT modules.

A. INPUTS
   1. Switches.
   2. Motion detector.
   3. Keyswitch.

B. OUTPUTS
   1. Visual alarm.
   2. Audible alarm.

C. FUNCTIONS
   1. System is armed and reset by keyswitch.
   2. Visual alarm is actuated by either
      (a) Tripping the switches, or
      (b) Continuous activation of the motion detector for at least five seconds.
   3. Audible alarm is actuated sixty seconds after the visual alarm is actuated if the system is not reset by the keyswitch during this interval.

Figure 3-2. Functional specification for the burglar alarm system.

In our example we can identify four distinct modules from the FUNCTIONS part of the functional specification, as follows:

1. The state of a switch or the motion detector input is read and saved by a procedure in the INPUT module. But the state of these inputs must be examined or tested before any action can be taken. We group together into a TEST module the procedures that implement the testing and that determine what further action should be taken as a result of the outcome of each test.
2. During operation it is necessary to test the keyswitch and to wait for it to be armed or reset before a particular action can be taken. We group the procedures that implement these waiting functions into a WAIT module.

3. A timer must be started and stopped, and its state must be read during the course of system operation. The procedures that implement these timer functions belong in a TIMER module.
4. When a test in one of the procedures of the TEST module indicates that an intruder has been detected, a procedure is invoked to actuate the visual alarm, to start a sixty-second timer and, upon expiration of the timer, to actuate the audible alarm. This procedure is contained in an INTRUDER DETECTED module.

In addition to these four modules, a fifth functional module whose presence cannot be deduced from the functional specification is needed. When the burglar alarm system is first turned on, or following a power interruption, or when it is disarmed by the keyswitch, the system must be initialized and all of the alarms and the timer must be reset. For convenience, the procedures that implement these functions are grouped together into a RESET module.

The module structure that we now have for the burglar alarm system is shown in Figure 3-3. We have placed each module on one of four levels in the top-down hierarchy. We know that the EXECUTIVE module is at the top level and that the INPUT, OUTPUT, and TIMER modules are at the bottom level. It is reasonable to assume, moreover, that the INTRUDER DETECTED module is at a lower level than the TEST module, but it cannot be definitely stated that the relationship between the modules on the second and third levels is exactly as illustrated in Figure 3-3. When the procedures that belong to the modules are fully defined and the interactions between them are known, then we will be able to specify the level of each module more precisely, as we shall see.

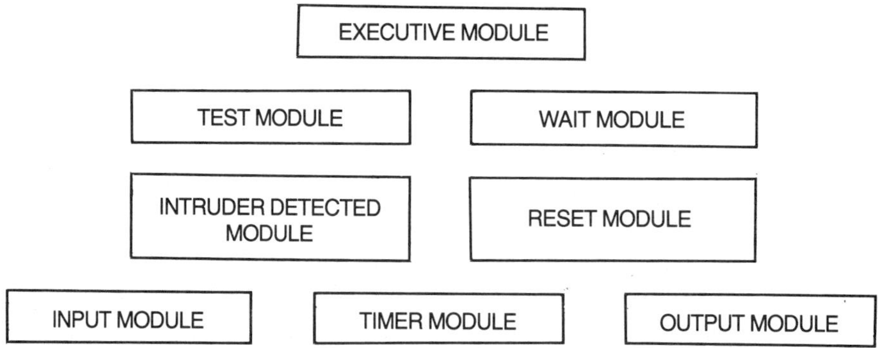

Figure 3-3. Functional modularization of the burglar alarm system.

The reader may have noticed that we chose each module name so that it has a relationship to the functions implemented by the procedures contained in the module. This way of choosing module names is strongly recommended. In many cases, several names are equally reasonable for a particular module. In such cases, choose the name you prefer. It is not necessary to be overly concerned with what someone else would do since there is no *right* way to select a module name. For example, the OUTPUT module in our system could just as easily be called the ALARM module since the only outputs in the burglar alarm system are the alarms.

It should also be noted that the way in which functions or procedures are assigned to a module also depends on one's personal preference. If a module contains too many procedures, it can be split into several modules. If several modules each contain a small number of unrelated procedures, they can be combined into a single module (the MISCELLANEOUS module?) to prevent the system from becoming unduly complex. In our system, for example, we could easily combine the TEST module, the WAIT module, and the INTRUDER DETECTED module. We chose not to do so because our system is not overly complex even with separate modules. As with every other aspect of system design, experience will help you find a reasonable modular decomposition of a system more quickly. Experience will also help you to choose module names that are meaningful to you and that can be understood by those working with you. Modularizing a system makes it easy to add functions to a design or to modify or delete parts of a design at any time during the system design cycle. Functional modularization is not the only way to divide software into modules. An alternate method, which can be used in conjunction with functional modularization, is called *data modularization*.

To avoid breaking up the continuity of our description at this point, let us next describe how to break modules into procedures and, in the first part of Chapter 4, describe how to design the procedures for the burglar alarm system. Then, after we complete the description of how the design language is used to implement the procedures of the burglar alarm system, we will describe data modularization.

PROCEDURES

A software module consists of a set of functions that belongs to that module. For each module, we define a set of procedures to implement the functions belonging to the module. To illustrate, let us describe how to define the procedures for each module of the burglar alarm system.

As stated earlier, the EXECUTIVE module consists of a single procedure called the EXECUTIVE procedure.

In the INPUT module, input signals are read. Therefore, let us define a procedure for reading each of the three input signals. For ease of identification, we assign procedure names that are related to the functions performed by the procedures. Thus, we call the INPUT module procedures READ KEYSWITCH, READ SWITCHES, and READ MOTION DETECTOR.

Similarly, the procedures in the OUTPUT module actuate and reset the audible and visual alarms. The functions required in this module can be implemented by one, two, or four procedures. A separate procedure can be defined to implement each of the four output functions, that of actuating or resetting each of the two alarms. Or, a single procedure can be used to perform all four output functions. Or, two procedures can be defined, one to actuate the alarms and a second to reset them. In our design we choose the latter method and call the procedures in the OUTPUT

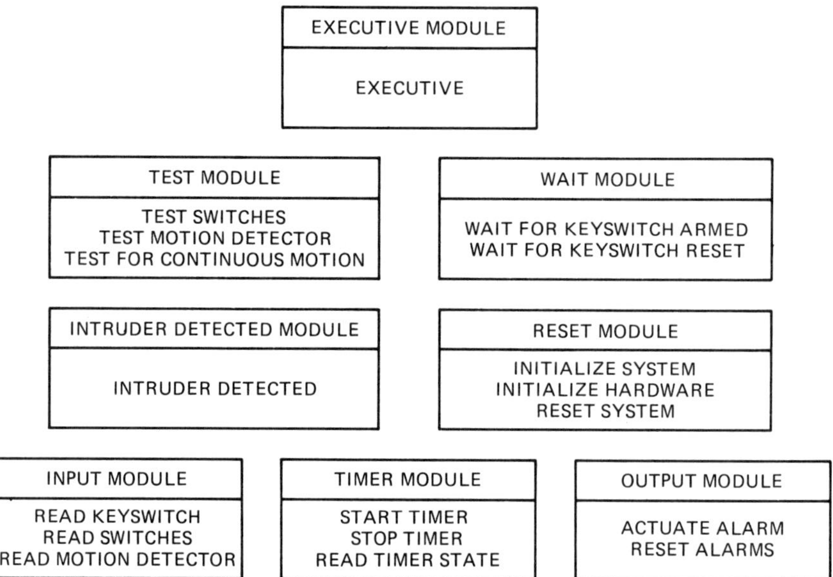

Figure 3-4. Module structure of the burglar alarm system showing the procedures that belong to each module.

module ACTUATE ALARM and RESET ALARMS. We discuss how to specify which alarm is to be actuated by the ACTUATE ALARM procedure when we describe how to design these procedures.

In the TEST module the switches and motion detector are tested. Thus, we call these procedures TEST SWITCHES, TEST MOTION DETECTOR, and TEST FOR CONTINUOUS MOTION. The TEST MOTION DETECTOR procedure tests whether or not the motion detector is tripped and the TEST FOR CONTINUOUS MOTION procedure determines whether or not the motion detector remains continuously tripped for at least five seconds to prevent false alarms.

In the WAIT module the keyswitch is tested and, if necessary, the system waits for its state to be changed from the reset state to the armed state, or vice versa. We call these procedures WAIT FOR KEYSWITCH ARMED and WAIT FOR KEYSWITCH RESET.

The TIMER module contains procedures that enable the system to start and stop a timer and to read the timer state to determine if it has expired. We call these procedures START TIMER, STOP TIMER, and READ TIMER STATE.

The procedure in the INTRUDER DETECTED module is called INTRUDER DETECTED.

Finally, the RESET module contains three procedures: a procedure to initialize the system when it is first turned on or after a power interruption, a procedure to initialize the hardware, and a procedure to reset the alarms and the timer. We call these procedures INITIALIZE SYSTEM, INITIALIZE HARDWARE, and RESET SYSTEM. The functions performed by INITIALIZE HARDWARE and RESET

SYSTEM are similar. We will see how these procedures are related to each other and to the INITIALIZE SYSTEM procedure shortly. The complete module structure for the burglar alarm system software showing the procedures that belong to each module is shown in Figure 3-4.

In some systems an additional level of subdivision is necessary to keep the complexity of the system reasonable. Let us now describe the use of *subsystems*.

SUBSYSTEMS

The burglar alarm system is small and therefore quite simple; in a more complex system the number of modules is much larger. As indicated in Chapter 2, in a more complex system the system should be divided into subsystems and a functional specification should be prepared for each subsystem. The modularization and design for each subsystem should then be carried out as if the subsystem were a small system.

Figure 3-5 illustrates how the subsystems and modules of a large system are related. The high-level subsystems have SUBSYSTEM EXECUTIVE modules that

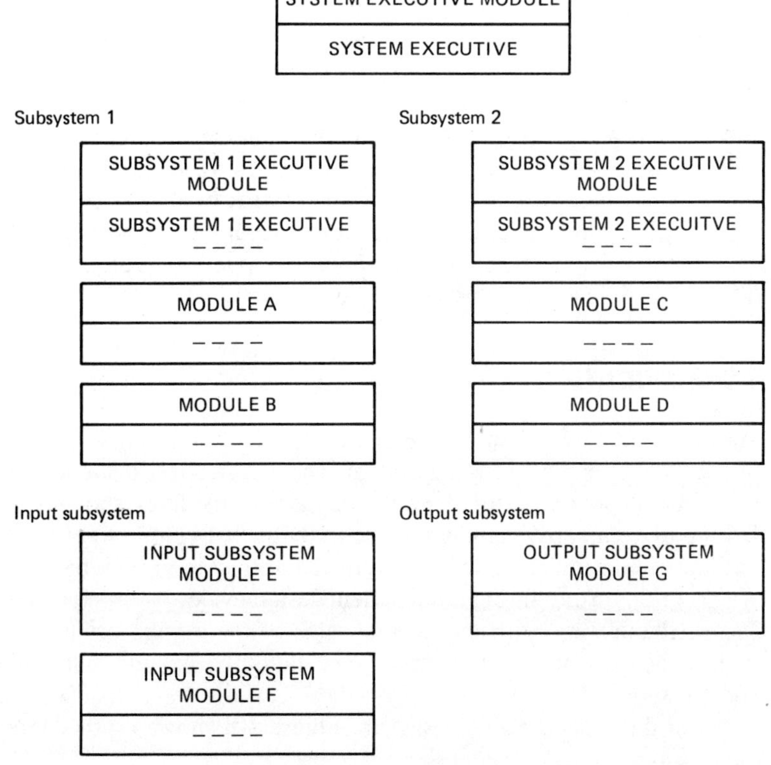

Figure 3-5. Subsystems.

contain the procedures called by the SYSTEM EXECUTIVE procedure in the SYSTEM EXECUTIVE module. The low-level subsystems may not have SUBSYSTEM EXECUTIVE modules if they provide utility functions for the other subsystems. The INPUT and OUTPUT subsystems are examples of low-level subsystems.

Let us next reexamine the relationship between the hardware and the software modules to see how hardware/software tradeoffs affect the modularization.

HARDWARE/SOFTWARE TRADEOFFS

Let us assume that the timer in the burglar alarm system is implemented completely in software except for a basic clock mechanism whose relationship to the microcomputer system is described later. In this case, the software modularization shown in Figure 3-3 is reasonable and is related to the hardware modularization as shown in Figure 3-6. The INPUT SIGNAL CONDITIONING module of Figure 3-1 has been replaced by the KEYSWITCH, SWITCHES, and MOTION DETECTOR modules and the OUTPUT SIGNAL CONDITIONING module has been replaced by the ALARMS module. The relationship between the software modules and the MICROCOMPUTER module is indicated by the double arrow since the software modules are implemented as procedures in the microcomputer. Since the information obtained from the inputs through the INPUT INTERFACE module is controlled by the software INPUT module, a relationship is shown by the dashed lines between these two modules. A similar relationship is shown between the software OUTPUT module and the OUTPUT INTERFACE module.

If we move the timer from the software into the hardware, a TIMER module is added to the hardware and the software TIMER module is deleted as shown in Figure 3-7. The three timer procedures are moved into the software INPUT and OUTPUT modules since their function now is to move information between the hardware TIMER module and the microcomputer.

DESIGN SPECIFICATION

As indicated in Chapter 2, the design specification contains specific information about the implementation of a system. The design specification, at this point, should contain a chart or list of the subsystems and modules showing the modules that belong to each subsystem and the procedures that belong to each module. As noted earlier, the design specification produced at this point may be subject to change as we progress further through the system design cycle.

Although it is difficult at this stage of the system design cycle to produce a hierarchical list of the procedures, one should be included ultimately in the design specification. This list, the *procedure calling tree*, indicates the relationship between the procedures in a system. Figure 3-8 shows a procedure calling tree for the burglar alarm system. After we have completed the design of the procedures for the burglar alarm system, we will return to the calling tree to show how it is obtained.

As we shall see, the data manipulated by a system is organized into *data structures*. A description of each data structure should also be included in the design specification. Each data structure description should contain information on how the data is organized, how it is accessed, and where it is stored in the system.

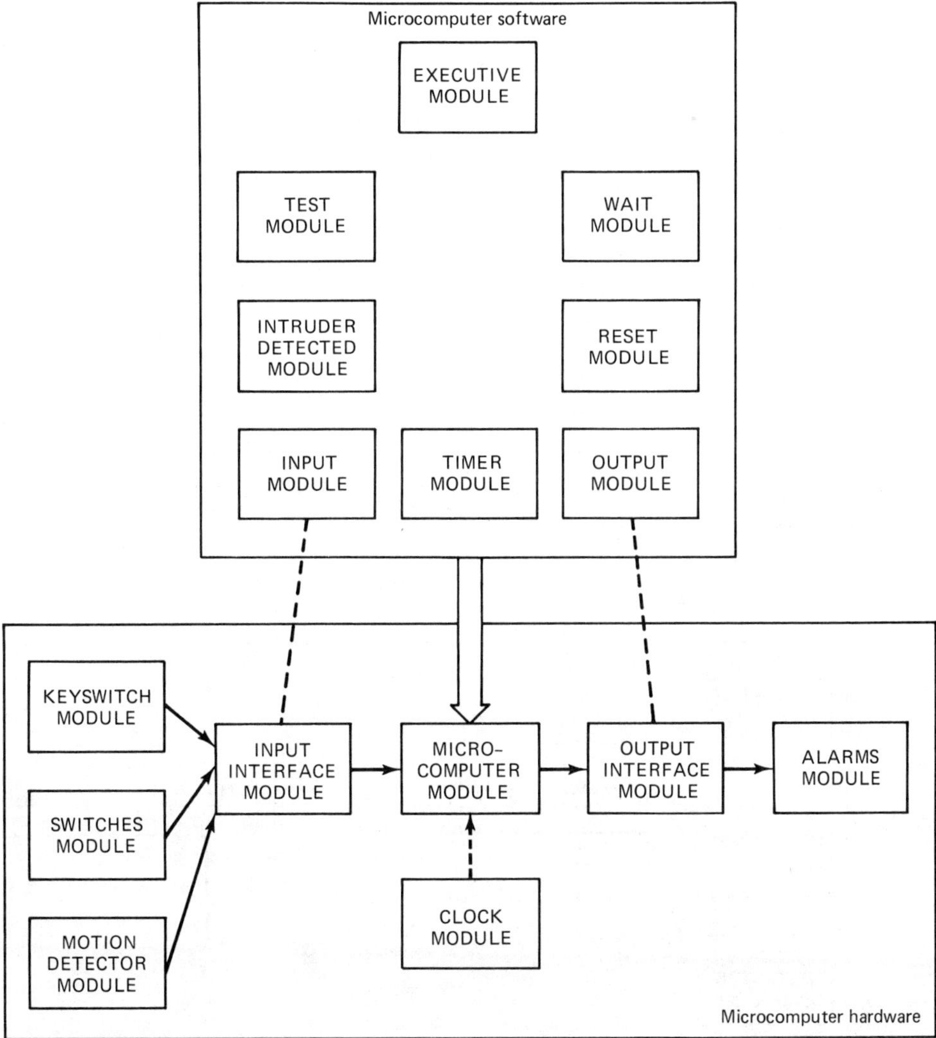

Figure 3-6. Burglar alarm system showing relationship between hardware and software modules.

In summary, the design specification for a system should contain the following:

- A subsystem list.
- A module list.
- A procedure calling tree.
- A description of each data structure.
- Other information necessary to understand the system at the design level that is not contained in the design language description of the system.

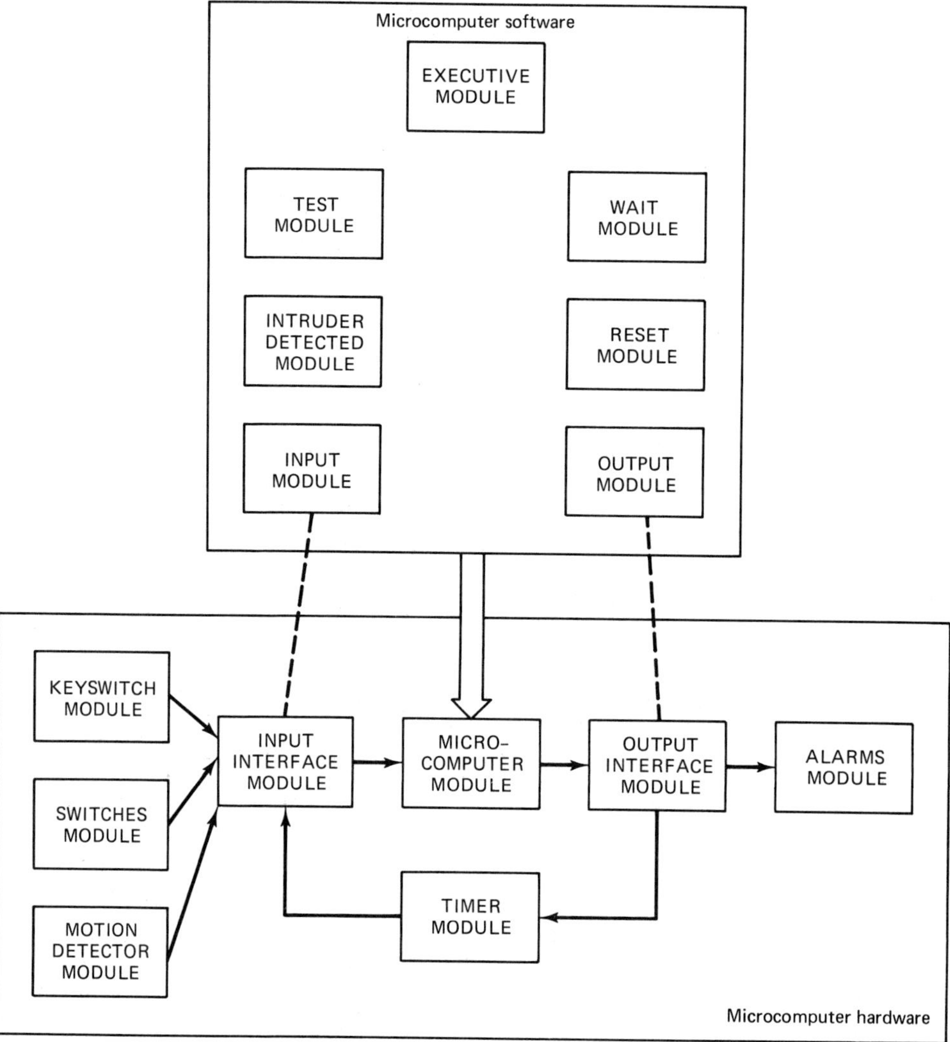

Figure 3-7. Modularization of burglar alarm system containing a hardware timer module.

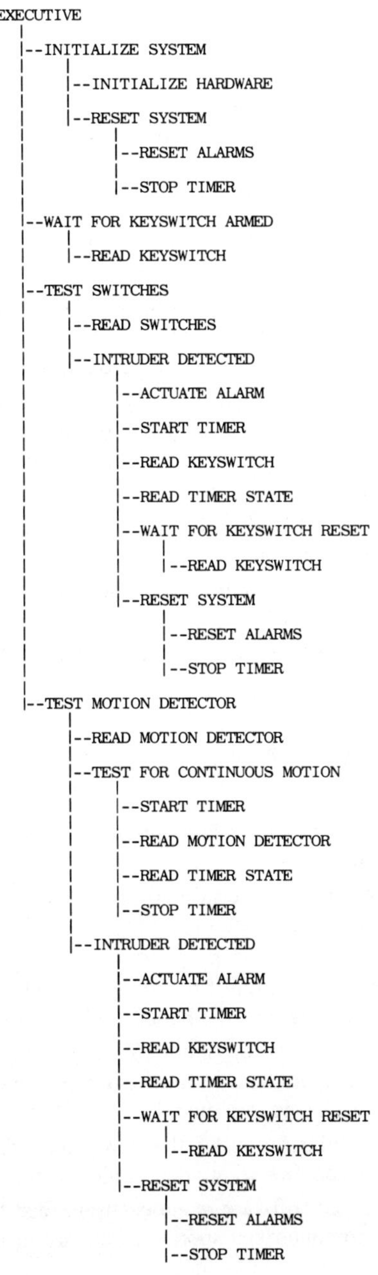

Figure 3-8. The procedure calling tree for the burglar alarm system.

DESIGN REVIEW

To develop and build a system that meets the needs of the user or customer, its design should be reviewed regularly during the system design cycle. As indicated in Chapter 2, user requirements and the functional specification should be reviewed frequently with the customer during development. Then, while the system is being modularized, while the functional specification is being converted into a design, and while the design is being implemented, additional design reviews should be conducted. If it is either undesirable or impossible for the customer or user to be involved in the latter reviews, competent *outsiders* should participate to ensure that user requirements and the functional specification are being met.

Sometimes, a problem will surface during a design review indicating that some part of the functional specification cannot be met reasonably or cost effectively. An alternative for that part of the functional specification can then be suggested and sent back to the customer for review. The latter step in the design review process is preferable to substituting an alternative design without the customer's review and consent; to do so would undoubtedly influence the acceptance of the system by the customer when it is completed.

In this chapter we modularized the burglar alarm system, defined the procedures in each of the software modules, and showed the relationship between the software and the hardware. Let us now proceed to design these procedures using design language.

EXERCISES

3-1. Divide the hardware implementation of a television set that does not contain a microcomputer into modules.

3-2. What software modules are needed to implement the functional specification for the computerized television set in Exercise 2-3? What procedures are needed for each software module?

3-3. Subject the modularization of the computerized television set to a hardware/software tradeoff study to determine if a better modularization is possible.

3-4. What hardware and software modules are needed to implement the functional specification for the computerized traffic light controller in Exercise 2-6? What procedures are needed for each software module?

3-5. Subject the modularization of the computerized traffic light controller to a hardware/software tradeoff study to determine if a better modularization is possible.

3-6. What hardware and software modules are needed to implement the functional specification for the computerized sports scoreboard in Exercise 2-9? What procedures are needed for each software module?

3-7. Subject the modularization of the computerized sports scoreboard to a hardware/software tradeoff study to determine if a better modularization is possible.

3-8. What hardware and software modules are needed to implement the functional specification for the computerized point-of-sale terminal in Exercise 2-12? What procedures are needed for each software module?

3-9. Subject the modularization of the computerized POS terminal to a hardware/software tradeoff study to determine if a better modularization is possible.

Chapter 4

Software Design

Part I
BURGLAR ALARM SYSTEM

This chapter consists of two parts. In the first part we show how the burglar alarm system is designed. As we proceed, we introduce a number of design language concepts that are needed. In part two of this chapter we consider the general principles of software design. The remaining design language concepts are then presented along with examples to illustrate how they are used.

EXECUTIVE PROCEDURE

Let us design each of the procedures of the burglar alarm system starting with the EXECUTIVE procedure. For clarity and ease of design, each procedure should also be designed in a top-down manner. That is, its operations should proceed step by step from top to bottom. The DO . . . END, IF . . . THEN . . . ELSE . . . and other constructs of the design language facilitate the top-down design of a procedure.

The EXECUTIVE procedure is used to ensure that the system performs the required functions in the proper sequence. If possible, the EXECUTIVE procedure should do no testing or low-level decision making. Just as the chief executive of a corporation delegates responsibilities, the EXECUTIVE procedure should also *delegate responsibilities* to the next lower level procedures. It should therefore contain the design language constructs needed to invoke these lower-level procedures and to cause them to be repeated in a suitable manner.

Let us see how an executive procedure is designed by examining the burglar alarm system EXECUTIVE shown in Figure 4-1. The name of the procedure is placed on the top line following the word PROCEDURE. This convention is used to identify the procedure and to permit *parameters* to be specified for the procedure.

```
PROCEDURE: EXECUTIVE (;)
BEGIN PROCEDURE
  CALL: INITIALIZE SYSTEM (;)
  DO FOREVER
    CALL: WAIT FOR KEYSWITCH ARMED (;)
    CALL: TEST SWITCHES (;)
    CALL: TEST MOTION DETECTOR (;)
  END
END PROCEDURE
```

Figure 4-1. The burglar alarm system EXECUTIVE procedure.

For the EXECUTIVE procedure, no parameters are specified; therefore only a semicolon appears within the parentheses. We discuss parameters shortly when we encounter an example in which parameters are actually specified.

The operations the EXECUTIVE procedure performs are contained between the phrases BEGIN PROCEDURE and END PROCEDURE. This convention permits us to insert descriptive information in the form of text into the procedure to provide additional documentation. This additional documentation is not confused with the design operations if it is placed between the procedure name and the BEGIN PROCEDURE constructs. For simplicity, we have omitted all additional documentation in the burglar alarm system examples; we discuss them further at the end of this chapter.

The first operation that the EXECUTIVE procedure performs causes the INITIALIZE SYSTEM procedure to be invoked. The operation:

```
CALL: INITIALIZE SYSTEM (;)
```

calls the INITIALIZE SYSTEM procedure. The latter procedure then performs its operations until it encounters a RETURN operation at which time it *returns* control back to the procedure from which it was called, in this case, to the EXECUTIVE procedure. The EXECUTIVE procedure then resumes performing its operations. In the EXECUTIVE procedure, the operations contained within the DO FOREVER . . . END construct are repeated indefinitely after control is returned from the INITIALIZE SYSTEM procedure. Thus, the burglar alarm system waits for the keyswitch to be armed (WAIT FOR KEYSWITCH ARMED) and then tests the sensors (TEST SWITCHES, TEST MOTION DETECTOR). It does this for as long as power is applied to the system. Note that if the system is armed, that is, the keyswitch is in the armed position, then, when the WAIT FOR KEYSWITCH ARMED procedure is called, control is immediately returned to the EXECUTIVE procedure. Thus, in this case, the switches and the motion detector are checked repeatedly; this is the desired action when the keyswitch is in the armed position. When the system is disarmed, that is, the keyswitch is in the reset position, control is not returned from the WAIT FOR KEYSWITCH ARMED procedure for as long as the keyswitch remains in the reset position. This causes the sensors to be ignored until the system is once again armed by the keyswitch.

As we shall see, if an intruder is detected during the operation of either the TEST SWITCHES procedure or the TEST MOTION DETECTOR procedure, suitable action is taken. The details of the action taken are contained within the latter procedures themselves. The EXECUTIVE ensures that high-level sequencing takes place; it does not concern itself with details that belong at the lower levels. Then, as we design the lower levels, these details are taken into account. Thus, the clarity of the design is enhanced by using the top-down approach in which details are relegated to the lower levels and the upper levels are kept relatively free of detail.

The EXECUTIVE procedure itself is *called* when power is first applied to the system or after power is reapplied after a power failure. The mechanism for doing this is described in Chapter 8. However, once it has been called, the EXECUTIVE procedure need never return to its caller; thus, no RETURN operation is provided. As we shall see, for proper operation of the system, every other procedure must contain at least one RETURN operation.

RESET AND INITIALIZE PROCEDURES

The RESET module contains procedures that perform initialization and reset functions. As a result, they are usually very simple and straightforward. We have identified three procedures in the burglar alarm system RESET module: INITIALIZE SYSTEM, INITIALIZE HARDWARE, and RESET SYSTEM. The INITIALIZE SYSTEM procedure called by the EXECUTIVE procedure is shown in Figure 4-2. It calls the INITIALIZE HARDWARE and the RESET SYSTEM procedures and then returns control to its calling procedure which, in this case, is the EXECUTIVE procedure.

```
PROCEDURE: INITIALIZE SYSTEM (;)
BEGIN PROCEDURE
  CALL: INITIALIZE HARDWARE (;)
  CALL: RESET SYSTEM (;)
  RETURN
END PROCEDURE
```

Figure 4-2. The INITIALIZE SYSTEM procedure.

The INITIALIZE HARDWARE procedure takes care of resetting and starting several built-in hardware functions. We defer a detailed discussion of hardware initialization to Chapter 8.

The RESET SYSTEM procedure is shown in Figure 4-3. It calls the RESET ALARMS and STOP TIMER procedures to turn off the alarms and the timer. We defer further discussion of the procedures in the INPUT module, OUTPUT module, and TIMER module to Chapter 6. Once the alarms and the timer are turned off, control is returned to the calling procedure. As we shall see, the RESET SYSTEM procedure is called from several other procedures and, in each case, when it is called it turns off the alarms and the timer and returns control to the procedure that called it. Thus, the benefits of using procedures are twofold: First, by using procedures, we divide the system into small parts each of which implements a single function that is easily understood. Second, because a procedure can be called from more than one place in the design, the operations of the procedure do not have to be repeated explicitly each place they are needed. When we have completed the design of the burglar alarm system procedures, it would be instructive for the reader to rewrite the EXECUTIVE procedure replacing each of the four calls with the specific operations contained in each of the called procedures and to consider the following questions: Is clarity sacrificed? Does repetition add anything to the design? The reader should consider these questions carefully to better appreciate the use of procedures in a modularized system.

```
PROCEDURE: RESET SYSTEM (;)
BEGIN PROCEDURE
  CALL: RESET ALARMS (;)
  CALL: STOP TIMER (;)
  RETURN
END PROCEDURE
```

Figure 4-3. The RESET SYSTEM procedure.

WAIT FOR KEYSWITCH ARMED PROCEDURE

In many systems, it is necessary to wait for an event to happen. One way to implement a wait function is to use the DO FOREVER . . . END construct with an internal test to terminate the procedure when the condition that is being waited for occurs. The WAIT FOR KEYSWITCH ARMED procedure for the burglar alarm system is shown in Figure 4-4. It calls the READ KEYSWITCH procedure in the INPUT module and tests the state of the keyswitch; if the keyswitch is not armed, the reading and testing of the keyswitch are repeated indefinitely until the keyswitch is armed. Then, control is returned to the calling procedure. Note that the ELSE part of the IF . . . THEN . . . ELSE . . . test construct is optional and can be omitted. In effect, this is equivalent to writing

```
ELSE  DO NOTHING
```

As we indicated, the use of a test construct with a RETURN operation provides a simple way to terminate a repetitive function that has been implemented with a DO FOREVER . . . END construct. Additional examples of this concept are provided in other procedures of the burglar alarm system; other constructs which can be used to terminate the operation of a repetitive function are introduced later. The operation

```
CALL: READ KEYSWITCH (;KEYSWITCH)
```

constitutes our first encounter with a *parameter*, which, in this case, permits information to be conveyed from the READ KEYSWITCH procedure to the WAIT FOR KEYSWITCH ARMED procedure. Let us, therefore, examine the concept of parameters in more detail.

```
PROCEDURE: WAIT FOR KEYSWITCH ARMED (;)
BEGIN PROCEDURE
  DO FOREVER
    CALL: READ KEYSWITCH (;KEYSWITCH)
    IF KEYSWITCH IS ARMED
      THEN RETURN
  END
END PROCEDURE
```

Figure 4-4. The WAIT FOR KEYSWITCH ARMED procedure.

PARAMETERS

Parameters are used for communication between a calling procedure and its called procedures. In the burglar alarm system, for example, the READ KEYSWITCH procedure reads the state of the keyswitch, that is, it examines whether the keyswitch is in the armed or reset position. This information is then conveyed to the calling procedure through the KEYSWITCH parameter that follows the semicolon inside the parentheses. Parameters that convey information from a called procedure to a calling procedure (from the READ KEYSWITCH procedure to the WAIT FOR KEYSWITCH ARMED procedure in the example) are known as *output parameters* and are placed after the semicolon. If more than one parameter is used, the individual parameters are separated by commas. Parameters that convey information in the other direction, that is, from the calling procedure to the called procedure, are known as *input parameters* and precede the semicolon. Shortly we will encounter examples of input parameters. The relationship between two procedures and their input and output parameters is illustrated in Figure 4-5. Note that *input* and *output* are defined with respect to the called procedure.

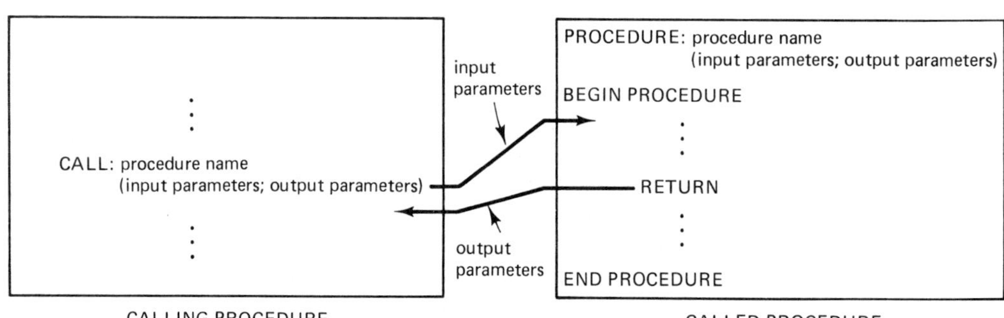

Figure 4-5. Relationship of input and output parameters to the related procedures.

As with all names, parameter names are chosen for readability. Any name can convey the necessary information as long as it is used consistently. If we choose the name SWITCH rather than KEYSWITCH to represent the state of the keyswitch in the example, the pertinent operations in Figure 4-4 become:

```
CALL: READ KEYSWITCH (; SWITCH)
IF SWITCH IS ARMED
  THEN RETURN
```

The information conveyed from the READ KEYSWITCH procedure to the WAIT FOR KEYSWITCH ARMED procedure by the output parameter SWITCH represents the state of the keyswitch; SWITCH should then be tested to determine whether or not to return to the calling procedure. Thus, the consistent use of an unambiguous parameter name, such as either SWITCH or KEYSWITCH, ensures that the correct information is tested by the IF . . . THEN . . . construct. As we shall see, all information manipulated in the microcomputer must be unambiguously identified to ensure that the system functions correctly. The use of a unique name to identify each item of information in a system is discussed further in the section on data structures.

Let us now continue our discussion of the design of the burglar alarm system with the procedures in the TEST module.

TEST SWITCHES PROCEDURE

A test procedure contains the constructs needed to determine if a particular condition exists. The test procedure also calls the other procedures that must be invoked to ensure that the desired actions are carried out in response to the outcome of the test. This protocol follows the corporate analogy of delegating responsibility introduced earlier in the chapter.

In the TEST SWITCHES procedure of the burglar alarm system, which is shown in Figure 4-6, the READ SWITCHES procedure is called first. A test is then performed to determine whether or not the switches are tripped. If the switches are tripped, the INTRUDER DETECTED procedure is called since the presence of an intruder has been detected. As we shall see, the alarms are manipulated within the INTRUDER DETECTED procedure and, when the system has been disarmed and

```
PROCEDURE: TEST SWITCHES (;)
BEGIN PROCEDURE
  CALL: READ SWITCHES (; SWITCHES)
  IF SWITCHES ARE TRIPPED
    THEN CALL: INTRUDER DETECTED (;)
  RETURN
END PROCEDURE
```

Figure 4-6. The TEST SWITCHES procedure.

reset, control is returned to the TEST SWITCHES procedure which, in turn, returns control to its calling procedure to wait for the system to be armed once again. If the switches are not tripped when the TEST SWITCHES procedure is called, it immediately returns control to the calling procedure.

INTRUDER DETECTED PROCEDURE

Up to now the design of each procedure in the burglar alarm system has consisted of only a few operations. The action needed when an intruder is detected is more complex. From the description of the INTRUDER DETECTED module, we see that the visual alarm is actuated and a sixty-second timer is started. Then, when the timer expires, the audible alarm is actuated. From the functional specification, we know that the keyswitch must be tested repeatedly since, when it is reset, the alarms must be turned off and the system returned to a quiescent state to wait for the keyswitch to be armed again.

Examining Figure 4-7, we see that the ACTUATE ALARM and START TIMER procedures are called first. Here we have two examples of the use of input parameters. Since there are two alarms in the system, it is necessary to indicate which of the two should be actuated by the ACTUATE ALARM procedure. Thus, the operations

```
SET ALARM TO VISUAL
CALL: ACTUATE ALARM (ALARM; )
```

cause the visual alarm to be actuated since the input parameter ALARM is *set* to VISUAL before being used in the calling sequence. In a similar manner, the audible alarm is actuated by setting ALARM to AUDIBLE before calling the ACTUATE ALARM procedure. As we shall see, the SET construct is also used to set output parameters before returning from a called procedure.

The input parameter for the START TIMER procedure is the desired time, in seconds, between when the timer is started and when it expires. In this case, the actual time (60 SECONDS) is inserted in place of a name and used directly as an input parameter. Both of these methods of specifying the *value* of an input parameter are equivalent and can be used interchangeably.

Having turned on the visual alarm and started the timer, it is necessary to wait for either the keyswitch to be reset or the timer to expire. The waiting action is accomplished within the procedure by setting up a DO FOREVER . . . END construct within which the keyswitch state and the timer state are tested. The keyswitch is tested first; if it remains in the armed position, the timer state is checked by calling the READ TIMER STATE procedure. Note that the DO . . . END construct is used as a set of *brackets* to indicate which operations belong to the THEN part and which belong to the ELSE part of the IF . . . THEN . . . ELSE . . . construct. The operations within the DO . . . END brackets are not repeated as in the case of the DO FOREVER . . . END construct. The indentation that we have used indicates that the operations within each set of DO . . . END brackets belong together; however, the

```
PROCEDURE: INTRUDER DETECTED (;)
BEGIN PROCEDURE
  SET ALARM TO VISUAL
  CALL: ACTUATE ALARM (ALARM;)
  CALL: START TIMER (60 SECONDS;)
  DO FOREVER
    CALL: READ KEYSWITCH (;KEYSWITCH)
    IF KEYSWITCH IS ARMED
      THEN DO
             CALL: READ TIMER STATE (;TIMER STATE)
             IF TIMER STATE IS EXPIRED
               THEN DO
                      SET ALARM TO AUDIBLE
                      CALL: ACTUATE ALARM (ALARM;)
                      CALL: WAIT FOR KEYSWITCH RESET (;)
                      CALL: RESET SYSTEM (;)
                      RETURN
                    END
           END
      ELSE DO
             CALL: RESET SYSTEM (;)
             RETURN
           END
  END
END PROCEDURE
```

Figure 4-7. The INTRUDER DETECTED procedure.

use of the DO . . . END construct ensures that no ambiguity exists regardless of indentation. We discuss indentation further in the section on documentation. In the example, when the operations within the THEN part of the IF . . . THEN . . . ELSE . . . construct are performed, if the timer has not yet expired, then no other operations remain to be performed. The function within the DO FOREVER . . . END construct is then repeated, causing the keyswitch and timer to be tested repeatedly. If, at any time before the timer expires, the keyswitch is found to be reset, then the two operations in the ELSE part of the IF . . . THEN . . . ELSE . . . construct are performed. The system is thereby reset, and control is returned to the calling procedure.

If, during operation the keyswitch remains armed for sixty seconds, then the timer expires and the operations

```
SET ALARM TO AUDIBLE
CALL: ACTUATE ALARM (ALARM;)
CALL: WAIT FOR KEYSWITCH RESET (;)
CALL: RESET SYSTEM (;)
RETURN
```

are performed. As a result, the audible alarm is actuated and remains actuated until the keyswitch is reset in the WAIT FOR KEYSWITCH RESET procedure. The alarms and the timer are turned off by the RESET SYSTEM procedure and control is then returned to the calling procedure.

WAIT FOR KEYSWITCH RESET PROCEDURE

The WAIT FOR KEYSWITCH RESET procedure, shown in Figure 4-8, is similar to the WAIT FOR KEYSWITCH ARMED procedure except that the test is made for the reset position instead of for the armed position of the keyswitch.

```
PROCEDURE: WAIT FOR KEYSWITCH RESET (;)
BEGIN PROCEDURE
  DO FOREVER
    CALL: READ KEYSWITCH (;KEYSWITCH)
    IF KEYSWITCH IS RESET
      THEN  RETURN
  END
END PROCEDURE
```

Figure 4-8. The WAIT FOR KEYSWITCH RESET procedure.

TEST MOTION DETECTOR PROCEDURE

The TEST MOTION DETECTOR procedure is shown in Figure 4-9. It calls the READ MOTION DETECTOR procedure and tests whether or not the motion detector is tripped. If the motion detector is not tripped, the TEST MOTION DETECTOR procedure returns control to the calling procedure. If it is tripped, then the TEST FOR CONTINUOUS MOTION procedure is called to determine whether or not the motion detector will remain tripped continuously for at least five seconds. If continuous motion is not detected, then the TEST MOTION DETECTOR procedure returns control to the calling procedure. If continuous motion is detected, then the INTRUDER DETECTED procedure is called to activate the alarms as described earlier. Note that the parameter CONTINUOUS, which is an output parameter of the TEST FOR CONTINUOUS MOTION procedure, indicates whether or not the motion detector remained tripped continuously for five seconds.

```
PROCEDURE: TEST MOTION DETECTOR (;)
BEGIN PROCEDURE
  CALL: READ MOTION DETECTOR (;MOTION DETECTOR)
  IF MOTION DETECTOR IS TRIPPED
    THEN  DO
            CALL: TEST FOR CONTINUOUS MOTION (;CONTINUOUS)
            IF CONTINUOUS IS SET
              THEN  CALL: INTRUDER DETECTED (;)
          END
  RETURN
END PROCEDURE
```

Figure 4-9. The TEST MOTION DETECTOR procedure.

TEST FOR CONTINUOUS MOTION PROCEDURE

When the motion detector is tripped, it is necessary to ensure that it remains tripped continuously for at least five seconds to prevent a false alarm. The TEST FOR CONTINUOUS MOTION procedure performs this test as shown in Figure 4-10.

```
PROCEDURE: TEST FOR CONTINUOUS MOTION (;CONTINUOUS)
BEGIN PROCEDURE
  CALL: START TIMER (5 SECONDS;)
  DO FOREVER
    CALL: READ MOTION DETECTOR (;MOTION DETECTOR)
    IF MOTION DETECTOR IS TRIPPED
      THEN  DO
              CALL: READ TIMER STATE (;TIMER STATE)
              IF TIMER STATE IS EXPIRED
                THEN  DO
                        CALL: STOP TIMER (;)
                        SET CONTINUOUS
                        RETURN
                      END
            END
      ELSE  DO
              CALL: STOP TIMER (;)
              RESET CONTINUOUS
              RETURN
            END
  END
END PROCEDURE
```

Figure 4-10. The TEST FOR CONTINUOUS MOTION procedure.

The START TIMER procedure is called to initiate the timing of a five-second interval. It is then necessary to wait for one of two possible situations to occur: either the motion detector reverts to its untripped state or the timer expires. The waiting action is accomplished within the procedure by setting up a DO FOREVER . . . END construct within which the motion detector state and the timer state are tested. If the motion detector remains tripped, then the timer is checked by the READ TIMER STATE procedure. If the timer has not yet expired, then no other operations are performed, and the motion detector state and timer state are retested. If, at any time before the timer expires, the motion detector reverts to its untripped state, then the operations

```
CALL: STOP TIMER (;)
RESET CONTINUOUS
RETURN
```

in the ELSE part of the IF . . . THEN . . . ELSE . . . construct are performed. Thus, the timer is stopped, the parameter CONTINUOUS is reset, and control is returned to the calling procedure.

If the motion detector remains tripped continuously for five seconds, then the timer expires and the operations

```
CALL: STOP TIMER (;)
SET CONTINUOUS
RETURN
```

are performed. As a result, the timer is stopped, the parameter CONTINUOUS is set, and control is returned to the calling procedure.

This completes our discussion of the design of the procedures for the burglar alarm system. Let us now examine aspects of design language not covered in the burglar alarm system example.

Part II
GENERAL PRINCIPLES

We have now completed our introduction to design language using the simple burglar alarm system example. In this part of the chapter we complete our discussion of design language and consider the subject of software design in general.

LOOPS

The DO FOREVER . . . END construct is commonly known as a *loop* since the operations between the DO FOREVER and the END phrases are executed repeatedly as if they were an endless loop. As we have seen, the endless (or infinite) loop is extremely useful in implementing the executive function of a real-time system such as the burglar alarm system. We have also used it to implement a loop that terminates when an internal test causes a RETURN operation to be performed. An alternative construct for a terminating loop is provided by the *conditional* loop construct DO WHILE . . . END. To illustrate the use of the latter construct, we have rewritten the WAIT FOR KEYSWITCH ARMED procedure in Figure 4-11 using the DO WHILE . . . END construct in place of the DO FOREVER . . . END construct. The operations contained within the DO WHILE . . . END construct are then repeated as long as the condition KEYSWITCH IS RESET is *true*. As soon as the keyswitch is armed, the condition becomes *false*, the loop terminates, and the operation following the END is performed. In this case, control is returned to the calling procedure since a RETURN operation follows the DO WHILE . . . END construct. Note that a call to the READ KEYSWITCH procedure must be inserted prior to the start of the conditional loop to ensure that the parameter KEYSWITCH is set to a valid state before it is tested. A common design error occurs if this operation is omitted thereby causing the system to behave in an unpredictable manner when it is built.

```
PROCEDURE: WAIT FOR KEYSWITCH ARMED (;)
BEGIN PROCEDURE
  CALL: READ KEYSWITCH (;KEYSWITCH)
  DO WHILE KEYSWITCH IS RESET
    CALL: READ KEYSWITCH (;KEYSWITCH)
  END
  RETURN
END PROCEDURE
```

Figure 4-11. Example of the DO WHILE ... END construct.

This example also illustrates that there are many correct ways to implement the software design for a system. Both of the designs for the WAIT FOR KEYSWITCH ARMED procedure provide identical functional behavior. Which construct is used is entirely a matter of personal preference. Again, experience and what seems easier and more logical are the best guides in deciding which is preferable in any particular situation.

Another very useful conditional loop construct is the DO FOR EACH . . . END construct. This construct permits us to indicate that the operations contained in the loop should be repeated a specific number of times without specifying an exact number at the design level. To illustrate, let us examine the READ SWITCHES procedure in the INPUT module of the burglar alarm system. The number of switches connected to the system may not be known until just before the system is installed. Yet, we must be able to indicate that each switch should be tested and, if *any* switch is tripped, the alarms should be actuated. The READ SWITCHES procedure is shown implemented using the DO FOR EACH construct in Figure 4-12. When the procedure is executed, the state of each switch is examined and tested. If it is tripped, the output parameter SWITCHES is set to TRIPPED and the procedure is terminated by the RETURN operation. If none of the switches is found to be tripped, the operations following the loop are executed causing the parameter SWITCHES to be set to NOT TRIPPED and terminating the execution of the pro-

```
PROCEDURE: READ SWITCHES (;SWITCHES)
BEGIN PROCEDURE
  DO FOR EACH SWITCH
    EXAMINE SWITCH AND SAVE ITS STATE
    IF SWITCH IS TRIPPED
      THEN  DO
              SET SWITCHES TO TRIPPED
              RETURN
            END
  END
  SET SWITCHES TO NOT TRIPPED
  RETURN
END PROCEDURE
```

Figure 4-12. Example of the DO FOR EACH ... END construct.

cedure. The actual number of switches to be tested can then be specified or a mechanism for specifying the number can be provided when the design language is converted into a programming language; alternately, the number can be provided when the system is installed.

COMPOUND CONDITIONS

A compound condition can be used in a test construct or in a loop construct. Examples of compound conditions are:

```
IF KEYSWITCH IS ARMED AND TIMER STATE IS EXPIRED
```

and

```
DO WHILE KEYSWITCH IS ARMED AND TIMER STATE IS EXPIRED
```

The connective OR can also be used in a compound condition as can any combination of the two connectives. The conditions can be positive as in the above examples or negative as in the following example:

```
IF KEYSWITCH IS RESET OR TIMER STATE IS NOT EXPIRED
```

This completes our introduction to design language. Let us now summarize the design language constructs.

SUMMARY OF DESIGN LANGUAGE

The design language constructs that we defined can be divided into the following categories: assignment constructs, test constructs, loop constructs, control constructs, and documentation constructs. We summarize the constructs for each category below and illustrate each construct with an example.

Assignment constructs

```
SET . . . TO . . .                    SET TIME TO FIVE O'CLOCK

SET . . .                             SET CONTINUOUS

RESET . . .                           RESET CONTINUOUS
```

Test constructs

```
IF a condition is true                IF KEYSWITCH IS ARMED
  THEN  do something                    THEN  RETURN

IF a condition is true                IF ALL RECORDS BUT THE LAST ONE HAVE BEEN SELECTED
  THEN  do something                    THEN  RETURN
  ELSE  do something different          ELSE  SELECT THE NEXT RECORD IN FILE
```

Loop constructs

```
                                   IF TIMER STATE IS EXPIRED
 DO                                  THEN  DO
   .                                         CALL: STOP TIMER (;)
   .                                         SET CONTINUOUS
   .                                         RETURN
 END                                       END

DO FOR EACH of a set of things     DO FOR EACH SWITCH
                                     EXAMINE SWITCH AND SAVE ITS STATE
        .                            IF SWITCH IS TRIPPED
        .                              THEN  DO
        .                                      SET SWITCHES TO TRIPPED
                                               RETURN
                                             END
END                                END

DO FOREVER                         DO FOREVER
        .                            CALL: READ KEYSWITCH (;KEYSWITCH)
        .                            IF KEYSWITCH IS ARMED
        .                              THEN  RETURN
END                                END

DO WHILE a test condition is true  DO WHILE KEYSWITCH IS RESET
        .                            CALL: READ KEYSWITCH (;KEYSWITCH)
        .
        .
END                                END
```

Control constructs

```
CALL: procedure name (input parameters;output parameters)
                                   CALL: ACTUATE ALARM (ALARM;)

RETURN                             RETURN
```

Documentation constructs

```
PROCEDURE: procedure name (input parameters;output parameters)
                                   PROCEDURE: ACTUATE ALARM (ALARM;)
BEGIN PROCEDURE                    BEGIN PROCEDURE
        .                                  .
        .                                  .
        .                                  .
END PROCEDURE                      END PROCEDURE
```

Additional documentation is needed in the *header* between the first line of the procedure and the BEGIN PROCEDURE line, as we shall see shortly.

Let us now complete the discussion of modularization that we started in Chapter 3.

MODULARIZATION CONTINUED

Having completed the procedure design phase for the burglar alarm system, we can now redraw the module structure of Figure 3-3 to show the correct top-down relationship between the software modules. Since the INTRUDER DETECTED procedure calls procedures in both the WAIT module and the RESET module, it is necessary to move these modules to new locations, as shown in Figure 4-13. None of the other relationships between modules is changed from what we assumed initially. The rules for establishing the level of a module are:

- A procedure may be called by procedures belonging to higher-level modules.
- A procedure may be called by a procedure within its own module.

The reader should verify that Figure 4-13 correctly represents the module structure for the burglar alarm system. One way to do this is to build a *procedure calling tree*, which shows the relationship between the procedures as we indicated when we introduced the concept in Chapter 3. The procedure calling tree for the burglar alarm system is shown in Figure 4-14. The format used in the figure is one that can be produced automatically, as we shall see in Chapter 7. Note that if a procedure is called more than once, it is duplicated in the calling tree.

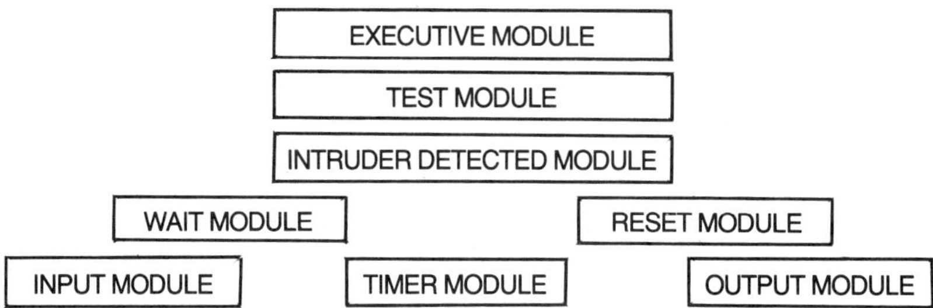

Figure 4-13. Corrected module structure for the burglar alarm system software.

The burglar alarm system provided us with an example whose modularization was relatively straightforward. Moreover, it was also straightforward to decompose each module into procedures. Unfortunately, most systems cannot be designed as easily. In most cases, a first-cut modularization is produced and each software module is decomposed into procedures. Then, after some of the procedure designs are completed, a second-cut modularization and decomposition are produced. Additional iterations may then be needed after more of the design is completed.

The procedure calling tree can also be used to show how parameters are passed between procedures. Part of the burglar alarm system calling tree is redrawn in Figure 4-15 showing parameters being passed between the procedures. The labeled

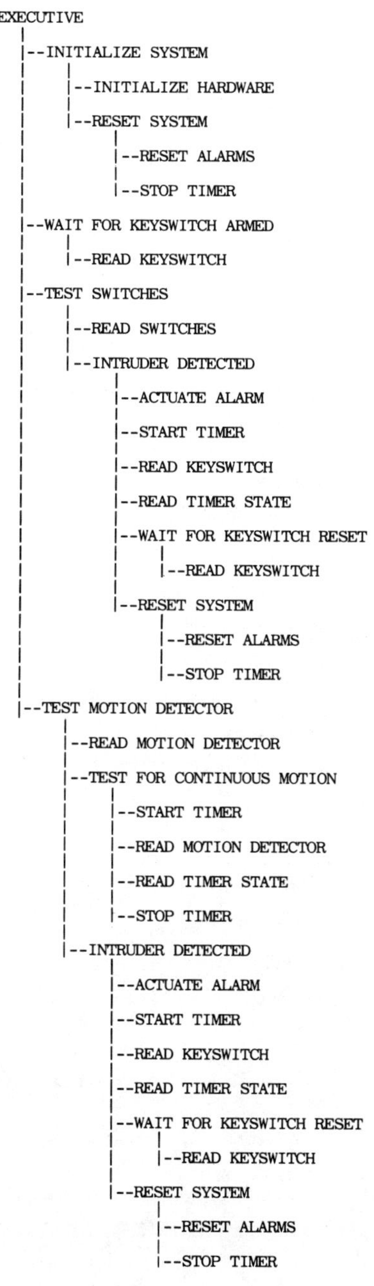

Figure 4-14. The procedure calling tree for the burglar alarm system software.

```
EXECUTIVE
   |
   |--INITIALIZE SYSTEM
   |
   |--WAIT FOR KEYSWITCH ARMED
   |    |
   |    |     <--- KEYSWITCH ---
   |    |--------------------------READ KEYSWITCH
   |
   |--TEST SWITCHES
   |    |
   |    |     <--- SWITCHES ---
   |    |--------------------------READ SWITCHES
   |    |
   |    |--INTRUDER DETECTED
   |         |
   |         |        --- ALARM --->
   |         |----------------------------ACTUATE ALARM
   |         |
   |         |         --- TIME --->
   |         |----------------------------START TIMER
   |         |
   |         |    <--- KEYSWITCH ---
   |         |----------------------------READ KEYSWITCH
   |         |
   |         |    <--- TIMER STATE ---
   |         |----------------------------READ TIMER STATE
   |         |
   |         |----------------------------WAIT FOR KEYSWITCH RESET
   |                                        |
   |                                        |    <--- KEYSWITCH ---
   |                                        |--------------------------READ KEYSWITCH
   |
   |--TEST MOTION DETECTOR
        |
        | <--- MOTION DETECTOR ---
        |--------------------------READ MOTION DETECTOR
        |
        |   <--- CONTINUOUS ---
        |--------------------------TEST FOR CONTINUOUS MOTION
        |                            |
        |                            |       --- TIME --->
        |                            |--------------------------START TIMER
        |                            |
        |                            | <--- MOTION DETECTOR ---
        |                            |--------------------------READ MOTION DETECTOR
        |                            |
        |                            |   <--- TIMER STATE ---
        |                            |--------------------------READ TIMER STATE
        |
        |--INTRUDER DETECTED
             |
             |        --- ALARM --->
             |----------------------------ACTUATE ALARM
             |
             |         --- TIME --->
             |----------------------------START TIMER
             |
             |    <--- KEYSWITCH ---
             |----------------------------READ KEYSWITCH
             |
             |    <--- TIMER STATE ---
             |----------------------------READ TIMER STATE
             |
             |----------------------------WAIT FOR KEYSWITCH RESET
                                            |
                                            |    <--- KEYSWITCH ---
                                            |--------------------------READ KEYSWITCH
```

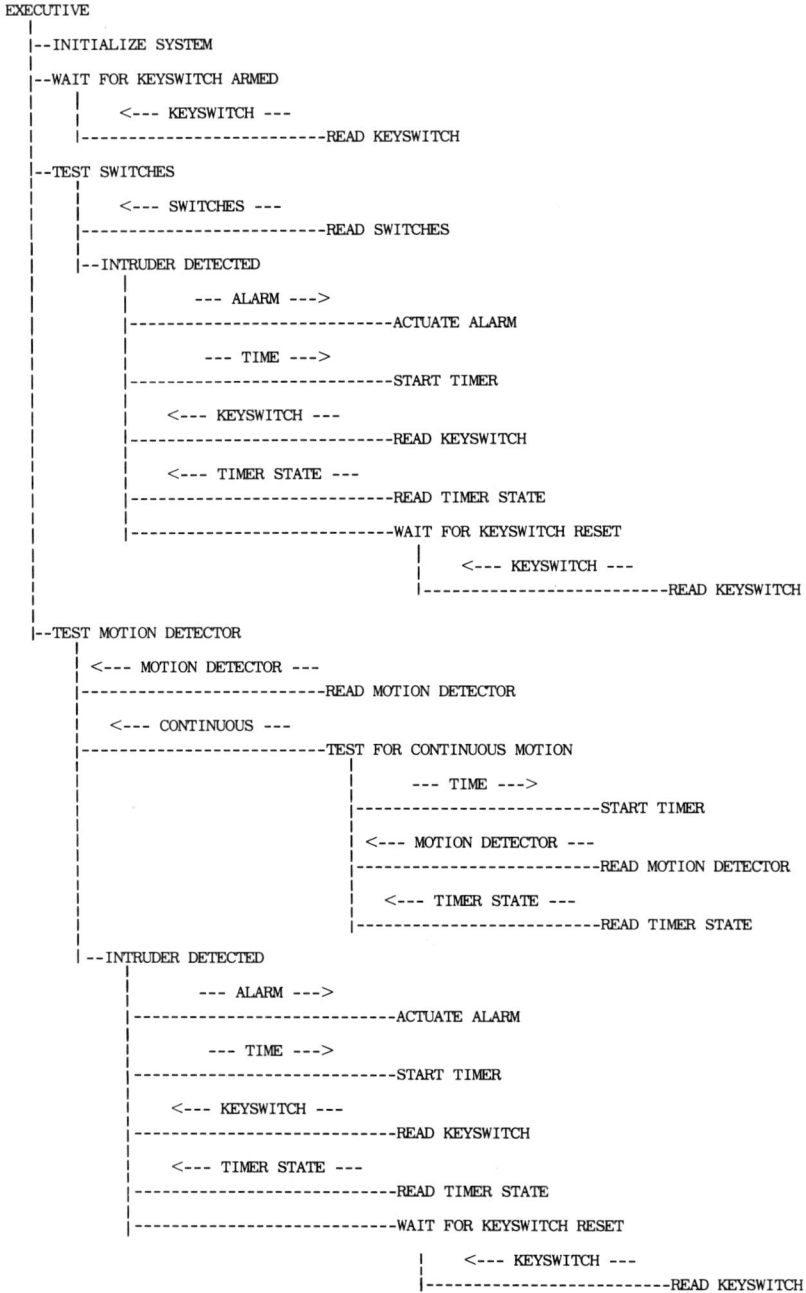

Figure 4-15. Partial procedure calling tree showing parameters.

arrows indicate whether parameters are input or output parameters and specify the names of the parameters. For example, SWITCHES is an output parameter of the READ SWITCHES procedure. Since the TEST SWITCHES procedure calls READ SWITCHES, the arrow labeled SWITCHES between the two procedures illustrates the complete relationship between them.

Since there are no precise rules to follow to modularize a system, it is useful to consider the concept of *data modularization* that can be used in conjunction with functional modularization to produce a first-cut design.

DATA MODULARIZATION

In most systems, information is stored in *data structures* and is retrieved from them during operation. A data structure is a collection of data records or information that is stored in the microcomputer in a systematic manner. In a later section we examine how information is organized into data structures. Here we wish to examine the relationship between data structures and modularization.

To ensure the integrity of the data in a data structure, we design a separate module to contain each data structure; we then stipulate that the procedures in other modules cannot directly access the data stored in the data structure within a module. For each module that contains a data structure, we then provide procedures through which the data in the module can be accessed. For example, let us assume that the system we are designing contains a data structure called RECORD. For now it is unimportant what kind of information RECORD contains since we want to examine how the information is manipulated, not what it means. We define a MAINTAIN RECORD module for the RECORD data structure and further define a READ RECORD procedure in that module which reads the information from the RECORD data structure. Then, if a procedure in another module requires information from RECORD, it calls the READ RECORD procedure that accesses the data structure on its behalf. This concept is illustrated in Figure 4-16 which shows how the READ RECORD procedure *reads* a record from the RECORD data structure for use by a procedure in the PROCESS module.

Other procedures in the MAINTAIN RECORD module may also be defined to write information into the RECORD data structure or to search for or otherwise manipulate the information in the data structure. We examine the latter concepts further in the section on data structures.

DESIGN CHECKOUT

We have seen how to modularize a system and how to design the procedures belonging to each module. Now we would like to check the correctness of the design to find and eliminate as many errors as possible before the system is built. Two techniques that can be used to help *checkout* a system at the design language level are: the *design walkthrough* and *data flow verification*. These techniques can also be used during a design review.

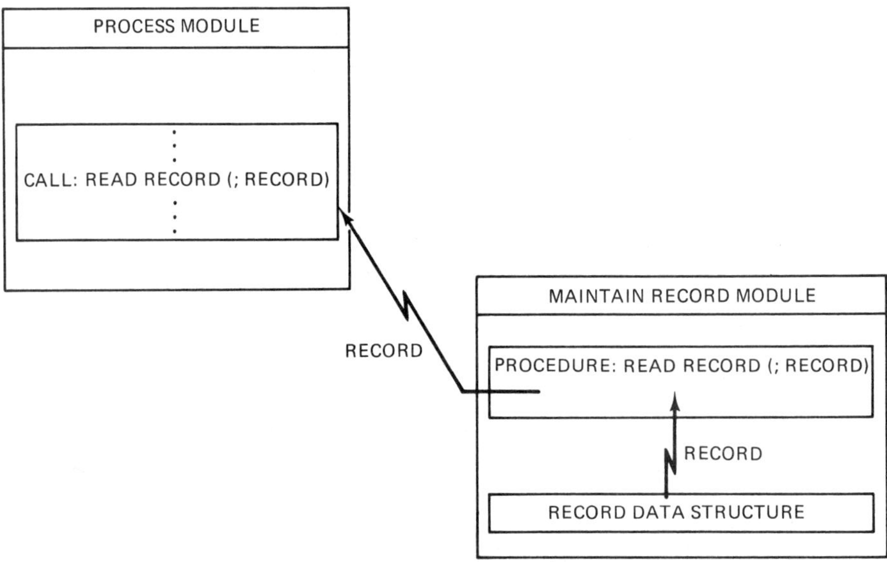

Figure 4-16. Reading a data record from the RECORD data structure in the MAINTAIN RECORD MODULE.

DESIGN WALKTHROUGH

At this stage in the design cycle there is generally no easy way to perform design language operations by machine to check the correctness of the design. Therefore, we must manually *walkthrough* and *execute* each operation of each procedure to test the system design as thoroughly as possible. Before describing how to walkthrough a design, let us discuss what it is that we want to check during the walkthrough.

If a procedure contains no test or loop constructs, then verifying that the procedure performs correctly is straightforward. Design language operations are examined sequentially and they either yield the desired action or they do not. It is also necessary to verify that correct input and output parameters are passed between each procedure and its called procedures.

If a procedure contains one or more conditional loops, we must verify that, when the operation of a loop is completed, the desired function has been performed. It may be sufficient to verify that the operations in the loop are repeated for a specified number of iterations or it may be necessary to verify that a particular calculation has been completed or that an anticipated event has taken place.

If a procedure contains test constructs, then it is necessary to ensure that the operations within each path of each test branch are performed when a suitable set of conditions is fulfilled. We must also verify that the operations cause the expected action to take place in each path. The outcome of a test depends on the values of parameters derived from either procedure input parameters or from output parameters obtained from called procedures. These input and output parameters often depend on external conditions whose values are unknown during the walkthrough. Therefore, we should assume that they take on suitable values that are representative of what can be expected during the actual operation of the system. It is usually impossible to check each complete path through the system since a very large number of possibilities exist. If the system is designed modularly, by selecting suitable values for the input and output parameters, we can verify each *part* of each path. Although a walkthrough cannot provide us with complete verification, it can assure us that all but the most subtle errors are found.

Since many design projects require the cooperation of all members of the design team, walkthroughs should be conducted by the whole team. The team member who designed the procedures of a particular module should conduct the walkthrough and describe what should happen at each step of each procedure. The other team members should critique the design and act as *devil's advocates* to try to find design errors. If a design error is found, either the designer can correct it or the design team can suggest ways to correct it. The walkthrough for a module is completed successfully when no errors can be found in the design of the complete module. Let us examine how to walk through the TEST module of the burglar alarm system. Refer to Figures 4-6, 4-9, and 4-10 for the individual procedures of this module.

In the TEST SWITCHES procedure the switches are read and a single test is performed. The only potential hazard in this procedure is that the wrong test is applied. Since the switches are tripped only when an intruder is present, the test shown in Figure 4-6 is correctly designed.

The TEST MOTION DETECTOR procedure contains two tests that are nested and therefore produce three possible paths in the procedure. First, the motion detector is read and its state is tested. If the motion detector is not tripped, the RETURN operation is performed, thereby immediately terminating the procedure. This is one of the paths and can be seen to function correctly. If the motion detector is tripped, the system tests for continuous motion. If continuous motion is not detected, the RETURN operation is again performed, thus terminating the procedure. This is the second path and also functions correctly in the design. Finally, if continuous motion is detected, the INTRUDER DETECTED procedure is called to actuate the alarms. Eventually, the system is reset in the INTRUDER DETECTED procedure, control is returned to the TEST MOTION DETECTOR procedure, and the RETURN operation is performed to terminate the procedure. This is the third path through the procedure. Thus, even in this more complex example, a simple discussion of the alternatives is sufficient to convince ourselves that no design errors are present.

The TEST FOR CONTINUOUS MOTION procedure contains a loop and two nested tests. Thus, we must check the three possible paths through the procedure as well as ensure that the loop terminates correctly. We must also verify that the procedure passes correct information back to its calling procedure via the parameter CONTINUOUS. In this procedure, a five-second timer is started and the operation of the loop is initiated. During the operation of the loop, the motion detector is read and its state is tested. If its state changes so that it is no longer tripped, then the timer is stopped and the parameter CONTINUOUS is reset to indicate that motion was not sustained for five seconds. Control is then returned to the calling procedure, thereby terminating the loop. This first path is illustrated in Figure 4-17(a). In the presence of continuous motion, the loop is repeated until the timer expires. This second path is shown in Figure 4-17(b). When the timer expires, it is stopped and the parameter CONTINUOUS is set to indicate that motion was sustained for five seconds. Control is then returned to the calling procedure to terminate the loop. This third path is illustrated in Figure 4-17(c). In each part of the figure, operations that are not part of the path under investigation are deleted for clarity and the pertinent constructs are shown in **boldface** type for emphasis.

The discussion we presented is indicative of the type of argument that should be presented by the designer during a walkthrough. The designer may also present visual aids such as the charts shown in Figure 4-17 which illustrate the three paths through the TEST FOR CONTINUOUS MOTION procedure.

A *walkthrough emulator* has been built by the authors to automate the walkthrough. The emulator *steps through* the design language operations and displays each in turn so that the walkthrough team can easily follow the sequence. The designer need only indicate which branch a test should take and whether the condition specified in a conditional loop construct is true or false. It should be noted that even the automated walkthrough is incapable of exhaustively testing each possible path through the system. It is a *tool* that the designer can use to help assure himself or herself that the system has been designed according to the desired specifications.

The walkthrough technique works well because we have modularized the system and divided each module into relatively small procedures. Thus, we have reduced the complexity of the system to an understandable level that can be discussed

```
PROCEDURE: TEST FOR CONTINUOUS MOTION (;CONTINUOUS)
BEGIN PROCEDURE
  CALL: START TIMER (5 SECONDS;)
  DO FOREVER
    CALL: READ MOTION DETECTOR (;MOTION DETECTOR)
    IF MOTION DETECTOR IS TRIPPED
      THEN DO
             ---
           END
      ELSE DO
             CALL: STOP TIMER (;)
             RESET CONTINUOUS
             RETURN
           END
  END
END PROCEDURE
```

Figure 4-17(a). The first walkthrough path in the TEST FOR CONTINUOUS MOTION procedure.

```
PROCEDURE: TEST FOR CONTINUOUS MOTION (;CONTINUOUS)
BEGIN PROCEDURE
  CALL: START TIMER (5 SECONDS;)
  DO FOREVER
    CALL: READ MOTION DETECTOR (;MOTION DETECTOR)
    IF MOTION DETECTOR IS TRIPPED
      THEN  DO
              CALL: READ TIMER STATE (;TIMER STATE)
              IF TIMER STATE IS EXPIRED
                THEN  DO
                        ---
                      END
            END
      ELSE  DO
              ---
            END
  END
END PROCEDURE
```

Figure 4-17(b). The second walkthrough path in the TEST FOR CONTINUOUS MOTION procedure.

```
PROCEDURE: TEST FOR CONTINUOUS MOTION (;CONTINUOUS)
BEGIN PROCEDURE
  CALL: START TIMER (5 SECONDS;)
  DO FOREVER
    CALL: READ MOTION DETECTOR (;MOTION DETECTOR)
    IF MOTION DETECTOR IS TRIPPED
      THEN  DO
              CALL: READ TIMER STATE (;TIMER STATE)
              IF TIMER STATE IS EXPIRED
                THEN  DO
                        CALL: STOP TIMER (;)
                        SET CONTINUOUS
                        RETURN
                      END
            END
      ELSE  DO
              ---
            END
  END
END PROCEDURE
```

Figure 4-17(c). The third walkthrough path in the TEST FOR CONTINUOUS MOTION procedure.

easily during a walkthrough. The other technique that can be used to help verify the correctness of a design is called *data flow verification*.

DATA FLOW VERIFICATION

A successful walkthrough verifies that the control paths through the system are executed correctly. Data flow verification verifies that information is manipulated correctly within the system. This includes information passed between procedures through parameters as well as information stored into and retrieved from data structures.

Data flow diagrams can be used to help visualize the flow of information through the system. They illustrate how information passes through the procedures on its way to and from data structures. Figure 4-18 is a data flow diagram for an inventory control system. From the illustration, it can be seen that an INVENTORY data structure is updated for each item that is purchased or returned. By preparing the data flow diagrams before the design walkthrough, it is possible during the walkthrough to verify that the data does pass through the system correctly. Alternately, data flow can be monitored and data flow diagrams showing the movement of the data can be produced during the walkthrough. The diagrams can then be analyzed to determine if data moves through the system correctly. In either case, we use data flow diagrams to verify that information moves through the system correctly.

The walkthrough emulator introduced in the last section can produce a data flow diagram for each walkthrough. A data flow diagram is only produced for each path taken during the walkthrough. But by suitably choosing the paths taken during a walkthrough, a comprehensive set of data flow diagrams can be produced.

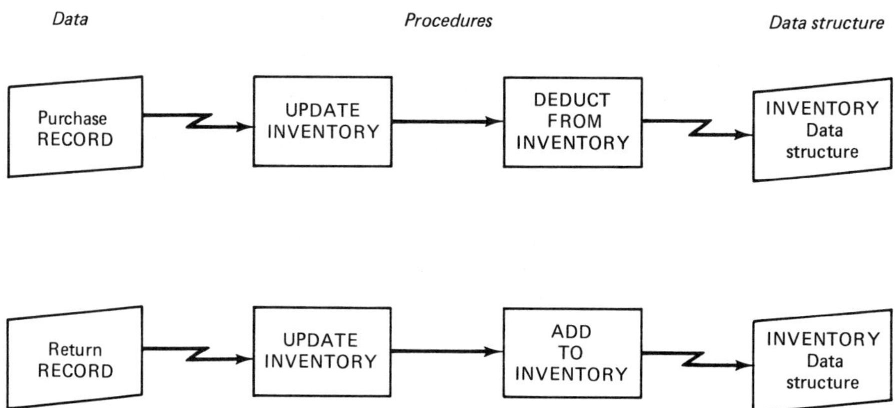

Figure 4-18. Data flow diagrams for INVENTORY data structure.

DATA STRUCTURES

During operation, the microcomputer manipulates information as data records. For convenience and to minimize problems, it is desirable to group together each set of related data records and store them in a *data structure*. Thus, a single data structure may contain a large quantity of related information. How the data structure is organized depends on what the data represents and how it is manipulated by the system.

The simplest data structure consisting of more than one item of information is called a *list*. Information is stored in sequence in a list, usually in the same order that the information is created or generated. The INPUT RECORD data structure of a system that uses keyboard entry of information is an example of a list. As each push-button key is depressed by the operator, a *character code* that corresponds to the depressed key is stored in the list. When an input sequence is completed by the operator, the list contains the character codes corresponding to the sequence of keys depressed by the operator. An example of a push-button layout for a keyboard intended for use in a point-of-sale system was shown in Figure 2-2. In this type of system, an input sequence may consist of the characters of a charge account number or an item price. Let us examine how the procedures that manipulate the INPUT RECORD data structure in the MAINTAIN INPUT RECORD module for such a system are designed.

The GET INPUT RECORD procedure, shown in Figure 4-19, is called whenever it is necessary for a *numeric* input sequence to be keyed in by the operator.

```
PROCEDURE: GET INPUT RECORD (;INPUT RECORD)
BEGIN PROCEDURE
  CALL: CLEAR INPUT RECORD (;)
  DO FOREVER
    CALL: READ KEYBOARD (;CHARACTER)
    IF CHARACTER CONTAINS 'CLEAR INPUT' CODE
      THEN  CALL: CLEAR INPUT RECORD (;)
    IF CHARACTER CONTAINS A NUMERIC CODE
      THEN  DO
              CALL: TEST IF INPUT RECORD FULL (;STATUS)
              IF STATUS INDICATES INPUT RECORD IS NOT FULL
                THEN  CALL: ADD TO INPUT RECORD (CHARACTER;)
                ELSE  CALL: BEEP (;)
            END
    IF CHARACTER CONTAINS A TERMINATOR CODE
      THEN  RETURN
    IF CHARACTER CONTAINS ANY OTHER CODE
      THEN  CALL: BEEP (;)
  END
END PROCEDURE
```

Figure 4-19. The GET INPUT RECORD procedure

INPUT RECORD is first cleared of previous information and a loop is used to repetitively read the character codes generated when the operator presses the keys on the keyboard, save these numeric character codes in INPUT RECORD, and terminate the procedure when a terminator key is depressed. If the CLEAR INPUT key is depressed at any time, the INPUT RECORD data structure is cleared and the input sequence is effectively restarted. When the operation of the procedure is terminated, the information read into the data structure is passed to the calling procedure through the output parameter INPUT RECORD.

The GET INPUT RECORD procedure calls several procedures. The READ KEYBOARD procedure is in the INPUT module. When called it waits until a key is depressed and returns the character code corresponding to the depressed key through its output parameter CHARACTER. The BEEP procedure is in the OUTPUT module. It causes a beep tone to be generated to inform the operator of an error condition. In our example, a beep tone is generated whenever the operator enters a numeric sequence containing more than the maximum permissible number of characters. Similarly, a beep tone is also generated if a key other than a numeric key, a terminator key, or the CLEAR INPUT key is depressed. The remaining procedures that are called by GET INPUT RECORD are CLEAR INPUT RECORD, ADD TO INPUT RECORD, and TEST IF INPUT RECORD FULL, all of which belong to the MAINTAIN INPUT RECORD module.

The CLEAR INPUT RECORD procedure is shown in Figure 4-20. It sets each element of the INPUT RECORD data structure to the *zero* character code, thereby deleting the information stored in the data structure. It also sets the FULL INDICATOR parameter to *empty*. The latter parameter is used by the TEST IF INPUT RECORD FULL procedure to determine when the INPUT RECORD data structure is full. The number of elements provided in the INPUT RECORD data structure for storing character codes is determined by the number of characters in the longest input sequence that may be keyed in by the operator. It is unnecessary to specify this maximum number during the early stages of design. The design language operation DO FOR EACH ELEMENT IN INPUT RECORD allows us to design the CLEAR INPUT RECORD procedure without knowing the size of the data structure.

```
PROCEDURE: CLEAR INPUT RECORD (;)
BEGIN PROCEDURE
  DO FOR EACH ELEMENT IN INPUT RECORD
    SET ELEMENT TO 'ZERO' CODE
  END
  SET FULL INDICATOR TO EMPTY
  RETURN
END PROCEDURE
```

Figure 4-20. The CLEAR INPUT RECORD procedure.

The ADD TO INPUT RECORD procedure is illustrated in Figure 4-21. It moves each of the character codes stored in the INPUT RECORD data structure to

```
PROCEDURE: ADD TO INPUT RECORD (CHARACTER; )
BEGIN PROCEDURE
  SHIFT INPUT RECORD CODES TO LEFT
  SET RIGHT-HAND INPUT RECORD ELEMENT TO CHARACTER
  INCREMENT FULL INDICATOR
  RETURN
END PROCEDURE
```

Figure 4-21. The ADD CHARACTER TO INPUT RECORD procedure.

the *left*, inserts the new character code (from the input parameter CHARACTER) into the vacated element on the *right* of the data structure, and increments FULL INDICATOR. Figure 4-22 illustrates how the characters in the data structure are manipulated by this procedure.

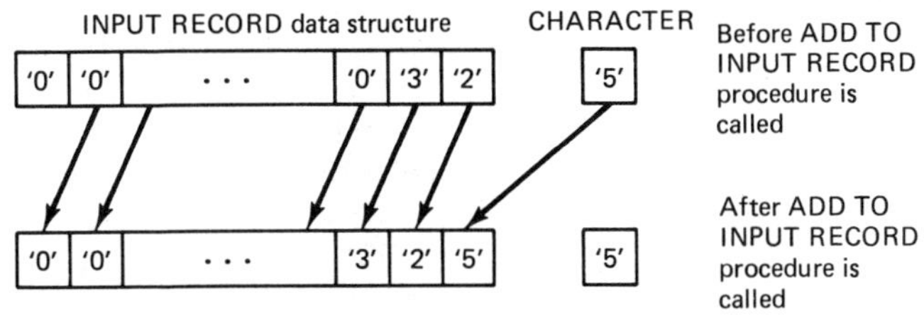

Figure 4-22. The operation of the ADD CHARACTER TO INPUT RECORD procedure.

The TEST IF INPUT RECORD FULL procedure is shown in Figure 4-23. It examines the FULL INDICATOR and reports its status as either FULL or NOT FULL through the output parameter STATUS.

```
PROCEDURE: TEST IF INPUT RECORD FULL (; STATUS)
BEGIN PROCEDURE
  IF FULL INDICATOR SHOWS THAT INPUT RECORD IS FULL
    THEN  SET STATUS TO FULL
    ELSE  SET STATUS TO NOT FULL
  RETURN
END PROCEDURE
```

Figure 4-23. The TEST IF INPUT RECORD FULL procedure.

As we have indicated, a data structure may consist of a large quantity of related information. Although the information may be stored in a single list or group of lists, the natural organization of the data is not always easy to see. But if the information is organized into a *hierarchical data structure*, the relationship between the data may be made clear. We illustrate this concept with a simple example.

Let us assume that the overall data structure, which we will call FILE, consists of a set of records. Moreover, let each record consist of a serial number, a name, and a street address. The relationship between the parts of this data structure is illustrated below:

```
FILE
  RECORD
    SERIAL NUMBER
    NAME
    STREET ADDRESS
```

If any part of the record consists of several entities, it can be subdivided further. For example, if we divide each name into first name, middle initial, and surname, and each street address into house number and street name, then the hierarchical relationship for the data structure FILE becomes:

```
FILE
  RECORD
    SERIAL NUMBER
    NAME
      FIRST NAME
      MIDDLE INITIAL
      SURNAME
    STREET ADDRESS
      HOUSE NUMBER
      STREET NAME
```

Thus, the organization of data in a hierarchical data structure is easily represented by a set of indented names. These names represent the levels of information contained in the data structure.

To complete the documentation of a data structure, it is necessary to add a *data structure definition* containing design information for each part of the data structure. An example of a data structure definition for the FILE data structure is illustrated below:

```
MODULAR DATA STRUCTURE: FILE

NAME                    SIZE    TYPE    CONTENTS            NOTES
----                    ----    ----    --------            -----
FILE                                                          1
  RECORD
    SERIAL NUMBER        10     BYTE    NUMERIC CODES
    NAME
      FIRST NAME         10     BYTE    ALPHABETIC CODES
      MIDDLE INITIAL      1     BYTE    ALPHABETIC CODES
      SURNAME            14     BYTE    ALPHABETIC CODES
    STREET ADDRESS
      HOUSE NUMBER        5     BYTE    NUMERIC CODES
      STREET NAME        20     BYTE    ALPHABETIC CODES
NOTE 1. FILE CONSISTS OF 256 RECORDS.
```

Although, as we indicated earlier, some of the information in the data structure definition can be omitted at this point, we have shown it for completeness. The header MODULAR DATA STRUCTURE identifies FILE as a *major* data structure for a module. Similar headers are used for defining data structures for use as input or output parameters or to store *local* data within a procedure. Local data can only be accessed by the procedure that contains the local data structure. SIZE indicates how many data items, in this case, how many character codes, can be stored in each entity of the data structure. Note that size is only shown for the lowest levels of the data structure hierarchy since that is where the data is actually stored. TYPE refers to how the data structure will be implemented in a programming language. For illustration, we use BYTE, which is a TYPE designation for the PL/M programming language. CONTENTS indicates what information is stored in each entity of the data structure. NOTES permits additional design information about each part of a data structure to be included in the data structure definition. Notes are placed below the design information for the data structure and are referenced by number. When we describe the second documentation level at the end of this chapter, we show how the data structure definitions are incorporated into the documentation.

In order to facilitate searching for information in a hierarchical data structure, it is often desirable that the records be stored in either alphabetical or numerical order with respect to some *key* information in the data structure. In the preceding example the serial number is an example of a *numeric key*; the surname is an example of an *alphabetic key*. In such a system, whenever the data structure is updated, it must be sorted to maintain the correct ordering of the data records. We discuss *sorting* and *searching* data structures in the next two sections.

SORTING A DATA STRUCTURE

Many methods have been devised for sorting a data structure into order. The design we present uses a simple algorithm to rearrange a set of records so that they are in numerical order. We assume that the records are contained in the data structure called FILE introduced in the preceding section and that the records are to be sorted numerically using the serial number as the key. The term KEY is used in the example for generality; assume KEY refers to the serial number. Figure 4-24 illustrates the SORT procedure that works in the following manner. The first record in FILE is selected. Then the key in the selected record is compared to the key in each of the other records in FILE. If a record is found in which the key is less than the key in the selected record, the two records are exchanged to put them into order. The comparisons are then continued using the key in the exchanged record. When all of the data records have been examined once, the first record in FILE is in the correct position. The same process is repeated for the next record and for each succeeding record. Then, when only one record remains, the records in the data structure will be in correct numerical order with respect to the selected key, the serial number.

```
PROCEDURE: SORT (;)
BEGIN PROCEDURE
  SELECT FIRST RECORD IN FILE
  DO FOREVER
    DO FOR EACH RECORD IN FILE FOLLOWING SELECTED RECORD
      IF KEY IN RECORD IS LESS THAN KEY IN SELECTED RECORD
        THEN  EXCHANGE RECORD AND SELECTED RECORD AND CONTINUE USING EXCHANGED RECORD
    END
    IF ALL RECORDS BUT THE LAST ONE HAVE BEEN SELECTED
      THEN  RETURN
      ELSE  SELECT NEXT RECORD IN FILE
  END
END PROCEDURE
```

Figure 4-24. Sorting a data structure into order.

SEARCHING A DATA STRUCTURE

If a data structure is randomly ordered, the only way to search for a particular item is to examine the records one at a time until a match is found. Although the same technique can be used with a sorted data structure, there are more efficient methods. Figure 4-25 illustrates the design for a SEARCH procedure that works well in many cases.

```
PROCEDURE: SEARCH (SEARCH KEY;RECORD)
BEGIN PROCEDURE
  SELECT RECORD IN CENTER OF FILE
  DO FOREVER
    IF SEARCH KEY IS EQUAL TO KEY IN SELECTED RECORD
      THEN  DO
              SET RECORD TO SELECTED RECORD
              RETURN
            END
    IF SEARCH KEY IS LESS THAN KEY IN SELECTED RECORD
      THEN  IGNORE RECORDS WHICH FOLLOW SELECTED RECORD
      ELSE  IGNORE RECORDS WHICH PRECEDE SELECTED RECORD
    IF RECORDS REMAIN IN FILE
      THEN  SELECT RECORD IN CENTER OF REMAINING RECORDS
      ELSE  DO
              SET RECORD TO 'NO MATCH FOUND'
              RETURN
            END
  END
END PROCEDURE
```

Figure 4-25. Searching a sorted data structure.

Since the records in the data structure FILE are sorted and in numerical order by serial number, we examine the record in the center of the data structure first. If the search key matches the key in the center record, we are done. If the search key is less than the key in the center record, we can eliminate from further consideration all of the records following it in the data structure. If the search key is greater than the key in the center record, we can eliminate from further consideration all of the records preceding it in the data structure. Thus, even in the absence of a match at this point, we eliminate the need to examine one-half of the records in the data structure. By examining the middle record of the remaining records, we can eliminate one-half of the remaining records. Continuing in this manner, we are guaranteed to either find a match or determine that a match does not exist in at most $\log_2 n$ steps as compared to $n/2$ steps on the average when searching straight through. If a data structure contains 2000 records, for example, the technique just described takes no more than 11 steps as compared to an average of 1000 steps using the straight through search. Of course, searching time must be balanced against sorting time to determine whether or not it is cost effective to do the sorting. If many searches are needed between sorts, the methods just described are worth implementing. Otherwise, the unsorted data structure can be searched directly. If an alphabetic key is used, the two phrases *is less than* and *is greater than* in the SORT and SEARCH procedures can be replaced by *alphabetically precedes* and *alphabetically follows*, respectively.

In the earlier discussion of the burglar alarm system, we ignored the details of how the TIMER module is implemented in the software. One way in which a timer can be implemented is by using an *interrupt* mechanism. Let us now examine the interrupt concept and how it affects system design.

INTERRUPT

Let us consider a familiar situation: We are working at a task and know that, periodically, we must stop to perform another chore. There are two ways to ensure that the latter chore gets done on time. We can repeatedly watch for the presence of the external stimulus that indicates when the chore should be performed. Or we can arrange to be *interrupted* whenever the stimulus occurs. In the former case, we repeatedly break our train of thought to watch for the stimulus; we also risk missing its occurrence if we are in deep concentration. In the latter case, we are free to concentrate on the task at hand knowing that we will be interrupted in time to perform the chore. Thus, the interrupt technique is more effective because it enables us to utilize our time efficiently. A similar situation exists in the microcomputer; we illustrate these concepts using the timer mechanism in the burglar alarm system.

In Figure 3-6 a CLOCK module is shown in the hardware part of the system. This clock generates a periodic signal using either the power line or a stable oscillator as the timing source. The microcomputer software can be designed to decrement a number that is represented by the parameter TIMER VALUE whenever the clock signal occurs. Thus, if a clock signal is generated every one-sixtieth of a second, then, to set the timer to run for five seconds, TIMER VALUE is set initially to the value 300, and, after five seconds have elapsed, it will be equal to zero. The microcomputer can determine when to decrement TIMER VALUE by either repeatedly checking for the presence of the clock signal or by using an interrupt mechanism that operates in a manner analogous to that described above for a human being.

If we examine the INTRUDER DETECTED and the TEST FOR CONTINUOUS MOTION procedures, we see that there are no provisions for *watching* the clock signal. In a system as straightforward as the burglar alarm system, such a provision can easily be added by inserting the operation

```
CALL: CHECK CLOCK SIGNAL (;)
```

into each procedure so that it immediately precedes the

```
CALL: READ TIMER STATE (;TIMER STATE)
```

operation. In other systems, however, this approach would necessitate the insertion of many such operations to ensure that the system decrements TIMER VALUE for each occurrence of the clock signal. Moreover, if a rapid response to the clock signal were needed (which is not the case in our example), such a response could not be assured unless the CHECK CLOCK SIGNAL operation were replicated many times. The increased system complexity coupled with the potentially poor response time of this type of design indicates that an interrupt mechanism should be considered instead.

We discuss the details of how the clock signal *interrupts* the microcomputer in Chapter 6. For now, it is sufficient to understand that whenever the clock signal occurs, the operation being performed is interrupted and a *CALL* to an INTERRUPT EXECUTIVE procedure takes place. The operations needed to respond to the clock signal are then carried out under the control of the INTERRUPT EXECUTIVE procedure. Then, after TIMER VALUE has been decremented, a RETURN operation causes the interrupted operation to be resumed and the original sequence of operations continued as if they were not interrupted. The procedures needed to implement the interrupt mechanism in the burglar alarm system are illustrated in the partial modularization shown in Figure 4-26. A second executive level module, the INTERRUPT EXECUTIVE module, has been added as well as an INTERRUPT CONTROL module. The only other change in the system is in the TIMER module where a PROCESS TIMER INTERRUPT procedure has been added.

The TIMER module procedures can now be designed and are shown in Figures 4-27 through 4-30. The design of the INTERRUPT EXECUTIVE procedure is illustrated in Figure 4-31. The two operations SAVE SYSTEM STATUS and RESTORE SYSTEM STATUS in the INTERRUPT EXECUTIVE procedure are needed to ensure that the operations of the INTERRUPT EXECUTIVE and its called procedures do not interfere with the correct resumption of the operations that were interrupted; we examine the implications of this statement in detail in Chapter 6.

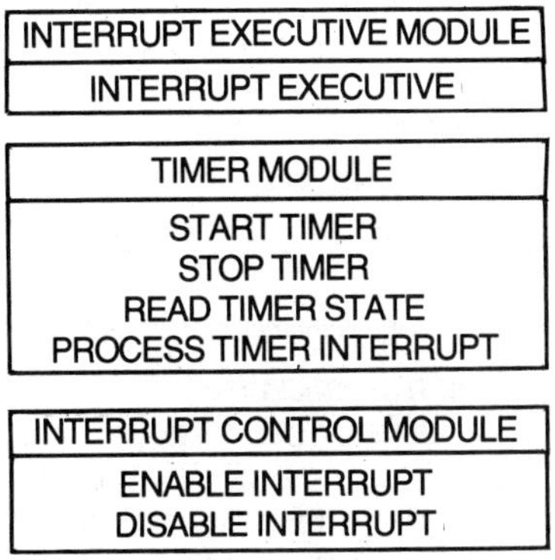

INTERRUPT EXECUTIVE MODULE
INTERRUPT EXECUTIVE

TIMER MODULE
START TIMER STOP TIMER READ TIMER STATE PROCESS TIMER INTERRUPT

INTERRUPT CONTROL MODULE
ENABLE INTERRUPT DISABLE INTERRUPT

Figure 4-26. Partial modularization of the burglar alarm system.

```
PROCEDURE: START TIMER (SECONDS;)
BEGIN PROCEDURE
  SET TIMER VALUE TO 60 * SECONDS
  SET TIMER STATE TO NOT EXPIRED
  CALL: ENABLE INTERRUPT (;)
  RETURN
END PROCEDURE
```

Figure 4-27. The START TIMER procedure.

```
PROCEDURE: STOP TIMER (;)
BEGIN PROCEDURE
  CALL: DISABLE INTERRUPT (;)
  RETURN
END PROCEDURE
```

Figure 4-28. The STOP TIMER procedure.

```
PROCEDURE: READ TIMER STATE (;TIMER STATE)
BEGIN PROCEDURE
  GET TIMER STATE VALUE
  RETURN
END PROCEDURE
```

Figure 4-29. The READ TIMER STATE procedure.

```
PROCEDURE: PROCESS TIMER INTERRUPT (;)
BEGIN PROCEDURE
  DECREMENT TIMER VALUE
  IF TIMER VALUE IS ZERO
    THEN DO
           CALL: STOP TIMER (;)
           SET TIMER STATE TO EXPIRED
         END
  RETURN
END PROCEDURE
```

Figure 4-30. The PROCESS TIMER INTERRUPT procedure.

```
PROCEDURE: INTERRUPT EXECUTIVE (;)
BEGIN PROCEDURE
  SAVE SYSTEM STATUS
  CALL: ENABLE INTERRUPT (;)
  CALL: PROCESS TIMER INTERRUPT (;)
  RESTORE SYSTEM STATUS
  RETURN
END PROCEDURE
```

Figure 4-31. The INTERRUPT EXECUTIVE procedure.

Several important aspects of an interrupt-driven system can be seen from the modularization and the procedure designs of the burglar alarm system.

- A separate procedure calling tree exists for the interrupt part of the system. This is illustrated for the burglar alarm system in Figure 4-32.
- A procedure such as STOP TIMER may appear in both of the procedure calling trees if it is called from procedures in both trees.
- Information is communicated between the two parts of the system through parameters such as TIMER VALUE and TIMER STATE which are manipulated in both parts of the system.

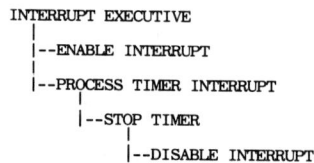

```
INTERRUPT EXECUTIVE
  |
  |--ENABLE INTERRUPT
  |
  |--PROCESS TIMER INTERRUPT
          |
          |--STOP TIMER
                 |
                 |--DISABLE INTERRUPT
```

Figure 4-32. Burglar alarm system interrupt procedure calling tree.

In operation, the clock signal does not cause any interrupts until the START TIMER procedure is called; the latter procedure sets TIMER VALUE to the correct value and calls the ENABLE INTERRUPT procedure. The latter procedure initializes the interrupt mechanism so that the clock signal interrupts the microcomputer every one-sixtieth of a second. Then, whenever an interrupt occurs, the system status is saved, the clock interrupt is reenabled having been automatically disabled at the occurrence of the interrupt, TIMER VALUE is decremented, the system status is restored, and the system returns to the interrupted operations. If TIMER VALUE becomes zero, then, in addition to the above operations, the clock interrupt is disabled and TIMER STATE is set to indicate that the desired time interval has elapsed. Once the clock interrupt is disabled in this manner, it remains in the inactive state until it is again enabled by the START TIMER procedure.

One last point should be made about the interrupt concept. Since the STOP TIMER procedure is called in both of the calling trees, it is possible for the following situation to occur:

- The STOP TIMER procedure is called from either the RESET SYSTEM procedure or the TEST FOR CONTINUOUS MOTION procedure.
- While the STOP TIMER procedure is operating and before the DISABLE INTERRUPT operation is reached, a clock interrupt occurs and the interrupt processing software (INTERRUPT EXECUTIVE) is called in response to the interrupt.
- During the execution of the PROCESS TIMER INTERRUPT procedure, which is called by the INTERRUPT EXECUTIVE procedure, the STOP TIMER procedure is again called.

That is, a procedure can be called while its own operation is interrupted. This situation is permissible if certain precautions are taken when the software is constructed. We discuss this concept further in Chapter 6. For now, we wish to indicate that it is not necessary to avoid such a situation in a microcomputer system; nevertheless, we must be aware of its existence.

This completes our description of interrupt from the software design viewpoint. We examine it again from the high-level programming language viewpoint in Chapter 5 and from the architecture and assembly language viewpoint in Chapter 6.

SECOND DOCUMENTATION LEVEL

The first documentation level consists of user requirements and the functional specification; the latter may consist of a user's manual whenever appropriate. The second documentation level includes both the software design specification described in Chapter 3 as well as the design language version of the software procedures, modules, and subsystems. Before we discuss how to complete the design level documentation, let us examine the concept of *indentation* that we have used extensively.

In every procedure we presented we indented the operations to show their relationship to one another. It should be pointed out that design language is completely unambiguous without indentation. Indentation improves readability, especially when several constructs are nested, and its use is strongly encouraged. The TEST

```
PROCEDURE: TEST FOR CONTINUOUS MOTION (;CONTINUOUS)
BEGIN PROCEDURE
CALL: START TIMER (5 SECONDS;)
DO FOREVER
CALL: READ MOTION DETECTOR (;MOTION DETECTOR)
IF MOTION DETECTOR TRIPPED
THEN DO
CALL: READ TIMER STATE (;TIMER STATE)
IF TIMER STATE EXPIRED
THEN DO
CALL: STOP TIMER (;)
SET CONTINUOUS
RETURN
END
END
ELSE DO
CALL: STOP TIMER (;)
RESET CONTINUOUS
RETURN
END
END
END PROCEDURE
```

Figure 4-33. The TEST FOR CONTINUOUS MOTION procedure written without indentation.

FOR CONTINUOUS MOTION procedure of the burglar alarm system is rewritten without indentation in Figure 4-33 to illustrate that clarity is indeed sacrificed.

The *rules* of indentation we use are shown below. An example is included to illustrate each rule.

1. All *brackets*, such as BEGIN PROCEDURE . . . END PROCEDURE, and DO . . . END, are lined up.

```
DO WHILE KEYSWITCH IS NOT ARMED
  CALL: READ KEYSWITCH (;KEYSWITCH)
END
```

2. All of the basic operations contained inside a set of *brackets* are indented by a fixed amount.

```
BEGIN PROCEDURE
  CALL: INITIALIZE HARDWARE (;)
  CALL: RESET SYSTEM (;)
  RETURN
END PROCEDURE
```

3. The words THEN and ELSE of a test construct are placed on separate lines and both are indented from the IF part of the construct by a fixed amount. When a single operation occurs within the THEN or the ELSE part of a test construct, it is placed on the same line as the THEN or ELSE.

```
IF ALL RECORDS BUT THE LAST ONE HAVE BEEN SELECTED
  THEN  RETURN
  ELSE  SELECT NEXT RECORD IN FILE
```

4. If more than one operation is contained within the THEN or ELSE part of a test construct, then a set of DO . . . END *brackets* must be used around these operations with the DO being placed on the same line as the THEN or ELSE.

```
IF TIMER STATE IS EXPIRED
  THEN  DO
          CALL: STOP TIMER (;)
          SET CONTINUOUS
          RETURN
        END
```

When design language procedures are written using these rules, then, together with the design specification, they are very nearly self-documenting. However, the following information is still needed at the procedure and module level:

- Procedure and module identification numbers if they are used.
- The name of the person who designed each procedure and module.
- The date on which the procedure or module was designed.
- The names of all persons who modified the design.
- The date on which each person last modified the design.
- A short statement of what the procedure or module does if the name of the procedure or module is not sufficient for this purpose.
- The name of the module to which the procedure belongs.
- The names of all of the procedures that the procedure calls.
- The names of all of the procedures that call the procedure.
- A data structure definition for each data structure and parameter that is manipulated by the procedure.
- A note to explain what each parameter in a data structure is for if it is not clear from the context.

This information can be inserted in the space between the procedure identification line and the BEGIN PROCEDURE phrase. Figure 4-34 illustrates a fully documented version of the RESET SYSTEM procedure of Figure 4-3. The optional lines

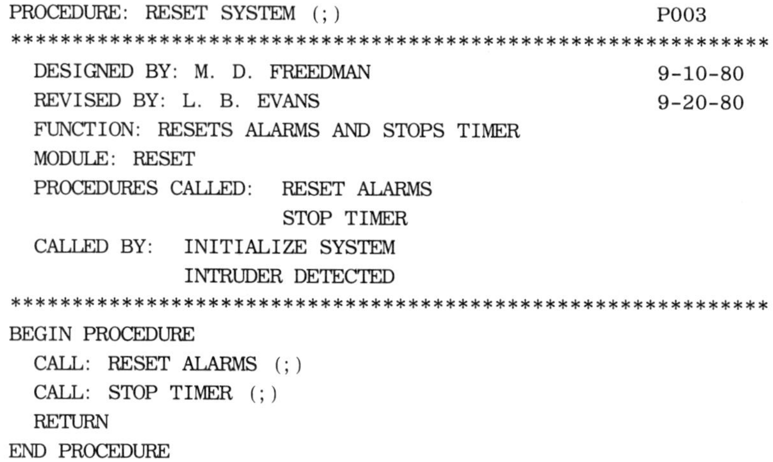

```
PROCEDURE: RESET SYSTEM (;)                                P003
**************************************************************
  DESIGNED BY: M. D. FREEDMAN                                9-10-80
  REVISED BY: L. B. EVANS                                    9-20-80
  FUNCTION: RESETS ALARMS AND STOPS TIMER
  MODULE: RESET
  PROCEDURES CALLED:  RESET ALARMS
                      STOP TIMER
  CALLED BY:  INITIALIZE SYSTEM
              INTRUDER DETECTED
**************************************************************
BEGIN PROCEDURE
  CALL: RESET ALARMS (;)
  CALL: STOP TIMER (;)
  RETURN
END PROCEDURE
```

Figure 4-34. Documented version of RESET SYSTEM procedure.

of asterisks are used to offset the documentation area for readability and may be omitted.

Many of the items listed above are also required as documentation at the module level. For this purpose, a *module description* can be put together as part of the documentation. One of the most important items that belongs in the module description is a data structure definition for each data structure contained in the module. Since the modular data structures can be manipulated by any procedure belonging to the module, the data structure definitions would be duplicated in each procedure if they were not contained in the module description. An example of a module description is shown in Figure 4-35 for the MAINTAIN INPUT RECORD module. Note that the designs for all of the procedures belonging to the module are included in the module description following the module header. In the interest of clarity, some of the documentation has been omitted from the *procedure* headers in the figure.

The reader should observe that even for a simple system many names are defined and used during the design process. Every subsystem, module, procedure, data structure, and parameter has a name. To prevent names from being confused with one another, it is helpful to build up a *name list* and enter each name into the list as it is defined. An indication of what each name represents can optionally be placed into the list which can then act as a *dictionary* for the system. An example of a partial name list for the burglar alarm system is shown in Figure 4-36. If a name is used in two different ways, as in the case of the name EXECUTIVE, it should be listed twice. The name list is part of the second documentation level and should be

```
MODULE: MAINTAIN INPUT RECORD                                   M004
----------------------------------------------------------------------
  DESIGNED BY: M. D. FREEDMAN                                   9-30-78
  PROCEDURES:  CLEAR INPUT RECORD
               ADD TO INPUT RECORD
               TEST IF INPUT RECORD FULL
               GET INPUT RECORD

  EXTERNAL PROCEDURES CALLED:  BEEP
                               READ KEYBOARD

  MODULAR DATA STRUCTURE:  INPUT RECORD

  NAME                SIZE   TYPE   CONTENTS             NOTES
  ----                ----   ----   --------             -----
  INPUT RECORD         10    BYTE   NUMERIC CODES
    FULL INDICATOR      1    BYTE   COUNTER
----------------------------------------------------------------------
PROCEDURE:  CLEAR INPUT RECORD (;)
**********************************************************************
BEGIN PROCEDURE
  DO FOR EACH ELEMENT IN INPUT RECORD
    SET ELEMENT TO 'ZERO' CODE
  END
  SET FULL INDICATOR TO EMPTY
  RETURN
END PROCEDURE
----------------------------------------------------------------------
PROCEDURE:  ADD TO INPUT RECORD (CHARACTER;)
**********************************************************************
  INPUT PARAMETER: CHARACTER

  NAME                SIZE   TYPE   CONTENTS             NOTES
  ----                ----   ----   --------             -----
  CHARACTER             1    BYTE   NUMERIC CODE
**********************************************************************
BEGIN PROCEDURE
  SHIFT INPUT RECORD CODES TO LEFT
  SET RIGHT-HAND INPUT RECORD ELEMENT TO CHARACTER
  INCREMENT FULL INDICATOR
  RETURN
END PROCEDURE
----------------------------------------------------------------------
```

Figure 4-35. Module description for the MAINTAIN INPUT RECORD module.

```
PROCEDURE:  TEST IF INPUT RECORD FULL (;STATUS)
**************************************************************************
  OUTPUT PARAMETER: STATUS

  NAME                   SIZE    TYPE    CONTENTS                  NOTES
  ----                   ----    ----    --------                  -----
  STATUS                   1     BYTE    FLAG
**************************************************************************
BEGIN PROCEDURE
  IF FULL INDICATOR SHOWS THAT INPUT RECORD IS FULL
    THEN  SET STATUS TO FULL
    ELSE  SET STATUS TO NOT FULL
  RETURN
END PROCEDURE
--------------------------------------------------------------------------
PROCEDURE:  GET INPUT RECORD (;INPUT RECORD)
**************************************************************************
  OUTPUT PARAMETER: INPUT RECORD

  NAME                   SIZE    TYPE    CONTENTS                  NOTES
  ----                   ----    ----    --------                  -----
  INPUT RECORD            10     BYTE    NUMERIC CODES               1

  NOTE 1: SEE MODULAR DATA STRUCTURE

  LOCAL PARAMETERS: CHARACTER
                    STATUS

  NAME                   SIZE    TYPE    CONTENTS                  NOTES
  ----                   ----    ----    --------                  -----
  CHARACTER                1     BYTE    ALPHANUMERIC CODE
  STATUS                   1     BYTE    FLAG
**************************************************************************
BEGIN PROCEDURE
  CALL: CLEAR INPUT RECORD (;)
  DO FOREVER
    CALL: READ KEYBOARD (;CHARACTER)
    IF CHARACTER CONTAINS 'CLEAR INPUT' CODE
      THEN  CALL: CLEAR INPUT RECORD (;)
    IF CHARACTER CONTAINS A NUMERIC CODE
      THEN  DO
              CALL: TEST IF INPUT RECORD FULL (;STATUS)
              IF STATUS INDICATES INPUT RECORD IS NOT FULL
                THEN  CALL: ADD TO INPUT RECORD (CHARACTER;)
                ELSE  CALL: BEEP (;)
            END
    IF CHARACTER CONTAINS A TERMINATOR CODE
      THEN  RETURN
    IF CHARACTER CONTAINS ANY OTHER CODE
      THEN  CALL: BEEP (;)
  END
END PROCEDURE
--------------------------------------------------------------------------
END MODULE
```

Figure 4-35. (Continued).

EXECUTIVE	MODULE
EXECUTIVE	PROCEDURE
INPUT	MODULE
READ KEYSWITCH	PROCEDURE
KEYSWITCH	OUTPUT PARAMETER
READ MOTION DETECTOR	PROCEDURE
MOTION DETECTOR	OUTPUT PARAMETER
READ SWITCHES	PROCEDURE
SWITCHES	OUTPUT PARAMETER
INTRUDER DETECTED	MODULE
INTRUDER DETECTED	PROCEDURE
TEST	MODULE
TEST FOR CONTINUOUS MOTION	PROCEDURE
CONTINUOUS	OUTPUT PARAMETER
TEST MOTION DETECTOR	PROCEDURE
TEST SWITCHES	PROCEDURE

Figure 4-36. Partial name list for the burglar alarm system.

included with the design specification and the design language description of the procedures.

Thus, a complete set of second-level documentation includes:

- A hierarchical list of subsystem, module, and procedure names. The name list, which also includes all data structure and parameter names, may serve this purpose.
- A procedure calling tree.
- A data structure definition for each data structure used in the system.
- A design language description of each procedure.
- Other pertinent information needed to understand the system at the design level; this information can either be put into the module or procedure headers or put into separate documents as needed.

EXERCISES

4-1. Are data structures needed for the computerized television set? If so, design these data structures and, if necessary, modify the software modularization developed in Exercise 3-2 to include the data modules. Determine what new procedures are needed for the modified modularization.

4-2. Design each of the procedures in the software modules of the computerized television set.

4-3. Are data structures needed for the computerized traffic light controller? If so, design these data structures and, if necessary, modify the software modularization produced in Exercise 3-4 to include the data modules. What new procedures are needed for this purpose?

4-4. Design each of the procedures in the software modules of the computerized traffic light controller.

4-5. Are data structures needed for your design of the computerized sports scoreboard? If so, design the data structures and, if necessary, modify the software modularization in Exercise 3-6 to include the data modules. What new procedures are needed for the modified modularization?

4-6. Design each of the procedures in the software modules of the computerized sports scoreboard.

4-7. Design the data structures needed for the computerized point-of-sale terminal in Exercise 3-8. Modify the software modularization to include the data modules. What new procedures are needed in these modules?

4-8. Design each of the procedures in the software modules of the computerized point-of-sale terminal.

4-9. If you are working on one of these systems as a group (design team), assign each module to one of the participants of the group and have each participant prepare and conduct a design walkthrough for the procedures in the assigned module(s). If the system contains a data structure, prepare data flow diagrams for each walkthrough.

4-10. Does the system you have designed require that an interrupt subsystem be used? If so, why? If you have not done so, modularize and design the interrupt subsystem.

4-11. Produce a procedure calling tree for the part of the system you have designed.

Chapter 5

Converting a Software Design into High-Level Language

We have now reached the point where the first-cut software design is complete. The design language is understandable and documents the design of the software. However, microcomputers are unable to interpret design language. As we have seen, except for a few well-defined constructs, design language is natural language and therefore meaningless to the microcomputer. What we must now do is translate the design language description of the system into a *microcomputer language*. The resulting set of microcomputer language procedures constitutes the *software* that gives the microcomputer the functional characteristics needed by the system.

In this chapter and in Chapters 6 and 7 we examine the different types of languages available for microcomputers. We also describe the *tools* available to aid in converting the design into a microcomputer language and for finding and eliminating errors in the completed software.

MICROCOMPUTER LANGUAGES

The relationship between the different languages we are going to discuss is illustrated in Figure 5-1. At the top is design language, which we described in detail in Chapter 4. The design language implementation of a system can be translated either into a high-level *compiler language* or into a low-level *assembly language*. Ultimately, we must end up with a *machine language* version of the software since, as we shall see, that is the language the microcomputer executes. Both compiler and assembly languages can be automatically translated into machine language using *tools* called *compilers* and *assemblers*. The compiler can translate either into assembly language, which requires further translation, or into machine language directly, as shown in Figure 5-1.

In many cases, the most cost-effective way to convert a design into a microcomputer language is to translate design language into a high-level compiler

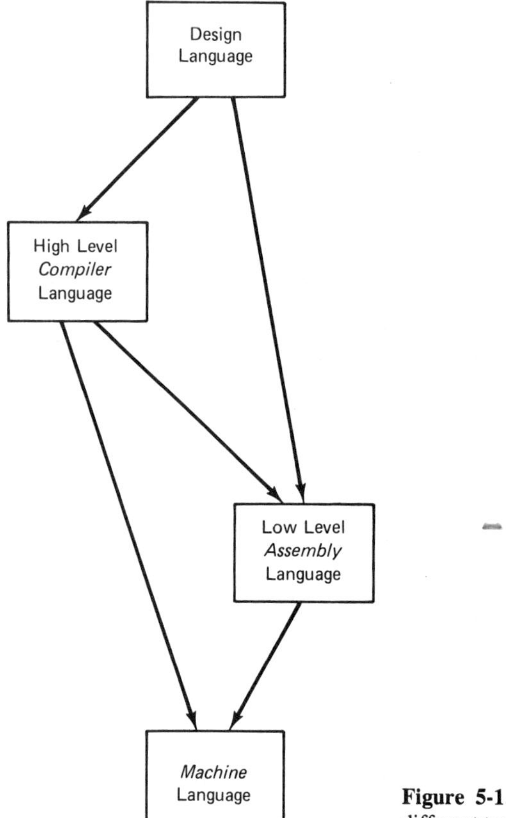

Figure 5-1. The relationship between different types of languages.

language. Since PL/M is an example of a compiler language that is especially suitable for use with microcomputers, we describe it in this chapter. An introduction to several other high-level languages is presented in Appendix D to enable the reader to work in whatever language is available.

This is not a text on how to program microcomputers; therefore, our treatment of programming is incomplete. We do provide sufficient material, however, to enable the reader to work the exercises and understand the concepts. Refer to one of the programming texts in the bibliography for a more detailed treatment of this subject.

PL/M LANGUAGE

PL/M is a subset of a high-level language called PL/I. It was developed by the Intel Corporation as an aid for programming their microcomputers. Thus, it contains a number of features that permit the development of efficient software for a microcomputer. At the same time, it possesses features that permit software to be developed in a systematic, modular, and top-down manner. In the following sections we describe the features of the PL/M language in sufficient detail to enable the reader to convert design language constructs into PL/M.

PL/M COMMENTS

PL/M *comments* are designated by the *brackets* /* and */. Thus, a comment in PL/M takes the form:

```
/*
                    THIS IS A COMMENT
                                                  */
```

and can be any number of lines in length. Comments are ignored by the PL/M compiler and are copied unchanged to the output listing produced by the compiler.

Thus, we can retain the design language operations by converting them into PL/M comments. The PL/M operations corresponding to each design language operation can then be placed immediately below each comment. The PL/M implementation of the software along with the design language comments constitute well-documented software that is easy to understand and work with.

First, we describe how to convert each of the design language constructs introduced in Chapter 4 into its corresponding PL/M operation. Next, we examine some PL/M constructs that do not have counterparts in design language but are needed for the software to execute on the microcomputer.

ASSIGNMENT CONSTRUCTS

Examples of the design language assignment constructs are shown below:

```
SET STATUS TO FULL
SET STATUS TO NOT FULL
SET CONTINUOUS
RESET CONTINUOUS
```

In PL/M, however, specific numeric or symbolic values must be used in place of terms like FULL. For example, let us assume that a zero value of STATUS represents the NOT FULL state and that any nonzero value of STATUS represents the FULL state. Then the PL/M operation

```
STATUS = 0;
```

causes STATUS to be set to the value zero and is therefore equivalent to SET STATUS TO NOT FULL. Similarly,

```
STATUS = 1;
```

causes STATUS to be set to the value one and so is equivalent to SET STATUS TO FULL.

For the SET and RESET constructs, let us assume that a PL/M parameter is *reset* if its value is zero and *set* if its value is one. Thus, the PL/M operation

```
CONTINUOUS = 0;
```

is equivalent to RESET CONTINUOUS and the PL/M operation

```
CONTINUOUS = 1;
```

is equivalent to SET CONTINUOUS.

Note that a *semicolon* terminates each PL/M operation. Semicolons are used as delimiters in PL/M to enable a single operation to occupy several lines unambiguously. Thus, it is necessary to insert the semicolons in the proper places to ensure that the PL/M operations are interpreted correctly. PL/M entities such as STATUS and CONTINUOUS which can be assigned different values at different times are called *variables*. Entities, such as 0 and 1, which do not vary are called *constants*.

LOOP CONSTRUCTS

The design language loop constructs are:

```
DO . . . END
DO WHILE . . . END
DO FOR EACH . . . END
DO FOREVER . . . END
```

The equivalent PL/M construct for DO . . . END is:

```
DO;
 .
 .
 .
END;
```

The DO WHILE ... END construct has an almost identical counterpart in PL/M which is:

```
DO WHILE expression;
  .
  .
  .
END;
```

But instead of a descriptive phase such as KEYSWITCH IS NOT ARMED, an *expression* is used in PL/M. The expression, in this case, is a *logical expression* whose *value* is either true or false at any time. An example of a logical expression is the phrase KEYSWITCH = 0 in the operation

```
DO WHILE KEYSWITCH = 0;
```

We have assumed that KEYSWITCH is equal to the value zero when the keyswitch is in the reset state and to a nonzero value when it is in the armed state. The logical expression KEYSWITCH = 0 is true whenever the keyswitch is not armed and the PL/M operation is therefore equivalent to the design language operation:

```
DO WHILE KEYSWITCH IS NOT ARMED
```

We introduced the PL/M expression here in order to be able to describe loop constructs; PL/M expressions are discussed in detail in a later section of this chapter.

The DO FOR EACH . . . END construct is related to and can be converted into the PL/M construct:

```
DO index = expression 1 TO expression 2;
  .
  .
  .
END;
```

Here a descriptive phrase is replaced by an *index* and two expressions. The design language operation DO FOR EACH SWITCH in a situation in which there are five switches can be implemented in PL/M by an operation of the form:

```
DO INDEX = 1 TO 5;
```

In this case, INDEX is a PL/M variable that is initially set to *expression 1*, which in the example is the constant 1. The loop is then executed, the value of INDEX is increased by 1, and the loop is executed again. This is repeated until the value of INDEX exceeds *expression 2*, which is the constant 5. The execution of the loop is terminated after having been executed exactly five times.

A variation of this PL/M construct permits the index to be increased by a value other than the value 1 each time the loop is executed. The latter version of this construct is given by:

```
DO index = expression 1 TO expression 2 BY expression 3;
  .
  .
  .
END;
```

Expression 3 provides a value by which the index should be increased for each execution of the loop. In the example,

```
DO INDEX = 1 TO 5 BY 2;
```

INDEX is initially set equal to 1. Then it is increased to 3 and finally to 5. Thus, the loop is executed three times instead of five times as in the previous example.

The DO FOREVER . . . END construct has no counterpart in PL/M. It can be implemented, however, by using the PL/M DO WHILE construct with an expression that is always true. Since the expression 1 = 1 is always true, the PL/M construct:

```
DO WHILE 1 = 1;
  .
  .
  .
END;
```

is equivalent to the DO FOREVER . . . END design language construct.

CONTROL CONSTRUCTS

Control constructs in design language are:

```
CALL:
RETURN
```

Corresponding constructs in PL/M are similar, namely:

```
CALL procedure name;
RETURN;
```

Examples of these constructs in PL/M along with their equivalent design language constructs are:

```
CALL: STOP TIMER (;)        CALL STOP$TIMER;
RETURN                      RETURN;
```

The PL/M compiler does not permit spaces to be used in a name such as STOP TIMER. However, dollar signs may be inserted into a name to make it more readable. Since the dollar signs are ignored by the compiler, they do not affect the interpretation of the name.

TEST CONSTRUCTS

Test constructs in design language are:

```
IF a test condition is true
  THEN  do something
```

and

```
IF a test condition is true
  THEN  do something
  ELSE  do something different
```

Corresponding PL/M constructs are similar:

```
IF expression
  THEN  statement;
```

and

```
IF expression
  THEN  statement 1;
  ELSE  statement 2;
```

No semicolon follows the expression since the PL/M compiler considers the complete IF . . . THEN . . . phrase to be a single construct. An example of a PL/M test construct is given by:

```
IF KEYSWITCH = 0
  THEN  RETURN;
```

which is equivalent to the design language construct:

```
IF KEYSWITCH IS RESET
  THEN  RETURN
```

An expression can specify a compound condition as in the example:

```
IF KEYSWITCH <> 0 AND TIMER$STATE = 0
```

This PL/M operation is equivalent to the design language operation:

```
IF KEYSWITCH IS ARMED AND TIMER STATE IS EXPIRED
```

The symbol <> means *is not equal to* and we have assumed that the variable TIMER$STATE is equal to zero whenever the timer is in the expired state.

An example of a test construct using the complete IF . . . THEN . . . ELSE . . . construct is given in Figure 5-2. Both the design language version of the operations and the corresponding PL/M operations are shown. We have assumed that the data structure INPUT RECORD contains ten characters and therefore is full when the PL/M variable FULL$INDICATOR is equal to ten.

```
/*  IF FULL INDICATOR SHOWS THAT INPUT RECORD IS FULL          */
                                          IF FULL$INDICATOR = 10
/*     THEN  SET STATUS TO FULL                                */
                                            THEN  STATUS = 1;
/*     ELSE  SET STATUS TO NOT FULL                            */
                                            ELSE  STATUS = 0;
```

Figure 5-2. Example of PL/M test construct.

Test constructs may be nested in PL/M. An example of a nested test construct is shown in Figure 5-3. Note that the DO . . . END brackets may sometimes be omitted in the PL/M realization of a procedure.

```
/*  IF CHARACTER CONTAINS A NUMERIC KEY CODE                         */
                                        IF CHARACTER >= '0' AND CHARACTER <= '9'
/*    THEN DO                                                        */
                                          THEN
/*            IF STATUS INDICATES INPUT RECORD IS NOT FULL           */
                                                IF STATUS = 0;
/*              THEN  CALL: ADD TO INPUT RECORD (CHARACTER;)         */
                                                  THEN  CALL ADD$TO$INPUT$RECORD (CHARACTER);
/*              ELSE  CALL: BEEP(;)                                  */
                                                  ELSE  CALL BEEP;
/*          END                                                      */
```

Figure 5-3. Example of nested PL/M test constructs.

In the example we see that a PL/M ELSE may follow two THEN's without any brackets. Whenever this situation occurs, the ELSE is *always* paired with the immediately preceding THEN. Since DO . . . END brackets help clarify the interpretation of the PL/M operations, we recommend that they always be used to avoid misinterpreting what the microcomputer will do. Figure 5-4 presents the previous example with the DO . . . END brackets inserted. Note that if the design specifies that the ELSE be paired with the first THEN, the DO . . . END brackets *must* be used, as shown in Figure 5-5. Changing the indentation to line the ELSE up with the desired THEN without suitable brackets may result in incorrect system operation. As with design language, indentation of the PL/M operations improves readability; their interpretation is unambiguous regardless of indentation.

Note that to test if a character code represents a numeric digit, it must lie between the character codes for zero and nine inclusive. In PL/M, the character codes for zero through nine are designated by '0', '1', '2', . . . , '9' where the apostrophes differentiate between the character codes and the numeric values for the numbers. We discuss the use of character codes in more detail in Chapter 6 and in Appendix B. Since the symbol >= means *greater than or equal to* and the symbol

```
/*  IF CHARACTER CONTAINS A NUMERIC KEY CODE                         */
                                        IF CHARACTER >= '0' AND CHARACTER <= '9'
/*    THEN DO                                                        */
                                          THEN  DO;
/*            IF STATUS INDICATES INPUT RECORD IS NOT FULL           */
                                                IF STATUS = 0
/*              THEN  CALL: ADD TO INPUT RECORD (CHARACTER;)         */
                                                  THEN  CALL ADD$TO$INPUT$RECORD (CHARACTER);
/*              ELSE  CALL: BEEP(;)                                  */
                                                  ELSE  CALL BEEP;
/*          END                                                      */
                                              END;
```

Figure 5-4. Alternate realization of example of Figure 5-3.

```
/*  IF CHARACTER CONTAINS A NUMERIC KEY CODE                           */
                                    IF CHARACTER >= '0' AND CHARACTER <= '9'
/*    THEN  DO                                                         */
                                      THEN  DO;
/*         IF STATUS INDICATES INPUT RECORD IS NOT FULL                */
                                            IF STATUS = 0;
/*          THEN  CALL: ADD TO INPUT RECORD (CHARACTER; )              */
                                             THEN  CALL ADD$TO$INPUT$RECORD (CHARACTER);
/*         END                                                         */
                                          END;
/*    ELSE  CALL: BEEP(; )                                             */
                                      ELSE  CALL BEEP;
```

Figure 5-5. Example showing ELSE paired with first THEN.

<= means *less than or equal to*, the test for a numeric key code in PL/M is provided by the operation:

```
IF CHARACTER >= '0' AND CHARACTER <= '9'
```

Note also that a single input parameter can be passed to a called procedure in PL/M by enclosing the parameter name in parentheses as illustrated by the operation:

```
CALL ADD$TO$INPUT$RECORD (CHARACTER);
```

We discuss PL/M parameters in more detail shortly.

In the figures we used to illustrate the conversion of design language into PL/M, the PL/M operations were shown offset to the right of the corresponding design language operations. The offset is used to improve readability and we use it in all of the examples in this book.

PL/M expressions and assignment constructs were introduced through examples in the previous sections. These concepts are developed further in the next section.

EXPRESSIONS

A PL/M expression consists of a set of PL/M variables and constants joined together by *operators*. For example, the design language phrase

```
60 * SECONDS
```

which was used in the START TIMER procedure of the burglar alarm system is also a PL/M expression denoting the product of the constant 60 and the variable SECONDS. The asterisk (*) is the multiplication operator; the plus sign (+), the minus sign (−), and the slash (/) are the addition, subtraction, and division operators, respectively. Another example showing the use of the *arithmetic operators* is given by:

```
3600 * HOURS + 60 * MINUTES + SECONDS
```

This expression is used to calculate time in seconds from its equivalent value in hours, minutes, and seconds. In PL/M, multiplication and division take *precedence* over addition and subtraction. Therefore, in the absence of parentheses, this expression is evaluated as if it were written with the parentheses shown below:

```
(3600 * HOURS) + (60 * MINUTES) + SECONDS
```

Interpreting this expression in any other manner requires the explicit use of parentheses. Expressions such as this one are called *arithmetic expressions*.

Examples of *logical expressions* were presented in the sections that described loop constructs and test constructs. Operators used in logical expressions can be *logical operators, relational operators,* or arithmetic operators. The PL/M logical operators are AND, OR, and NOT. The PL/M relational operators are shown in the chart below:

Operator	Interpretation
=	is equal to
<	is less than
>	is greater than
<=	is less than or equal to
>=	is greater than or equal to
<>	is not equal to

When a logical expression is used in a conditional loop or in a test construct, it has a *value* that is either true or false at any time. To determine whether to reexecute the operations in a loop or whether the operations in the THEN part or the ELSE part of a test construct should be executed, the logical expression is evaluated. If it is true, the loop operations are reexecuted or the THEN operations are executed. If it is false, the loop is terminated or the ELSE operations, if an ELSE part exists, are executed.

A precedence relation exists among all operators, as shown below:

Precedence	Operator
1	* / (multiply, divide)
2	+ − (add, subtract)
3	relational
4	NOT
5	AND
6	OR

As before, parentheses can be used to change the natural order of the precedence relationship or to increase clarity to avoid misinterpreting what the microcomputer will do. When used to increase clarity, parentheses fulfill a role similar to that of the DO . . . END brackets. The DO . . . END brackets group operations together; the parentheses group parts of expressions together. In both cases, the grouping helps to ensure that what the microcomputer does is what we want it to do.

This completes our discussion of PL/M expressions. Let us now turn to the PL/M assignment construct. The general format for the PL/M assignment construct is given by:

variable = expression;

where expression is an arithmetic expression. After the operation specified by the assignment construct is executed, the variable will be equal to the value computed from the expression. An example of a PL/M assignment construct is:

```
TIME = 3600 * HOURS + 60 * MINUTES + SECONDS;
```

which calculates the time in seconds from its equivalent value in hours, minutes, and seconds.

DATA DECLARATIONS

As we have seen, there are two different categories of data in PL/M: constants and variables. For each variable, the PL/M compiler must know the range of values that the variable may represent. All PL/M compilers provide at least two such ranges. If a variable need only be capable of differentiating up to 256 different values (0 to 255, say), then it is called a *byte* variable. If its usage requires that it differentiate up to 65,536 different values, then it is called an *address* variable. An address variable consists of two bytes that are treated as a single entity in PL/M. The *data type*, byte or address, of each variable must be *declared* to the compiler prior to its use in a procedure. PL/M *data declarations* take the form:

```
DECLARE SECONDS BYTE;
DECLARE TIME ADDRESS;
```

These two declarations can be combined into the single data declaration:

```
DECLARE SECONDS BYTE, TIME ADDRESS;
```

Declarations for variables of the same data type may be combined even further, as follows:

```
DECLARE (SECONDS,MINUTES,HOURS) BYTE;
```

PL/M has provision for grouping variables into data structures. The list data structure is called an *array* in PL/M. A type of hierarchical data structure, called a *structure*, can also be defined in PL/M. We examine how to declare and use PL/M arrays and structures in the next sections.

PL/M ARRAYS

In Chapter 4 we introduced the list data structure INPUT RECORD as a modular data structure for storing numeric character codes in the MAINTAIN INPUT RECORD module. To declare a PL/M array for this purpose, it is necessary to specify the maximum number of character codes that have to be stored in the array. Let us assume that this number is ten, as shown below in the data structure definition for INPUT RECORD.

```
MODULAR DATA STRUCTURE:  INPUT RECORD

NAME              SIZE   TYPE   CONTENTS          NOTES
----              ----   ----   --------          -----
INPUT RECORD       10    BYTE   NUMERIC CODES
```

Using this information, the INPUT RECORD data structure can then be declared as a PL/M array, as follows:

```
DECLARE INPUT$RECORD (10) BYTE;
```

The individual elements in the array can then be manipulated using an *index* that can be either a constant, a variable, or an expression. As an example, the CLEAR INPUT RECORD procedure of Figure 4-20 is reproduced in Figure 5-6, which shows the operations needed to convert the design language procedure into PL/M. In the example, the variable INDEX is used as the PL/M loop index as well as the array index and the variable FULL$INDICATOR is set to zero to indicate that the array is empty. Since the PL/M variable INDEX does not appear in design language, the *data structure definition* for INDEX contains header information which is added during conversion. The reader should note again how apostrophes differentiate between the character code zero, '0', and the numeric value for zero. Finally, note that the declarations for the INPUT$RECORD array and the FULL$INDICATOR variable are not contained within the procedure itself. Since they are modular data structures, their PL/M declarations are placed at the module level so that they are accessible to the other procedures in the module; the declaration for the variable INDEX is placed within the procedure itself since it is a local parameter and does not contain any modular information.

PL/M STRUCTURES

In Chapter 4 we presented a design for a SORT procedure that manipulated records in a data structure called FILE. We now show how to declare FILE as a PL/M structure and how to manipulate information in a PL/M structure.

```
/*    MODULAR DATA STRUCTURE:   INPUT RECORD                                      */
/*                                                                                */
/*    NAME                     SIZE    TYPE    CONTENTS          NOTES            */
/*    ----                     ----    ----    --------          -----            */
/*    INPUT RECORD              10     BYTE    NUMERIC CODES                      */
                                                   DECLARE INPUT$RECORD (10) BYTE;
/*      FULL INDICATOR           1     BYTE    COUNTER                            */
                                                   DECLARE FULL$INDICATOR BYTE;
                                               .
                                               .
                                               .

/*  PROCEDURE:   CLEAR INPUT RECORD (;)                                           */
/*  ******************************************************************        */
/*    LOCAL PARAMETER NOT USED IN DESIGN LANGUAGE                                 */
/*                                                                                */
/*    NAME                     SIZE    TYPE    CONTENTS          NOTES            */
/*    ----                     ----    ----    --------          -----            */
/*    INDEX                      1     BYTE    INDEX                              */
                                                   DECLARE INDEX BYTE;
/*  ******************************************************************        */
/*  BEGIN PROCEDURE                                                               */
/*    DO FOR EACH ELEMENT IN INPUT RECORD                                         */
                                                     DO INDEX = 0 TO 9;
/*      SET ELEMENT TO 'ZERO' CODE                                                */
                                                       INPUT$RECORD (INDEX) = '0';
/*    END                                                                         */
                                                     END;
/*    SET FULL INDICATOR TO EMPTY                                                 */
                                                     FULL$INDICATOR = 0;
/*    RETURN                                                                      */
                                                     RETURN;
/*  END PROCEDURE                                                                 */
```

Figure 5-6. Example illustrating the use of a PL/M array.

As before, let us assume that each record in FILE contains a name, a street address, and a serial number and that the serial number is used as a key. Furthermore, unlike the example in Chapter 4, let us assume that each serial number is a positive number that is less than 65,536 and represented by an address variable and that the name and street address each consist of up to 20 alphabetic or numeric characters that are represented by character codes. Then, each record consists of three entities that can be declared in a single PL/M declaration, as follows:

```
DECLARE SERIAL$NUMBER ADDRESS, NAME (20) BYTE, STREET$ADDRESS (20) BYTE;
```

Assuming that there are 256 such records in FILE, we specify the size of FILE by using a PL/M *structure declaration* in place of the above declaration, as follows:

```
DECLARE FILE (256) STRUCTURE (SERIAL$NUMBER ADDRESS, NAME (20) BYTE, STREET$ADDRESS (20) BYTE);
```

This structure declaration indicates that FILE is a PL/M structure containing 256 records, each of which consists of a two-byte serial number, a 20-byte name, and a 20-byte street address. The individual records in FILE can then be manipulated using an index whose value specifies a record number from 0 through 255. For example, the serial number in the *tenth* record of the structure FILE is given by

```
FILE (9).SERIAL$NUMBER
```

where the *dot* ties the name of the entity in the record to the name of the structure. The elements of the two arrays in each record are manipulated using indices whose values range from 0 through 19. For example, the first character code stored in the name part of the *fifteenth* record in FILE is given by

```
FILE (14).NAME (0)
```

and the *thirteenth* character code stored in the street address part of the *twenty-first* record of FILE is given by

```
FILE (20).STREET$ADDRESS (12)
```

We have reproduced the SORT procedure of Chapter 4 in Figure 5-7 to illustrate how a PL/M structure is used.

In our PL/M examples thus far, we have omitted the declarations needed to specify the names of the procedures and to identify their input and output parameters. We discuss these topics next.

```
/*  MODULAR DATA STRUCTURE: FILE                                                     */
/*                                                                                   */
/*  NAME                    SIZE    TYPE      CONTENTS              NOTES            */
/*  ----                    ----    ----      --------              -----            */
/*  FILE                                                              1              */
/*    RECORD                                                                         */
/*      SERIAL NUMBER         1     ADDRESS   NUMBER                                 */
/*      NAME                 20     BYTE      ALPHABETIC CODES                       */
/*      STREET ADDRESS       20     BYTE      ALPHANUMERIC CODES                     */
/*                                                                                   */
/*  NOTE 1. FILE CONSISTS OF 256 RECORDS.                                            */
                          DECLARE FILE (256) STRUCTURE (SERIAL$NUMBER ADDRESS, NAME (20) BYTE,
                                                                  STREET$ADDRESS (20) BYTE);
/*  -------------------------------------------------------------------------------  */
```

Figure 5-7. Example illustrating the use of a PL/M structure.

```
/*  PROCEDURE: SORT (;)                                                                         */
/*  ***************************************************************************************    */
/*    LOCAL PARAMETERS NOT USED IN DESIGN LANGUAGE                                              */
/*                                                                                              */
/*    NAME                    SIZE   TYPE       CONTENTS              NOTES                     */
/*    ----                    ----   ----       --------              -----                     */
/*    INDEX1                    1    BYTE       INDEX                                           */
                                                   DECLARE INDEX1 BYTE;
/*    INDEX2                    1    BYTE       INDEX                                           */
                                                   DECLARE INDEX2 BYTE;
/*    INDEX3                    1    BYTE       INDEX                                           */
                                                   DECLARE INDEX3 BYTE;
/*    SAVE SERIAL NUMBER        1    ADDRESS    SAVE ADDRESS                                    */
                                                   DECLARE SAVE$SERIAL$NUMBER ADDRESS;
/*    SAVE NAME                 1    BYTE       SAVE BYTE                                       */
                                                   DECLARE SAVE$NAME BYTE;
/*    SAVE STREET               1    BYTE       SAVE BYTE                                       */
                                                   DECLARE SAVE$STREET BYTE;
/*  ***************************************************************************************    */
/*  BEGIN PROCEDURE                                                                             */
/*    SELECT FIRST RECORD IN FILE                                                               */
                                                      INDEX1 = 0;
/*    DO FOREVER                                                                                */
                                                      DO WHILE 1 = 1;
/*      DO FOR EACH RECORD IN FILE FOLLOWING SELECTED RECORD                                    */
                                                        DO INDEX2 = INDEX1 + 1 TO 255;
/*        IF KEY IN RECORD IS LESS THAN KEY IN SELECTED RECORD                                  */
                                                          IF FILE (INDEX2).SERIAL$NUMBER < FILE (INDEX1).SERIAL$NUMBER
/*          THEN  EXCHANGE RECORD AND SELECTED RECORD AND CONTINUE USING EXCHANGED RECORD       */
                                                            THEN DO;
                                                                   SAVE$SERIAL$NUMBER = FILE(INDEX1).SERIAL$NUMBER;
                                                                   FILE(INDEX1).SERIAL$NUMBER = FILE(INDEX2).SERIAL$NUMBER;
                                                                   FILE(INDEX2).SERIAL$NUMBER = SAVE$SERIAL$NUMBER;
                                                                   DO INDEX3 = 0 TO 19;
                                                                     SAVE$NAME = FILE(INDEX1).NAME (INDEX3);
                                                                     FILE(INDEX1).NAME (INDEX3) = FILE(INDEX2).NAME(INDEX3);
                                                                     FILE(INDEX2).NAME (INDEX3) = SAVE$NAME;
                                                                     SAVE$STREET = FILE(INDEX1).STREET$ADDRESS (INDEX3);
                                                                     FILE(INDEX1).STREET$ADDRESS (INDEX3) =
                                                                                     FILE(INDEX2).STREET$ADDRESS (INDEX3);
                                                                     FILE(INDEX2).STREET$ADDRESS (INDEX3) = SAVE$STREET;
                                                                   END;
                                                                 END;
                                                        END;
/*      IF ALL RECORDS BUT THE LAST ONE HAVE BEEN SELECTED                                      */
                                                        IF INDEX1 = 254
/*        THEN  RETURN                                                                          */
                                                          THEN RETURN;
/*        ELSE  SELECT NEXT RECORD IN FILE                                                      */
                                                          ELSE INDEX1 = INDEX1 + 1;
/*    END                                                                                       */
                                                      END;
/*  END PROCEDURE                                                                               */
```

Figure 5-7. (Continued).

PROCEDURE DECLARATIONS

For a procedure such as the CLEAR INPUT RECORD procedure which has no input or output parameters, the PL/M *procedure declaration* takes the following form:

```
CLEAR$INPUT$RECORD: PROCEDURE;
```

The end of the procedure is designated by an END phrase of the form:

```
END CLEAR$INPUT$RECORD;
```

The procedure name need not be repeated in the END phrase, but if it is used, it must match the name used in the procedure declaration.

If a procedure is called only from within its own module, the procedure declaration presented above is adequate. But if the procedure is called from a procedure contained in another module, the PL/M compiler must be so informed; a *public attribute* is used for this purpose. An example showing how to assign a public attribute to a procedure is given by the procedure declaration for the BEEP procedure, as follows:

```
BEEP: PROCEDURE PUBLIC;
```

In addition to assigning the public attribute to the BEEP procedure, an *external procedure declaration* is needed for the BEEP procedure in every module containing a procedure that calls it. This external procedure declaration takes the form:

```
BEEP: PROCEDURE EXTERNAL;
END BEEP;
```

We will illustrate the use of the public attribute and the external procedure declaration shortly. First, let us discuss how a PL/M procedure declaration is used to identify the input parameters for a procedure and how output parameters are returned from a PL/M procedure.

PARAMETERS

Input parameters, which can be constants or variables, are identified for a procedure through its procedure declaration. This is done by placing the names of the input parameters into the procedure declaration between a set of parentheses. For example, the PL/M procedure declaration for the ADD TO INPUT RECORD procedure is given by:

```
ADD$TO$INPUT$RECORD: PROCEDURE (CHARACTER);
```

If more than one input parameter is used, the input parameter names inside the parentheses are separated by commas. In a previous section we saw how a calling procedure identifies and passes the values of input parameters to a called procedure. The reader will recall that the ADD TO INPUT RECORD procedure is called in the following manner:

```
CALL ADD$TO$INPUT$RECORD (CHARACTER);
```

These examples illustrate how a variable input parameter, CHARACTER, is identified and its value passed to a called procedure in PL/M. An example for a constant input parameter is given by the procedure declaration and the PL/M call operation for the START TIMER procedure:

```
START$TIMER: PROCEDURE (SECONDS) PUBLIC;

CALL START$TIMER (5);
```

If an external procedure declaration is needed for a procedure to which a variable input parameter is passed, it takes the form:

```
ACTUATE$ALARM: PROCEDURE (ALARM) EXTERNAL;
  DECLARE ALARM BYTE;
END ACTUATE$ALARM;
```

Note that a data type must be declared for the input parameter in the external procedure declaration even though the data type must also be declared in the procedure or module itself. If a constant parameter is passed to a procedure, a name must be assigned to the constant in the external procedure declaration to permit it to have the correct data type. This is illustrated below for the START TIMER procedure.

```
START$TIMER: PROCEDURE (SECONDS) EXTERNAL;
  DECLARE SECONDS BYTE;
END START$TIMER;
```

If more than one input parameter is passed to a procedure, the number of input parameters in each PL/M call operation and in the corresponding procedure declaration and in each external procedure declaration must be the same. Moreover, the same data type must be assigned to an input parameter in the call operation and to the corresponding input parameter in each of the related procedure declarations. That is, if data type BYTE is assigned to the first input parameter in a PL/M call operation, data type BYTE must be assigned to the first input parameter in all of the related procedure declarations.

A single output parameter can be returned by a PL/M procedure in a straightforward manner. First, the procedure declaration must specify the data type of the output parameter, as shown below:

```
TEST$IF$INPUT$RECORD$FULL: PROCEDURE BYTE;
```

Thus, the TEST IF INPUT RECORD FULL procedure returns a byte variable as an output parameter. Then, the *value* of the output parameter is identified by the modified PL/M RETURN construct:

```
RETURN expression;
```

Thus, in the TEST IF INPUT RECORD FULL procedure, the value of the variable STATUS is returned by using the RETURN construct:

```
RETURN STATUS;
```

The PL/M call operation is *not* used to call a procedure that returns an output parameter. Instead, an operation similar to a PL/M assignment construct is used, as illustrated below:

```
STATUS = TEST$IF$INPUT$RECORD$FULL;
```

The complete TEST IF INPUT RECORD FULL procedure is illustrated in Figure 5-8 along with sufficient additional constructs to show how these concepts are used. Since FULL INDICATOR is part of a modular data structure, its PL/M data declaration is placed in the module description. The PL/M data declaration and the call operation which are shown below the TEST IF INPUT RECORD FULL procedure are part of the GET INPUT RECORD procedure. They are shown to illustrate how the the former procedure is called by the latter procedure. Note that a procedure that is called by another procedure in the same module *must* precede it as illustrated in the example. Note also that STATUS is declared twice: once in each of the procedures. Thus, two versions of the variable STATUS exist and each procedure manipulates its own version. Information is passed from one version of STATUS to the other only when the TEST IF INPUT RECORD FULL procedure is called with STATUS as an output parameter. In effect, information is then *copied* from one version of STATUS to the other, thus ensuring the integrity of the former regardless of how the latter is manipulated.

Finally, if a procedure that returns an output parameter is called from another module, it must be assigned the public attribute. An example is given by the READ KEYBOARD procedure:

```
READ$KEYBOARD: PROCEDURE BYTE PUBLIC;
```

Every module containing a procedure that calls the READ KEYBOARD procedure must contain an external procedure declaration of the form:

```
READ$KEYBOARD: PROCEDURE BYTE EXTERNAL;
END READ$KEYBOARD;
```

The methods just described do not work well with PL/M arrays and structures. To list each element of a PL/M array or structure as an input parameter is not only

```
/*    MODULAR DATA STRUCTURE:   INPUT RECORD                                      */
/*                                                                                */
/*    NAME                SIZE    TYPE    CONTENTS              NOTES             */
/*    ----                ----    ----    --------              -----             */
/*    INPUT RECORD         10     BYTE    NUMERIC CODES                           */
/*      FULL INDICATOR      1     BYTE    COUNTER                                 */
                                              DECLARE FULL$INDICATOR BYTE;
                              .
                              .
                              .
/* ------------------------------------------------------------------------------ */
/* PROCEDURE:   TEST IF INPUT RECORD FULL  (;STATUS)                              */
                                              TEST$IF$INPUT$RECORD$FULL: PROCEDURE BYTE;
/* ****************************************************************************** */
/*    OUTPUT PARAMETER:  STATUS                                                   */
/*                                                                                */
/*    NAME                SIZE    TYPE    CONTENTS              NOTES             */
/*    ----                ----    ----    --------              -----             */
/*    STATUS                1     BYTE    FLAG                                    */
                                                DECLARE STATUS BYTE;
/* ****************************************************************************** */
/* BEGIN PROCEDURE                                                                */
/*    IF FULL INDICATOR SHOWS THAT INPUT RECORD IS FULL                           */
                                                IF FULL$INDICATOR = 10
/*      THEN   SET STATUS TO FULL                                                 */
                                                  THEN  STATUS = 1;
/*      ELSE   SET STATUS TO NOT FULL                                             */
                                                  ELSE  STATUS = 0;
/*    RETURN                                                                      */
                                                RETURN STATUS;
/* END PROCEDURE                                                                  */
                                              END TEST$IF$INPUT$RECORD$FULL;
/* ------------------------------------------------------------------------------ */
                                      .
                                      .
                                      .
/*    LOCAL PARAMETER:  STATUS                                                    */
/*                                                                                */
/*    NAME                SIZE    TYPE    CONTENTS              NOTES             */
/*    ----                ----    ----    --------              -----             */
/*    STATUS                1     BYTE    FLAG                                    */
                                      .         DECLARE STATUS BYTE;
                                      .
                                      .
/*      CALL:  TEST IF INPUT RECORD FULL  (;STATUS)                               */
                                                     STATUS = TEST$IF$INPUT$RECORD$FULL;
```

Figure 5-8. Illustration of output parameter passing in PL/M.

tedious but also highly inefficient. Since a PL/M procedure can only return a single output parameter, it cannot be used to return an array or structure. Several methods are available for passing the information in an array or structure from one procedure to another in PL/M. The method that best suits our purpose uses a concept known as *based variables*.

BASED VARIABLES

Since it is difficult to pass the information contained in a PL/M array or structure to a procedure as an input parameter and impossible to return it as an output parameter, we instead pass a *pointer* that indicates *where* the information is located. This enables a procedure to access or manipulate the information in the PL/M array or structure as if it had received a copy of it. Let us use the SEARCH AND PRINT RECORD procedure, whose design language implementation is shown in Figure 5-9, to illustrate this concept.

```
PROCEDURE: SEARCH AND PRINT RECORD (SEARCH KEY; )
BEGIN PROCEDURE
  CALL: SEARCH (SEARCH KEY; RECORD)
  CALL: PRINT (RECORD; )
  RETURN
END PROCEDURE
```

Figure 5-9. Procedure to illustrate the use of based variables.

In the SEARCH AND PRINT RECORD procedure, the SEARCH procedure is called to search the data structure FILE for a match with SEARCH KEY. If a match is found, the complete record (serial number, name, and street address) corresponding to the match is returned through the output parameter RECORD. Otherwise, the NAME part of RECORD is set to 'NO MATCH FOUND' before RECORD is returned to its calling procedure as an output parameter. RECORD is then passed to the PRINT procedure as an input parameter and the appropriate information is printed as required. We have seen how the data structure FILE can be declared as a PL/M structure. The data structure RECORD, which is used as an output parameter in the SEARCH procedure, is declared as a PL/M structure, as follows:

```
DECLARE RECORD STRUCTURE (SERIAL$NUMBER ADDRESS, NAME (20) BYTE, STREET$ADDRESS (20) BYTE);
```

Then, when a match is found, the corresponding record is moved from FILE to RECORD using PL/M assignment constructs of the form:

```
RECORD.SERIAL$NUMBER = FILE (INDEX1).SERIAL$NUMBER;
RECORD.NAME (INDEX2) = FILE (INDEX1).NAME (INDEX2);
```

In the example, INDEX1 is used to select the record in FILE for which a match was found; INDEX2 is used to move each of the characters in the selected NAME to the

NAME part of RECORD. A pointer to RECORD is then returned as an output parameter. The pointer, RECORD$POINTER in this case, must be declared as a PL/M ADDRESS variable in the procedure. In addition, during the execution of the SEARCH procedure, RECORD$POINTER must be set to a suitable value that points to the PL/M structure RECORD. The latter operation is accomplished by an assignment construct of the form:

```
RECORD$POINTER = .RECORD;
```

Figure 5-10 illustrates these concepts for the SEARCH procedure.

```
/*  PROCEDURE: SEARCH (SEARCH KEY;RECORD)                                    */
                                   SEARCH: PROCEDURE (SEARCH$KEY) ADDRESS PUBLIC;
/*  ********************************************************************** */
                                   .
                                   .
                                   .
/*   OUTPUT PARAMETER: RECORD                                                */
/*                                                                           */
/*   NAME              SIZE   TYPE      CONTENTS              NOTES         */
/*   ----              ----   ----      --------              -----         */
/*   RECORD                                                                  */
/*     SERIAL NUMBER     1    ADDRESS   NUMBER                               */
/*     NAME             20    BYTE      ALPHABETIC CODES                     */
/*     STREET ADDRESS   20    BYTE      ALPHANUMERIC CODES                   */
                                   DECLARE RECORD STRUCTURE (SERIAL$NUMBER ADDRESS, NAME (20) BYTE,
                                                                  STREET$ADDRESS (20) BYTE);

/*   LOCAL PARAMETER: RECORD POINTER                                         */
/*                                                                           */
/*   NAME              SIZE   TYPE      CONTENTS              NOTES         */
/*   ----              ----   ----      --------              -----         */
/*   RECORD POINTER      1    ADDRESS   POINTER                              */
                                   DECLARE RECORD$POINTER ADDRESS;
/*  ********************************************************************** */
                                   .
                                   .
                                   .
/*       SET RECORD TO SELECTED RECORD                                       */
                                   .
                                   .
                                   .
/*       RETURN                                                              */
                                       RECORD$POINTER = .RECORD;
                                       RETURN RECORD$POINTER;
                                   .
                                   .
                                   .
```

Figure 5-10. Passing PL/M structure information through an output parameter using a pointer.

Figure 5-11 illustrates how the SEARCH AND PRINT RECORD procedure is converted into PL/M. This procedure shows how the pointer that is returned from the SEARCH procedure as an output parameter is passed to the PRINT procedure as an input parameter. Note that a PL/M declaration is not needed for the RECORD

```
/*  PROCEDURE:  SEARCH AND PRINT RECORD  (SEARCH KEY; )                              */
                                     SEARCH$AND$PRINT$RECORD: PROCEDURE (SEARCH$KEY) PUBLIC;
/*  *******************************************************************************  */
/*    INPUT PARAMETER:  SEARCH KEY                                                   */
/*                                                                                   */
/*    NAME                  SIZE     TYPE        CONTENTS               NOTES       */
/*    ----                  ----     ----        --------               -----       */
/*    SEARCH KEY             1       ADDRESS     KEY                                 */
                                          DECLARE SEARCH$KEY ADDRESS;
/*                                                                                   */
/*    LOCAL PARAMETER:  RECORD POINTER                                               */
/*                                                                                   */
/*    NAME                  SIZE     TYPE        CONTENTS               NOTES       */
/*    ----                  ----     ----        --------               -----       */
/*    RECORD POINTER         1       ADDRESS     POINTER                             */
                                          DECLARE RECORD$POINTER ADDRESS;
/*  *******************************************************************************  */
/*  BEGIN PROCEDURE                                                                  */
/*    CALL:  SEARCH  (SEARCH KEY; RECORD)                                            */
                                          RECORD$POINTER = SEARCH (SEARCH$KEY);
/*    CALL:  PRINT  (RECORD; )                                                       */
                                          CALL PRINT (RECORD$POINTER);
/*    RETURN                                                                         */
                                          RETURN;
/*  END PROCEDURE                                                                    */
                                     END SEARCH$AND$PRINT$RECORD;
```

Figure 5-11. Passing a pointer from one procedure to another.

structure in the SEARCH AND PRINT RECORD procedure since the information in the structure is not used explicitly in the latter procedure.

Figure 5-12 shows how the information in the RECORD structure is made available for use in the PRINT procedure. In the latter procedure the RECORD structure is declared to be *based* or located where the pointer, RECORD$POINTER, indicates it is located. The use of the keyword BASED in the PL/M declaration causes all references to RECORD to be made to the RECORD structure that was declared in the SEARCH procedure. Thus, the information stored in the RECORD structure by the SEARCH procedure can be used by the operations in the PRINT procedure in a straightforward manner.

The concept of based variables that we have just described allows information in one PL/M module to be directly accessed by a procedure in another PL/M module. This violates our design rule of isolating a data structure within a module, but passing a copy of a complete structure from one PL/M procedure to another cannot be done automatically and to insist on it would add to the complexity of the software. Moreover, a certain degree of isolation is provided by the use of pointers enabling only those procedures to which a pointer is passed to access the corresponding data. In our example, by copying the data from FILE to RECORD and then passing the PL/M pointer, RECORD$POINTER, to the PRINT procedure, the data in FILE is adequately isolated. For these reasons, we tolerate the *sharing* of data which is implied by the concept of based variables in PL/M. Note that the

```
/*  PROCEDURE:  PRINT  (RECORD; )                                          */
                                      PRINT:  PROCEDURE  (RECORD$POINTER)  PUBLIC;
/*  ********************************************************************** */
/*    LOCAL PARAMETER:  RECORD POINTER                                     */
/*                                                                         */
/*    NAME                 SIZE    TYPE       CONTENTS             NOTES   */
/*    ----                 ----    ----       --------             -----
/*    RECORD POINTER         1     ADDRESS    STRUCTURE POINTER            */
                                      DECLARE RECORD$POINTER ADDRESS;
/*                                                                         */
/*    INPUT PARAMETER:  RECORD                                             */
/*                                                                         */
/*    NAME                 SIZE    TYPE       CONTENTS             NOTES   */
/*    ----                 ----    ----       --------             -----   */
/*    RECORD                                                         1     */
/*      SERIAL NUMBER        1     ADDRESS    NUMBER                       */
/*      NAME                20     BYTE       ALPHABETIC CODES             */
/*      STREET ADDRESS      20     BYTE       ALPHANUMERIC CODES           */
/*                                                                         */
/*  NOTE 1:  RECORD IS BASED AT RECORD POINTER.                            */
                                      DECLARE  (RECORD BASED RECORD$POINTER)  STRUCTURE
                                          (SERIAL$NUMBER ADDRESS,  NAME  (20)  BYTE
                                              BYTE,  STREET$ADDRESS  (20)  BYTE);
/*    LOCAL PARAMETER:  INDEX                                              */
/*                                                                         */
/*    NAME                 SIZE    TYPE       CONTENTS             NOTES   */
/*    ----                 ----    ----       --------             -----   */
/*    INDEX                  1     BYTE       INDEX                        */
                                      DECLARE INDEX BYTE;
/*  ********************************************************************** */
                                 .
                                 .
                                 .
/*    DO FOR EACH CHARACTER IN THE NAME PORTION OF RECORD                  */
                                         DO INDEX = 0 TO 19;
/*      CALL:  OUTPUT CHARACTER  (CHARACTER; )                             */
                                           CALL OUTPUT$CHARACTER  (RECORD.NAME(INDEX));
/*    END                                                                  */
                                         END;
                                 .
                                 .
                                 .
```

Figure 5-12. Example showing how to use a pointer to access a PL/M structure.

PL/M declaration for RECORD$POINTER *must precede* its use in the PL/M declaration for the RECORD data structure.

In our example the data structure was a PL/M structure consisting of a single RECORD. To complete our discussion of based variables, let us show how a PL/M *array* or a PL/M structure consisting of *many records* can be passed from one procedure to another. In each case, a pointer must be set to an appropriate value and the pointer passed from one procedure to another as an input or output parameter. For the array INPUT$RECORD, the pointer is set by the operation:

```
INPUT$RECORD$POINTER = .INPUT$RECORD;
```

and for the structure FILE, the pointer is set by the operation

```
FILE$POINTER = .FILE;
```

Then, to use the information contained in the data structures, we use the pointers in PL/M declarations to establish the locations of the data structures, as follows:

```
DECLARE (INPUT$RECORD BASED INPUT$RECORD$POINTER) (10) BYTE;

DECLARE (FILE BASED FILE$POINTER) (256) STRUCTURE (SERIAL$NUMBER ADDRESS,NAME (20) BYTE, STREET$ADDRESS (20) BYTE);
```

Remember that whenever pointers are used in PL/M, they must first be declared as *address* variables.

INITIALIZATION

When we described the CLEAR INPUT RECORD procedure, we showed how to initialize an array of PL/M *variables* during the operation of a system. In some cases, the information stored in a data structure represents *constant* data that is never changed during the operation of the system. An example of constant data is the *control schedule* data used by a microcomputerized fuel injection system to control the fuel flow for an internal combustion engine. The data structure containing the control schedule need only be changed if the engine type is changed; this does not normally occur during the lifetime of an automobile.

To initialize a constant data structure in PL/M, the DATA attribute is included in the data declaration along with a list of the values to be used. An example illustrating how a CONTROL$SCHEDULE array is initialized in PL/M is shown below:

```
DECLARE CONTROL$SCHEDULE (10) BYTE DATA (10, 15, 25, 40, 60, 76, 88, 98, 106, 110);
```

To initialize BYTE constants, as in the above example, values between 0 and 255 must be used. For the initialization of ADDRESS constants, values between 0 and 65,535 can be used. Alternately, strings of character codes can be used to initialize a data structure; one character code is needed to initialize each BYTE constant and two character codes are needed to initialize each ADDRESS constant. An example illustrating how a PL/M array named MESSAGE is initialized by a string of character codes is shown below:

```
DECLARE MESSAGE (17) BYTE DATA ('PUSH START BUTTON');
```

In the example, during execution of the system, MESSAGE (0) contains the character code 'P', MESSAGE (1) contains the character code 'U', and so forth.

This completes our description of how data and data structures are manipulated in PL/M. A summary of the PL/M programming language is given in Appendix C.

PL/M MODULES

When the procedures and data structure definitions belonging to a module are converted into PL/M, it is necessary to convert the *rest* of the module description into PL/M as well. By examining the module description for the MAINTAIN INPUT RECORD module of Figure 4-35, we see that the first and last lines of the module description remain to be converted. The PL/M version of the *module declaration*

```
MODULE: MAINTAIN INPUT RECORD
```

is given by:

```
MAINTAIN$INPUT$RECORD: DO;
```

and the corresponding end phrase

```
END MODULE
```

is converted into

```
END MAINTAIN$INPUT$RECORD;
```

The module name need not be repeated in the latter case, but if it is used, it must match the name used in the module declaration.

The external procedure declarations follow the module declaration and are, in turn, followed by the modular data structures. The procedures themselves follow the module header in the order in which they occur in the module description. The converted MAINTAIN INPUT RECORD module is shown in Figure 5-13 to illustrate what a complete PL/M module looks like. The reader should note the following:

- Some header information, such as the *called by list*, is omitted in the example to reduce the size of the figure.
- The data structure heading LOCAL PARAMETER NOT USED IN DESIGN LANGUAGE is provided to permit PL/M declarations to be inserted for parameters which are used as indices or counters but do not occur in design language.
- In practice, each procedure is printed on a separate page to improve readability although the complete module is treated as a single entity by the PL/M compiler. We have not done so in the example to help illustrate the relationship of the parts of the module to one another.

OTHER CONSIDERATIONS

The concepts of input, output, and interrupt were discussed in earlier chapters. There are PL/M operations that permit us to implement these and other related functions directly in PL/M, but these PL/M operations will be more easily understood if

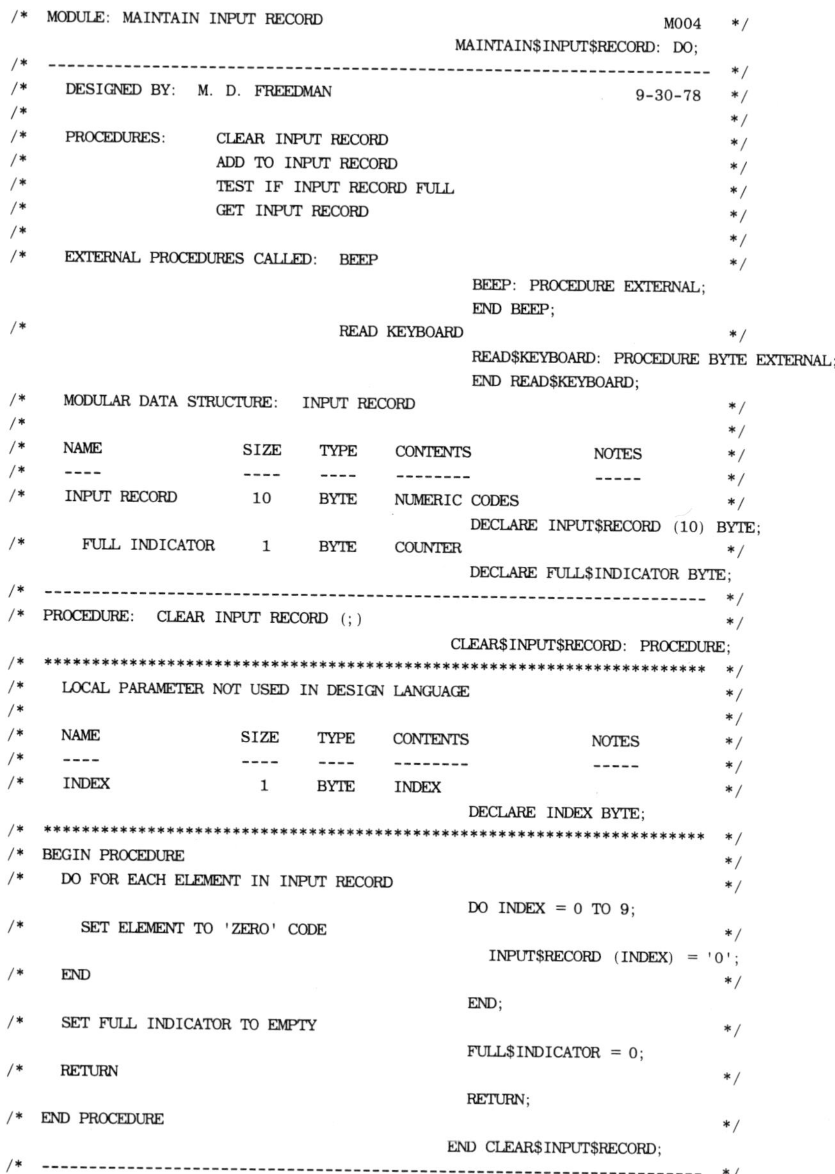

```
/*  MODULE: MAINTAIN INPUT RECORD                                    M004    */
                                           MAINTAIN$INPUT$RECORD: DO;
/*  ------------------------------------------------------------------------ */
/*    DESIGNED BY:  M. D. FREEDMAN                                  9-30-78  */
/*                                                                           */
/*    PROCEDURES:     CLEAR INPUT RECORD                                     */
/*                    ADD TO INPUT RECORD                                    */
/*                    TEST IF INPUT RECORD FULL                              */
/*                    GET INPUT RECORD                                       */
/*                                                                           */
/*    EXTERNAL PROCEDURES CALLED:  BEEP                                      */
                                             BEEP: PROCEDURE EXTERNAL;
                                             END BEEP;
/*                                 READ KEYBOARD                             */
                                             READ$KEYBOARD: PROCEDURE BYTE EXTERNAL;
                                             END READ$KEYBOARD;
/*    MODULAR DATA STRUCTURE:  INPUT RECORD                                  */
/*                                                                           */
/*    NAME              SIZE    TYPE    CONTENTS          NOTES              */
/*    ----              ----    ----    --------          -----              */
/*    INPUT RECORD       10     BYTE    NUMERIC CODES                        */
                                             DECLARE INPUT$RECORD (10) BYTE;
/*      FULL INDICATOR    1     BYTE    COUNTER                              */
                                             DECLARE FULL$INDICATOR BYTE;
/*  ------------------------------------------------------------------------ */
/*  PROCEDURE:  CLEAR INPUT RECORD (;)                                       */
                                           CLEAR$INPUT$RECORD: PROCEDURE;
/*  ************************************************************************ */
/*    LOCAL PARAMETER NOT USED IN DESIGN LANGUAGE                            */
/*                                                                           */
/*    NAME              SIZE    TYPE    CONTENTS          NOTES              */
/*    ----              ----    ----    --------          -----              */
/*    INDEX               1     BYTE    INDEX                                */
                                             DECLARE INDEX BYTE;
/*  ************************************************************************ */
/*  BEGIN PROCEDURE                                                          */
/*    DO FOR EACH ELEMENT IN INPUT RECORD                                    */
                                             DO INDEX = 0 TO 9;
/*      SET ELEMENT TO 'ZERO' CODE                                           */
                                               INPUT$RECORD (INDEX) = '0';
/*    END                                                                    */
                                             END;
/*    SET FULL INDICATOR TO EMPTY                                            */
                                             FULL$INDICATOR = 0;
/*    RETURN                                                                 */
                                             RETURN;
/*  END PROCEDURE                                                            */
                                           END CLEAR$INPUT$RECORD;
/*  ------------------------------------------------------------------------ */
```

Figure 5-13. The MAINTAIN INPUT RECORD module.

```
/*  PROCEDURE:  ADD TO INPUT RECORD (CHARACTER;)                               */
                                        ADD$TO$INPUT$RECORD: PROCEDURE (CHARACTER);
/*  *********************************************************************   */
/*    INPUT PARAMETER: CHARACTER                                               */
/*                                                                             */
/*    NAME              SIZE    TYPE    CONTENTS            NOTES              */
/*    ----              ----    ----    --------            -----              */
/*    CHARACTER           1     BYTE    NUMERIC CODE                           */
                                          DECLARE CHARACTER BYTE;
/*    LOCAL PARAMETER NOT USED IN DESIGN LANGUAGE                              */
/*                                                                             */
/*    NAME              SIZE    TYPE    CONTENTS            NOTES              */
/*    ----              ----    ----    --------            -----              */
/*    INDEX               1     BYTE    INDEX                                  */
                                          DECLARE INDEX BYTE;
/*  *********************************************************************   */
/*  BEGIN PROCEDURE                                                            */
/*    SHIFT INPUT RECORD CODES TO LEFT                                         */
                                          DO INDEX = 0 TO 8;
                                            INPUT$RECORD (INDEX) = INPUT$RECORD (INDEX + 1);
                                          END;
/*    SET RIGHT-HAND INPUT RECORD ELEMENT TO CHARACTER                         */
                                          INPUT$RECORD (9) = CHARACTER;
/*    INCREMENT FULL INDICATOR                                                 */
                                          FULL INDICATOR = FULL$INDICATOR + 1;
/*    RETURN                                                                   */
                                          RETURN;
/*  END PROCEDURE                                                              */
                                        END ADD$TO$INPUT$RECORD;
/*  ---------------------------------------------------------------------   */
/*  PROCEDURE: TEST IF INPUT RECORD FULL (;STATUS)                             */
                                        TEST$IF$INPUT$RECORD$FULL: PROCEDURE BYTE;
/*  *********************************************************************   */
/*    OUTPUT PARAMETER: STATUS                                                 */
/*                                                                             */
/*    NAME              SIZE    TYPE    CONTENTS            NOTES              */
/*    ----              ----    ----    --------            -----              */
/*    STATUS              1     BYTE    FLAG                                   */
                                          DECLARE STATUS BYTE;
/*  *********************************************************************   */
/*  BEGIN PROCEDURE                                                            */
/*    IF FULL INDICATOR SHOWS THAT INPUT RECORD IS FULL                        */
                                          IF FULL$INDICATOR = 10
/*      THEN  SET STATUS TO FULL                                               */
                                            THEN  STATUS = 1;
/*      ELSE  SET STATUS TO NOT FULL                                           */
                                            ELSE  STATUS = 0;
/*    RETURN                                                                   */
                                          RETURN STATUS;
/*  END PROCEDURE                                                              */
                                        END TEST$IF$INPUT$RECORD$FULL;
/*  ---------------------------------------------------------------------   */
```

Figure 5-13. (Continued).

```
/*  PROCEDURE: GET INPUT RECORD (; INPUT RECORD)                                 */
                                        GET$INPUT$RECORD: PROCEDURE ADDRESS PUBLIC;
/*  ***************************************************************************  */
/*    OUTPUT PARAMETER: INPUT RECORD                                             */
/*                                                                               */
/*    NAME                SIZE    TYPE    CONTENTS              NOTES            */
/*    ----                ----    ----    --------              -----            */
/*    INPUT RECORD         10     BYTE    NUMERIC CODES           1              */
/*                                                                               */
/*    NOTE 1: MODULAR DATA STRUCTURE                                             */
/*                                                                               */
/*    LOCAL PARAMETERS: CHARACTER                                                */
/*                      STATUS                                                   */
/*                                                                               */
/*    NAME                SIZE    TYPE    CONTENTS              NOTES            */
/*    ----                ----    ----    --------              -----            */
/*    CHARACTER            1      BYTE    ALPHANUMERIC CODE                      */
                                          DECLARE CHARACTER BYTE;
/*    STATUS               1      BYTE    FLAG                                   */
                                          DECLARE STATUS BYTE;
/*  ***************************************************************************  */
/*  BEGIN PROCEDURE                                                              */
/*    CALL: CLEAR INPUT RECORD (;)                                               */
                                          CALL CLEAR$INPUT$RECORD;
/*    DO FOREVER                                                                 */
                                          DO WHILE 1 = 1;
/*      CALL: READ KEYBOARD (; CHARACTER)                                        */
                                            CHARACTER = READ$KEYBOARD;
/*      IF CHARACTER CONTAINS 'CLEAR INPUT' CODE                                 */
                                            IF CHARACTER = 'C'
/*        THEN  CALL: CLEAR INPUT RECORD (;)                                     */
                                              THEN  CALL CLEAR$INPUT$RECORD;
/*      IF CHARACTER CONTAINS A NUMERIC CODE                                     */
                                            IF CHARACTER >= '0' AND CHARACTER <= '9'
/*        THEN  DO                                                               */
                                              THEN  DO;
/*              CALL: TEST IF INPUT RECORD FULL (; STATUS)                       */
                                                  STATUS = TEST$IF$INPUT$RECORD$FULL;
/*              IF STATUS INDICATES INPUT RECORD IS NOT FULL                     */
                                                  IF STATUS = 0
/*                THEN  CALL: ADD TO INPUT RECORD (CHARACTER; )                  */
                                                    THEN  CALL ADD$TO$INPUT$RECORD (CHARACTER);
/*                ELSE  CALL: BEEP (;)                                           */
                                                    ELSE  CALL BEEP;
/*            END                                                                */
                                                END;
/*      IF CHARACTER CONTAINS A TERMINATOR CODE                                  */
                                            IF CHARACTER = 'T'
/*        THEN  RETURN                                                           */
                                              THEN  DO;
                                                  INPUT$RECORD$POINTER = .INPUT$RECORD;
                                                  RETURN INPUT$RECORD$POINTER;
                                                END;
/*      IF CHARACTER CONTAINS ANY OTHER CODE                                     */
                                            IF (CHARACTER < '0' OR CHARACTER > '9') AND
                                                  CHARACTER <> 'C' AND CHARACTER <> 'T'
/*        THEN  CALL: BEEP (;)                                                   */
                                              THEN  CALL BEEP;
/*    END                                                                        */
                                          END;
/*  END PROCEDURE                                                                */
                                        END GET$INPUT$RECORD;
/*  -------------------------------------------------------------------------   */
/*  END MODULE                                                                   */
                                        END MAINTAIN$INPUT$RECORD;
```

Figure 5-13. (Continued).

we defer their description until after our discussion of microcomputer architecture and assembly language. Thus, we will complete the description of PL/M at the end of Chapter 6. Before we discuss the latter topic, let us summarize the programming language documentation requirements.

THIRD DOCUMENTATION LEVEL

The third documentation level consists of the programming language version of the procedures and modules of the system. Since the programming language version of the documentation contains the design language version as comments, much of the second documentation level is contained in the third documentation level. Note that the design language documentation should not be maintained separately once it has been converted into a programming language. Attempting to maintain two identical copies of the design language documentation, one of which contains the programming language version of the system, can lead to troublesome discrepancies. Moreover, it is always possible to recover the second documentation level from the third documentation level by extracting and selectively printing only the design language part of the documentation. We discuss this further in Chapter 7.

EXERCISES

5-1. Convert the procedures of the computerized television set into a high-level language such as PL/M.

5-2. Convert the procedures of the computerized traffic light controller into a high-level language such as PL/M.

5-3. Convert the procedures of the computerized sports scoreboard into a high-level language such as PL/M.

5-4. Convert the procedures of the computerized POS terminal into a high-level language such as PL/M.

Chapter 6

Microcomputer Architecture

Part I
ASSEMBLY LANGUAGE

We are now going to broaden our knowledge of microcomputer software to the assembly language level. However, it is necessary to study the *architecture* of the microcomputer in order to understand assembly language. We use the Intel 8085 microcomputer as an example for this purpose.

As in the case of high-level language software, we are not attempting to exhaustively cover all aspects of microcomputer architecture or assembly language software. Although it may be necessary under some circumstances to convert the software from design language into assembly language, we assume that most of the software is converted into a high-level language, such as PL/M, and then translated into machine language automatically by a compiler. But even when using PL/M, it is often necessary to understand what the microcomputer is doing when it *executes* the PL/M operations. Our introduction to microcomputer architecture and assembly language software is intended to give the reader the ability to understand these topics. For further information on assembly language software or microcomputer architecture, refer to the references in the bibliography.

MICROCOMPUTER ARCHITECTURE AND ASSEMBLY LANGUAGE

Just as the architecture of a building determines how the building is seen by the observer, the architecture of a microcomputer determines how the microcomputer is seen by someone who understands its assembly language and who designs its interface hardware. We are not concerned with bricks and mortar, that is, we are not concerned with how to build a microcomputer, only with how it works in our system. Thus, we must know not only how it is organized physically but also what operations it can execute. Let us first examine the physical nature of the Intel 8085 microcomputer architecture and add details of how it operates as we need them.

A block diagram of the physical part of the architecture of the Intel 8085 microcomputer is shown in Figure 6-1. The INPUT INTERFACE module consists of a *multiplexer* that is responsible for selecting one set of input lines from all of the inputs whenever an input instruction is executed. A number or *address* which is part of each input instruction specifies the particular *input port*, or set of input lines, to be selected. Thus, the input instruction takes the form

> Read input port *n* and move the data read from the input port into the ACCUMULATOR REGISTER.

where *n* is the *address* of the specific input port. When the execution of the input instruction has been completed, the information read from the selected lines is contained in a specific location in the MICROCOMPUTER module called the ACCUMULATOR REGISTER. The OUTPUT INTERFACE module consists of a multiplexer that passes output information produced by the MICROCOMPUTER module to a selected *output port*, or set of output lines. A number or *address* is used to specify which output port should be selected. The output instruction takes the form

> Move data from the ACCUMULATOR REGISTER to output port *m*.

where *m* is the *address* of the specific output port. The data to be sent to the selected output port is obtained from the ACCUMULATOR REGISTER in the MICROCOMPUTER module.

The MICROCOMPUTER module is illustrated in more detail in Figure 6-2. The ARITHMETIC LOGIC UNIT performs the arithmetic operations in the microcomputer. It is capable of performing hundreds of thousands of operations per second and therefore must be fed instructions and data automatically to take advantage of its speed.

The MEMORY acts as a storage bank for both data and instructions. It is capable of operating at a sufficiently rapid rate to keep up with the ARITHMETIC LOGIC UNIT. A unit of information in the Intel 8085 is the 8-bit *byte*. Each *location* in the MEMORY is capable of storing one byte, which comprises either an

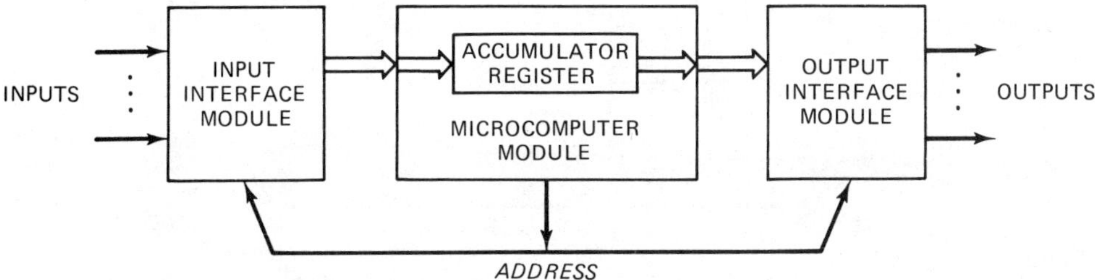

Figure 6-1. Block diagram of the Intel 8085 MICROCOMPUTER architecture.

instruction or a data item or a part of either. Since the MEMORY contains many storage locations, *addresses* are used to differentiate between the storage locations. The *memory address* is a number that specifies a particular memory location in a similar manner that the input or output *address* specifies a particular input or output port. The ACCUMULATOR REGISTER is functionally a memory location capable of storing a byte of data; but, since it is not located in the MEMORY, an address is not needed to specify that it should be used. It should be noted that the Intel 8085 and most other microcomputers have more than one register and provision is made for specifying which register is to be used at any given time.

The DATA BUS is the common data path through which the information moves between any two of the blocks of the MICROCOMPUTER module. It should be noted that the paths between the INPUT INTERFACE module, the ACCUMULATOR REGISTER, and the OUTPUT INTERFACE module are shown as being separate from the DATA BUS in the figures. In the Intel 8085, the DATA BUS is actually used to implement all of these paths. However, it simplifies our discussion to think of them as separate entities and we shall do so in this chapter.

The CONTROL UNIT is responsible for retrieving instructions from the MEMORY, determining what action should be taken to execute each instruction, and actuating suitable control lines, shown as dashed lines in Figure 6-2, to ensure

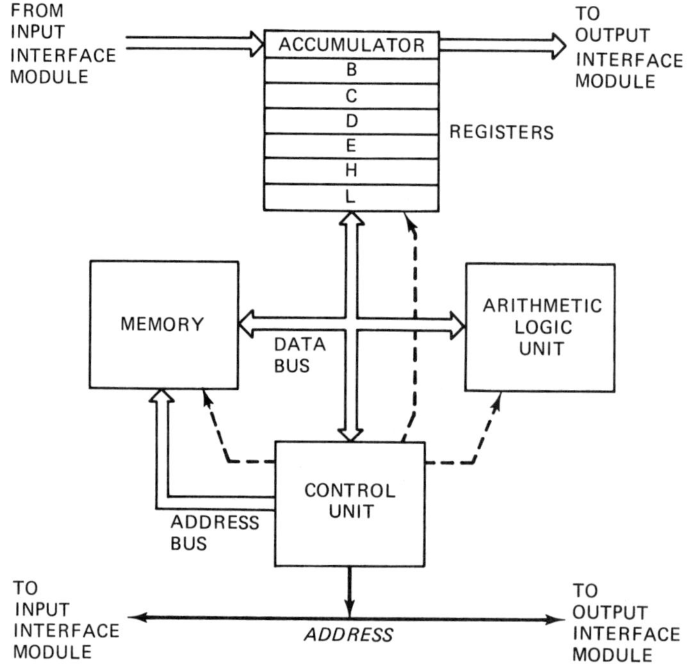

Figure 6-2. The Intel 8085 MICROCOMPUTER module.

that each instruction is executed correctly. We use the design language procedure which was introduced in Chapter 1 and which is reproduced in Figure 6-3 as an example to illustrate how the CONTROL UNIT works. The operation

```
EXAMINE INPUT 1 AND SAVE ITS VALUE
```

is the first operation within the loop in the procedure. The *two* assembly language instructions needed to implement this operation are:

> Read input port 1 and move the data read from the input port into the ACCUMULATOR REGISTER.
>
> Store the data contained in the ACCUMULATOR REGISTER into the memory location whose address is given by VALUE1.

We have assumed that the state of INPUT 1 is read through input port 1 and that the memory address is represented symbolically as VALUE1. Eventually, a number equal to the memory address will be assigned to VALUE1. Thus, we see that assembly language instructions specify the movement of information within the microcomputer architecture. For convenience, assembly language instructions are abbreviated into mnemonic forms; in the Intel 8085, for example, the two assembly language instructions shown above become:

```
IN     1
STA    VALUE1
```

A summary of the mnemonic instructions along with their interpretation is provided in Figure 6-36 later in the chapter. The reader should use this summary for reference, as needed.

The instructions themselves must also be stored in the MEMORY. Let us assume that they are stored in sequence starting in memory location 2000 in our example. Thus, the input instruction, which requires 16 bits or 2 bytes of memory, will occupy memory locations 2000 and 2001; the store instruction, which requires

```
DO FOREVER
  EXAMINE INPUT 1 AND SAVE ITS VALUE
  EXAMINE INPUT 2 AND SAVE ITS VALUE
  IF THE VALUE OF INPUT 1 IS GREATER THAN 4 AND LESS THAN 8
    THEN  SET OUTPUT 1 TO THE VALUE 6
    ELSE  SET OUTPUT 1 TO THE VALUE 0
  IF THE VALUE OF INPUT 2 IS GREATER THAN 2 AND LESS THAN 6
    THEN  SET OUTPUT 2 TO THE VALUE 4
    ELSE  SET OUTPUT 2 TO THE VALUE 0
END
```

Figure 6-3. Example procedure from Chapter 1.

24 bits or 3 bytes of memory, will occupy memory locations 2002, 2003, and 2004. To indicate how the MEMORY is allocated to instructions, we place the addresses of the memory locations containing the instructions alongside the instructions themselves as shown below:

```
2000  IN    1
2002  STA   VALUE1
2005  ...
```

Although it is not necessary to consider the addresses of the memory location explicitly when writing assembly language programs, the presence of these addresses alongside the instructions can help us to understand how the CONTROL UNIT works.

During the execution of these first two instructions, the following operations take place within the microcomputer:

1. The input instruction IN 1 is read from memory locations 2000 and 2001 by the CONTROL UNIT. This step is called the *fetch cycle*.
2. The CONTROL UNIT sends the input port *address* 1 to the INPUT INTERFACE module and commands the INPUT INTERFACE module to select input port 1, read the logical state of its input lines, and send a data byte containing these states to the ACCUMULATOR REGISTER.
3. The CONTROL UNIT commands the ACCUMULATOR REGISTER to save the information it receives from the INPUT INTERFACE module. These latter two steps constitute the *execute cycle*.

This completes the execution of the input instruction. Note that the execution of an instruction consists of a fetch cycle and an execute cycle.

4. The store instruction, STA VALUE1, is then read from memory locations 2002, 2003, and 2004 by the CONTROL UNIT.
5. The CONTROL UNIT commands the ACCUMULATOR REGISTER to send a copy of its data to the MEMORY. The information stored in the ACCUMULATOR REGISTER is not destroyed by this operation.
6. The CONTROL UNIT simultaneously sends the memory address represented by VALUE1 to the MEMORY.
7. The MEMORY is commanded by the CONTROL UNIT to save the information it receives from the ACCUMULATOR REGISTER in the location specified by the address.

The execution of these two instructions which illustrate how information is manipulated by the CONTROL UNIT is illustrated pictorially in Figure 6-4. The circled numbers in the figure correspond to the numbered steps shown above.

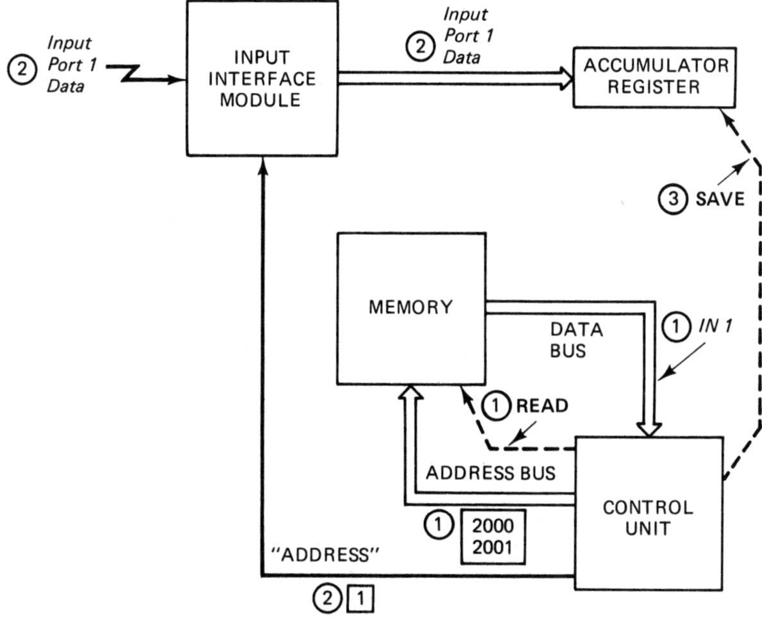

Figure 6-4(a). Execution of the INPUT 1 instruction.

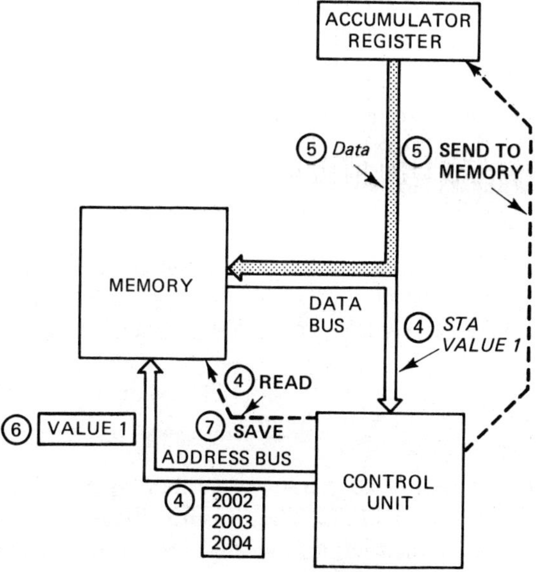

Figure 6-4(b). Execution of the STORE VALUE 1 instruction.

Addresses are shown enclosed in boxes, commands issued to other parts of the microcomputer by the CONTROL UNIT are shown in **boldface** type, and data and instructions which are moved between the parts of the microcomputer are shown in *italic* type. It should be noted that, in Figures 6-2 and 6-4, the ADDRESS BUS and the DATA BUS are shown as being separate buses. As we shall see later, they are not physically separate. But it simplifies our discussion to think of them as being separate buses and we shall do so in this chapter.

In a manner similar to that described above, the operation

```
EXAMINE INPUT 2 AND SAVE ITS VALUE
```

is equivalent to the two assembly language instructions:

```
2005  IN    2
2007  STA   VALUE2
2010  ...
```

The third operation in the example procedure is the test operation:

```
IF THE VALUE OF INPUT 1 IS GREATER THAN 4 AND LESS THAN 8
  THEN  SET OUTPUT 1 TO THE VALUE 6
  ELSE  SET OUTPUT 1 TO THE VALUE 0
```

Recall that the value of INPUT 1 is stored in the memory location represented symbolically by VALUE1. Thus, it is first necessary to read the value of INPUT 1 from memory location VALUE1 and compare it to the number 4. This is functionally equivalent to the *four* assembly language instructions:

```
2010  LDA   VALUE1
2013  CPI   4
2015  JZ    ELSE1
2018  JC    ELSE1
2021  ...
```

The instruction LDA VALUE1 is similar to the instruction STA VALUE1. However, data is moved in the opposite direction, that is, data is *loaded* into the ACCUMULATOR REGISTER from the MEMORY. The CPI 4 instruction is equivalent to:

> Compare the value of the number stored in the ACCUMULATOR REGISTER to the number 4 and note the result by setting the *flags*.

The *flags* are bits that are set or reset to keep track of certain types of information. For example, if the number in the ACCUMULATOR REGISTER is equal to 6, then, during the execution of the compare instruction, the flags are set to indicate that 6 is greater than 4. The two instructions, JZ ELSE1, *Jump to ELSE1 if zero flag is set*, and JC ELSE1, *Jump to ELSE1 if carry flag is set*, test these flags in the following manner:

> If the zero flag is set to indicate that the value in the ACCUMULATOR REGISTER is equal to the value of the compare operand, which is 4 in the example, then the next instruction to be executed is identified by the *label* ELSE1. Otherwise, the JC ELSE1 instruction is executed to test the carry flag. If the carry flag is set to indicate that the value in the ACCUMULATOR REGISTER is less than the operand, the instruction at ELSE1 is executed next. Otherwise, the instruction in location 2021 is executed next.

Thus, the combined result of these two instructions is to continue with the execution of the instruction in location 2021 only if the value in the ACCUMULATOR REGISTER is greater than 4.

For the other part of the design language test operation, the following instructions are used:

```
2021  CPI   8
2023  JZ    ELSE1
2026  JNC   ELSE1
2029  ...
```

The execution of these instructions is similar to that described above except for the JNC ELSE1, *Jump to ELSE1 if carry flag is not set*, instruction. As a result, the instructions starting in memory location 2029 are executed only if the value in the ACCUMULATOR REGISTER is less than 8 as well as greater than 4. The latter instructions therefore correspond to the THEN part of the test operation SET OUTPUT 1 TO THE VALUE 6 and are given by the assembly language instructions:

```
2029  MVI   A,6
2031  OUT   1
2033  JMP   CONT1
2036  ...
```

The number 6 is placed in the ACCUMULATOR REGISTER by the instruction MVI A,6, *Move the number 6 into the ACCUMULATOR REGISTER*. The OUT 1 instruction is equivalent to:

> Move data from the ACCUMULATOR REGISTER to output port 1.

and therefore causes the number 6 to be sent to output port 1. The instruction JMP CONT1, *Jump to CONT1*, is necessary to avoid executing the ELSE part of the test instruction along with the THEN part. It causes the instruction labeled CONT1 to be executed next regardless of how the flags are set. Note that CONT1 is short for CONTINUE1 since the Intel 8085 assembler restricts symbols to six characters although many assemblers have less stringent restrictions on the length of symbols.

The instructions needed for the ELSE part of the test operation are:

```
2036  ELSE1:  MVI   A,0
2038          OUT   1
2040  CONT1:  ...
```

which causes the number 0 to be sent to output port 1.

The remainder of the procedure consists of similar operations, as shown in Figure 6-5. Comments in an assembly language procedure are preceded by a semicolon and continue to the end of the line. The design language operations for our example are shown as comments in Figure 6-5.

In our description of the Intel 8085 architecture and in the example we used only the ACCUMULATOR REGISTER, but as mentioned earlier, other registers are provided in the Intel 8085. The organization of these registers is illustrated in Figure 6-2. Some are general-purpose registers such as the ACCUMULATOR REGISTER; some have special-purpose functions. In the next section we describe the different mechanisms that can be used to specify operands or to compute memory addresses in the Intel 8085. In so doing we will see what the specific functions of each of the registers are and how they are used.

ADDRESSING

An instruction must either contain an operand or it must specify where to obtain the data to use as an operand. Alternately, in the case of store or move instructions, the instruction must specify where to put the data it manipulates. In this section we examine the methods for specifying operands directly or for computing the addresses of memory locations that contain operands or are used as destinations.

Immediate addressing. In some instructions, as in the example MVI A,6, the number specified in the instruction is used directly during the execution of the instruction; it is not interpreted as an address. This is called *immediate addressing* since the number is stored in the instruction in the place normally reserved for an address but is used immediately as an operand instead. Either an 8-bit or a 16-bit immediate address is possible depending on the instruction. In the example MVI A,6, the number 6 is stored as an 8-bit number since the 8-bit ACCUMULATOR REGISTER is intended to receive the operand. In the Intel 8085 only one instruction uses a 16-bit immediate address since a 16-bit register pair is intended to receive the operand. In the instruction LXI H,6, *Load the number 6 into the H and L register pair*, the number 6 is stored in the instruction as a 16-bit number since the 16-bit register pair consisting of the H and L registers is intended to receive the operand.

```
;                                   DO FOREVER
;                                     EXAMINE INPUT 1 AND SAVE ITS VALUE
  2000   START:   IN     1
  2002            STA    VALUE1
;                                     EXAMINE INPUT 2 AND SAVE ITS VALUE
  2005            IN     2
  2007            STA    VALUE2
;                                     IF THE VALUE OF INPUT 1 IS GREATER THAN 4 AND LESS THAN 8
  2010            LDA    VALUE1
  2013            CPI    4
  2015            JZ     ELSE1
  2018            JC     ELSE1
  2021            CPI    8
  2023            JZ     ELSE1
  2026            JNC    ELSE1
;                                       THEN  SET OUTPUT 1 TO THE VALUE 6
  2029            MVI    A,6
  2031            OUT    1
  2033            JMP    CONT1
;                                       ELSE  SET OUTPUT 1 TO THE VALUE 0
  2036   ELSE1:   MVI    A,0
  2038            OUT    1
;                                     IF THE VALUE OF INPUT 2 IS GREATER THAN 2 AND LESS THAN 6
  2040   CONT1:   LDA    VALUE2
  2043            CPI    2
  2045            JZ     ELSE2
  2048            JC     ELSE2
  2051            CPI    6
  2053            JZ     ELSE2
  2056            JNC    ELSE2
;                                       THEN  SET OUTPUT 2 TO THE VALUE 4
  2059            MVI    A,4
  2061            OUT    2
  2063            JMP    CONT2
;                                       ELSE  SET OUTPUT 2 TO THE VALUE 0
  2066   ELSE2:   MVI    A,0
  2068            OUT    2
;                                   END
  2070   CONT2:   JMP    START
  2073            . . .
```

Figure 6-5. Example of an assembly language procedure.

Direct addressing. In some instructions a 16-bit number is used to specify a memory address directly. In this manner, up to 65,536 different locations in the MEMORY can be specified. This is called *direct addressing*. Examples of direct addressing were given by the instructions LDA VALUE1 and JZ ELSE1. In the first example, VALUE1 symbolically represents the 16-bit address of the memory location containing the operand to be used. In the second example, ELSE1 symbolically represents the 16-bit address of the memory location containing the next instruction to be executed if the zero flag is set. In both cases, the symbol is replaced by a 16-bit address when the software is translated into machine language by the assembler. In our example, ELSE1 will be replaced by the number 2036 represented as a 16-bit binary number.

Although a 16-bit number is always required to specify a direct address, the *size of the operand* depends on the instruction. The LDA VALUE1 instruction specifies that the single byte of data stored in memory location VALUE1 should be moved into the ACCUMULATOR REGISTER. In the Intel 8085 the only direct-address instructions that specify 16-bit operands are the LHLD, *Load the HL register pair from the MEMORY*, and the SHLD, *Store the HL register pair into the MEMORY*, instructions. In the LHLD instruction the byte in the memory location specified by the direct address is moved into the L register and the byte in the memory location whose address is one greater than the direct address is moved into the H register. The SHLD instruction is similar except that two bytes are moved from the HL register pair into the MEMORY.

Indirect addressing. Another type of addressing used in the Intel 8085 is called *indirect addressing*. In this case, the direct address of the memory location to be used by the instruction is contained in a second location. In some microcomputers the second location is a memory location and the address of this *second location* is specified in the instruction. In the Intel 8085 the memory location containing the direct address is one of the register pairs, BC, DE, or HL, and an explicit indirect address is not needed. An example of an instruction using indirect addressing is given by the instruction MOV A,M, which is equivalent to:

> Move the data stored in the memory location whose address is stored in the HL register pair into the ACCUMULATOR REGISTER.

The letter M following the comma in the instruction indicates that the data to be moved is to be obtained from a memory location. For the Intel 8085 assembly language, the second item, M in the example, always designates what the data is or where it comes from; the first item, A in the example, always designates where it goes to. Note that the two instructions

```
LXI    H,VALUE1
MOV    A,M
```

are equivalent to the single instruction

```
LDA    VALUE1
```

since the address represented symbolically by VALUE1 is placed into the HL register pair by the LXI H,VALUE1 instruction before the MOV A,M instruction is executed.

The instructions LDAX B and LDAX D are examples of indirect addressing where the direct address is stored in either register pair BC or DE. In either case, data is moved from the MEMORY to the ACCUMULATOR REGISTER since the instructions are equivalent to:

> Load the ACCUMULATOR REGISTER with data from the memory location whose address is contained in the BC or DE register pair.

Register addressing. There is also a group of instructions in the Intel 8085, the *register-to-register* instructions for which no memory addresses are required. An example of a register-to-register instruction is given by the move instruction MOV A,H. When this instruction is executed, the data in the H register is copied into the ACCUMULATOR REGISTER without changing the contents of the H register itself.

Indexing. Before we leave the topic of addressing, let us examine how a loop index is manipulated in assembly language for the Intel 8085. The CLEAR INPUT RECORD procedure introduced in Chapter 4 provides us with a simple example of a loop for this purpose. One of two approaches can be used: The index can be stored in the MEMORY and loaded into a register each time it is needed; or it can be loaded into a register initially and manipulated directly. We illustrate the latter approach in Figure 6-6 for the design language loop:

```
DO FOR EACH ELEMENT IN INPUT RECORD
  SET ELEMENT TO 'ZERO' CODE
END
```

Note that the first three assembly language instructions initialize the registers; the C register is set up as a counter, the B register is loaded with the character code for zero, and the HL register pair is loaded with the address of the first byte of INPUT RECORD. During each execution of the loop, a copy of the zero character code is moved from the B register into the memory location whose address is contained in the HL register pair, the address in the HL register pair is incremented by the

```
;                           DO FOR EACH ELEMENT IN INPUT RECORD
        MVI   C,10
        MVI   B,'0'
        LXI   H,INREC
;                             SET ELEMENT TO 'ZERO' CODE
 LOOP:  MOV   M,B
        INX   H
        DCR   C
;                           END
        JNZ   LOOP
```

Figure 6-6. Assembly language implementation of a design language loop.

INX H instruction, and the counter is decremented by the DCR C instruction. A compare instruction is not needed since the DCR instruction causes the zero flag to be set if the number being decremented becomes equal to zero. Thus, if the counter is not equal to zero, the loop is repeated. The reader should compare the assembly language implementation of the loop with the PL/M implementation of the same loop shown in Figure 5-6 to see how PL/M compares with assembly language.

In the preceding examples we have shown how the Intel 8085 addresses the MEMORY, moves information, performs simple tests, and executes input and output instructions. In so doing, we introduced how the REGISTERS, MEMORY, DATA BUS, and CONTROL UNIT work. We ignored the operation of the ARITHMETIC LOGIC UNIT which, as we stated earlier, performs the arithmetic operations in the microcomputer. Let us now turn our attention to the ARTHMETIC LOGIC UNIT.

ARITHMETIC LOGIC UNIT

The ARITHMETIC LOGIC UNIT performs operations on data transmitted to it via the DATA BUS from both the MEMORY and the REGISTERS. It also sends results back to the MEMORY and to the REGISTERS via the DATA BUS. The ARITHMETIC LOGIC UNIT not only performs arithmetic operations on the data but can also perform logic operations.

The arithmetic instructions available in the Intel 8085 include the add and subtract instructions as well as variations of these instructions which are used for special purposes, as we shall see. There are no multiplication or division instructions in the Intel 8085 although such instructions do exist in other microcomputers. We describe shortly how the the add instruction can be used to implement a multiplication algorithm in the Intel 8085.

With one exception, all of the add and subtract instructions involve the use of the ACCUMULATOR REGISTER. The two basic add and subtract instructions are:

Add operand to ACCUMULATOR REGISTER.
Subtract operand from ACCUMULATOR REGISTER.

The operand to be added or subtracted can be in a register or in the MEMORY or it can be specified in the instruction itself as an immediate address. If the MEMORY is specified, then indirect addressing through the HL register pair is implied. Direct addressing for the add and subtract instructions is not provided in the Intel 8085. Examples of the add and subtract instructions are shown in Figure 6-7. The instructions which add or subtract the carry flag permit multibyte operands to be added and subtracted easily. In the case of subtraction, the carry flag represents a *borrow* rather than a carry; thus, SBI stands for *Subtract with borrow*. Figure 6-8 illustrates how the ADC instruction is used to perform multibyte addition in the Intel 8085.

ADD	M	Add the operand stored in the memory location whose address is stored in the HL register pair to the operand in the ACCUMULATOR REGISTER.
SUB	D	Subtract the operand stored in the D register from the operand in the ACCUMULATOR REGISTER.
ADI	20	Add the number 20 to the operand in the ACCUMULATOR REGISTER.
ADC	M	Add the operand stored in the memory location whose address is stored in the HL register pair to the operand in the ACCUMULATOR REGISTER and also add the carry flag to the least-significant bit of the sum.
SBI	35	Subtract the number 35 from the operand in the ACCUMULATOR REGISTER and also subtract the carry flag from the least-significant bit of the difference.

Figure 6-7. Examples of the Intel 8085 add and subtract instructions.

In the example, two 32-bit numbers are stored in memory locations OP1, OP1+1, OP1+2, OP1+3 and OP2, OP2+1, OP2+2, OP2+3. The least-significant bytes of each number are stored in the high address memory locations OP1+3 and OP2+3 and the most-significant bytes are stored in the low address memory locations OP1 and OP2. The C register is used as a counter and the DE and HL register pairs are used for indirect addressing. The SUB A instruction is used to clear the carry flag since a carry is not generated when a number is subtracted from itself. Within the loop, the bytes are added one at a time from least-significant to most-significant along with the carry flag to take care of the carry between the bytes. The resulting sum then replaces OP1 in the MEMORY.

To expand the example to any length multibyte number, only the three initialization instructions must be changed. The loop itself does not change. A similar method can be used for multibyte subtraction by replacing the ADC instruction with an SBB or *Subtract with borrow* instruction. The reader should note that the decre-

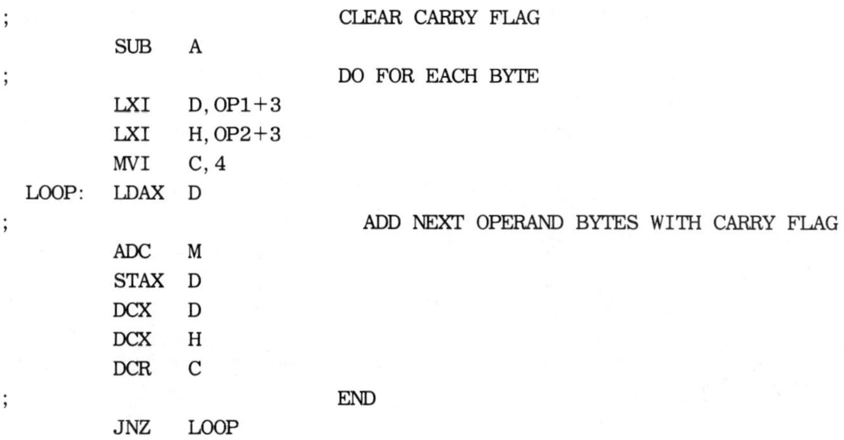

```
;                          CLEAR CARRY FLAG
         SUB   A
;                          DO FOR EACH BYTE
         LXI   D,OP1+3
         LXI   H,OP2+3
         MVI   C,4
  LOOP:  LDAX  D
;                            ADD NEXT OPERAND BYTES WITH CARRY FLAG
         ADC   M
         STAX  D
         DCX   D
         DCX   H
         DCR   C
;                          END
         JNZ   LOOP
```

Figure 6-8. Assembly language example for multibyte addition.

ment instructions do not alter the carry flag so that it cannot change between successive executions of the ADC or SBB instructions in the loop.

The DAD instruction is the only add instruction that does not use the ACCUMULATOR REGISTER. It is equivalent to:

Add the contents of the specified register pair to the HL register pair.

Since these are double byte operands, DAD stands for *Double length add*.

For single byte operands, the instruction

```
ADD   A
```

causes the 8-bit number in the ACCUMULATOR REGISTER to be *doubled* in value. A similar instruction

```
DAD   H
```

causes the 16-bit number in the HL register pair to be doubled. In both cases, this is equivalent to shifting each bit in the operand to the left by one bit position and shifting the most-significant bit into the carry flag. We use this feature in the multiplication procedure shown in Figure 6-9.

In the multiplication example the multiplier and multiplicand are both assumed to be 8-bit positive numbers. The multiplier is assumed to have been placed in the H register and the multiplicand in the C register. The E register is used as a counter and the HL register pair is used to accumulate the partial product sum as it is formed. Note that the multiplier is shifted out of the H register as the partial product sum is formed in the HL register pair, thereby making room for the latter. The DAD H instruction is used for this purpose. The DAD B instruction is used to add

```
;                           CONVERT MULTIPLICAND TO 16 BITS
         MVI    B,0
;                           INITIALIZE PARTIAL PRODUCT SUM
         MVI    L,0
;                           DO FOR EACH BIT IN MULTIPLIER
         MVI    E,8
;                             SHIFT PARTIAL PRODUCT SUM AND MULTIPLIER LEFT BY ONE BIT
  LOOP:  DAD    H
;                             IF MOST-SIGNIFICANT BIT OF MULTIPLIER IS A ONE
         JNC    SKIP
;                               THEN  ADD MULTIPLICAND TO PARTIAL PRODUCT SUM
         DAD    B
;                           END
  SKIP:  DCR    E
         JNZ    LOOP
```

Figure 6-9. Assembly language multiplication example.

the multiplicand that has been converted into its equivalent 16-bit number to the partial product sum whenever a nonzero multiplier bit is shifted into the carry flag.

The other arithmetic instructions in the Intel 8085 that use the ARITHMETIC AND LOGIC UNIT are the increment and decrement instructions. We have seen many examples of how they work and therefore do not pursue them further here. The compare instructions are identical to the subtract instructions and a subtraction does take place; however, the result is discarded and only the flag states are saved. We have used the compare immediate, CPI, instruction several times; the other compare instruction, CMP, compares a byte in one of the REGISTERS or in the MEMORY to the byte in the ACCUMULATOR REGISTER. For all of the compare instructions, the zero flag is set if the two bytes are equal and the carry flag is set if the specified byte is greater than the byte in the ACCUMULATOR REGISTER. Note that both bytes are treated as if they were positive numbers when a compare instruction is executed.

This completes our description of the arithmetic instructions that can be peformed by the ARITHMETIC LOGIC UNIT. Let us now turn to the logic instructions.

LOGIC INSTRUCTIONS

The Intel 8085 logic instructions fall into three groups: two-operand instructions, one-operand instructions, and carry flag instructions.

Two-operand instructions. The *two-operand* instructions cause the information contained in the ACCUMULATOR REGISTER to be modified in a bit-by-bit manner depending on the information contained in the second operand. The truth table below indicates how the *value* of each bit in the result is determined for both the *AND with ACCUMULATOR REGISTER* instruction, ANA, and the *OR with ACCUMULATOR REGISTER* instruction, ORA.

Bit in ACCUMULATOR REGISTER	Bit in second operand	Bit in AND result	Bit in OR result
0	0	0	0
0	1	0	1
1	0	0	1
1	1	1	1

Both of these instructions have immediate addressing versions, namely, ANI and ORI. Let us look at examples that illustrate how these instructions are used.

When a button is depressed on a keyboard, a character code is generated. We have shown how to work with character codes directly. However, it is useful to be able to convert the character codes representing numeric keys into the numbers which they represent so that they can be manipulated arithmetically. The AND instruction can be used for the conversion since each numeric character code consists of an 8-bit code whose least-significant four bits are equal to the numeric value of the character. This can be seen by examining the character codes for the digits 0 through 9 as shown in the table below:

'0'	0011 0000	'5'	0011 0101
'1'	0011 0001	'6'	0011 0110
'2'	0011 0010	'7'	0011 0111
'3'	0011 0011	'8'	0011 1000
'4'	0011 0100	'9'	0011 1001

The representation illustrated in the table is part of the American Standard Code for Information Interchange, commonly referred to by its initials, ASCII.

To convert these character codes into numbers, the most-significant or leftmost four bits must be changed to zeros and the remaining bits left untouched. If an ASCII character code is contained in the ACCUMULATOR REGISTER, the ANI 15 instruction converts it into its equivalent numeric value since the decimal number 15 is equivalent to 0000 1111 in binary.

The inverse operation, that of converting a 4-bit number into an ASCII character code, can be accomplished by an OR instruction. Since the decimal number 48 is equivalent to 0011 0000 in binary, then, if a 4-bit number from 0 through 9 is in the ACCUMULATOR REGISTER, it will be converted into the corresponding ASCII character code by the ORI 48 instruction. The latter operation is useful when we need to convert a number into a character code in order to display it on an output device that accepts ASCII character codes.

One-operand instructions. The *one-operand* logic instructions are the rotate instructions that cause the information contained in the ACCUMULATOR REGISTER to be moved within the register itself. In particular, each bit is moved to the left or to the right by a single bit position. The bit moved out of the extreme left-hand or right-hand bit position is moved into the vacated bit position at the other end as well as into the carry flag. In a variation of the rotate instructions, the carry flag is appended to the end of the ACCUMULATOR REGISTER during execution and treated as if it were part of the register. The rotate instructions are:

RLC	Rotate the ACCUMULATOR REGISTER to the left.
RRC	Rotate the ACCUMULATOR REGISTER to the right.
RAL	Rotate the ACCUMULATOR REGISTER to the left with the carry flag appended.
RAR	Rotate the ACCUMULATOR REGISTER to the right with the carry flag appended.

The AND and OR instructions are used with the rotate instructions to convert character codes into 4-bit numbers and to *pack* two of these numbers into a byte.

```
;                   CONVERT FIRST CHARACTER CODE INTO FOUR-BIT NUMBER
        MOV   A,C
        ANI   15
;                   MOVE FOUR-BIT NUMBER INTO OTHER HALF OF ACCUMULATOR REGISTER
        RLC
        RLC
        RLC
        RLC
;                   SAVE NUMBER TEMPORARILY
        MOV   C,A
;                   CONVERT SECOND CHARACTER CODE INTO FOUR-BIT NUMBER
        MOV   A,D
        ANI   15
;                   PACK TWO NUMBERS TOGETHER
        ORA   C
;                   SAVE PACKED NUMBERS
        MOV   C,A
```

Figure 6-10. Converting character codes into four-bit numbers and packing the numbers into bytes.

These instructions are also used to *unpack* numbers and to convert them into character codes. The assembly language procedures for this purpose are shown in Figures 6-10 and 6-11; Figure 6-12 illustrates how the packing procedure works in a step-by-step manner. We assume that the two character codes are initially contained in the C and D registers and that the packed numbers are saved in the C register. For

```
;                   ELIMINATE THE LEFT-HAND OF THE PACKED NUMBERS
        MOV   A,C
        ANI   15
;                   CONVERT THE RIGHT-HAND NUMBER INTO A CHARACTER CODE
        ORI   48
;                   SAVE THE CHARACTER CODE
        MOV   D,A
;                   ELIMINATE THE RIGHT-HAND OF THE PACKED NUMBERS
        MOV   A,C
        ANI   240
;                   MOVE THE LEFT-HAND NUMBER INTO THE OTHER HALF OF ACCUMULATOR REGISTER
        RLC
        RLC
        RLC
        RLC
;                   CONVERT THE NUMBER INTO A CHARACTER CODE
        ORI   48
;                   SAVE THE CHARACTER CODE
        MOV   C,A
```

Figure 6-11. Unpacking four-bit numbers and converting them into character codes.

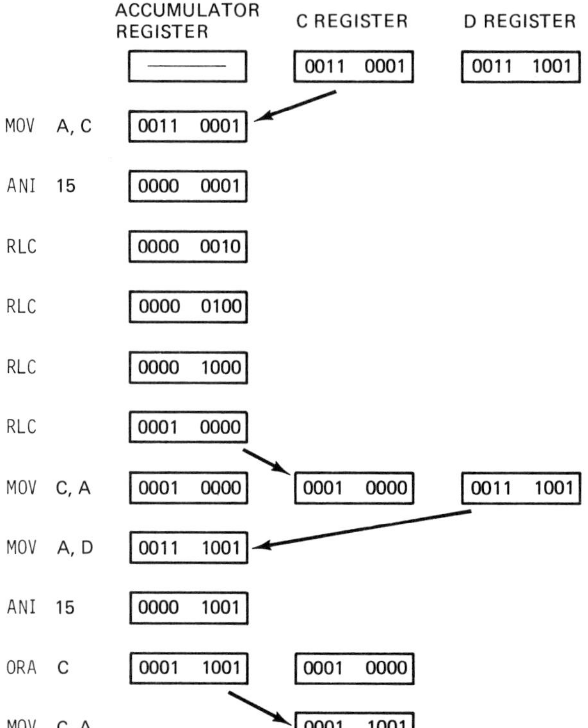

Figure 6-12. Step-by-step illustration of packing.

the unpacking example, we assume that the packed numbers are initially contained in the C register and that the unpacked codes are saved in the C and D registers.

Carry flag instructions. The carry flag instructions are used to *Set the carry flag*, STC, and to *Complement* (change the state of) *the carry flag*, CMC. In a previous example, in Figure 6-8, we used the instruction SUB A to clear the carry flag. However, the subtraction also clears the ACCUMULATOR REGISTER. If we want to clear the carry flag without affecting the information in the ACCUMULATOR REGISTER, the instruction STC followed by the instruction CMC can be used. Thus, complete control of the carry flag is possible with these two instructions.

We have seen several examples of the Intel 8085 jump instructions. Let us now examine all of the control instructions.

CONTROL INSTRUCTIONS

In the Intel 8085 the control instructions include the *jump* instructions as well as the *call* and *return* instructions. All three may be *unconditional*, that is, they are executed whenever they are encountered, or they may be *conditional*, in which case, they are executed only if a specified condition is true. The test conditions are specified by the carry, zero, sign, and parity flags, as indicated in Figure 6-13.

The unconditional control instructions are *jump*, JMP, *call*, CALL, and *return*, RET. The conditional control instructions in the Intel 8085 are represented by the letters J, C, or R followed by one of the condition specifiers, as follows:

C	Execute the instruction only if the carry flag is set.
NC	Execute the instruction only if the carry flag is *not* set.
Z	Execute the instruction only if the zero flag is set.
NZ	Execute the instruction only if the zero flag is *not* set.
M	Execute the instruction only if the sign bit is set, that is, if the result is negative (minus).
P	Execute the instruction only if the sign bit is *not* set, that is, if the result is positive.
PE	Execute the instruction only if the parity flag is set, that is, if parity is even.
PO	Execute the instruction only if the parity flag is *not* set, that is, if parity is odd.

Thus, as we have seen, JZ, JC, and JNC mean *Jump if the zero flag is set, Jump if the carry flag is set*, and *Jump if the carry flag is not set*. Similarly, CZ, CC, and CNC mean *Call the specified procedure if the zero flag is set, Call the specified procedure if the carry flag is set*, and *Call the specified procedure if the carry flag is not set*. Also, RZ and RC mean *Return to calling procedure if the zero flag is set* and *Return to calling procedure if the carry flag is set*.

An example of the conditional *return* instruction is provided by the design language construct

```
IF KEYSWITCH IS RESET
  THEN  RETURN
```

Carry Flag	The carry flag is set to indicate that a carry or borrow has taken place during the execution of an add, subtract, compare, or double add instruction. A rotate instruction can move a ONE bit into the carry flag, thereby *setting* the flag. The carry flag is always reset when an AND or an OR instruction is executed.
Zero Flag	The zero flag is set to indicate that a zero result has been generated by the execution of an add, subtract, compare, AND, OR, increment byte, or decrement byte instruction.
Sign Flag	The sign flag is set to indicate that a negative result has been generated by the execution of an add, subtract, compare, AND, OR, increment byte, or decrement byte instruction.
Parity Flag	The parity flag is set to indicate that there are an even number of ONE bits in the result generated by the execution of an add, subtract, compare, AND, OR, increment byte, or decrement byte instruction.

Figure 6-13. Conditions that affect the Intel 8085 flags.

Let us assume, as we did in Chapter 5, that the variable KEYSWITCH is equal to zero when it is in the reset state. Then the preceding design language construct is equivalent to the following assembly language instructions:

```
;                               IF KEYSWITCH IS RESET
        LDA   KEYSW
        CPI   0
;                                 THEN  RETURN
        RZ
```

The *value* of KEYSWITCH is placed into the ACCUMULATOR REGISTER and compared to zero, thereby setting the zero flag if KEYSWITCH is zero. The *return* instruction is then executed only if the zero flag is set, that is, if the keyswitch is reset.

This completes our basic introduction to the Intel 8085 architecture and to assembly language programming. However, in order to understand how the microcomputer actually executes the control instructions and how interrupts are handled, we must understand how a *stack* operates. We examine the stack next.

THE STACK

The stack is a special-purpose memory used primarily for storing information related to calling and returning from procedures. Let us first describe how the stack operates functionally, then how it is implemented in the Intel 8085 microcomputer, and, finally, how it is used during the operation of a system.

Functionally, a stack is a *last in-first out* memory. As such, it does not require explicit addresses and uses only the two basic operations PUSH and POP (sometimes called PULL) to manipulate information. Data is moved into the stack whenever a PUSH operation is executed and moved out of the stack whenever a POP operation is executed. The operation of the stack is illustrated in Figure 6-14. As each item is pushed into the stack, all of the items below it move *down* one level. As an item is popped from the top of the stack, all of the items below it move *up* one level. Thus, information is stored in the stack in the order it is received but is retrieved from the stack in reverse order.

When a microcomputer system is in operation, CALL and RETURN operations are executed to start and stop the execution of the procedures. Since a procedure may be called from different places in different procedures, it is necessary to keep track of which CALL operation invoked the execution of a procedure. This permits the operation that follows the CALL operation that started the execution of a procedure to be executed immediately following the execution of a RETURN operation in the called procedure. Figure 6-15 illustrates this concept for a procedure called three times from another procedure. The control paths that must be followed each time the procedure is executed are illustrated by arrows in the figure. The stack provides a convenient way to keep track of the information needed to enable the

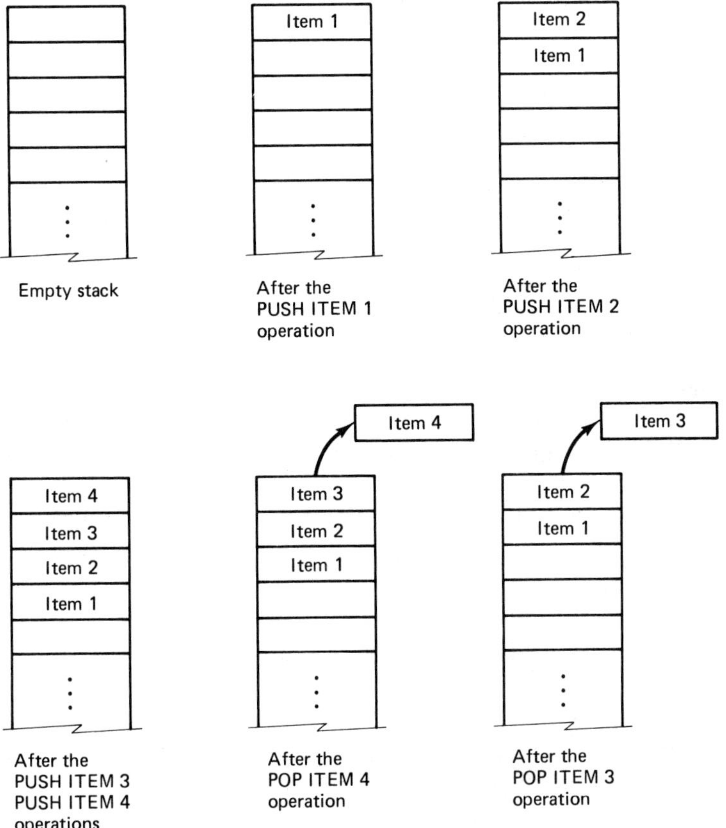

Figure 6-14. Functional operation of a stack.

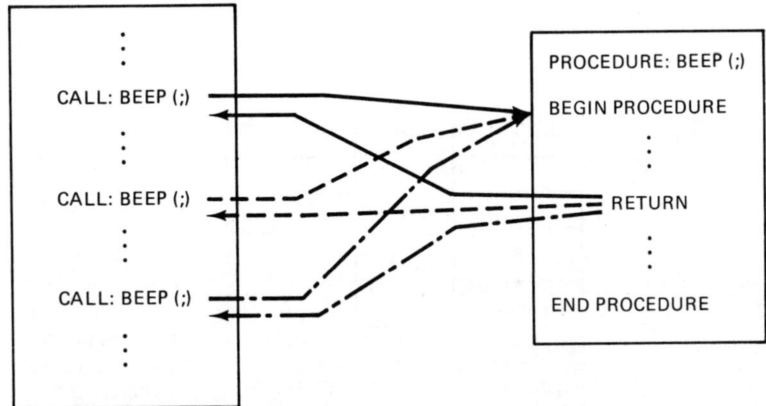

Figure 6-15. Example to illustrate multiple execution of a procedure.

correct path to be taken when a RETURN operation is executed. To enable the stack to be used for this purpose, the CALL operation is equivalent to the two operations:

PUSH a pointer that points to the operation that follows the CALL operation into the stack.

Start the execution of the called procedure.

and the RETURN operation is equivalent to the two operations:

POP a pointer from the stack.

Execute the operation indicated by the pointer.

Figure 6-16 illustrates how the pointers and the stack are manipulated in the example.

We have seen that, during the operation of a system, procedure calls are *nested*. That is, a called procedure may call other procedures. The use of a stack to keep track of procedure calls as described above also works for nested procedure calls. Figure 6-17 illustrates how the stack keeps track of nested procedure calls dur-

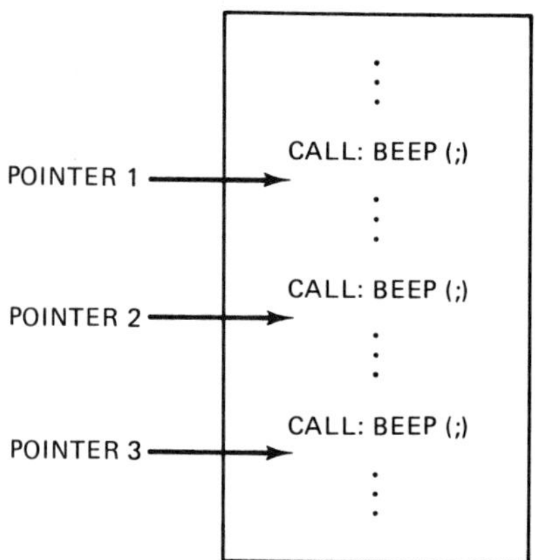

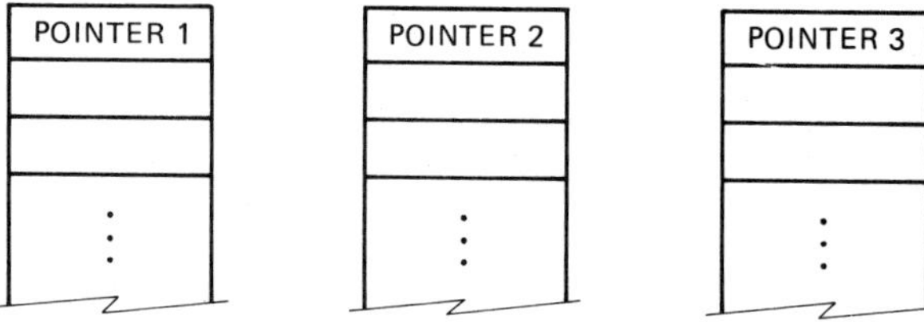

Figure 6-16. Manipulation of stack and pointers for multiple execution of a procedure.

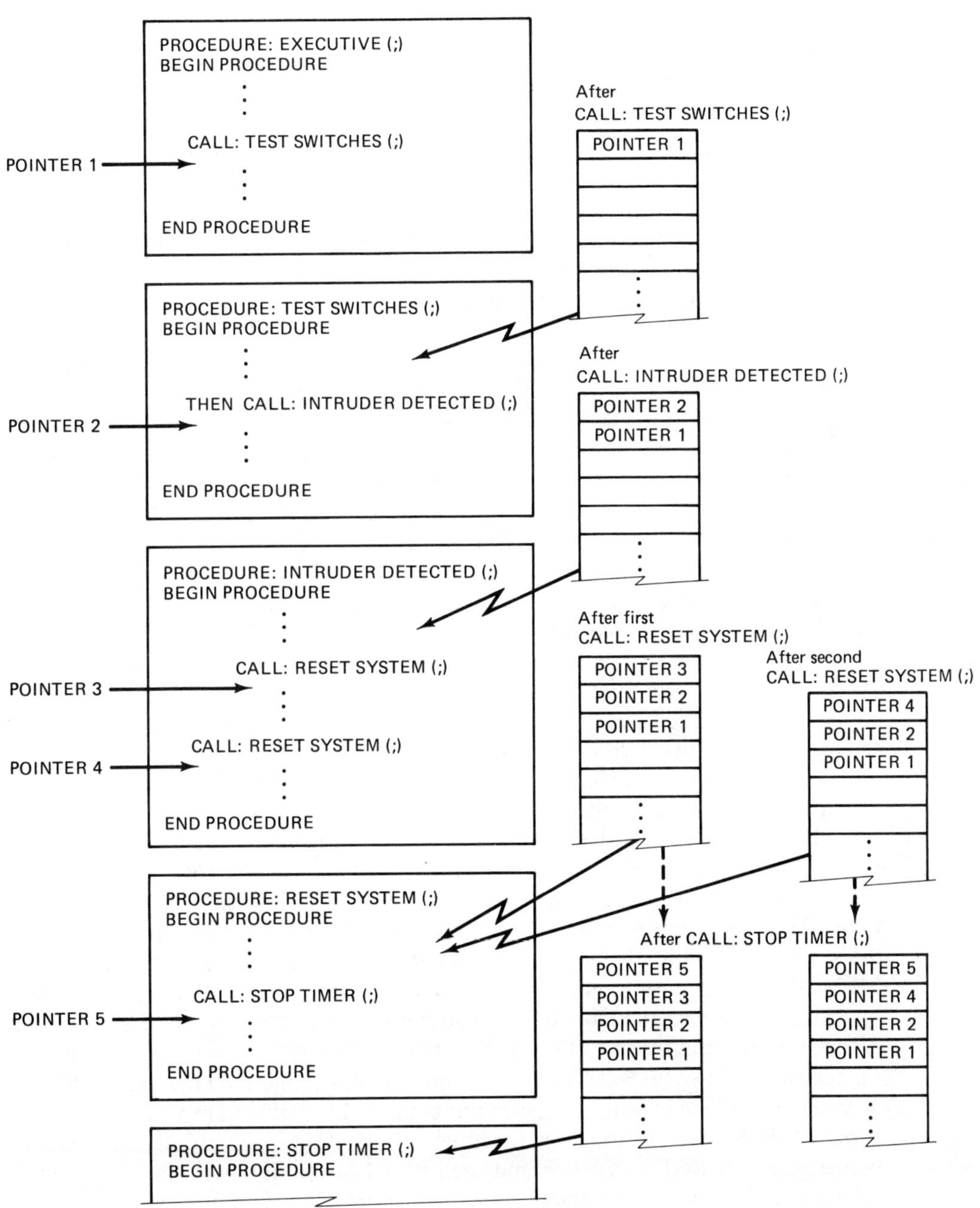
PROCEDURE: EXECUTIVE (;)
BEGIN PROCEDURE
CALL: TEST SWITCHES (;)
POINTER 1
END PROCEDURE
After
CALL: TEST SWITCHES (;)
POINTER 1
PROCEDURE: TEST SWITCHES (;)
BEGIN PROCEDURE
THEN CALL: INTRUDER DETECTED (;)
POINTER 2
END PROCEDURE
After
CALL: INTRUDER DETECTED (;)
POINTER 2
POINTER 1
PROCEDURE: INTRUDER DETECTED (;)
BEGIN PROCEDURE
CALL: RESET SYSTEM (;)
POINTER 3
CALL: RESET SYSTEM (;)
POINTER 4
END PROCEDURE
After first
CALL: RESET SYSTEM (;)
POINTER 3
POINTER 2
POINTER 1
After second
CALL: RESET SYSTEM (;)
POINTER 4
POINTER 2
POINTER 1
PROCEDURE: RESET SYSTEM (;)
BEGIN PROCEDURE
CALL: STOP TIMER (;)
POINTER 5
END PROCEDURE
After CALL: STOP TIMER (;)
POINTER 5
POINTER 3
POINTER 2
POINTER 1
POINTER 5
POINTER 4
POINTER 2
POINTER 1
PROCEDURE: STOP TIMER (;)
BEGIN PROCEDURE

Figure 6-17. Nested procedure calls.

ing the operation of the burglar alarm system. Note that in each case, the pointer at the top of the stack causes the execution of the calling procedure to be resumed correctly when a RETURN operation is executed in the called procedure.

The description we presented for the stack illustrates how the stack works functionally. In practice, stacks are not implemented in this manner for two reasons:

- Every item of data stored in the stack would need to be moved *down* or *up* whenever a PUSH or POP operation were executed. This requirement is costly both in execution time and in complexity of hardware.
- The size of the stack cannot be unlimited in size as we have assumed.

In the Intel 8085, as in most microcomputers that provide a built-in implementation for a stack, the operation of the stack is simulated in a straightforward manner. A section of the MEMORY is set aside for the stack and a *stack pointer* is provided. In the Intel 8085 the stack pointer is stored in a 16-bit *stack pointer register* whose function it is to keep track of where the *top* of the stack is currently located. As each PUSH or POP instruction is executed, the stack pointer is adjusted appropriately. Although the MEMORY in the Intel 8085 is organized in bytes, each item of information manipulated by the stack is always 16 bits long. The latter information is either an address that is used as a pointer by the RET instruction or it is data that has been obtained from a register pair. Thus, each stack operation takes two steps, as illustrated in Figure 6-18. In the example the PUSH B instruction moves two bytes from register pair BC into the stack and the PUSH D instruction moves two bytes from register pair DE into the stack. The POP B instruction then moves the latter two bytes from the stack into register pair BC and the POP D instruction moves the former two bytes into register pair DE. The end result in our example is that the data in the two register pairs is exchanged.

The Intel 8085 instructions that use the stack or manipulate the stack pointer include the CALL, RET, PUSH, POP, SPHL or *Load the STACK POINTER from the HL register pair*, and LXI SP or *Load the STACK POINTER immediate* instructions. The latter two instructions are used to initialize the stack pointer before the stack is used. Initializing the stack pointer ensures that the specific part of the MEMORY set aside for use as a stack is used correctly. Thus, the stack pointer must be initialized *before* the first CALL instruction is executed by the EXECUTIVE procedure. For this reason, the operation to initialize the stack pointer *must* be implemented in the EXECUTIVE procedure and *not* in the INITIALIZE SYSTEM procedure as implied by the examples presented in Chapter 4. The reader may have noticed that the stack instructions function in pairs. That is, each CALL instruction is matched by a RET instruction and each PUSH instruction is matched by a POP instruction. This *pairing* of stack instructions normally occurs in a natural manner. But if a design or programming error causes the pairing to be disturbed, then one of two malfunctions may occur:

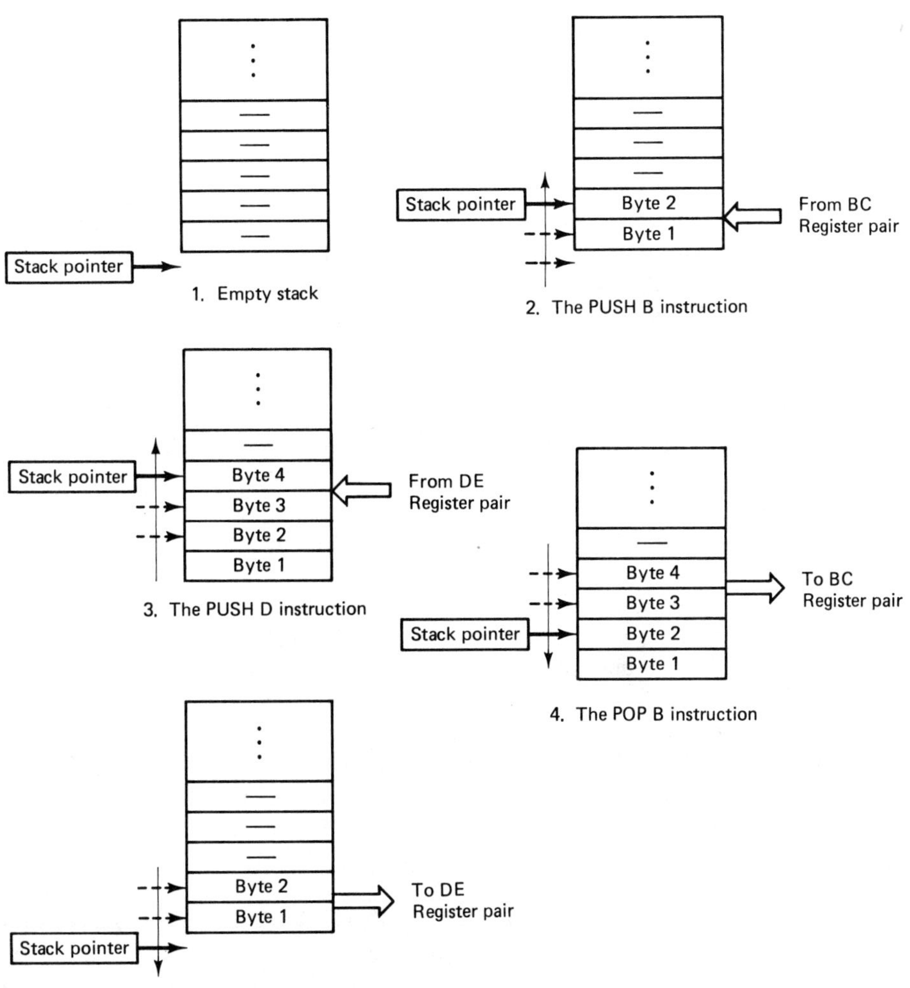

Figure 6-18. The operation of a simulated stack.

- A RET instruction may use an incorrect pointer or it may use data that is not a valid address as a pointer.
- The stack pointer may be adjusted so that it points to a location outside the memory region allocated for use as a stack.

The latter difficulty may also arise if the stack is inadvertently filled and an attempt is made to execute a PUSH or CALL instruction. The Intel 8085 microcomputer does not provide a way to automatically detect these situations in order to prevent them from occurring; the reader should be aware that they can occur.

The stack is also used to pass input parameters to a procedure, to return an output parameter from a procedure, and to simplify the operation of the system in the presence of interrupts. We examine these concepts in the following sections.

PARAMETER PASSING

We have seen that input parameters are passed to procedures and output parameters are returned from procedures during the operation of a system containing a microcomputer. When PL/M is used, the programmer need not be concerned with how parameters are passed since the compiler takes care of the details. When assembly language is used, the responsibility for manipulating parameters falls on the programmer. To simplify the use of parameters, the Intel Corporation has established a set of standards so that parameter passing is carried out uniformly. Thus, the assembly language programmer should know and use these standards so that both PL/M and assembly language procedures operate uniformly and the procedures can call one another. The standards described below apply only to programs developed using the ISIS operating system on the Intel Microcomputer Development System. Other conventions are in use on other systems.

Output parameters are passed through registers. The data to be returned as an output parameter is moved into the ACCUMULATOR REGISTER if it is a byte variable or constant and into the HL register pair if it is an address variable or constant. The calling procedure then retrieves the data from the corresponding register or register pair immediately following the execution of the RET instruction. Figure 6-19 illustrates how an output parameter is passed from the TEST IF INPUT RECORD FULL (TINREC) procedure to its calling procedure in assembly language. These instructions implement the PL/M construct

```
RETURN STATUS;
```

in the TEST IF INPUT RECORD FULL (TINREC) procedure and the construct

```
STATUS = TEST$IF$INPUT$RECORD$FULL;
```

in the calling procedure where STATUS is a byte variable.

Both the registers and the stack are used for passing input parameters. If a single input parameter is passed into a procedure, it is passed through the BC register pair regardless of whether it is a byte or an address variable or constant. If two input parameters are passed into a procedure, the first is passed through the BC register pair and the second is passed through the DE register pair. If more than two input parameters are passed into a procedure, all but the last two are pushed into the stack; the last two are passed through the BC and DE register pairs as described above. Figure 6-20 illustrates input parameter passing for the PL/M example

```
CALL ADD$TO$INPUT$RECORD (CHARACTER1,CHARACTER2,CHARACTER3);
```

which for illustration has been modified from the corresponding burglar alarm system procedure.

```
        .
        .
        .
LDA     STATUS
RET
        .
        .
        .
```

Figure 6-19(a). The assembly language instructions for the PL/M operation, RETURN STATUS;, in the TEST IF INPUT RECORD FULL (TINREC) procedure.

```
        .
        .
        .
CALL    TINREC
STA     STATUS
        .
        .
        .
```

Figure 6-19(b). The assembly language instructions for the PL/M operation, STATUS = TESTIFINPUT$RECORD$FULL;, in the calling procedure.

In the example a copy of CHAR1 is moved into the L register by the LHLD instruction. Since the LHLD instruction moves a 16-bit operand, the H register is also affected but the data placed into the latter register is extraneous and is ignored. The HL register pair is then pushed into the stack. A copy of CHAR2 is next moved into the L register and then placed into the C register by the MOV C,L instruction. A copy of CHAR3 is moved into the E register in a similar manner. Finally, the ADD TO INPUT RECORD (ADDREC) procedure is called; this step pushes a pointer into the stack and starts the execution of the called procedure.

In the ADD TO INPUT RECORD procedure the *address* of the memory location that will be used to store the copy of CHAR3 is moved into the HL register pair by the LXI H,CHAR3 instruction. Then the copy of CHAR3, which is in the E register, is moved into this memory location by the MOV M,E instruction. In a similar manner, the copy of CHAR2, which is in the C register, is moved into the memory location that has been designated to store it. The address pointer stored at the top of the stack is then moved into the DE register pair temporarily. The copy of CHAR1 is retrieved from the stack by the POP B instruction which moves it into the C register; the byte moved into the B register by this instruction is ignored. The byte in the C register is then moved into the memory location designated to store the copy of CHAR1. Finally, the address pointer that was stored temporarily in the DE register pair is pushed back into the stack so that it will be available when a RET instruction is executed to terminate the execution of the procedure.

The stack therefore provides a simple mechanism for passing an arbitrary number of parameters into a procedure. If the number of input parameters is fairly

```
      .
      .
      .
LHLD  CHAR1
PUSH  H
LHLD  CHAR2
MOV   C,L
LHLD  CHAR3
MOV   E,L
CALL  ADDREC
      .
      .
      .
```

Figure 6-20(a). Input parameter calling sequence for calling the ADD TO INPUT RECORD (ADDREC) procedure.

```
      .
      .
      .
LXI   H,CHAR3
MOV   M,E
LXI   H,CHAR2
MOV   M,C
POP   D
POP   B
LXI   H,CHAR1
MOV   M,C
PUSH  D
      .
      .
      .
```

Figure 6-20(b). Saving the input parameters in the ADD TO INPUT RECORD (ADDREC) procedure.

large or if more than two bytes must be returned from a procedure as output parameters, it is often better to pass a pointer in the manner described in Chapter 5. The assembly language instructions which are used for this purpose and which are therefore equivalent to the PL/M operation

```
RECORD$POINTER = .RECORD;
```

are

```
LXI   H,RECORD
SHLD  RECPTR
```

and RECPTR can then be passed between the two procedures as described above. To see how to use RECPTR, let us first examine how the data structure RECORD is accessed directly in the MAINTAIN RECORD MODULE. In this case, the instructions

```
LXI    H,RECORD
MOV    A,M
```

move the first byte in RECORD into the ACCUMULATOR REGISTER. Other bytes in RECORD are then accessed by adding suitable *offset* values to the HL register pair before executing the move instruction. In the procedure to which the parameter is passed, the instructions

```
LHLD   RECPTR
MOV    A,M
```

also cause the first byte in RECORD to be moved into the ACCUMULATOR REGISTER. This is because the contents of the HL register pair is the same after the LXI H,RECORD instruction is executed in a procedure in the MAINTAIN RECORD MODULE or after the LHLD RECPTR instruction is executed in a procedure to which RECPTR is passed as a parameter. What we have just described is the assembly language mechanism which is equivalent to the based variable mechanism used for passing structures or arrays between procedures in PL/M.

INTERRUPT

The concept of interrupt was discussed in general in Chapter 4. In this section we discuss how interrupt works, how the stack is used during an interrupt, and several assembly language instructions whose operation is directly related to the interrupt function. Let us start by describing how the CONTROL UNIT implements the interrupt capability.

Recall that before an instruction can be executed, it must first be read from the MEMORY by the CONTROL UNIT. Before doing so, however, the CONTROL UNIT tests an *interrupt request signal* supplied by the INTERRUPT module, as shown in Figure 6-21. If this signal is *off*, the CONTROL UNIT reads the next instruction from the MEMORY and executes it as we described earlier. If the interrupt request signal is *on*, the CONTROL UNIT instead executes an instruction whose function is equivalent to the CALL instruction. As we shall see later, this instruction is sent to the CONTROL UNIT by the INTERRUPT module through the DATA BUS when the INTERRUPT ACKNOWLEDGE signal is turned *on*. The procedure *called* in this manner starts in a memory location whose address is also specified by the INTERRUPT module. It is the INTERRUPT EXECUTIVE procedure and controls the execution of the procedures needed to respond to the interrupt. Since the instruction supplied by the INTERRUPT module that starts the execution of the INTERRUPT EXECUTIVE procedure is effectively a CALL instruction, the address of the interrupted instruction is automatically pushed into the stack. This information enables the system to continue execution with the interrupted instruc-

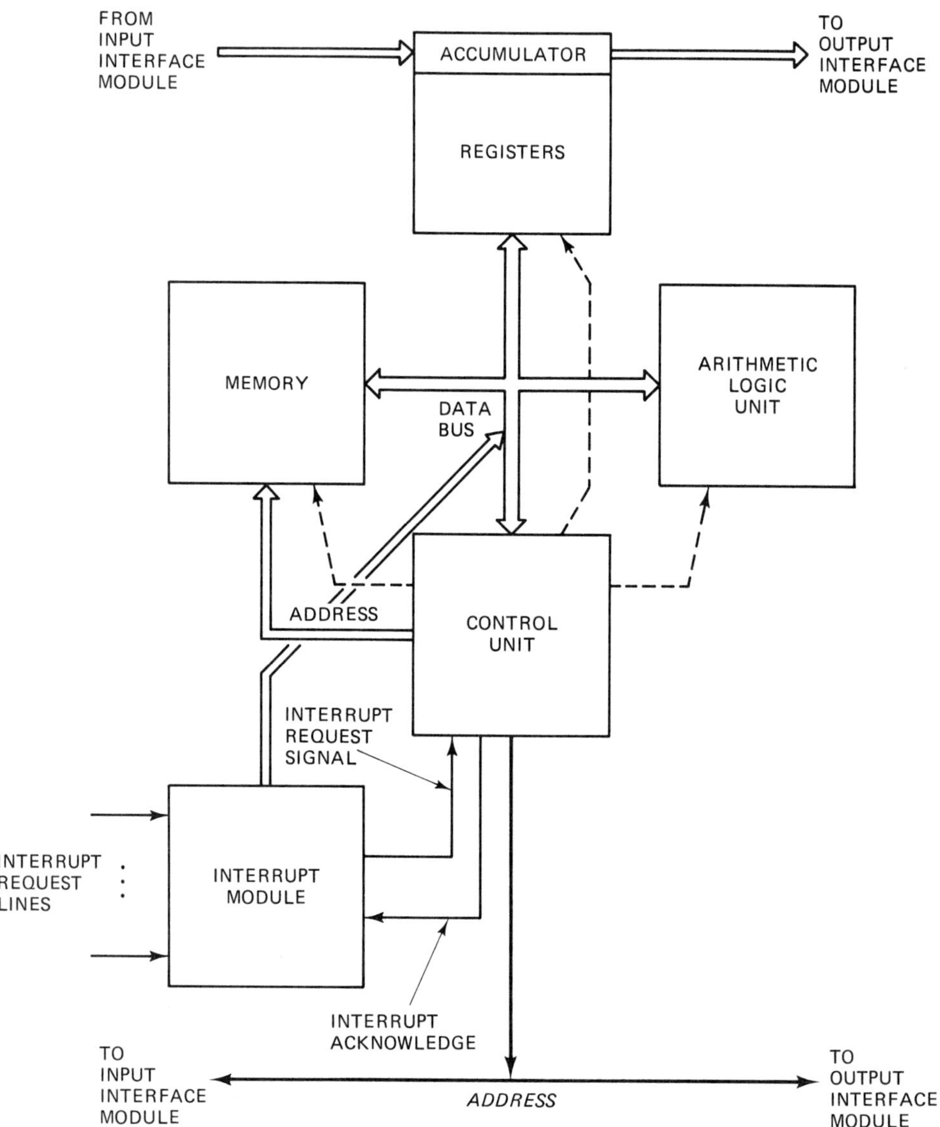

Figure 6-21. The INTERRUPT module and its relationship to the Intel 8085 MICROCOMPUTER module.

tion when a RET instruction is executed to terminate the execution of the INTERRUPT EXECUTIVE procedure.

The burglar alarm system INTERRUPT EXECUTIVE procedure is reproduced in Figure 6-22. In Chapter 4 we were not able to explain why the SAVE SYSTEM STATUS and RESTORE SYSTEM STATUS operations are needed. Now that we

```
PROCEDURE: INTERRUPT EXECUTIVE (;)
BEGIN PROCEDURE
  SAVE SYSTEM STATUS
  CALL: ENABLE INTERRUPT (;)
  CALL: PROCESS TIMER INTERRUPT (;)
  RESTORE SYSTEM STATUS
  RETURN
END PROCEDURE
```

Figure 6-22. The INTERRUPT EXECUTIVE procedure for the burglar alarm system.

have described the architecture of the microcomputer and how it is related to interrupt, we can discuss why these operations are used.

An interrupt request can occur at any time. Thus, there is no way to ensure that the internal registers or flags in the microcomputer do not contain information which, if destroyed, would cause the system to malfunction. It is therefore necessary to provide a way to save the contents of the registers and flags immediately after the execution of the INTERRUPT EXECUTIVE procedure begins and then to restore their contents just prior to returning to the execution of the interrupted procedure. The stack provides a convenient way to do so, as illustrated in Figure 6-23. Note that the POP instructions are not executed in the same order as the PUSH instructions. The reversal of order is necessary to ensure that each saved item is restored correctly. The symbol PSW in the example refers to the PROGRAM STATUS WORD which consists of both the ACCUMULATOR REGISTER and the flags.

```
;                          PROCEDURE: INTERRUPT EXECUTIVE (;)
;                          BEGIN PROCEDURE
;                            SAVE SYSTEM STATUS
        PUSH  H
        PUSH  D
        PUSH  B
        PUSH  PSW
;                            CALL: ENABLE INTERRUPT (;)
        CALL  ENABLE
;                            CALL: PROCESS TIMER INTERRUPT (;)
        CALL  PROCES
;                            RESTORE SYSTEM STATUS
        POP   PSW
        POP   B
        POP   D
        POP   H
;                            RETURN
        RET
;                          END PROCEDURE
```

Figure 6-23. Assembly language version of the INTERRUPT EXECUTIVE procedure.

In the burglar alarm system we provided an INTERRUPT CONTROL module containing the ENABLE INTERRUPT and DISABLE INTERRUPT procedures. For our simple example, using the Intel 8085, the ENABLE INTERRUPT procedure need contain only the EI, *Enable interrupt*, and RET instructions. Similarly, the DISABLE INTERRUPT procedure need contain only the DI, *Disable interrupt*, and RET instructions. As discussed in Chapter 4, the interrupt mechanism is automatically disabled when an interrupt occurs. Thus, it is necessary to reenable it in one of the interrupt procedures to ensure that the system responds to future interrupt requests. The interrupt system is reenabled when the ENABLE INTERRUPT procedure is called by the INTERRUPT EXECUTIVE procedure, as shown in Figure 6-23.

The burglar alarm system contains a single interrupt source, the clock signal. Many microcomputer systems, however, need to respond to requests from more than a single interrupt source. We consider this situation and how it is handled in the Intel 8085 next.

MULTIPLE INTERRUPTS

In a system that must respond to requests from multiple interrupt sources, a mechanism is needed to differentiate between the different interrupt requests. Figure 6-24 illustrates how this is done functionally in design language. The names of the interrupt requests were chosen for illustration only and no significance should be attached to them. What is illustrated is that test operations must be performed to determine which request caused the interrupt and procedures must be provided to handle each interrupt request. The test operations can be implemented in the software by translating the design language literally; however, the Intel 8085 interrupt hardware provides a more direct mechanism for this purpose.

```
PROCEDURE: INTERRUPT EXECUTIVE (;)
BEGIN PROCEDURE
  SAVE SYSTEM STATUS
  CALL: ENABLE INTERRUPT (;)
  CALL: TEST INTERRUPT REQUEST (;REQUEST)
  IF REQUEST IS 'CLOCK'
    THEN  CALL: PROCESS TIMER INTERRUPT (;)
  IF REQUEST IS 'SWITCH'
    THEN  CALL: PROCESS SWITCH INTERRUPT (;)
  IF REQUEST IS 'PANIC BUTTON'
    THEN  CALL: PROCESS PANIC BUTTON INTERRUPT (;)
  RESTORE SYSTEM STATUS
  RETURN
END PROCEDURE
```

Figure 6-24. A functional INTERRUPT EXECUTIVE procedure for a multiple interrupt system.

As illustrated in Figure 6-25, in order to cause an interrupt, the interrupt request lines are connected either to the Interrupt Request Signal, to one of the RESTART signals, or to the TRAP signal. If any of these five signals is turned *on* by an interrupt request line, the interrupt request is recognized by the CONTROL UNIT and the interrupt system is activated. The method of activation for each of these signals differs.

If an interrupt request line connected to the Interrupt Request Signal is activated, then, when the CONTROL UNIT completes execution of the current instruction, it does not execute the next instruction. Instead, it turns on the INTERRUPT ACKNOWLEDGE signal to request that the INTERRUPT module supply a CALL instruction to execute. The latter instruction is sent to the CONTROL UNIT via the DATA BUS. When the CALL instruction sent to the CONTROL UNIT is executed, it causes the address of the interrupted instruction to be pushed onto the stack and the instruction in the memory location specified in the CALL instruction to be executed next. In general, an *interrupt vector*, which is implemented by an unconditional *jump* instruction, should be placed in each of the memory locations specified in a CALL instruction supplied by the INTERRUPT module. Each interrupt vector then causes the appropriate interrupt procedure to be executed. Note that the SAVE SYSTEM STATUS, CALL: ENABLE INTERRUPT (;), RESTORE SYSTEM STATUS and RETURN operations of Figure 6-24 must now be duplicated in each of the PROCESS procedures. The duplication is necessary because the test and the resulting call operations are now *hardware* operations and are carried out in a different sequence, as shown in the modified INTERRUPT EXECUTIVE *procedure* illustrated in Figure 6-26. The PROCESS TIMER INTERRUPT procedure is shown in Figure 6-27 to illustrate the format of this procedure. This figure should be compared to Figure 4-30. The assembly language instructions needed to implement part

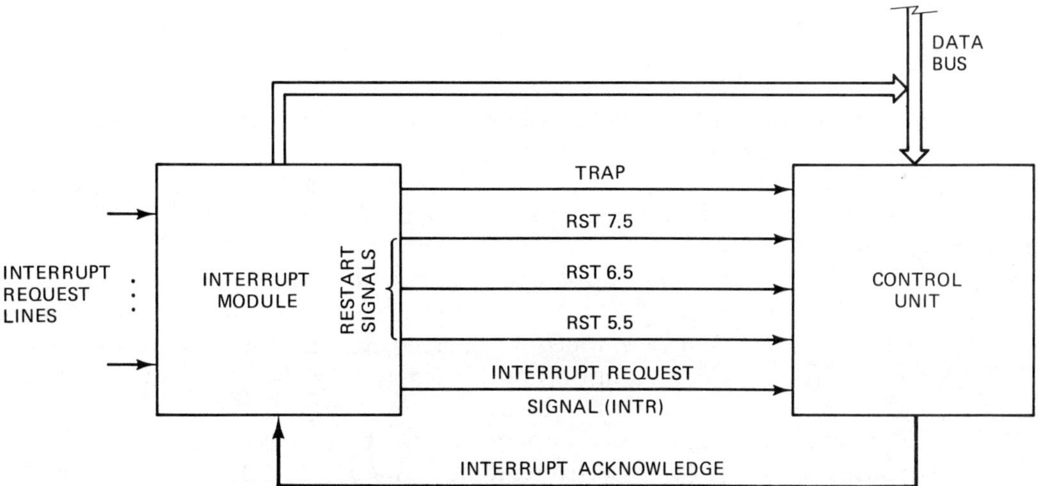

Figure 6-25. The INTERRUPT module for a multiple interrupt system.

```
PROCEDURE; INTERRUPT EXECUTIVE (;)
*****************************************************
  THIS PROCEDURE IS HARDWARE IMPLEMENTED
*****************************************************
BEGIN PROCEDURE
  CALL: TEST INTERRUPT REQUEST (;REQUEST)
  IF REQUEST IS 'CLOCK'
    THEN CALL: PROCESS TIMER INTERRUPT (;)
  IF REQUEST IS 'SWITCH'
    THEN CALL: PROCESS SWITCH INTERRUPT (;)
  IF REQUEST IS 'PANIC BUTTON'
    THEN CALL: PROCESS PANIC BUTTON INTERRUPT (;)
END PROCEDURE
```

Figure 6-26. INTERRUPT EXECUTIVE *procedure* for a hardware-implemented interrupt system.

```
PROCEDURE: PROCESS TIMER INTERRUPT(;)
*****************************************************
BEGIN PROCEDURE
  SAVE SYSTEM STATUS
  CALL: ENABLE INTERRUPT (;)
  DECREMENT TIMER VALUE
  IF TIMER VALUE IS ZERO
    THEN DO
            CALL: STOP TIMER (;)
            SET TIMER STATE TO EXPIRED
         END
  RESTORE SYSTEM STATUS
  RETURN
END PROCEDURE
```

Figure 6-27. The PROCESS TIMER INTERRUPT procedure.

of this procedure along with the corresponding *jump* instructions in memory locations 0 through 63 for several of the interrupt vectors are shown in Figure 6-28. The interrupt technique that automatically invokes the execution of interrupt procedures using predefined memory addresses and interrupt vectors is known as *vectored interrupt*.

Four other interrupt request signals are also illustrated in Figure 6-25: TRAP, RST 7.5, RST 6.5, and RST 5.5. The odd names for the latter three signals were chosen for historical reasons which are unimportant to us. These interrupt signals do not require that a CALL instruction be supplied by the INTERRUPT module. Instead, the CONTROL UNIT automatically executes a RESTART instruction to *call* the instruction in memory location 36 if the TRAP signal is *on* and in memory locations 60, 52, or 44, respectively, if the RST 7.5, RST 6.5, or RST 5.5 signal is

```
;                                   INTERRUPT VECTOR FOR CALL 0
    0   JMP   TIMER
;                                   INTERRUPT VECTOR FOR CALL 8
    8   JMP   SWITCH
;                                   INTERRUPT VECTOR FOR CALL 16
   16   JMP   PANIC
         :                                 :
;                                   INTERRUPT VECTOR FOR CALL 56
   56   JMP   . . .
                                           :
---------------------------------------------------------------------
                                           :
;                                   PROCEDURE: PROCESS TIMER INTERRUPT (;)
;                                   BEGIN PROCEDURE
;                                     SAVE SYSTEM STATUS
TIMER:  PUSH  H
        PUSH  D
        PUSH  B
        PUSH  PSW
;                                     CALL: ENABLE INTERRUPT (;)
        CALL  ENABLE
         :                                 :
;                                     RESTORE SYSTEM STATUS
        POP   PSW
        POP   B
        POP   D
        POP   H
;                                     RETURN
        RET
;                                   END PROCEDURE
```

Figure 6-28. How vectored interrupt is set up.

on. Thus, these four signals provide additional vectored interrupt capability. Since the operation of a RESTART interrupt is handled completely by the CONTROL UNIT, these interrupts are often called *internal* interrupts; the other vectored interrupts are called *external* interrupts. Note that both interrupts provide the capability to respond to one of a set of multiple interrupt requests without the need for a software test to determine which interrupt request line is *on*.

If two interrupt requests are turned *on* simultaneously, the system must decide which to respond to first. For this purpose, each interrupt request signal has been assigned a *priority* by the Intel Corporation. The signal with the higher priority is recognized first if two signals are *on* together. The relative priorities for the Intel 8085 signals are shown below:

TRAP	highest
RST 7.5	·
RST 6.5	·
RST 5.5	·
INTR	lowest

Thus, the TRAP interrupt signal should be used to recognize external events that are sufficiently urgent to require an extremely rapid response when they occur.

An example of a high-priority event is the detection that a power supply is losing power which indicates that the system should be shut down. The microcomputer is capable of executing many instructions between the time when failing power is first sensed and when insufficient power is available to enable the system to continue operation. The system is therefore able to shut itself down systematically during this time interval. When power is restored to a system that has been turned off or shut down, an interrupt can be used to start execution after sufficient power is available for proper operation.

The lowest priority interrupt is assigned to the INTR signal. However, this signal can be connected to many interrupt request lines. Priority is selected for the latter lines by the INTERRUPT module which selects a different CALL instruction to send to the CONTROL UNIT if two of these lines are actuated at the same time. The specific priorities selected by the INTERRUPT module are assigned by the system designer and, depending on the INTERRUPT module hardware, may even be changed during system operation.

The interrupt priority mechanisms just described determine which of several simultaneous interrupt requests the system responds to first. They do not prevent an interrupt procedure that is being executed from being interrupted. As we indicated earlier, the interrupt mechanism is automatically disabled when an interrupt occurs. Thus, if the interrupt mechanism is not reenabled until after the execution of the interrupt procedure is completed, the latter procedure cannot be interrupted. It is neither necessary nor desirable, however, to design a system in this manner since a delay in responding to an interrupt could result in inefficient operation. We discuss the subject of *concurrent interrupts* next.

CONCURRENT INTERRUPTS

If the processing of an interrupt request can be interrupted by another interrupt request, then several interrupt procedures can be in the process of being executed at any given time. Since the processing of these interrupt requests are overlapped, they are called *concurrent interrupts*.

Using the stack for handling the processing of the interrupt procedures permits concurrent interrupts to be handled correctly without additional effort. In every interrupt driven system, however, some interrupt requests have greater urgency than others. A priority system must be established to prevent the processing of an interrupt request from being interrupted by a request of lesser urgency. In the Intel 8085, as described in the last section, the determination of which of several simultaneous interrupt requests the system responds to first is a hardware function. The determination of whether to permit the processing of an interrupt request to be interrupted by another interrupt request is implemented by a combination of hardware and software functions.

The interrupt processing priorities assigned by the hardware are:

- The TRAP interrupt request is always active and cannot be disabled. Thus, it has the highest priority with respect to interrupt processing as well as with respect to response.
- The remaining interrupt requests are all disabled either automatically following an interrupt request or when a DI, *Disable interrupt*, instruction is executed.

Of the latter group of interrupts, however, the RST 5.5, RST 6.5, and RST 7.5 interrupt requests can be turned off selectively or *masked* by the software. Thus, the INTR interrupt request has a higher processing priority than the RESTART interrupt requests since it cannot be masked. To mask the RESTART interrupt requests, the *Set interrupt mask*, SIM, instruction is used along with a suitable mask byte in the ACCUMULATOR REGISTER. Each execution of the SIM instruction can either mask (if the mask bit is ONE) or unmask (if the mask bit is ZERO) any of the three RESTART interrupt requests. The mask byte, which must be placed into the ACCUMULATOR REGISTER before the SIM instruction is executed, determines the action to be taken according to the chart shown in Figure 6-29. As shown in the figure, if the *mask enable* bit is ZERO, the mask bits are ignored. This capability is provided since the SIM instruction is used for other purposes as specified by the remaining bits, as we shall see later. If the *mask enable* bit is ONE, the mask bits in the CONTROL UNIT are set or reset if the corresponding mask bits in the ACCU-

				MASK ENABLE	RST 7.5 MASK BIT	RST 6.5 MASK BIT	RST 5.5 MASK BIT

```
IF MASK ENABLE BIT IS 'ONE'
  THEN  DO FOR EACH MASK BIT
           SET MASK BIT IN CONTROL UNIT TO VALUE OF MASK BIT IN ACCUMULATOR REGISTER
        END
```

Figure 6-29. Interpretation of byte in ACCUMULATOR REGISTER when SIM instruction is executed.

MULATOR REGISTER are ONE or ZERO, respectively. For example, the instruction sequence:

```
MVI    A,13
SIM
```

causes the mask bits for RST 7.5 and RST 5.5 to be set, thereby disabling these interrupt request lines, and causes the mask bit for RST 6.5 to be reset, thereby enabling the RST 6.5 interrupt request line, since the number 13 is equivalent to 0000 1101 in binary. Thus, the interrupt processing priorities for the RESTART interrupt requests can be established when the software is designed.

It is sometimes necessary for the software to examine the states of the interrupt mask bits. A *Read interrupt mask*, RIM, instruction provides this capability in the Intel 8085 microcomputer. When the RIM instruction is executed, the ACCUMULATOR REGISTER is loaded with a byte of information whose interpretation is illustrated in Figure 6-30. The three mask bit states are placed into the three least-significant bits of the byte in the ACCUMULATOR REGISTER. If the *enable flag* is a ONE bit, it indicates that the interrupt system is enabled. If the *enable flag* is a ZERO bit, it indicates that the interrupt system has been disabled either automatically or by execution of the DI, *Disable interrupt*, instruction. Each *pending flag*

	RST 7.5 PENDING FLAG	RST 6.5 PENDING FLAG	RST 5.5 PENDING FLAG	ENABLE FLAG	RST 7.5 MASK BIT	RST 6.5 MASK BIT	RST 5.5 MASK BIT

Figure 6-30. Interpretation of interrupt status byte which is placed into ACCUMULATOR REGISTER when a RIM instruction is executed.

indicates that the corresponding RESTART interrupt request has been turned *on* but has not yet caused an interrupt to take place. This situation occurs either when the interrupt system is disabled or when the corresponding interrupt mask bit is set. Note that a pending interrupt request is not ignored; its ability to interrupt the system is only deferred until the processing of all higher priority interrupt requests is completed.

This completes our general description of microcomputer architecture. We have thus far concentrated on describing the Intel 8085 architecture from an assembly language viewpoint. Let us next consider some advanced architecture topics.

Part II
RELATED TOPICS

In Part I of this chapter we presented the basic architecture of the Intel 8085 microcomputer. In this part of the chapter we present several architecture-related topics such as how interrupt enhances input-output. We also complete our discussion of PL/M by showing how input-output and interrupt are treated in PL/M.

REENTRANCY

In Chapter 4 we discussed the fact that a procedure can be called and executed while its own execution is interrupted. In order for the system to operate correctly when such a situation occurs, the following criteria must be fulfilled by the procedure.

- The stack must be used to save all the pointers, registers, and flags when the procedure is interrupted.
- The stack must be used to store all of the variables manipulated by the procedure during normal execution.

A procedure that fulfills these criteria is called a *reentrant* procedure. Note that all procedures called by a reentrant procedure must also be reentrant. This is necessary because any of the latter procedures may also be called while their execution is interrupted. Note that it is not necessary for all of the procedures in a module to be reentrant; only those procedures appearing in both the calling tree headed by the EXECUTIVE procedure and the calling tree headed by the INTERRUPT EXECUTIVE procedure must be reentrant.

INPUT-OUTPUT AND INTERRUPT

The operations carried out by the input and output instructions introduced earlier are commonly called *programmed input-output*. In this section we reexamine this input-output mechanism to see how interrupt can be used to improve the efficiency of input and output.

In the example of Chapter 1 both input and output are performed asynchronously. That is, there is no waiting for either input or output; the values of the bits at an input port at the instant that the INPUT instruction is executed are used. Similarly, an output is updated whenever the OUTPUT instruction is executed. In many systems, however, we must deal either with a synchronous input or output device or with a device for which a fixed minimum waiting time must be observed between the reading of successive inputs or the updating of successive outputs. In either case, we must ensure that successive executions of the INPUT or the OUTPUT instructions are spaced in time to ensure correct system operation. We use an example to illustrate this concept.

Let us assume that the microcomputer is sending a message consisting of a string of character codes for printing on a typewriter. Let us assume that the typewriter can print 30 characters per second, which is about the maximum rate for an electromechanical typewriter. Thus, unless the characters being transmitted to the typewriter by the microcomputer are spaced at least 33 milliseconds apart, there is a high probability that some of the character codes sent to the typewriter may not be printed. The most straightforward way to ensure that every character is typed is to wait until a character has been printed before the next character code is sent to the typewriter. Functionally, a BUSY signal from the typewriter can be examined and tested repeatedly by the microcomputer and, when the signal changes to indicate that the typewriter is no longer busy, the next character code can be sent to the typewriter. The process of testing and waiting can then be repeated for the remaining characters until the entire message is printed. The design language procedures shown in Figures 6-31 and 6-32 illustrate this concept.

In this example a great deal of microcomputer effort is wasted checking the typewriter BUSY signal. As indicated earlier, the wasted effort could mean the difference between a system that operates well and one that does not. If, instead, we use the BUSY signal to generate an interrupt request to the microcomputer whenever it changes from the busy state to the nonbusy state, then an interrupt procedure can be used to send the character codes to the typewriter. The microcomputer need not concern itself with the typewriter except in response to an interrupt. Thus, not only is the efficiency of the microcomputer improved, but the use of interrupt also provides the ability to interleave input and output transfers between the microcomputer and a number of low-speed input and output devices. Figure 6-33 illustrates a design language procedure that prepares a system to send a message to a typewriter via interrupt. Note that if another message is in the process of being printed, the message is placed into a queue. Otherwise, the message is saved, the first character code is sent to the typewriter, and the interrupt system is unmasked and enabled. Figure 6-34 is the PROCESS TYPEWRITER INTERRUPT procedure that is executed whenever a typewriter interrupt request occurs. This procedure does one of three things: If a character still remains in the current message, it sends the character to the typewriter. If the printing of the current message has been completed and if a message is waiting in the queue, the procedure initiates the printing of the latter

```
PROCEDURE: SEND MESSAGE TO TYPEWRITER (MESSAGE;)
BEGIN PROCEDURE
  DO FOR EACH CHARACTER IN MESSAGE
    CALL: WAIT FOR TYPEWRITER NOT BUSY (;)
    CALL: OUTPUT TO TYPEWRITER (CHARACTER;)
  END
  RETURN
END PROCEDURE
```

Figure 6-31. The SEND MESSAGE TO TYPEWRITER procedure.

```
PROCEDURE: WAIT FOR TYPEWRITER NOT BUSY (;)
BEGIN PROCEDURE
  DO FOREVER
    CALL: READ TYPEWRITER BUSY SIGNAL (;BUSY)
    IF BUSY IS NOT SET
      THEN RETURN
  END
END PROCEDURE
```

Figure 6-32. The WAIT FOR TYPEWRITER NOT BUSY procedure.

```
PROCEDURE: PREPARE TO SEND TYPEWRITER MESSAGE (MESSAGE; )
BEGIN PROCEDURE
  CALL: TEST IF MESSAGE BEING PRINTED (; STATUS)
  IF STATUS INDICATES MESSAGE IS BEING PRINTED
    THEN DO
           CALL: PLACE MESSAGE INTO QUEUE (MESSAGE; )
           RETURN
         END
    ELSE DO
           CALL: SET MESSAGE BEING PRINTED (; )
           CALL: SAVE CURRENT MESSAGE (MESSAGE; )
           CALL: GET CHARACTER FROM CURRENT MESSAGE (; CHARACTER)
           CALL: OUTPUT TO TYPEWRITER (CHARACTER; )
           CALL: UNMASK AND ENABLE TYPEWRITER INTERRUPT (; )
           RETURN
         END
END PROCEDURE
```

Figure 6-33. The PREPARE TO SEND TYPEWRITER MESSAGE procedure.

message. Otherwise, it masks the typewriter interrupt. Similar interrupt procedures can be used for other input and output devices.

Since the *DMA block transfer* is more efficient than either programmed input-output or interrupt driven input-output, it is used for high-speed input and output devices.

DMA BLOCK TRANSFER

As described above, programmed input-output is more efficient when it is interrupt driven. Nevertheless, it is still necessary to execute an interrupt procedure for each byte transferred between the microcomputer and each input or output device. The time needed to perform the steps to interrupt the microcomputer, save system status, get the next byte and cxecute the OUTPUT instruction (or execute the INPUT instruction and save the byte read), and restore system status can be substantial. Thus, programmed input-output, even if interrupt driven, is suitable only for relatively slow input or output devices. The *Direct Memory Access* or DMA block transfer does not require that an input-output instruction or interrupt procedure be executed for each byte. Therefore, it is used for high-speed input or output devices.

The DMA block transfer is implemented in hardware and requires that microcomputer instructions be executed only at the beginning and at the end of a complete transfer of a data block. The hardware consists of a DMA module as shown in Figure 6-35. It keeps track of where the data comes from or goes to in the MEMORY, whether an input or output DMA block transfer is in progress, and how many additional bytes must be sent or received to complete the transfer. To initiate a DMA block transfer, programmed input-output instructions are executed to send the

```
PROCEDURE: PROCESS TYPEWRITER INTERRUPT (;)
BEGIN PROCEDURE
  SAVE SYSTEM STATUS
  CALL: ENABLE INTERRUPT (;)
  CALL: TEST IF CURRENT MESSAGE COMPLETED (;STATUS)
  IF STATUS INDICATES CURRENT MESSAGE IS NOT COMPLETED
    THEN DO
           CALL: GET CHARACTER FROM CURRENT MESSAGE (;CHARACTER)
           CALL: OUTPUT TO TYPEWRITER (CHARACTER;)
           RESTORE SYSTEM STATUS
           RETURN
         END
    ELSE DO
           CALL: TEST IF MESSAGE IN QUEUE (;STATUS)
           IF STATUS INDICATES MESSAGE IS IN QUEUE
             THEN DO
                    CALL: GET MESSAGE FROM QUEUE (;MESSAGE)
                    CALL: SAVE CURRENT MESSAGE (MESSAGE;)
                    CALL: GET CHARACTER FROM CURRENT MESSAGE (;CHARACTER)
                    CALL: OUTPUT TO TYPEWRITER (CHARACTER;)
                    RESTORE SYSTEM STATUS
                    RETURN
                  END
             ELSE DO
                    CALL: MASK TYPEWRITER INTERRUPT (;)
                    CALL: RESET MESSAGE BEING PRINTED (;)
                    RESTORE SYSTEM STATUS
                    RETURN
                  END
         END
END PROCEDURE
```

Figure 6-34. The PROCESS TYPEWRITER INTERRUPT procedure.

address of the first location of a memory block and the length of the block to the DMA module. Actually, the *block length minus one* is used in the Intel 8085 microcomputer system. A command to start the DMA block transfer is also sent to the DMA module, thereby completing the operations needed to initiate the block transfer. The microcomputer is then free to execute other tasks during the block transfer and the DMA module is responsible for completing the block transfer.

Let us examine how the DMA module carries out the steps needed to complete an output block transfer.

1. The BUSY signal from the output device is monitored by the DMA module until it indicates that the device is not busy.
2. The DMA module then requests permission from the CONTROL UNIT to use the DATA bus by turning *on* the HOLD signal.

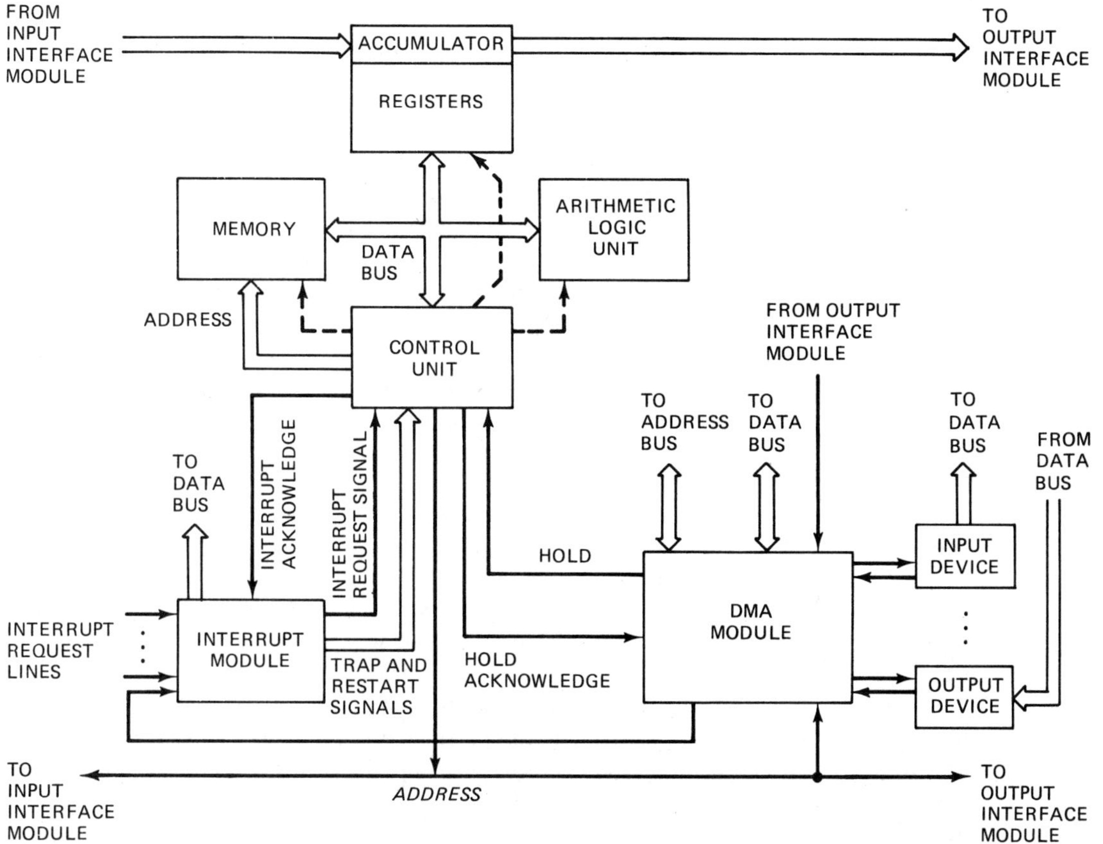

Figure 6-35. The DMA module and its relationship to the Intel 8085 MICROCOMPUTER module.

3. When the CONTROL UNIT is done using the DATA bus and can relinquish the bus, it turns *on* the HOLD ACKNOWLDEGE signal. This action grants permission to the DMA module to use the DATA bus.
4. When the DMA module receives this permission, it sends the address of the next location in the block to the MEMORY via the ADDRESS bus. The byte in the corresponding memory location is then read from the MEMORY and sent to the output device on the DATA bus. The DMA module simultaneously commands the output device to accept the data from the bus.
5. The block length in the DMA module is then tested.
6. If it is not zero, the block length in the DMA module is decremented in preparation for the next test and the block address in the DMA module is incremented to point to the next memory location in the block in preparation for the next byte transfer. Operation then continues with step 1.

7. If the block length is zero, the block transfer is complete and DMA operation is suspended until it is once again initiated, as described above.

It should be pointed out that the overall operation of the microcomputer system is affected only slightly during a DMA block transfer. The microcomputer can function at maximum speed except when the MEMORY is being read in step 4 above. This contrasts with programmed output that requires the execution of an interrupt procedure for each byte transferred to the output device.

The DMA module operates in a similar manner when performing an input block transfer. When the BUSY signal indicates that a byte is ready to be transferred from the input device to the MEMORY, a sequence of operations similar to that described above takes place. The major differences are: The byte must be available in the input device before the request to use the DATA bus is made to the CONTROL UNIT. And, when the DATA bus is made available to the DMA module, the byte is sent from the input device to the MEMORY and stored in the memory location whose address is supplied by the DMA module. Again, the effect of a DMA block transfer on the operation of the microcomputer system is minimal. Before leaving this subject, let us examine the role that interrupt plays in facilitating the operation of DMA block transfers.

Consider the following situation: The microcomputer completes the preparation of information for an output block transfer while a previous DMA block transfer to the same output device is still in progress. Since the output device is busy, the block transfer of the new information must be postponed until the current block transfer is completed. The microcomputer then places the request for the new block transfer into a queue and proceeds to perform other tasks while waiting for the current block transfer to be completed. For efficiency, it is desirable to initiate the new block transfer as soon as the current one is completed. Thus, the considerations for the use of interrupt are relevant here. The microcomputer should be interrupted when the current block transfer is completed and an interrupt process procedure executed to determine if a block transfer is in the queue. If so, the interrupt process procedure should execute the instructions needed to initiate the block transfer in the queue. A similar mechanism can be used to ensure that input block transfers are also initiated efficiently.

MACHINE LANGUAGE

We introduced microcomputer architecture and assembly language to enable the reader to understand the details of interrupt and input-output. However, a high-level language, such as PL/M, is preferred over assembly language for converting a software design into a microcomputer language. Only if a system involving a critical timing loop, for example, cannot be made to work properly using PL/M should assembly language be used. And then it should be used only to implement the critical loop. Because of the relatively poor understandability of machine language and the fact that there is a one-to-one correspondence between it and assembly language, machine language should *never* be used to produce microcomputer software.

As illustrated in Figure 5-1, however, machine language is what we must ultimately end up with since the microcomputer executes only machine language instructions. Also, as we shall see, it is useful to be able to recognize and understand machine language instructions during the integration phases of the system design cycle. For this reason, we include a brief discussion of machine language instructions in this section.

Assembly language instructions are written using alphabetic and numeric characters so that we can easily read them. However, it would be very inefficient to try to make the microcomputer *understand* the assembly language instructions directly. Thus, each assembly language instruction is translated into a machine language *code* that the microcomputer can understand and execute.

As an example, consider the assembly language instruction IN 1. This instruction is represented in machine language by the bit sequence 1101 1011 0000 0001 where 1101 1011 represents the instruction part IN and 0000 0001 represents the number 1. Since bit sequences are hard for us to work with, hexadecimal notation is often used to represent machine language instructions (see Appendix A). For example, IN 1 is equivalent to DB 01 in hexadecimal. Figure 6-36 lists the Intel 8085 machine language instructions for many of the assembly language instructions introduced in this chapter. The interpretation of each instruction is included in the figure so that it can be used for reference. Note that the list is not intended to be complete.

In the figure we use the following conventions:

- The letter M in an assembly language instruction indicates that the memory address to be used is contained in the HL register pair (indirect addressing).
- We have used the symbol PROC to designate the name of a called procedure. The first instruction of PROC is assumed to be located in memory location 04 05, hexadecimal.

  NOTE: In every Intel 8085 instruction that uses direct addressing, the bytes of the address are stored in reverse order in the instruction.
- We use the symbol ELSE to designate the direct address of the memory location containing the instruction to be executed next if the specified condition of a conditional *jump* instruction is true. In our examples this address is assumed to be 27 13, hexadecimal.
- We have used the symbol VALUE to designate the direct address of the memory location that contains an operand or where an operand should be stored. In the LXI instruction the address represented by the symbol VALUE is itself the operand (immediate addressing). In our examples this address is assumed to be 28 2E, hexadecimal. Note that the bytes of the immediate address are also stored in reverse order in the LXI instruction.

Assembly language		Machine language	Instruction interpretation
ADC	M	8E	Add the 8-bit number in the memory location whose address is in the HL register pair to the ACCUMULATOR REGISTER along with the carry flag.
ADD	C	81	Add the 8-bit number in the C register to the ACCUMULATOR REGISTER.
ADD	M	86	Add the 8-bit number in the memory location whose address is in the HL register pair to the ACCUMULATOR REGISTER.
ADI	20	C6 14	Add the number 20 to the ACCUMULATOR REGISTER.
ANI	15	E6 0F	AND each bit in the number 15 with the corresponding bit in the ACCUMULATOR REGISTER.
CALL	PROC	CD 05 04	Call the procedure whose first instruction is in memory location PROC.
CC	PROC	DC 05 04	Call the procedure whose first instruction is in memory location PROC if the carry flag is set.
CMC		3F	Complement (change the state of) the carry flag.
CMP	C	B9	Compare the 8-bit number in the C register to the number in the ACCUMULATOR REGISTER and set the flags.
CNC	PROC	D4 05 04	Call the procedure whose first instruction is in memory location PROC if the carry flag is not set.
CPI	4	FE 04	Compare the number 4 to the number in the ACCUMULATOR REGISTER and set the flags.
CZ	PROC	CC 05 04	Call the procedure whose first instruction is in memory location PROC if the zero flag is set.
DAD	D	19	Add the 16-bit number in the DE register pair to the HL register pair.
DCR	C	0D	Decrement the 8-bit number in the C register.
DCX	D	1B	Decrement the 16-bit number in the DE register pair.
DI		F3	Disable interrupt.
EI		FB	Enable interrupt.
IN	1	DB 01	Read input port 1 and move the data into the ACCUMULATOR REGISTER.
INX	H	23	Increment the 16-bit number in the HL register pair.
JC	ELSE	DA 13 27	Jump to the instruction in memory location ELSE if the carry flag is set.
JMP	ELSE	C3 13 27	Jump to the instruction in memory location ELSE.
JNC	ELSE	D2 13 27	Jump to the instruction in memory location ELSE if the carry flag is not set.
JNZ	ELSE	C2 13 27	Jump to the instruction in memory location ELSE if the zero flag is not set.
JZ	ELSE	CA 13 27	Jump to the instruction in memory location ELSE if the zero flag is set.
LDA	VALUE	3A 2E 28	Load (move) into the ACCUMULATOR REGISTER data from memory location VALUE.

Figure 6-36. A Subset of the Intel 8085 machine language instructions.

LDAX	B	0A	Load (move) into the ACCUMULATOR REGISTER data from the memory location whose address is in the BC register pair.
LHLD	VALUE	2A 2E 28	Load (move) into the HL register pair data from memory location VALUE.
LXI	H, VALUE	21 2E 28	Load (move) into the HL register the address of memory location VALUE.
MOV	A, H	7C	Move data from the H register into the ACCUMULATOR REGISTER.
MOV	A, M	7E	Move data from the memory location whose address is in the HL register pair into the ACCUMULATOR REGISTER.
MOV	M, A	77	Move data from the ACCUMULATOR REGISTER into the memory location whose address is in the HL register pair.
MVI	A, 6	3E 06	Move the number 6 into the ACCUMULATOR REGISTER.
ORA	C	B1	OR each bit in the C register with the corresponding bit in the ACCUMULATOR REGISTER.
ORI	48	F6 30	OR each bit in the number 48 with the corresponding bit in the ACCUMULATOR REGISTER.
OUT	1	D3 01	Move data from the ACCUMULATOR REGISTER to output port 1.
POP	PSW	F1	Pop the stack and store the data into the Program Status Word (ACCUMULATOR REGISTER and flags).
PUSH	H	E5	Push the HL register pair into the stack.
RAL		17	Rotate the bits in the ACCUMULATOR REGISTER to the left with the carry flag appended.
RAR		1F	Rotate the bits in the ACCUMULATOR REGISTER to the right with the carry flag appended.
RC		D8	Return if the carry flag is set.
RET		C9	Return.
RIM		20	Read the interrupt mask and move the data into the ACCUMULATOR REGISTER.
RLC		07	Rotate the bits in the ACCUMULATOR REGISTER to the left.
RRC		0F	Rotate the bits in the ACCUMULATOR REGISTER to the right.
RZ		C8	Return if the zero flag is set.
SBI	35	DE 23	Subtract the number 35 from the ACCUMULATOR REGISTER and also subtract the carry flag.
SHLD	VALUE	22 2E 28	Store (move) into memory location VALUE data from the HL register pair.
SIM		30	Set the interrupt mask using the data in the ACCUMULATOR REGISTER.
SPHL		F9	Load (move) into the stack pointer register the address from the HL register pair.
STA	VALUE	32 2E 28	Store (move) into memory location VALUE data from the ACCUMULATOR REGISTER.

Figure 6-36. (Continued).

STAX D	12	Store (move) into the memory location whose address is in the DE register pair data from the ACCUMULATOR REGISTER.
STC	37	Set the carry flag.
SUB C	91	Subtract the 8-bit number in the C register from the ACCUMULATOR REGISTER.

Figure 6-36. (Continued).

This completes our discussion of microcomputer architecture, but before concluding the chapter we would like to show how some of the operations introduced in this chapter can be executed in PL/M.

PL/M COMPLETED

In Chapter 5 we left the PLM operations that deal with input-output, interrupt, and other related functions for completion in this chapter. These operations can now be related to their equivalent assembly language instructions.

The assembly language instructions for the design language operation

```
EXAMINE INPUT 1 AND SAVE ITS VALUE
```

are given by

```
IN    1
STA   VALUE1
```

The equivalent PL/M operation is

```
VALUE1 = INPUT (1);
```

The parameter contained within the parentheses is the input port number. After the data is read from the input port, it is assigned to the variable VALUE1. The variable to the left of the equal sign in the PL/M input operation may be an element of a PL/M array or structure.

The design language operation

```
SET OUTPUT1 TO THE VALUE 0
```

is equivalent to the assembly language instructions

```
MVI   A,0
OUT   1
```

The equivalent PL/M operation is given by

```
OUTPUT (1) = 0;
```

The parameter within the parentheses is the output port number. The expression to the right of the equal sign specifies the data value that should be sent to the output port. Any valid PL/M expression can be used to specify this value.

The stack is manipulated in PL/M in the same way that it is manipulated in assembly language. In fact, since the PL/M CALL and RETURN operations are translated into corresponding instructions in assembly language, the use of the stack is exactly as described for the assembly language instructions. The initialization of the stack pointer can be left to be done automatically by the PL/M compiler or it can be done by the programmer. In either case, it must be done in the EXECUTIVE procedure before any other procedures are called. The stack is then assigned to a memory region whose location is specified later by the person who determines where the completed program should be located in the MEMORY. We discuss *locating* in Chapter 7.

As we have indicated, the passing of parameters through the stack is done automatically by the PL/M compiler using the data declarations. The compiler inserts suitable assembly language instructions in both the calling procedure and the called procedure to ensure that all parameters are passed correctly.

For interrupt processing, the *process* procedure for each of the interrupt requests must be identified to enable the compiler to implement these procedures correctly. This identification is provided in the procedure declaration, as illustrated by the example below:

```
PROCESS$TIMER$INTERRUPT: PROCEDURE INTERRUPT 0;
```

The information provided in this declaration permits the compiler to automatically insert into memory location 0 a *jump* instruction to the PROCESS$TIMER$INTERRUPT procedure as shown in Figure 6-28. The compiler also inserts the instructions that correspond to the design language operations SAVE SYSTEM STATUS and RESTORE SYSTEM STATUS, as shown in Figure 6-28. For interrupt vectors in locations 8, 16, . . . , 56, the numbers used in the procedure declarations should be 1, 2, . . . , 7, respectively.

For the TRAP, RST 5.5, RST 6.5, and RST 7.5 interrupt requests, the PL/M compiler must be instructed to set up the interrupt vectors at locations 36, 44, 52, and 60, respectively. Similarly, interrupt vectors can also be set up in other memory locations, but it is beyond the scope of our discussion to show how this is done.

The *Enable interrupt* and *Disable interrupt* instructions are provided in PL/M by the ENABLE and DISABLE operations and it is the responsibility of the programmer to insert them into the procedures if they are needed.

Operations equivalent to the SIM and RIM instructions for interrupt processing are provided in PL/M by two predefined PL/M procedures. The S$MASK procedure is used to set the masks and the R$MASK procedure is used to read the mask information. If either procedure is used, it must be declared in an external procedure declaration. The external procedure declaration for the S$MASK procedure takes the form:

```
S$MASK: PROCEDURE (MASK) EXTERNAL;
  DECLARE MASK BYTE;
END S$MASK;
```

And the external procedure declaration for the R$MASK procedure takes the form:

```
R$MASK: PROCEDURE BYTE EXTERNAL;
END R$MASK;
```

To set the interrupt masks, the variable MASK is first set to a value that is determined by the information shown in Figure 6-29. Then the S$MASK procedure is called with MASK as an input parameter. Thus, the following operations set the masks for the RST 7.5 and RST 5.5 interrupt requests and reset the mask for the RST 6.5 interrupt request.

```
MASK = 13;
CALL S$MASK (MASK);
```

To read interrupt mask information, a PL/M operation of the form

```
MASK = R$MASK;
```

is used. After this operation is executed, the variable MASK contains the interrupt mask information as defined in Figure 6-30.

Finally, to make a PL/M procedure reentrant, a procedure declaration of the form

```
STOP$TIMER: PROCEDURE REENTRANT;
```

is used. The PL/M compiler then assigns space on the stack for every variable, array, and structure declared within the procedure. This action permits the procedure to be called during interrupt processing even if its own execution has been interrupted. Remember that every procedure called by a reentrant procedure must also be declared to be reentrant.

We have now completed our discussion of microcomputer architecture and have presented the material that was left unfinished in Chapter 5. We next examine the tools available to help us develop, check out, and integrate the software.

EXERCISES

6-1. Select a *simple* procedure you have designed and convert it into the assembly language instructions for a microcomputer such as the Intel 8085. Use the microcomputer manufacturer's manual if you are not using the Intel 8085 or to supplement the material we have presented. Compare the difficulty of converting a design into assembly language with converting a design into a high-level language such as PL/M.

6-2. An individual procedure should not contain a mixture of high-level language constructs and assembly language instructions. However, it is possible to combine into a single system some procedures that have been converted into a high-level language with other procedures that have been converted into assembly language instructions. Of course, the conventions used for interfacing procedures and modules must be consistent in a system containing both types of procedures in order for the system to operate correctly. What advantages would there be to converting some procedures in a system into assembly language rather than into a high-level language? What disadvantages would there be? Under what circumstances would the advantages outweigh the disadvantages?

Chapter 7

Software Development, Check Out, and Integration

Part I
BASIC TOOLS

The system design cycle consists of developing a set of user requirements, converting the requirements into a functional specification for the system, creating a design, converting the design into a hardware/software realization, integrating the parts of the design, checking it out, and verifying that it works correctly. At each step of the design cycle, documentation must be produced and maintained. For the software, much of this documentation consists of *text*. Thus, we must be able to produce and modify text efficiently. We must be able to translate the software modules containing the procedures into machine language modules and connect them together into an operational system. We must also be able to thoroughly check the operation of the system to demonstrate that it operates correctly. *Tools* are available to help us at each step of the design cycle. In this chapter we examine some of these tools to see how they can be used to systematically develop, check out, and integrate the software for a microcomputer-based system. Tools available for checking out the hardware and for integrating the software into the hardware are described in Chapters 9 and 10.

SYSTEM DEVELOPMENT TOOLS

The system development tools we describe in the following sections and in Chapter 10 consist of software that is either implemented on a microcomputer development system, integrated into the system under development, or implemented on a large general-purpose computer system. Moreover, these tools have been developed under the same constraints that govern the development of all software. Thus, each tool satisfies a set of user requirements and a functional specification that were developed by the software group that designed the tool. As a result, tools that are designed for the same purpose often differ significantly in how they achieve their goals. Because of these differences we can only describe what the tools do in general. Whenever we do provide specific examples, it should be understood that they are for illustration only. The results produced by another similar tool may differ even if the two perform similar tasks. Although the descriptions of many of the tools are independent of the computers they are implemented on, we assume initially that the tools are implemented on a microcomputer development system or integrated into the system under development. Then, after we have described the basic tools, we will show how tools that are implemented on a large computer system are used to develop microcomputer software.

Figure 7-1 lists the tools according to their major function. The reader should refer to this figure as we describe the tools to see where they fit into the overall picture. Some of the tools, such as the editors, operate independently of the hardware under development. Other tools, such as the *in-circuit emulator*, are used in conjunction with the hardware being developed. Finally, tools such as the *common stub* are integrated into the application software itself and can be used during all phases of the software and hardware integration.

Most of the tools manipulate text information. The text information must be stored in a way that makes it easy to access and to work with. Let us therefore discuss methods for storing and accessing the text information used during the development of a microcomputer-based system.

Information management	Software design	Software construction	System integration
Operating system	Automated editor	Automated editor	Integration plan
Information files	Walkthrough emulator	Translator	Command files
	Calling tree generator	Linker and locater	Common stub
		Command files	Monitor
			In-circuit emulator
			Microcomputer analyzer

Figure 7-1. System development tools.

Software can be developed by writing out the design language operations and converting them into a programming language longhand using paper and pencil. However, in order to use automated tools to translate the programming language operations into machine language instructions, the former must exist in a machine readable format. Punched paper tape, punched cards, or magnetic storage devices can serve to store information in machine readable formats. Many systems now use *magnetic disc* storage devices for this purpose. We will assume that all of the information is stored on magnetic discs when it is first created and that it is manipulated in this format throughout the system design cycle. An *operating system* provides the capability needed to keep track of the information stored on the magnetic discs and to make it available to the tools.

To make it easy to access information stored on a magnetic disc through the operating system, the information is divided into *files*. Each file is assigned a *name* that consists of two parts: a symbolic *file name* and a *name extension*. The disc must be inserted into a mechanism called a *disc drive* so that information can be read from it or written onto it. Since a system may contain more than one disc drive, a *disc drive identifier* must be specified along with the file name and the name extension. An example of a file name for a file used to store the EXECUTIVE module of a system is EXEC. For the Intel microcomputer development system, file names are restricted to six characters. The name extensions used with each file name should be chosen to easily differentiate the different files associated with each module or procedure. For example, the files containing the design language/programming language text can be assigned the extension PLM. The files containing the machine language instructions produced by the PL/M compiler can be assigned the extension OBJ (for Object file). If the magnetic disc is inserted into disc drive number one, then the complete file specifiers for the design language/programming language file and the machine language file for the EXECUTIVE module are given by

```
:F1:EXEC.PLM

:F1:EXEC.OBJ
```

The convention we have described has been established for the ISIS operating system used on the Intel microcomputer development system. Other conventions using symbols other than colons and periods are in use on other systems.

In the following sections we assume that each of the tools described uses the operating system facilities to read information from a specified disc file and to write information to a second disc file. The latter disc file may be related to the former, that is, it may have the same name with a different extension, or it may have a completely different name. We begin with the *editor*, which is a tool for creating and modifying the information stored in a disc file.

EDITOR

The step in the system design cycle that follows the development of the functional specification is the creation of the system design. The creation of the software part of a design consists of producing text for each procedure and module and storing the text in suitably named files. The tool used for this purpose is the *editor* or *text editor*. The editor is also used for making changes in the text and correcting design or programming errors when necessary. Two types of editors are in common use: the *line-oriented* editor and the *cursor-based* editor.

Line-oriented editor. There are two ways a line-oriented editor manipulates information. In the simpler case, a line number is assigned to each line of text, whether it is a comment, such as a design language operation, or an operation in a programming language. Line numbers can be assigned by the operator or they can be assigned automatically by the editor in response to an operator request. For example, the operator could request that the first line number be the number 100 and that each successive line number be 10 greater than the previous one. The line numbers would then be 100, 110, 120, . . . , and so on, until the complete text is typed and a request is made to the editor by the operator to stop issuing line numbers. Errors are corrected by retyping the lines containing the errors. For example, if line 120 reads

```
120    BEGIN PROCDURE
```

then, by typing

```
120    BEGIN PROCEDURE
```

the corrected text automatically replaces the incorrect version. Alternately, a command of the form *Replace text string* CD *with text string* CED *on line 120* can be used to obtain the same result. If a line is omitted, it can be assigned any number between the numbers of the two adjacent lines between which it belongs. When it is typed using that line number, it is automatically inserted between the two lines.

To examine the corrected text, a *Display* or *List* command causes the complete text to be generated on the display device, which is usually a typewriter or a television-type display called a CRT terminal. Alternately, the text can be listed on a printer. If it becomes necessary to insert a line between two lines with adjacent line numbers, the editor can be commanded to *Resequence* the text and thereby assign new line numbers that are spaced out. The new line can then be inserted in the text as described above.

The second way that a line-oriented editor can keep track of information is by the use of *pointers*. Pointers indicate a specific character and a specific line. Editor commands then refer to the character and line indicated by the pointers. Typical text-modifying commands are *Delete the next four lines, Delete the next three characters,* and *Insert the following text.* Other commands are used to move the pointers without modifying the text. For example, *Move the pointers back (or ahead) five lines* and *Move the pointers to the beginning (or end) of the text* are commands of the latter type.

Line-oriented editors also have *Search* and *Replace* commands such as, *Search for and display the next occurrence of the text string* CALL and *Replace the next (or every) occurrence of the text string* CALL: *with the text string* CALL.

Since typing long commands is tedious, commands are usually shortened, often to single characters. For example, *Delete the next three characters* is often abbreviated to 3D or D3, *Delete the next four lines* to 4K or K4, for *Kill four lines*, and so on. Unfortunately, there is little standardization and different editors often use the same characters for different commands, and vice versa. This lack of standardization can lead to *disastrous* results when different editors are encountered by personnel working in a common engineering facility.

Cursor-based editor. The cursor-based editor displays text on a CRT terminal in the format typed by the operator. Changes are made by positioning a *cursor* (bar, highlight, or arrow) at the position where the changes are to be made and then typing the new text directly onto the display. Provision is made in most cursor-based editors to easily insert characters into an existing line or to delete characters from within an existing line without extensive retyping. Similarly, complete lines can be inserted into or deleted from the text with relative ease. Since there is a one-to-one correspondence between what is visible on the screen and the text in the file being created or edited, corrections are easy to make and the amount of typing is minimized as compared to the line-oriented editor.

The text editor is a general tool for generating and modifying text whether the text consists of general documentation, design language, or programming language. However, the text editor does not reduce the amount of typing associated with the production of new text. All new text must at one time or another be typed by the engineer, programmer or technician. A tool which is an extension of the cursor-based editor has been developed to help automate the task of text generation. We call this tool an *automated editor* and describe its operation below.

AUTOMATED EDITOR

In addition to the functions provided by a cursor-based editor, the automated editor can also provide the following functions: automatic generation of design language constructs, automatic generation of text strings, automatic indentation and reindentation, semiautomatic conversion of design language into programming language, and automatic extraction of design language.

It is not possible to completely automate the task of generating new text. However, many words, phrases, and constructs are repeated many times in the design language procedures and modules. The automated editor enables a complete word, phrase, or construct to be inserted into the text by pressing a *function key*. The text inserted by a function key can consist of a design language construct, a string that has been defined by the user, or a construct for the particular programming language being used. Design language text strings that can be generated automatically include the complete design language header which contains the programmer's name, the date, the procedure and module names, and so forth. User-defined strings include the names of subsystems, modules, procedures, data structures, and parameters so that these names do not have to be retyped whenever they are encountered. Standard programming language text strings include words such as BYTE and ADDRESS for the PL/M language. Thus, by assigning text strings to function keys and by using design language and programming language function keys, a great deal of typing can be saved by using the automated editor. The name table maintained in the automated editor contains the user-defined strings and can be printed and used as the name list for the second documentation level.

Automatic indentation causes the left margin to be repositioned automatically whenever a DO or END construct is inserted with a function key. This feature relieves the designer of the need to manually insert spaces or use the TAB key to indent text.

If a change necessitates changing the indentation, the automatic reindentation feature can be used. During reindentation, each line of text is repositioned, if necessary, to ensure proper indentation of the design language or programming language constructs. An error caused by an omitted or extraneous DO or END construct can be detected and brought to the attention of the operator during reindentation. Even in the absence of this type of error, it is possible that when the text is reindented, the design will differ from what the designer intended. If this happens, suitable DO . . . END *brackets* can be inserted by the designer as needed to correct the design; the text can then be reindented again to provide for the new *brackets*.

When a design language procedure or module is completed, it must be converted into a programming language. As we described earlier, this entails converting each design language operation into a comment and inserting suitable programming language operations into the text. The conversion of design language into comments, the spacing of these design language comments to permit the programming language text to be inserted, and the insertion of programming language constructs can be done automatically for the standard design language constructs. Similarly, design language names can automatically be converted into programming language symbols. The conversion is initiated by a function key. For PL/M, a set of /* and */ comment delimiters is added to each line. Then, for each standard design language construct, a new line is inserted below the construct and, where possible, the equivalent PL/M construct is inserted. For example, the DO FOREVER construct is *translated* into DO WHILE 1 = 1; as shown below:

```
/*          DO FOREVER                                  */
            DO WHILE 1 = 1;
```

The indentation of the programming language text is adjusted to correspond to the design language text. Names are converted into PL/M symbols by inserting appropriate dollar signs and periods. When the automated conversion has been carried out as far as possible, the remainder of the PL/M operations can be typed in manually to complete the conversion. In many cases, the latter step can be facilitated by using standard programming language or user-defined strings available through the function keys.

The text file now contains both the design language and the programming language versions of the procedure or module. The complete text can now be printed on a typewriter or printer. When it is printed, the programming language text is moved to the right, as shown below, to provide the documentation format we have used in the examples in this book.

```
/*          DO FOREVER                                              */
                                                DO WHILE 1 = 1;
```

For assembly language procedures, the *design language* is moved to the right, as shown in the examples in Chapter 6. In place of the combined listing, the user may request that a listing be produced that contains only the design language portion of the text. In this case, the programming language lines of text are omitted from the listing as are all characters designating that a design language statement is a comment. Thus, we can extract the original design language text even though it has been converted into a programming language. The latter feature of the automated editor enables us to maintain a single text file for both the design language and the programming language levels of documentation for each module and procedure.

WALKTHROUGH EMULATOR

As stated earlier, the sooner design errors are discovered in the system design cycle, the easier they can be corrected. The design walkthrough can help find errors at the design level. However, a great deal of concentration is demanded from the participants during a walkthrough to ensure that maximum benefit is obtained. The *walkthrough emulator* reduces some of the effort required during a walkthrough by automatically *stepping through* the design for the participants. Sequencing between procedures through *calls* and *returns* does not require the participants to shuffle from page to page as when a walkthrough is performed manually. For each test construct, the state of the walkthrough can optionally be saved and the walkthrough restarted later from the saved state so that both of the test alternatives can be evaluated under similar conditions. If desired, a data flow diagram for the walkthrough can be produced automatically after each walkthrough. The data flow diagram provides additional information about the design and helps to verify whether the design is correct or contains errors.

CALLING TREE GENERATOR

The procedure calling tree was introduced in Chapter 3. We suggested there that a procedure calling tree can be generated automatically. A tool has been developed for this purpose. It examines the design language version of the EXECUTIVE procedure and produces the first two levels of the calling tree, as illustrated in Figure 7-2. The calling tree generator then examines the design language versions of each of the procedures called by the EXECUTIVE procedure and produces the third level of the tree. The generator continues to examine each successive level of called procedures until the tree is completed; the complete procedure calling tree is then printed, as illustrated by the example shown in Figure 7-3. If procedure numbers are assigned to the procedures for debugging purposes, they can be inserted in the procedure calling tree although this is not shown in the figure. Even after the design is converted into a programming language, the procedure calling tree can be produced from the design language part of the text. Thus, we can generate a new procedure calling tree whenever design changes alter the tree.

```
EXECUTIVE
  |
  |--INITIALIZE SYSTEM
  |
  |--WAIT FOR KEYSWITCH ARMED
  |
  |--TEST SWITCHES
  |
  |--TEST MOTION DETECTOR
```

Figure 7-2. First two levels of the calling tree for the burglar alarm system.

The calling tree generator can also be used to optionally insert a *called by list* into each procedure header of the design.

COMPILER

A compiler translates modules and procedures written in a high-level programming language such as PL/M into machine language instructions. The relationship between the compiler and its inputs and outputs is illustrated functionally in Figure 7-4. The input to the compiler consists of a text file containing the high-level programming language operations derived from the design language version of the software. The compiler reads the input text one line at a time from the file. If a line contains a comment, it is ignored. If a line contains text that is not a comment, the compiler examines the text for *syntax* errors. If syntax errors are not detected, the text is translated into one or more machine language instructions. These instructions are then saved in a file for later use by the linker. The compiler also transmits each line of input text to a printing device to produce an input listing.

An example of an input listing produced by the PL/M compiler for the burglar alarm system EXECUTIVE module is shown in Figure 7-5. At the top of the listing is a *header block* containing the following pertinent information: the module name,

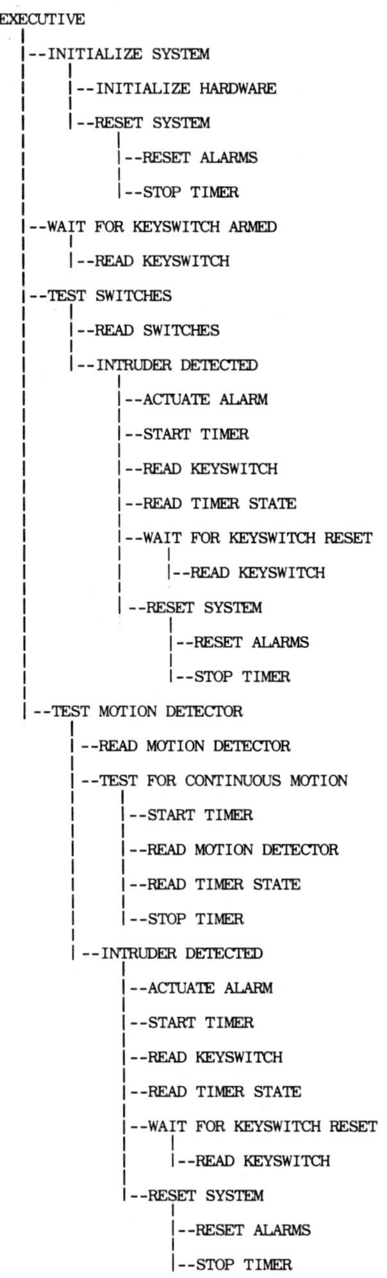

Figure 7-3. The procedure calling tree for the burglar alarm system software.

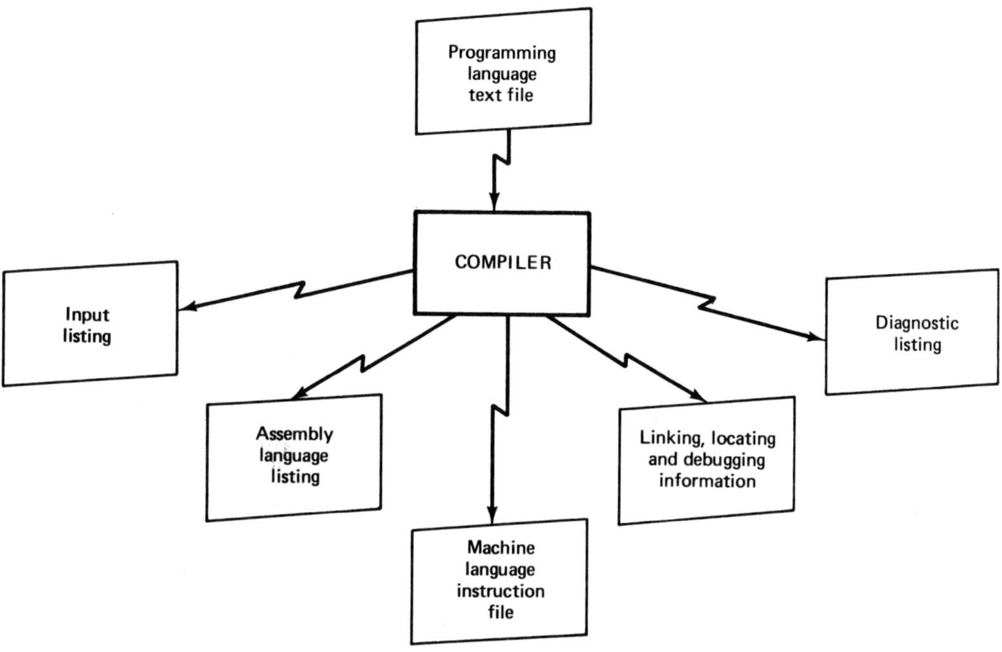

Figure 7-4. The compiler.

the name of the machine language instruction file, and the system command that initiated the execution of the compiler.

The header block is followed by the PL/M text with two columns of numbers appended on the left side. The first of these two columns contains a sequence number for every line of text that is not a comment. The second column contains a number that indicates the *nesting level* of each PL/M operation as established by the procedure declarations and the DO . . . END constructs. Thus, for example, line 11 is at level 2 indicating that it is inside the procedure, while line 13 is at level 3 indicating that it is inside both the procedure and the DO WHILE 1 = 1; . . . END; construct. Note that the END; phrases are treated as if they are nested within the constructs they terminate. Thus, the END; in line 16 is considered to be at nesting level 3.

At the end of the input listing is a *trailer block* containing additional information about the module. In the example, 23 bytes of memory are needed to store the instructions, no bytes are needed for storing PL/M variables since no variables are declared, and, at most, two additional stack levels will be needed by this module during execution. The trailer block indicates that the input to the compiler consisted of 43 lines of text including the design language comments and that the compiler detected no syntax errors during translation.

If an *assembly language listing* that also contains the corresponding machine language instructions produced by the compiler is requested, it is produced along

```
PL/M-80 COMPILER

ISIS-II PL/M-80 V3.1 COMPILATION OF MODULE EXECUTIVE
OBJECT MODULE PLACED IN :F1:EXEC.OBJ
COMPILER INVOKED BY:  PLM80 :F1:EXEC.PLM

              /*  MODULE: EXECUTIVE                                       MODULE #1   */
  1                                           EXECUTIVE: DO;
              /********************************************************************** */
              /*  DESIGNED BY: MDF                  15-OCT-80
              /********************************************************************** */
              /*    EXTERNAL PROCEDURE DECLARATIONS                                   */
              /*                                                                      */
  2  1                                          INITIALIZE$SYSTEM: PROCEDURE EXTERNAL;
  3  2                                          END INITIALIZE$SYSTEM;
              /*                                                                      */
  4  1                                          WAIT$FOR$KEYSWITCH$ARMED: PROCEDURE EXTERNAL;
  5  2                                          END WAIT$FOR$KEYSWITCH$ARMED;
              /*                                                                      */
  6  1                                          TEST$SWITCHES: PROCEDURE EXTERNAL;
  7  2                                          END TEST$SWITCHES;
              /*                                                                      */
  8  1                                          TEST$MOTION$DETECTOR: PROCEDURE EXTERNAL;
  9  2                                          END TEST$MOTION$DETECTOR;
              /*--------------------------------------------------------------------- */
              /*  PROCEDURE: EXECUTIVE (;)                                            */
 10  1                                        EXECUTIVE: PROCEDURE PUBLIC;
              /********************************************************************** */
              /*    DESIGNED BY: MDF                 15-OCT-80                        */
              /*    MODULE: EXECUTIVE                                                 */
              /********************************************************************** */
              /*  BEGIN PROCEDURE                                                     */
              /*    CALL: INITIALIZE SYSTEM (;)                                       */
 11  2                                          CALL INITIALIZE$SYSTEM;
              /*    DO FOREVER                                                        */
 12  2                                          DO WHILE 1 = 1;
              /*      CALL: WAIT FOR KEYSWITCH ARMED (;)                              */
 13  3                                            CALL WAIT$FOR$KEYSWITCH$ARMED;
              /*      CALL: TEST SWITCHES (;)                                         */
 14  3                                            CALL TEST$SWITCHES;
              /*      CALL: TEST MOTION DETECTOR (;)                                  */
 15  3                                            CALL TEST$MOTION$DETECTOR;
              /*    END;                                                              */
 16  3                                          END;
              /*  END PROCEDURE                                                       */
 17  2                                        END EXECUTIVE;
              /********************************************************************** */
              /*  END MODULE                                                          */
 18  1                                        END EXECUTIVE;

MODULE INFORMATION:

     CODE AREA SIZE       = 0017H     23D
     VARIABLE AREA SIZE   = 0000H      0D
     MAXIMUM STACK SIZE   = 0002H      2D
     43 LINES READ
     0 PROGRAM ERROR(S)
END OF PL/M-80 COMPILATION
```

Figure 7-5. PL/M input listing for burglar alarm system executive.

with the input listing. The assembly language listing for the burglar alarm system EXECUTIVE module is shown in Figure 7-6. It is requested by inserting the *keyword* CODE into the operating system command, as shown in the header block of the listing. The assembly language listing contains all of the information present in the input listing as well as the assembly language and the corresponding machine language instructions that are interleaved with the PL/M text lines. For example, the PL/M operation

```
CALL INITIALIZE$SYSTEM;
```

on line 11 has been translated into

```
0000  CD0000          CALL     INITIALIZESYSTEM
```

The first two columns contain the instruction address relative to the beginning of the module and the machine language instruction in hexadecimal; the third column contains the corresponding assembly language instruction CALL INITIALIZESYSTEM, which is almost identical to the PL/M operation in this case.

An assembly language comment can be placed anywhere on a line as long as it is preceded by a semicolon. For example, both

```
; STATEMENT # 10
```

and

```
; PROC  EXECUTIVE
```

are assembly language comments. A design language comment may become separated from its corresponding PL/M operation if the compiler inserts an assembly language instruction between the two. For example, the assembly language instruction

```
000D  CD0000          CALL     TESTSWITCHES
```

has been inserted between the PL/M comment

```
/*      CALL:   TEST MOTION DETECTOR (;)                                    */
```

and its corresponding PL/M operation

```
CALL TEST$MOTION$DETECTOR;
```

This is an idiosyncrasy of the PL/M compiler which sometimes prints a comment before it prints the assembly language instruction corresponding to the *preceding* PL/M operation. An example in which the PL/M operation and the corresponding assembly language instructions are adjacent to one another is provided by the PL/M operation

```
DO WHILE 1 = 1;
```

and its corresponding assembly language instructions.

Assembly language labels are inserted in the listing if needed by *jump* instructions. In the example, both @1: and @2: are labels needed by the two jump instructions JMP @1 and JNZ @2, respectively.

Before leaving this example let us make two more observations. The PL/M operation on line 12, the DO WHILE 1 = 1; operation, is the only one requiring more than one assembly language instruction in our simple example. As we stated earlier, this is not usually the case. Finally, the compiler inserted a RET or *return* instruction at the end of the procedure. This is done by the compiler for *every* procedure whether or not it is needed and whether or not there is already a PL/M RETURN operation at the end of the procedure. Again, this is an idiosyncrasy of this compiler. It is intended to prevent execution from erroneously *falling through the bottom* of the procedure, which would cause instructions or data that happen to follow in the MEMORY to be executed incorrectly. If such a situation were to occur, it would be difficult to detect during check out.

If the compiler detects syntax errors during compilation, it produces diagnostic messages along with the input listing. To illustrate, we introduced a syntax error into the burglar alarm system EXECUTIVE module and, in Figure 7-7, we have reproduced the input listing produced by the compiler for the *faulty* program. The name of the WAIT FOR KEYSWITCH ARMED procedure is misspelled so that the name in the *call* does not correspond to the name used in the external procedure

```
PL/M-80 COMPILER

ISIS-II PL/M-80 V3.1 COMPILATION OF MODULE EXECUTIVE
OBJECT MODULE PLACED IN :F1:EXEC.OBJ
COMPILER INVOKED BY: PLM80 :F1:EXEC.PLM CODE

               /*  MODULE: EXECUTIVE                                            MODULE #1  */
  1                                                     EXECUTIVE: DO;
               /**********************************************************************  */
               /*  DESIGNED BY: MDF                    15-OCT-80
               /**********************************************************************  */
               /*    EXTERNAL PROCEDURE DECLARATIONS                                        */
               /*                                                                           */
  2   1                                                   INITIALIZE$SYSTEM: PROCEDURE EXTERNAL;
  3   2                                                   END INITIALIZE$SYSTEM;
               /*                                                                           */
  4   1                                                   WAIT$FOR$KEYSWITCH$ARMED: PROCEDURE EXTERNAL;
  5   2                                                   END WAIT$FOR$KEYSWITCH$ARMED;
               /*                                                                           */
  6   1                                                   TEST$SWITCHES: PROCEDURE EXTERNAL;
  7   2                                                   END TEST$SWITCHES;
               /*                                                                           */
  8   1                                                   TEST$MOTION$DETECTOR: PROCEDURE EXTERNAL;
  9   2                                                   END TEST$MOTION$DETECTOR;
               /*----------------------------------------------------------------------   */
```

Figure 7-6. PL/M assembly language listing for burglar alarm system executive.

```
            /*  PROCEDURE: EXECUTIVE (;)                                              */
 10  1                                          EXECUTIVE: PROCEDURE PUBLIC;
                                              ; STATEMENT # 10
                    ; PROC  EXECUTIVE
            /************************************************************************ */
            /*    DESIGNED BY: MDF                      15-OCT-80                     */
            /*    MODULE: EXECUTIVE                                                   */
            /************************************************************************ */
            /*  BEGIN PROCEDURE                                                       */
            /*    CALL: INITIALIZE SYSTEM (;)                                         */
 11  2                                            CALL INITIALIZE$SYSTEM;
                                              ; STATEMENT # 11
            /*    DO FOREVER                                                          */
          0000  CD0000          CALL    INITIALIZESYSTEM
 12  2                                            DO WHILE 1 = 1;
                                              ; STATEMENT # 12
                    @1:
          0003  3E01            MVI     A,1H
          0005  FE01            CPI     1H
          0007  C21600          JNZ     @2
            /*      CALL: WAIT FOR KEYSWITCH ARMED (;)                                */
 13  3                                              CALL WAIT$FOR$KEYSWITCH$ARMED;
                                              ; STATEMENT # 13
            /*      CALL: TEST SWITCHES (;)                                           */
          000A  CD0000          CALL    WAITFORKEYSWITCHARMED
 14  3                                              CALL TEST$SWITCHES;
                                              ; STATEMENT # 14
            /*      CALL: TEST MOTION DETECTOR (;)                                    */
          000D  CD0000          CALL    TESTSWITCHES
 15  3                                              CALL TEST$MOTION$DETECTOR;
                                              ; STATEMENT # 15
            /*    END;                                                                */
          0010  CD0000          CALL    TESTMOTIONDETECTOR
 16  3                                            END;
                                              ; STATEMENT # 16
          0013  C30300          JMP     @1
                    @2
            /*  END PROCEDURE                                                         */
 17  2                                          END EXECUTIVE;
                                              ; STATEMENT # 17
          0016  C9              RET
            /************************************************************************ */
            /*  END MODULE                                                            */
 18  1                                          END EXECUTIVE;

MODULE INFORMATION:

     CODE AREA SIZE       = 0017H     23D
     VARIABLE AREA SIZE   = 0000H      0D
     MAXIMUM STACK SIZE   = 0002H      2D
     43 LINES READ
     0 PROGRAM ERROR(S)
END OF PL/M-80 COMPILATION
```

Figure 7-6. (Continued).

```
PL/M-80 COMPILER

ISIS-II PL/M-80 V3.1 COMPILATION OF MODULE EXECUTIVE
OBJECT MODULE PLACED IN :F1:EXEC.OBJ
COMPILER INVOKED BY: PLM80 :F1:EXEC.PLM

           /*  MODULE: EXECUTIVE                                        MODULE #1  */
  1                                          EXECUTIVE: DO;
           /*********************************************************************  */
           /*  DESIGNED BY: MDF                 15-OCT-80
           /*********************************************************************  */
           /*    EXTERNAL PROCEDURE DECLARATIONS                                   */
           /*                                                                      */
  2  1                                         INITIALIZE$SYSTEM: PROCEDURE EXTERNAL;
  3  2                                         END INITIALIZE$SYSTEM;
           /*                                                                      */
  4  1                                         WAIT$FOR$KEYSWITCH$ARMED: PROCEDURE EXTERNAL;
  5  2                                         END WAIT$FOR$KEYSWITCH$ARMED;
           /*                                                                      */
  6  1                                         TEST$SWITCHES: PROCEDURE EXTERNAL;
  7  2                                         END TEST$SWITCHES;
           /*                                                                      */
  8  1                                         TEST$MOTION$DETECTOR: PROCEDURE EXTERNAL;
  9  2                                         END TEST$MOTION$DETECTOR;
           /*--------------------------------------------------------------------  */
           /*  PROCEDURE: EXECUTIVE (;)                                            */
 10  1                                     EXECUTIVE: PROCEDURE PUBLIC;
           /*********************************************************************  */
           /*    DESIGNED BY: MDF               15-OCT-80                          */
           /*    MODULE: EXECUTIVE                                                 */
           /*********************************************************************  */
           /*  BEGIN PROCEDURE                                                     */
           /*    CALL: INITIALIZE SYSTEM (;)                                       */
 11  2                                       CALL INITIALIZE$SYSTEM;
           /*    DO FOREVER                                                        */
 12  2                                       DO WHILE 1 = 1;
           /*       CALL: WATCH FOR KEYSWITCH ARMED (;)                            */
 13  3                                         CALL WATCH$FOR$KEYSWITCH$ARMED;
*** ERROR #105, STATEMENT #13, NEAR 'WATCHFORKEYSWITCHARMED',  UNDECLARED IDENTIFIER
           /*       CALL: TEST SWITCHES (;)                                        */
*** ERROR #118, STATEMENT #13, NEAR 'WATCHFORKEYSWITCHARMED',  INVALID INDIRECT CALL, IDENTIFIER NOT AN ADDRESS SCALAR
 14  3                                         CALL TEST$SWITCHES;
           /*       CALL: TEST MOTION DETECTOR (;)                                 */
 15  3                                         CALL TEST$MOTION$DETECTOR;
           /*    END;                                                              */
 16  3                                       END;
           /*  END PROCEDURE                                                       */
 17  2                                     END EXECUTIVE;
           /*********************************************************************  */
           /*  END MODULE                                                          */
 18  1                                     END EXECUTIVE;

MODULE INFORMATION:

     CODE AREA SIZE       = 0014H     20D
     VARIABLE AREA SIZE   = 0001H      1D
     MAXIMUM STACK SIZE   = 0002H      2D
     43 LINES READ
     2 PROGRAM ERROR(S)
END OF PL/M-80 COMPILATION
```

Figure 7-7. PL/M input listing for a module containing an error.

declaration. Since the misspelled name or *identifier* is not declared in its misspelled form, the compiler indicates that ERROR #105 has been detected. Also, when the name in a *call* construct is contained in an external procedure declaration, it is automatically considered to be an ADDRESS variable by the PL/M compiler. Since the misspelled name does not appear in such a declaration, a second error, #118, indicates that the name is not declared to be an ADDRESS. This illustrates another idiosyncrasy of the PL/M compiler, that of thoroughness; a single syntax error often gives rise to several error messages. Note, also, that the error message specifies the number of the statement containing the syntax error. Unfortunately, an error message does not always follow the line containing the syntax error. Moreover, the statement number in an error message is not always a reliable indicator of the location of a syntax error. Usually, if the syntax error is not in the line indicated, it is in the line immediately following the error message. There are two exceptions: (1) Some syntax errors are not detected until after the last line of the procedure or module is examined. The error messages for these syntax errors then follow the end of the input listing just prior to the trailer block. (2) A syntax error in a line may not be detected until a contradiction is detected elsewhere in the procedure or module. The compiler cannot determine which of the two lines contains the syntax error; the error message therefore indicates that the syntax error is located in the second line where it was detected.

One other compiler output is shown in Figure 7-4 but does not appear in any of the listings. It contains the *Linking, Locating and Debugging Information*. This information is saved in the machine language instruction file and is used by the linker and locater and for debugging, that is, for eliminating *bugs* or errors, as we shall see later.

ASSEMBLER

The assembler translates assembly language instructions into machine language instructions. It functions in a manner similar to the compiler except that the input listing produced is the assembly language listing. Otherwise, the assembler reads the input text one line at a time from a disc file, ignores the assembly language comments, examines each instruction for syntax errors, and translates each instruction into a machine language instruction. It also produces information for the linker and locater and for debugging.

An example of an assembly language input listing for the Intel 8085 assembly language is shown in Figure 7-8. Each design language operation is preceded by a semicolon to indicate to the assembler that it is a comment. In the example, DS performs the same function as a byte data declaration does in PL/M. DSEG (data segment) and CSEG (code segment) are used to separate memory areas reserved for data from those reserved for instructions. Also, the D and C in the third column identifies whether the address part of the instruction refers to an address in the data segment or in the code segment of the memory. This information is needed during linking, as we shall see shortly.

```
ISIS-II 8080/8085 MACRO ASSEMBLER, V3.0
 LOC  OBJ         LINE        SOURCE STATEMENT

                      ;                          PROCEDURE: MICROCOMPUTER SYSTEM EXAMPLE (;)
                      ;                          ************************************************************
                      ;                          DESIGNED BY: MDF              LAST UPDATE: 08-07-81 LBE
                      ;
                      ;                          LOCAL PARAMETERS NOT USED IN DESIGN LANGUAGE:
                      ;                                         NAME           TYPE           SIZE
                      ;                                         ----           ----           ----
                      ;                                         VALUE1         BYTE           --
                               DSEG
 0000                 VALUE1:  DS    1
                      ;                                         VALUE2         BYTE           --
 0000                 VALUE2:  DS    1
                      ;                          ************************************************************
                      ;                          BEGIN PROCEDURE
                               CSEG
                      ;                            DO FOREVER
                      ;                              EXAMINE INPUT 1 AND SAVE ITS VALUE
 0000 DB01            START:   IN    1
 0002 320000    D              STA   VALUE1
                      ;                              EXAMINE INPUT 2 AND SAVE ITS VALUE
 0005 DB02                     IN    2
 0007 320100    D              STA   VALUE2
                      ;                              IF THE VALUE OF INPUT 1 IS GREATER THAN 4 AND LESS THAN 8
 000A 3A0000    D              LDA   VALUE1
 000D FE04                     CPI   4
 000F CA2400    C              JZ    ELSE1
 0012 DA2400    C              JC    ELSE1
 0015 FE08                     CPI   8
 0017 CA2400    C              JZ    ELSE1
 001A D22400    C              JNC   ELSE1
                      ;                                THEN  SET OUTPUT 1 TO THE VALUE 6
 001D 3E06                     MVI   A,6
 001F D301                     OUT   1
 0021 C32800    C              JMP   CONT1
                      ;                                ELSE  SET OUTPUT 1 TO THE VALUE 0
 0024 3E00            ELSE1:   MVI   A,0
 0026 D301                     OUT   1
                      ;                              IF THE VALUE OF INPUT 2 IS GREATER THAN 2 AND LESS THAN 6
 0028 3A0100    D     CONT1:   LDA   VALUE2
 002B FE02                     CPI   2
 002D CA4200    C              JZ    ELSE2
 0030 DA4200    C              JC    ELSE2
 0033 FE06                     CPI   6
 0035 CA4200    C              JZ    ELSE2
 0038 D24200    C              JNC   ELSE2
                      ;                                THEN  SET OUTPUT 2 TO THE VALUE 4
 003B 3E04                     MVI   A,4
 003D D302                     OUT   2
 003F C34600    C              JMP   CONT2
                      ;                                ELSE  SET OUTPUT 2 TO THE VALUE 0
 0042 3E00            ELSE2:   MVI   A,0
 0044 D302                     OUT   2
                      ;                            END
 0046 C30000    C     CONT2:   JMP   START
                      ;                          END PROCEDURE
 0000           C              END   START
```

Figure 7-8. An assembly language listing for the Intel 8085 microcomputer.

MACHINE LANGUAGE INSTRUCTION FILE

One of the outputs produced by both the compiler and the assembler is a file containing the machine language instructions for the module being translated. When they are executed, these instructions cause the programming language operations that were contained in the programming language text file to be performed. However, before the machine language instructions can be executed, it is necessary to put them into the microcomputer MEMORY. Since each procedure or module is translated into its machine language instructions separately, it is not known during translation where the instructions in the other modules will be located when they are put into the MEMORY. How then can the individual software modules be translated one at a time and the machine language instructions be combined into an executable software system? To answer this question, let us examine the concept of *relocatability* which then leads us into linking and locating.

A *relocatable* module is one which can be placed anywhere in the MEMORY *after* it has been translated. During translation, it is assumed that the first memory location to be occupied by the machine language instructions of each module is location zero; all of the memory locations needed by the module are then assigned as if this assumption were true. However, linking, locating, and debugging information is produced during translation to keep track of all memory reference instructions. Both the machine language instructions and the linking, locating, and debugging information are then stored in the machine language instruction file or *object file*. Later, when the modules are joined or *linked* together and when each is assigned to a specific area or *located* in the MEMORY, the address in each memory reference instruction is adjusted using the linking and locating information. Regardless of the order in which linking and locating take place, the result must be the same: each memory reference instruction must contain the actual memory address of the procedure, data structure, or instruction that is referenced.

To illustrate how relocation works, let us use the example of Figure 7-6, the assembly language listing of the EXECUTIVE module for the burglar alarm system. The instruction JMP @1 is an unconditional jump instruction to memory location 0003. But this memory location has been assigned relative to memory location zero, which is assumed by the compiler to contain the first instruction of the procedure. When the procedure is later assigned a specific location in the MEMORY by the locater, a *relocation constant* is added to the address part of the instruction, thereby assuring that the jump instruction will be executed correctly. For example, if the EXECUTIVE procedure is assigned to the memory so that its first instruction is located in memory location 1000, hexadecimal, then the address part of the unconditional jump instruction is adjusted by 1000, hexadecimal by the locater. The instruction executed will then be JMP 1003H or C3 03 10 as required for the correct operation of the system. Note that the linking, locating, and debugging information is not shown in the assembly language listing, that the address bytes are stored in reverse order in the machine language instruction (03 10 rather than 10 03), and that an H following a number indicates that the number should be interpreted as a hexadecimal number.

In the example of Figure 7-6 each of the *calls* has the same apparent address of zero. When each of the modules is assigned to a specific part of the memory and the procedures linked together, the address in each CALL instruction is then replaced by the actual address of the corresponding procedure. To ensure that these addresses are replaced correctly, the linking, locating, and debugging information contains the symbolic name of each called procedure. Information indicating which CALL instructions correspond to each of the symbolic names is also provided. It should be noted that the addresses in CALL instructions in the assembly language listing may not always be zero as they are in the example. The reason for this and the specific details of how the linking, locating, and debugging information is used is beyond the scope of our discussion.

LINKER, LOCATER, AND LOADER

As we have seen, linking is the process of *connecting* a procedure with its *calls* and locating is the process of assigning specific memory locations to the instructions in the software. In general, linking can be accomplished either before or after locating. However, this is very dependent on the linking and locating software provided by the manufacturer or vendor. We assume that the linker and locater can be used in either sequence. The linker and locater software provided for linking and locating object files produced by the Intel 8085 compilers and assemblers operate in this manner.

The inputs to the linker consist of the following:

- The names of the disc file containing the machine language instructions for each procedure or module to be linked together.
- The name of the disc file into which the linked software should be saved.
- A set of optional keywords, such as MAP, which requests that the linker produce a symbol list for the software.

In addition to the linked software, the linker also produces diagnostic messages if errors are detected during linking.

If the software being linked has not yet been located, the linker cannot assign absolute memory addresses to the calls or to the memory reference instructions. It does assign new relocatable addresses and adjusts all of the addresses in procedure calls and memory reference instructions relative to a new *origin*. It thereby produces a new relocatable machine language module from the individual procedures and modules that were linked together. Such linked modules can again be linked together until, finally, all calls are connected to their respective procedures. The locater then assigns specific memory locations to each instruction in the linked module and adjusts the address of each memory instruction, thereby completing the process of generating an executable software module for the complete system.

If the locater is used before the linker or to locate a module containing only a few linked modules, the procedures in these modules are assigned to absolute locations in the MEMORY. The calls in these modules are then connected to their respective procedures during a subsequent linking step. When used in this manner, the linking and locating steps should be iterated as needed to ensure that all of the software is completely linked together and correctly located in the MEMORY.

Once an executable software module is produced, it can be loaded into the memory and its instructions executed. If the memory consists of read-only memory devices, the loading process consists of permanently writing the machine language software into these devices. If read-write memory is used, such as during check out and integration, a *loader* is used to put the machine language software into the MEMORY. We discuss read-only memory devices and read-write memory devices in detail in Chapter 8.

AUTOMATIC CONSTRUCTION OF SOFTWARE

The execution of each tool we have described is initiated by an operating system command that indicates what the tool is to do. For example, the linker must be supplied with the names of the disc files containing the modules that should be linked together. For the Intel microcomputer development system, the operating system command to execute the linker in order to link the burglar alarm system together is given by

```
LINK :F1:EXEC.OBJ,:F1:TEST.OBJ,:F1:WAIT.OBJ,:F1:INTRUD.OBJ,:F1:RESET.OBJ,:F1:TIMER.OBJ,&
     :F1:INPUT.OBJ,:F1:OUTPUT.OBJ,PLM80.LIB,SYSTEM.LIB TO :F1:BURG.LNK
```

The ampersand character, &, permits a command to occupy more than one line. We have omitted optional keywords in the example. Thus, we see that typing operating system commands for a large system with many modules and optional keywords can be both tedious and potentially error prone. Therefore, many microcomputer development systems permit operating system commands to be stored in a *command file* so that they do not have to be retyped when they are needed. To execute the commands stored in a command file on the Intel microcomputer development system, an operating system command of the form

```
SUBMIT :F1:BURG
```

is typed. This causes the commands stored in the disc file named BURG.CSD on the magnetic disc in disc drive number one to be executed. CSD is the default extension for a file specified in an Intel SUBMIT command.

An example of a command file containing the sequence of system commands needed to execute the PL/M compiler, the linker, and the locater is given by

```
PLM80 :F1:%0.PLM
LINK :F1;EXEC.OBJ,:F1:TEST.OBJ,:F1:WAIT.OBJ,:F1:INTRUD.OBJ,:F1:RESET.OBJ,:F1:TIMER.OBJ,&
     :F1: INPUT.OBJ,:F1:OUTPUT.OBJ,PLM80.LIB,SYSTEM.LIB TO :F1:BURG.LNK
LOCATE :F1:BURG.LNK MAP
```

In this example the name of the disc file containing the PL/M module to be compiled is not specified directly; the symbol %0 is used instead. When the text in a single module or procedure is changed, such as to correct an error detected during integration, only the module or procedure that has been changed must be recompiled. However, the complete system must again be linked together to include the new version of the corrected module or procedure and the linked software must then be located. Let us assume that these commands are stored in the disc file named BURG.CSD on the magnetic disc in disc drive number one. The SUBMIT command that causes the symbol %0 to be replaced with the file name INPUT and the commands in the file to be executed is given by

```
SUBMIT :F1:BURG(INPUT)
```

This command has the same effect as if the command

```
PLM80 :F1:INPUT.PLM
```

were specified directly, followed by the LINK and LOCATE commands shown above.

USING A LARGE COMPUTER

In the preceding sections we assumed that the tools used for the design of software were implemented on a microcomputer development system. An alternative is to use tools that are implemented on a large computer for the initial phases of software design. Then the information stored in files on a magnetic disc in the large computer can be moved to a magnetic disc in the microcomputer development system to enable the remaining phases of the system design cycle to be completed. The step of moving information from a magnetic disc file on the large computer to a magnetic disc file on the microcomputer development system is called *downloading*. Let us briefly consider the advantages and disadvantages of using a large computer during the system design cycle.

On a microcomputer development system, the amount of magnetic disc storage capacity is limited. Thus, it may be necessary to divide the software among several magnetic discs. Then, to link the software together, the object files produced by the translator must be copied onto a common disc so that all of them are accessible to the linker at one time. A large computer can provide a large quantity of magnetic disc storage capacity, thus permitting all of the software to be accessible simultaneously. One efficient mode of operation is for the design language and programming language versions of the software to be maintained only on the large computer. When completed, each module is then downloaded onto a temporary or *scratch* disc, translated into machine language, and only the object file saved on a disc in the microcomputer development system. Alternately, if a suitable programming language translator is available on the large computer, then translation can be performed on the latter machine *before* downloading. In either case, the two systems should perform mutually exclusive functions for the software design team.

If the software design team consists of two or more persons, then, in the absence of a large computer, more than one microcomputer development system may be needed to minimize the time spent waiting for a system. Microcomputer development systems are considerably more expensive than workstations or terminals for a large computer. Thus, if a large computer is used, a separate terminal can be made available at reasonable cost for each person on the design team. The microcomputer development systems need be shared only during the latter phases of the system design cycle after the software is downloaded. Therefore, the use of a large computer system may reduce the capital equipment investment needed for a project.

When any computer system is in use, we must provide ways to recover from both system failures and power failures. We see how this is done for microcomputer-based systems such as the burglar alarm system in the next chapter. For a computer used for software development, it is necessary to ensure that the information stored on the magnetic disc files can be recovered if they are destroyed or altered during a system failure or power failure. The most common method of ensuring that the information stored on the magnetic disc files will not be lost when a failure occurs is to periodically copy them onto a *backup* magnetic disc or magnetic tape. This precaution assures that a duplicate version of the information is available should the primary copy be ruined. If the magnetic discs are *backed up* daily, then no more than one day's work is lost if a failure occurs. If a large computer is used for software development, periodic backup is the responsibility of the manager of the large computer facility. If a microcomputer development system is used, periodic backup is the responsibility of the manager of the microcomputer system design team. Thus, another advantage of using a large computer to store the design documentation is that there is no need to be concerned with backup; it is done automatically and routinely.

Finally, some of the special-purpose software tools, such as the calling tree generator, execute considerably more slowly on a microcomputer development system than on a large computer. Thus, the calling tree, for example, can be updated more often if a large computer is used.

A disadvantage of the large computer is that whenever a system failure occurs, the facilities of the large computer are unavailable to the project team and work may slow down or come to a halt. If more than one microcomputer development system is in use, then only one system is affected by a failure; work can continue on the remaining systems although it must proceed at a slower pace.

Thus, the large computer has several advantages over the microcomputer development system. It also has disadvantages. Which approach is used depends on the size of the project design team, the available resources, the duration of the project schedule, as well as on other factors that differ from project to project. It is up to the manager of the design team to decide which approach is better for a particular project.

We mentioned earlier that the compiler and assembler both produce debugging information as part of their output. Let us next examine how software is debugged, checked out, and integrated into a working system using both the debugging information as well as tools intended specifically for the debugging and integration of software.

Part II
SYSTEMATIC INTEGRATION OF SOFTWARE

Thus far, we have described a systematic way to design software and to convert a software design into a programming language. In Part I of this chapter we described the tools that are available to help us develop the software for a microcomputer-based system. Each of these tools can help detect a different class of error: The walkthrough emulator helps detect errors in the flow of control through a procedure as well as data flow errors. The calling tree generator detects when a procedure is called by a procedure in in a lower-level module; it also indicates which procedures should be made reentrant. The translators (the compiler and assembler) detect programming language syntax errors. Even with these tools, however, design and programming errors or *bugs* inevitably remain. Software debugging tools can then be used to help find and correct these remaining errors. In this part of the chapter we examine these debugging tools as well as a systematic methodology for debugging and integrating software. The use of this systematic integration methodology ensures that the debugging tools are used effectively; it also provides us with a high degree of confidence that the remaining errors are detected and eliminated.

SOFTWARE INTEGRATION

Once the errors detected by the walkthrough emulator, the calling tree generator, and the programming language translator are corrected, it is tempting to link the software together, locate it, load it into the memory, and execute it to see if it works. Such an approach is *not* recommended for two reasons: First, the software will very likely execute in an erratic manner, thus making it almost impossible to determine what errors remain. Second, if the software does execute in a reasonable manner, it will be difficult to test adequately to ensure that any remaining errors are detected.

A systematic approach to software integration consists of testing and integrating the software in a top-down manner, in phases, as follows:

- For the first phase of integration, we allow only the top-level EXECUTIVE procedure and the INITIALIZE SYSTEM procedure to execute to verify that they execute correctly and call lower-level procedures in the correct sequence. During this step, we prevent the other procedures called by the EXECUTIVE procedure from executing. We describe how to selectively execute procedures shortly.

- Having checked out the EXECUTIVE and INITIALIZE SYSTEM procedures, we proceed to phase two and allow one of the other procedures called by the EXECUTIVE procedure to execute to test its behavior.
- To complete phase two of integration, two courses of action are possible depending on the characteristics of the system being integrated. In some systems each of the remaining procedures called by the EXECUTIVE procedure can then be allowed to execute one at a time and thereby integrated into the system. Then the third-level procedures can be permitted to execute one at a time and integrated in the same manner. This approach can then be repeated for each remaining level until the software is completely checked out and integrated. Note that the correct execution of test constructs and conditional loop constructs in a procedure depend on information obtained from either the procedure's input parameters or from the output parameters returned by called procedures. It is therefore necessary to be able to vary the values of these parameters in order to test a procedure thoroughly. We show shortly how to vary parameters easily during check out.
- In a system consisting of several distinct subsystems the following approach may be preferred for phase two and the subsequent integration phases. After one of the SUBSYSTEM EXECUTIVE procedures called by the EXECUTIVE procedure is checked out, all of the procedures in the subsystem headed by this procedure are then checked out and integrated one level at a time. Then, each of the other SUBSYSTEM EXECUTIVE procedures called by the EXECUTIVE procedure is permitted to execute and its corresponding subsystem is integrated. Because of the interaction between subsystems, it may be necessary to integrate parts of some subsystems out of their natural sequence.
- When the integration of the subsystems and modules that are not interrupt driven is complete, the interrupt software can be integrated. This phase of integration is done either by initiating the execution of the INTERRUPT EXECUTIVE procedure, if one exists, or by using a software procedure to call the INTERRUPT EXECUTIVE procedure. The integration of the interrupt software is then carried out in the manner described above. If an INTERRUPT EXECUTIVE procedure does not exist, the execution of each of the PROCESS INTERRUPT procedures can be called individually and thereby integrated in a straightforward manner.

The integration steps described above can often be carried out by executing the software on a microcomputer development system. In order to do this, the microcomputer development system must be able to execute the software directly or it must be able to *emulate* the execution of the software. Alternately, if emulation capability is available on a large computer, software integration may be carried out on it. The integration phases during which the INPUT and OUTPUT modules and the INTERRUPT module are integrated may require that specific hardware be built and available for test before these integration phases can be completed. Thus, their description is deferred until we consider how the software is integrated into the hardware in Chapter 10. We also defer a description of an alternate approach that combines software integration with system integration until Chapter 10.

The integration methodology described above is straightforward. Nevertheless, it is necessary to plan each step in advance in order to ensure that the integration of a system is done thoroughly. It is also important to plan how to vary parameters to ensure that the integration proceeds smoothly. For this purpose, we prepare an *integration plan* before starting the integration of a system. Moreover, a technique has been developed to enable procedures to be selectively executed and to permit parameters to be easily varied. This technique makes use of a *tool* we call the *common stub*. In the next sections we discuss the integration plan and how to implement the common stub and use it for integration.

INTEGRATION PLAN

As indicated in the preceding section, the integration of a microcomputer-based system is best carried out by grouping the steps carried out during integration into phases. The goal of each integration phase should be to have a specific part of the system operational. For example, one of the integration phases could consist of the steps needed to integrate a complete subsystem. Alternately, an integration phase could involve the integration of a module or group of modules.

The integration plan documents the integration phases. It consists of a detailed description of each phase of the integration process and specifies what part of the system should be operational at the end of each phase. The description of an integration phase should indicate what procedures (or modules or subsystems) will be tested and what the system will be able to do functionally when the integration phase is complete. Moreover, suitable test values should be specified for those parameters which are varied during each integration phase. Also, if the values of calculated parameters can be estimated or otherwise determined, these values should be included in the integration plan documentation. This permits the system to be evaluated more objectively during integration.

Later in the chapter we discuss how to track the progress of system development through the system design cycle. The integration plan permits progress to be evaluated during check out and integration. Before discussing the management aspects of the system design cycle, let us look at the tools that can be used for check out and integration starting with the common stub.

COMMON STUB

The common stub is implemented as a software module that is linked together with the other modules of the system under development. It contains a data structure and several procedures that control the execution of the procedures of the system during integration. The common stub data structure consists of a SINGLE STEP parameter and three lists: a PROCEDURE CONTROL LIST, a PARAMETER LIST, and a PROCEDURES CALLED LIST. When SINGLE STEP is set, as each procedure is called, its identification number is displayed and the system waits for the operator to issue a command to proceed. The PROCEDURE CONTROL LIST contains integration control information for each procedure in the system being integrated. This information indicates whether the procedure should be executed, whether its execution should be skipped, or whether the execution of the system should be stopped when the procedure is called. The PROCEDURE CONTROL LIST also indicates whether the procedure identification number should be recorded in the PROCEDURES CALLED LIST. When the execution of a procedure is skipped, the values of its output parameters must be defined by the COMMON STUB procedure. The PARAMETER LIST contains test values for the output parameters that are used to enable testing to continue when a procedure is skipped.

The procedures communicate with the COMMON STUB module through a COMMON STUB procedure. The COMMON STUB procedure is called by every procedure in the system except the EXECUTIVE and INITIALIZE SYSTEM procedures. However, at the option of the designer, INITIALIZE SYSTEM may call COMMON STUB *after* it calls the INITIALIZE COMMON STUB procedure which we describe shortly. The design language operations that must be included in the procedures for this purpose take the following form:

```
CALL: COMMON STUB (ID NUMBER;PARAMETER 1,...,PARAMETER N,SKIP)
IF SKIP IS SET
  THEN  RETURN
```

The input parameter ID NUMBER is a number that is uniquely defined for each procedure to identify it to the COMMON STUB module. The output parameters, PARAMETER 1, . . . , PARAMETER N, are the output parameters of the calling procedure, thereby enabling their values to be set by the COMMON STUB procedure from the PARAMETER LIST. The SKIP parameter is used to enable the execution of the procedure to be skipped. An example illustrating how these operations are inserted into a procedure is shown in Figure 7-9.

```
PROCEDURE: TEST FOR CONTINUOUS MOTION (;CONTINUOUS)
BEGIN PROCEDURE
  CALL: COMMON STUB (4;CONTINUOUS,SKIP)
  IF SKIP IS SET
    THEN  RETURN
  CALL: START TIMER (5 SECONDS;)
        .
        .
        .
END PROCEDURE
```

Figure 7-9. Calling the common stub procedure.

The COMMON STUB module also contains an INITIALIZE COMMON STUB procedure which must be called by the INITIALIZE SYSTEM procedure. As indicated above, the INITIALIZE SYSTEM procedure may call the COMMON STUB procedure only after it has called the INITIALIZE COMMON STUB procedure. The INITIALIZE COMMON STUB procedure is used to set or reset SINGLE STEP and to initialize the lists in the common stub data structure to ensure that they contain meaningful information when they are used. Finally, procedures are needed to permit SINGLE STEP and the information in the PROCEDURE CONTROL LIST and the PARAMETER LIST to be updated and to permit the operator to interact with the system to examine the information in the PROCEDURES CALLED LIST. The latter procedures are called UPDATE SINGLE STEP, UPDATE PROCEDURE CONTROL LIST, UPDATE PARAMETER LIST, and INTERACT WITH OPERATOR. The design for the complete COMMON STUB module is shown in Figure 7-10. Let us now examine how the COMMON STUB module is used to facilitate system integration.

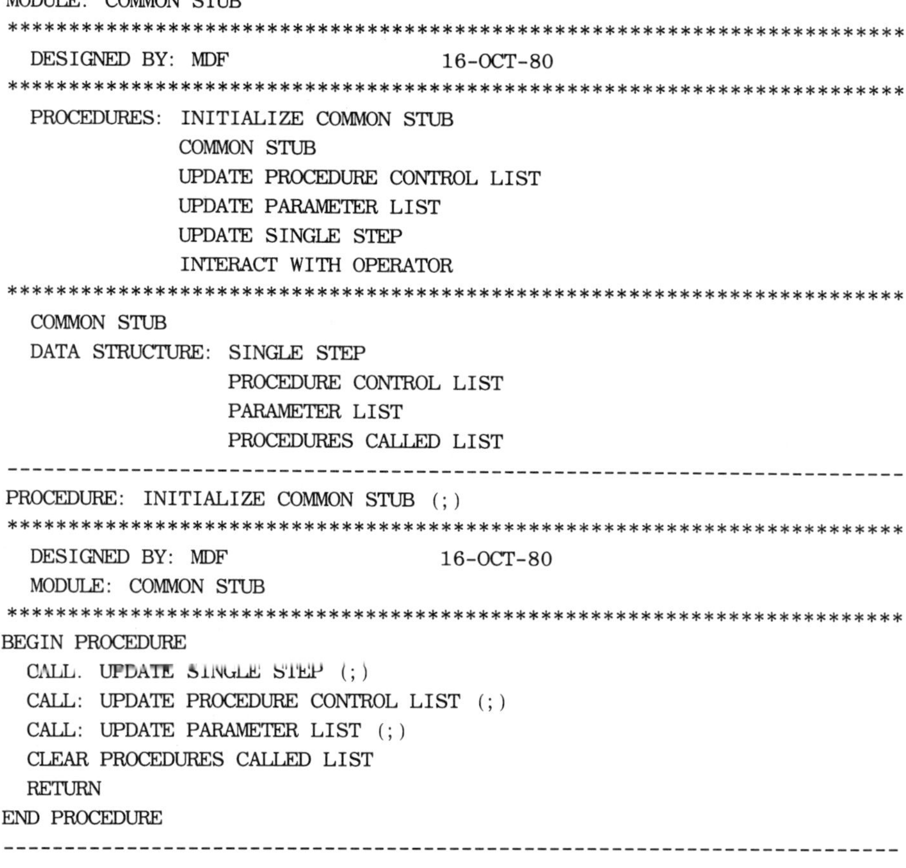

```
MODULE: COMMON STUB
*************************************************************************
  DESIGNED BY: MDF                        16-OCT-80
*************************************************************************
  PROCEDURES: INITIALIZE COMMON STUB
              COMMON STUB
              UPDATE PROCEDURE CONTROL LIST
              UPDATE PARAMETER LIST
              UPDATE SINGLE STEP
              INTERACT WITH OPERATOR
*************************************************************************
  COMMON STUB
  DATA STRUCTURE: SINGLE STEP
                  PROCEDURE CONTROL LIST
                  PARAMETER LIST
                  PROCEDURES CALLED LIST
-------------------------------------------------------------------------
PROCEDURE: INITIALIZE COMMON STUB (;)
*************************************************************************
  DESIGNED BY: MDF                        16-OCT-80
  MODULE: COMMON STUB
*************************************************************************
BEGIN PROCEDURE
  CALL: UPDATE SINGLE STEP (;)
  CALL: UPDATE PROCEDURE CONTROL LIST (;)
  CALL: UPDATE PARAMETER LIST (;)
  CLEAR PROCEDURES CALLED LIST
  RETURN
END PROCEDURE
-------------------------------------------------------------------------
```

Figure 7-10. Common stub module.

```
PROCEDURE: COMMON STUB (ID NUMBER;SKIP)
**********************************************************************
  DESIGNED BY: MDF                    16-OCT-80
  MODULE: COMMON STUB
**********************************************************************
BEGIN PROCEDURE
  IF CODE IN PROCEDURE CONTROL LIST FOR ID NUMBER INDICATES RECORD
                                                       PROCEDURE CALLED
    THEN  SAVE ID NUMBER IN NEXT LOCATION OF PROCEDURES CALLED LIST
  IF CODE IN PROCEDURE CONTROL LIST FOR ID NUMBER INDICATES STOP
    THEN  CALL: INTERACT WITH OPERATOR (;)
    ELSE  DO
            IF SINGLE STEP SET
              THEN  DO
                      CALL: DISPLAY ID (ID NUMBER;)
                      CALL: WAIT FOR CONTINUE COMMAND (;)
                    END
          END
  IF CODE IN PROCEDURE CONTROL LIST FOR ID NUMBER INDICATES SKIP
    THEN  SET SKIP
    ELSE  RESET SKIP
  RETURN
END PROCEDURE
----------------------------------------------------------------------
PROCEDURE: UPDATE PROCEDURE CONTROL LIST (;)
**********************************************************************
  DESIGNED BY: MDF                    16-OCT-80
  MODULE: COMMON STUB
  CALLED BY: INITIALIZE COMMON STUB
**********************************************************************
BEGIN PROCEDURE
  CALL: GET UPDATE DATA (;DATA)
  PUT DATA INTO PROCEDURE CONTROL LIST
  RETURN
END PROCEDURE
----------------------------------------------------------------------
PROCEDURE: UPDATE PARAMETER LIST (;)
**********************************************************************
  DESIGNED BY: MDF                    16-OCT-80
  MODULE: COMMON STUB
  CALLED BY: INITIALIZE COMMON STUB
**********************************************************************
BEGIN PROCEDURE
  CALL: GET UPDATE DATA (;DATA)
  PUT DATA INTO PARAMETER LIST
  RETURN
END PROCEDURE
----------------------------------------------------------------------
```

Figure 7-10. (Continued).

```
PROCEDURE: UPDATE SINGLE STEP (;)
*******************************************************************
  DESIGNED BY: MDF                    16-OCT-80
  MODULE: COMMON STUB
  CALLED BY: INITIALIZE COMMON STUB
*******************************************************************
BEGIN PROCEDURE
  CALL: GET UPDATE DATA (;DATA)
  IF DATA INDICATES THAT SINGLE STEP IS DESIRED
    THEN  SET SINGLE STEP
    ELSE  RESET SINGLE STEP
  RETURN
END PROCEDURE
-------------------------------------------------------------------
PROCEDURE: INTERACT WITH OPERATOR (;)
*******************************************************************
  DESIGNED BY: MDF                    16-OCT-80
  MODULE: COMMON STUB
  CALLED BY: COMMON STUB
*******************************************************************
BEGIN PROCEDURE
  CALL: OUTPUT MESSAGE ('PRINT ID LIST? ';)
  CALL: GET ANSWER (;ANSWER)
  IF ANSWER IS 'YES'
    THEN  DO FOR EACH ENTRY IN PROCEDURES CALLED LIST
              PRINT ENTRY
          END
  CALL: OUTPUT MESSAGE ('ENTER MONITOR? ';)
  CALL: GET ANSWER (;ANSWER)
  IF ANSWER IS 'YES'
    THEN  CALL: MONITOR (;)
  CALL: OUTPUT MESSAGE ('CONTINUE EXECUTION? ';)
  CALL: GET ANSWER (;ANSWER)
  IF ANSWER IS 'YES'
    THEN  RETURN
    ELSE  CALL: STOP EXECUTION (;)
END PROCEDURE
-------------------------------------------------------------------
END MODULE
```

Figure 7-10. (Continued).

Let us assume that data for SINGLE STEP and the PROCEDURE CONTROL LIST and PARAMETER LIST have been prepared and are stored either on a tape or in a disc file and can be read by the GET UPDATE DATA procedure. The details of how this is done vary with each system since they depend on how the data is stored. The data set used to initialize the system when integration is begun should cause the execution of every procedure to be skipped and the identification number of each called procedure to be recorded in the PROCEDURES CALLED LIST. To examine the PROCEDURES CALLED LIST, a STOP EXECUTION code should be placed into the PROCEDURE CONTROL LIST for one of the procedures called by the EXECUTIVE procedure. The SINGLE STEP parameter should also be reset when the COMMON STUB module is initialized for the first time.

The execution of the EXECUTIVE procedure is initiated to start integration. The system, including the COMMON STUB module, is initialized when the INITIALIZE SYSTEM procedure is called by the EXECUTIVE procedure. The EXECUTIVE procedure then calls the next level procedures in the usual manner. However, the execution of these procedures is skipped and their identification numbers recorded in the COMMON STUB module. When the procedure whose STOP EXECUTION code is set is called, the message

```
PRINT ID LIST?
```

is typed by the INTERACT WITH OPERATOR procedure (see Figure 7-10). If the operator responds in the affirmative, then a list of the identification numbers for the called procedures is printed or displayed. The option

```
ENTER MONITOR?
```

is then typed and the operator may elect to initiate the execution of the *monitor*. We describe the monitor and how it is used shortly. Finally, the message

```
CONTINUE EXECUTION?
```

is presented to the operator who may indicate whether to continue to the next stopping point or to stop execution completely. By running the system past the stopping point several times and examining the procedures called listings, the calling sequence of the procedures can be verified to be correct or a problem can be detected. If, during execution, the system does not reach the procedure for which the STOP EXECUTION code is set, then either SINGLE STEP or additional STOP EXECUTION codes can be set by modifying the PROCEDURE CONTROL LIST data. The reason for the problem can then be determined by either *single stepping* the system, thereby tracking execution on a procedure-by-procedure basis, or by examining the procedures called listings if the second approach is used. The problem can then be eliminated by correcting design language and programming language operations.

Once the first phase of software integration is complete, the remaining phases can be initiated in order by changing the control codes in the PROCEDURE CONTROL LIST accordingly. If a procedure that returns an output parameter is skipped, a value for the parameter must be provided when the PARAMETER LIST is updated. In fact, the system may be executed several times using different values for a parameter to check operation under a variety of conditions.

The common stub therefore provides a tool to facilitate the integration of the software in a highly systematic way. When used with a good integration plan, suitable sets of PROCEDURE CONTROL LIST and PARAMETER LIST data can be prepared in advance, thereby permitting integration to proceed quickly and efficiently. The computed results and the procedure called listings can be saved along with the integration plan to provide a record that enables progress to be tracked easily during integration. This record is invaluable for both the project team and project management. Every member of the project team can track the status of the project and know, in advance, when he or she will need to provide assistance during integration.

Finally, when the system is complete, the COMMON STUB module is disabled by setting SINGLE STEP and all of the control codes so that all of the procedures execute normally. If, however, an unforeseen change must be made to the system or if an undiagnosed fault is discovered later, the facilities provided by the common stub remain available. These facilities are then enabled either by setting SINGLE STEP or by providing new data containing appropriate control codes for the PROCEDURE CONTROL LIST.

IMPLEMENTATION OF THE COMMON STUB

We have now described the COMMON STUB module from a functional and design viewpoint. Implementing it is straightforward in most respects; the design language is converted into a programming language, compiled in the usual manner, and connected to the system during linking. But two aspects of the common stub implementation we described require further examination. The first is that we need a mechanism for handling calls to the COMMON STUB procedure for varying numbers of output parameters. The second is that we may need a more efficient mechanism for skipping procedures than the one described in the previous section which requires the use of the SKIP parameter and a test construct in the calling procedure.

A simple way to provide for a varying number of output parameters is to use a different COMMON STUB procedure for each case. Thus, we would implement a set of procedures which are called in the following manner:

```
CALL: COMMON STUB (ID NUMBER; SKIP)
CALL: COMMON STUB 1 (ID NUMBER; PARAMETER 1, SKIP)
CALL: COMMON STUB 2 (ID NUMBER; PARAMETER 1, PARAMETER 2, SKIP)
```

and so forth. Each of the COMMON STUB N procedures would then take the format shown in Figure 7-11. Although it appears that a large number of COMMON STUB procedures may be necessary, this is not usually the case. For example, as we have seen, if PL/M is used for the Intel 8085 microcomputer, only three possibilities exist: A PL/M procedure may return no parameters or it may return a single BYTE output parameter or a single ADDRESS output parameter. Thus, only three COMMON STUB procedures are needed for Intel 8085 PL/M.

```
PROCEDURE: COMMON STUB N (ID NUMBER;PARAMETER 1, ..., PARAMETER N,SKIP)
***********************************************************************
  DESIGNED BY: MDF                   16-OCT-80
  MODULE: COMMON STUB
***********************************************************************
BEGIN PROCEDURE
  IF CODE IN PROCEDURE CONTROL LIST FOR ID NUMBER INDICATES RECORD
                                                        PROCEDURE CALLED
    THEN  SAVE ID NUMBER IN NEXT LOCATION OF PROCEDURES CALLED LIST
  IF CODE IN PROCEDURE CONTROL LIST FOR ID NUMBER INDICATES STOP
    THEN  CALL: INTERACT WITH OPERATOR (;)
    ELSE  DO
             IF SINGLE STEP SET
               THEN  DO
                        CALL: DISPLAY ID (ID NUMBER;)
                        CALL: WAIT FOR CONTINUE COMMAND (;)
                     END
          END
  IF CODE IN PROCEDURE CONTROL LIST FOR ID NUMBER INDICATES SKIP
    THEN  DO
             GET N PARAMETERS FOR ID NUMBER FROM PARAMETER LIST
             SET SKIP
          END
    ELSE  RESET SKIP
  RETURN
END PROCEDURE
```

Figure 7-11. Common stub procedure modified for N output parameters.

Because of PL/M's limited output parameter capability, it is awkward to return a SKIP parameter every time the COMMON STUB procedure is called. Thus, we need a more efficient mechanism for skipping the execution of a procedure when PL/M is used. The stack provides such a mechanism. In Chapter 6 we saw how the stack is used in the Intel 8085 to save the pointers needed by the RETURN operations. When the COMMON STUB procedure is executing, the top item in the stack contains a pointer to the procedure that called the COMMON STUB procedure. Let us call this procedure the *test* procedure. The second item in the stack is a pointer to the procedure that called the test procedure. Therefore, the execution of the test procedure is skipped if an instruction equivalent to a POP instruction is executed before the RETURN operation in the COMMON STUB procedure is executed. Execution then continues directly with the procedure that called the test procedure. If the test procedure returns a BYTE output parameter, a test value from the PARAMETER LIST should be placed in the ACCUMULATOR REGISTER before the execution of the COMMON STUB procedure is terminated. Alternately, if the test procedure returns an ADDRESS output parameter, a test value from the PARAMETER LIST should be placed in the HL register pair. Figure 7-12 illustrates how this is done in PL/M for both BYTE and ADDRESS output parameters using the RETURN operation.

```
/*PROCEDURE: COMMON STUB RETURNING BYTE (ID NUMBER;PARAMETER)                    */
                          COMMON$STUB$RETURNING$BYTE: PROCEDURE (ID$NUMBER) BYTE PUBLIC;
/****************************************************************************   */
/*  DESIGNED BY: MDF                 16-OCT-80                                   */
/*  MODULE: COMMON STUB                                                          */
/*                                                                               */
/*  INPUT PARAMETER:                                                             */
/*                NAME          TYPE          SIZE                               */
/*                ----          ----          ----                               */
/*              ID NUMBER       BYTE           --                                */
                                              DECLARE ID$NUMBER BYTE;
/*                                                                               */
/*  OUTPUT PARAMETER:                                                            */
/*                NAME          TYPE          SIZE                               */
/*                ----          ----          ----                               */
/*              PARAMETER       BYTE           --                                */
                                              DECLARE PARAMETER BYTE;
/****************************************************************************   */
/*BEGIN PROCEDURE                                                                */
/*  IF CODE IN PROCEDURE CONTROL LIST FOR ID NUMBER INDICATES RECORD             */
/*                                                         PROCEDURE CALLED      */
/*    THEN  SAVE ID NUMBER IN NEXT LOCATION OF PROCEDURES CALLED LIST            */
/*  IF CODE IN PROCEDURE CONTROL LIST FOR ID NUMBER INDICATES STOP               */
/*    THEN  CALL: INTERACT WITH OPERATOR (;)                                     */
/*    ELSE  DO                                                                   */
/*            IF SINGLE STEP SET                                                 */
/*              THEN  DO                                                         */
/*                      CALL: DISPLAY ID (ID NUMBER;)                            */
/*                      CALL: WAIT FOR CONTINUE COMMAND (;)                      */
/*                    END                                                        */
/*          END                                                                  */
/*  IF CODE IN PROCEDURE CONTROL LIST FOR ID NUMBER INDICATES SKIP               */
/*    THEN DO                                                                    */
                                        THEN  DO;
/*            GET PARAMETER FOR ID NUMBER FROM PARAMETER LIST                    */
                                              PARAMETER = PARAMETER$LIST (ID$NUMBER);
/*            ADJUST STACK TO SKIP CALLING PROCEDURE                             */
                                              STACKPTR = STACKPTR + 2;
/*            RETURN                                                             */
                                              RETURN PARAMETER;
/*          END                                                                  */
                                              END;
/*  RETURN                                                                       */
/*END PROCEDURE                                                                  */
                                        END COMMON$STUB$RETURNING$BYTE;
```

Figure 7-12(a). Partially converted common stub procedure for a byte output parameter in PL/M.

A POP operation is not available in PL/M. But provision is made for manipulating the stack pointer directly. Thus, the PL/M operation

```
STACKPTR = STACKPTR + 2;
```

adjusts the stack pointer so that the second item in the stack becomes the top item and the effect of a POP instruction is achieved. We use the design language operation ADJUST STACK TO SKIP CALLING PROCEDURE for this purpose. Note

```
/*PROCEDURE:  COMMON STUB RETURNING ADDRESS (ID NUMBER;PARAMETER)              */
                                   COMMON$STUB$RETURNING$ADDRESS: PROCEDURE (ID$NUMBER) ADDRESS PUBLIC;
/**************************************************************************   */
/*  DESIGNED BY: MDF                    16-OCT-80                               */
/*  MODULE: COMMON STUB                                                         */
/*                                                                              */
/*  INPUT PARAMETER:                                                            */
/*                  NAME         TYPE          SIZE                             */
/*                  ----         ----          ----                             */
/*                  ID NUMBER    BYTE           --                              */
                                          DECLARE ID$NUMBER BYTE;
/*                                                                              */
/*  OUTPUT PARAMETER:                                                           */
/*                  NAME         TYPE          SIZE                             */
/*                  ----         ----          ----                             */
/*                  PARAMETER    ADDRESS        --                              */
                                          DECLARE PARAMETER ADDRESS;
/**************************************************************************   */
/*BEGIN PROCEDURE                                                               */
/*  IF CODE IN PROCEDURE CONTROL LIST FOR ID NUMBER INDICATES RECORD            */
/*                                                        PROCEDURE CALLED      */
/*    THEN  SAVE ID NUMBER IN NEXT LOCATION OF PROCEDURES CALLED LIST           */
/*  IF CODE IN PROCEDURE CONTROL LIST FOR ID NUMBER INDICATES STOP              */
/*    THEN  CALL: INTERACT WITH OPERATOR (;)                                    */
/*    ELSE  DO                                                                  */
/*            IF SINGLE STEP SET                                                */
/*              THEN  DO                                                        */
/*                      CALL: DISPLAY ID (ID NUMBER;)                           */
/*                      CALL: WAIT FOR CONTINUE COMMAND (;)                     */
/*                    END                                                       */
/*          END                                                                 */
/*  IF CODE IN PROCEDURE CONTROL LIST FOR ID NUMBER INDICATES SKIP              */
/*    THEN  DO                                                                  */
                                      THEN  DO;
/*            GET PARAMETER FOR ID NUMBER FROM PARAMETER LIST                   */
                                          PARAMETER = PARAMETER$LIST (ID$NUMBER);
/*            ADJUST STACK TO SKIP CALLING PROCEDURE                            */
                                          STACKPTR = STACKPTR + 2;
/*            RETURN                                                            */
                                          RETURN PARAMETER;
/*          END                                                                 */
                                        END;
/*  RETURN                                                                      */
/*END PROCEDURE                                                                 */
                                   END COMMON$STUB$RETURNING$ADDRESS;
```

Figure 7-12(b). Partially converted common stub procedure for an address output parameter in PL/M.

that the memory in the Intel 8085 which is used for the stack is arranged so that the first item pushed into the stack is stored in the two highest addressed bytes of the memory area reserved for the stack. The stack pointer must then be decremented by two for each PUSH (or equivalent) operation or incremented by two for each POP (or equivalent) operation. As noted earlier, the stack pointer is manipulated automatically in PL/M. Except for initializing the stack pointer and for implementing the skip function in the COMMON STUB procedure, we do not recommend that the stack pointer be manipulated directly by the applications software. Otherwise, it is possible for malfunctions to occur which are difficult to detect.

This completes our description of how the common stub is used during integration. Let us now consider other tools that can be used during integration as well as tools for automating the construction of software and for automating the management functions needed during the system design cycle.

OTHER INTEGRATION TOOLS

During integration, it is often desirable to be able to examine the current value that has been computed for a parameter. Since the *monitor* can provide this capability, we provided a way to call the monitor in the COMMON STUB procedure. The monitor is a software module which is installed in the microcomputer development system and which can also be installed in the system under development. The latter may be in the form of a removable module so that it is available only during integration and for later trouble-shooting. In addition to providing the ability to examine information in the memory, the monitor provides a method for the operator to communicate with the microcomputer at a lower level than that provided by the operating system in a microcomputer development system. Monitor commands available for use by the operator include the following:

- Display the contents of one or more memory locations or registers or read an input port. The display may be in hexadecimal, in decimal, or in any of several number systems that can be selected by the operator.
- Change the contents of a memory location or a register from its current value to a specified value or send the specified value to an output port.
- Execute the software in the memory starting with the instruction stored in a specified location.

Thus, the monitor provides communication with the microcomputer system at the machine language level. The reader should note, however, that to start execution from any instruction other than the first instruction in the EXECUTIVE procedure or the common stub instruction where execution was stopped is risky because parameter values may be undefined and the stack may contain incorrect or extraneous pointers.

As described, the monitor provides communication between the operator and the system at a low level. In order to use the monitor to examine the value of a parameter, such as KEYSWITCH, the address of its memory location must be known by the operator. An address for a parameter can be obtained from the symbol list or table produced by the locater. In some systems, however, the symbol table can be saved and placed into the memory when the software is loaded for execution. In this case, a monitor-like tool can access the symbol table when the system is stopped during integration. The operator can then directly request that the value of KEYSWITCH be displayed without knowing its memory location. A tool with this monitor-like capability is the *in-circuit emulator*. The in-circuit emulator also provides other functions which are useful during system integration and which are described in Chapter 10. We defer the description of another integration tool called the *microcomputer analyzer* until Chapter 9.

PROJECT MANAGEMENT

We have seen that it is important to plan each integration phase carefully before starting to check out a system. It is equally important to estimate when each step of the system design cycle will be completed. These estimates provide us with a schedule that should include completion dates for each of the following milestones:

- The completion of the documentation for the user requirements and the functional specification for the system and each subsystem.
- The acceptance of the user requirements and the functional specification by the customer.
- The completion of the preliminary system design.
- The completion of the modularization of the system.
- The completion of the software design for each procedure and module.
- The conversion of the design into a programming language and the elimination of all syntax errors.
- The completion of each integration phase.
- The verification of the performance of the system against the user requirements and the functional specification. This latter step may include formal acceptance testing if such testing is required by the customer.

In this section we describe how to prepare a project schedule. We also discuss how to track the steps in the system design cycle to ensure that the project is completed on schedule.

Estimating a schedule in advance of a project is difficult if an elaborate software system is involved. However, by using the systematic methods and tools we have described it is possible to provide a realistic schedule once the system is modularized and broken into procedures. Since the procedures are limited in complexity, the size and scope of each can be estimated (perhaps even before it is completely designed) and an estimate of the effort necessary to design, build, test, and integrate it into the system can be assigned to it. By using these estimates, subsystems and modules can be assigned to project personnel and a schedule with realistic milestone dates can be developed for the complete project.

By using this schedule, each step in the system design cycle can be monitored to ensure that the system is completed on time. A chart can also be prepared containing the names of the subsystems, modules, and procedures as well as the names of the persons responsible for completing the steps for each procedure and a completion date for each step. Similar information should be provided for each of the integration phases. Then, as each step is completed, it can be be noted on the chart, thereby permitting the project to be tracked. Any problems encountered in meeting a scheduled milestone can be noted and the effect on the remainder of the project can be evaluated. The schedule and cost estimates can also be modified, if necessary.

This method of managing a project containing software is especially useful if the design of a procedure, its conversion into a programming language, and its integration into the system are assigned to different people. Without a systematic project management technique, one of these steps may be overlooked and, as a result, may adversely affect the overall schedule.

FOURTH DOCUMENTATION LEVEL

The fourth documentation level initially consists of the integration plan and the management schedule chart. As integration proceeds, the test results obtained during each integration step can be saved and made a part of the fourth documentation level. In addition, all changes to the schedule and the reasons for these changes should be included in the fourth documentation level. Thus, the fourth level consists predominantly of project management information in contrast to the other levels which consist predominantly of design and implementation information.

We have now completed our discussion of software integration. The related topics of hardware integration and system integration are considered in Chapters 9 and 10, respectively. In the next chapter we describe how to design the hardware for a system containing a microcomputer.

EXERCISES

7-1. Figure 7-1 lists the tools that can be used during the system design cycle. However, all of them may not be available. Since a completely manual approach to system and software development is not cost-effective and all of the tools described are not available on every microcomputer system, list a minimum subset of tools that would be acceptable to you for developing a microcomputer system. Give reasons for each choice.

7-2. Starting with the minimum subset of Exercise 7-1, list each of the remaining tools in the order that you consider them important. For each tool, give the reason why you chose it over the remaining tools.

7-3. Design a software integration plan for the computerized television set (see the exercises in Chapters 2 through 5).

7-4. Design a software integration plan for the computerized traffic light controller (see the exercises in Chapters 2 through 5).

7-5. Design a software integration plan for the computerized sports scoreboard (see the exercises in Chapters 2 through 5).

7-6. Design a software integration plan for the computerized point-of-sale terminal (see the exercises in Chapters 2 through 5).

7-7. Modify the design of the computerized television set so that the common stub module can be used during integration.

7-8. Modify the design of the computerized traffic light controller so that the common stub module can be used during integration.

7-9. Modify the design of the computerized sports scoreboard so that the common stub module can be used during integration.

7-10. Modify the design of the computerized point-of-sale terminal so that the common stub module can be used during integration.

7-11. If your system uses Intel 8085 PL/M, complete the conversion from design language into PL/M for the common stub procedures.

7-12. If your system does not use Intel 8085 PL/M, then:

(a) If necessary, modify the design of the common stub procedures to work with the language and microcomputer you are using.

(b) Convert the design language version of the common stub procedures into the language you are using.

7-13. It is difficult to estimate the time and effort needed to complete each step of an integration plan even when working in a controlled industrial environment. This exercise illustrates the steps needed to do so even though the end result may not be able to be verified in your environment. For one of the software integration plans designed in Exercises 7-3 through 7-6,

(a) Determine the size and scope of each procedure needed to complete each step of the integration plan. (Use any reasonable measure, such as assign a *1* to the smallest, most straightforward procedure and assign *n* to a procedure which is *n* times more complex, that is, it should take *n* times as long to complete.)

(b) Add up these measures for all of the procedures and multiply by your estimate of how much time it should take to complete a procedure of measure 1. This estimate should include design time, walkthrough time, time to convert the design into a programming language, and the time to debug and integrate the procedure into the system.

The latter estimates should be prorated since procedures are rarely debugged and integrated one at a time. Also, be sure to allow time for correcting problems and for some redesign.

Chapter 8

Hardware Design

Before integrated circuit technology came into being, electronic systems were constructed from discrete components such as transistors, capacitors, and resistors. Hardware was designed at the circuit level and system complexity was constrained primarily by the cost of circuit design and packaging.

In the early sixties, integrated circuit elements were introduced and hardware design became more functional. Integrated circuit elements, such as gates, amplifiers, and flip-flops, became available and, for much of the hardware design cycle, the designer concentrated on interconnecting these elements into modules. At this point in time, the cost of hardware design was constrained primarily by the cost of module design. Many systems which were not practical previously now became cost-effective.

During the sixties and into the early seventies, it became possible to build integrated circuits containing a large number of component parts. As a result, a complete *module* containing a variety of gates, flip-flops, and buffers could now be built on a *single* integrated circuit chip. Thus, integrated circuit chip *modules*, such as adders, multiplexers, and shift registers became available for use as building blocks. Hardware design cost was now constrained primarily by the cost of system and subsystem design. Once again, it became cost-effective to build systems which were formerly not practical.

During this time, the increased use of integrated circuit technology caused the cost of a class of computers called *minicomputers* to decrease rapidly. Thus, for some applications, it became feasible to incorporate a computer into an electronic system and a new era of electronic system design had begun. The cost of an electronic system was no longer governed by hardware costs alone. It was necessary to provide software for the minicomputer in order for the system to operate properly. Hardware design, in many cases, was now limited to providing an interface between the minicomputer and its environment. Thus, hardware costs began to decrease in relation to the overall system cost which now included the cost of software development. Once again, a new class of sophisticated applications for electronic systems became cost-effective.

During the seventies, it became possible to build a complete computing system, a microcomputer, onto a small number of integrated circuit chips. With the availability of this microcomputer *component*, the cost of the hardware portion of a system dropped even more significantly with respect to the overall system cost. As in the minicomputer case, much of the hardware design was reduced to providing an interface between the microcomputer and its environment. However, unlike the minicomputer, which is usually purchased as a completely assembled subsystem, the microcomputer may be purchased either as a set of printed circuit boards or as a set of unconnected integrated circuit chips. In this chapter we discuss the hardware design of a microcomputer-based system from two viewpoints: how to design microcomputer system hardware using integrated circuit chips and how to design the interface between the microcomputer and its environment. As in the case of software, no attempt is made to provide a complete treatment of hardware design. We provide instead an introduction to microcomputer system hardware design and refer the reader to one of the references in the bibliography for a more detailed treatment of the subject. We begin by discussing hardware modularization, a topic first introduced in Chapter 3.

HARDWARE MODULARIZATION

A general hardware modularization for a microcomputer-based system was presented in Chapter 3 and is reproduced in Figure 8-1. The figure illustrates the relationship between the microcomputer module and its environment. It does not show those hardware modules which are connected to the signal conditioning modules and are part of the system under development. The relationship of the latter modules to the microcomputer are best illustrated by an example.

In the exercises at the end of Chapter 3 the reader was asked to develop a hardware modularization for a microcomputerized television set. In Figure 8-2 we show part of the modularization for the television set to illustrate how the hardware modules interact with the signal conditioning modules. The principles for modularizing a hardware system are similar to the principles presented for the modulariza-

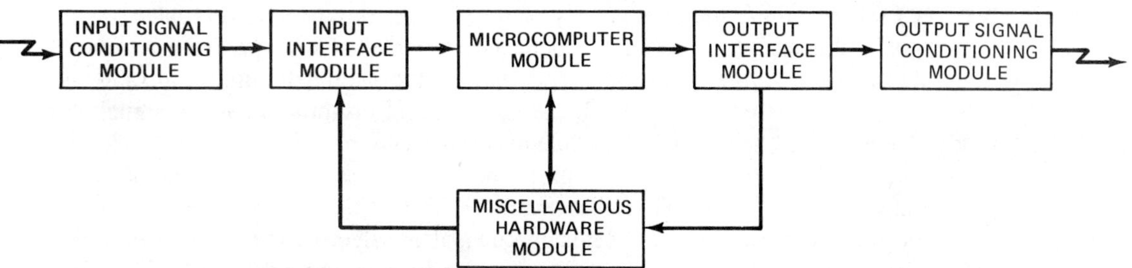

Figure 8-1. General hardware modularization for a microcomputer-based system.

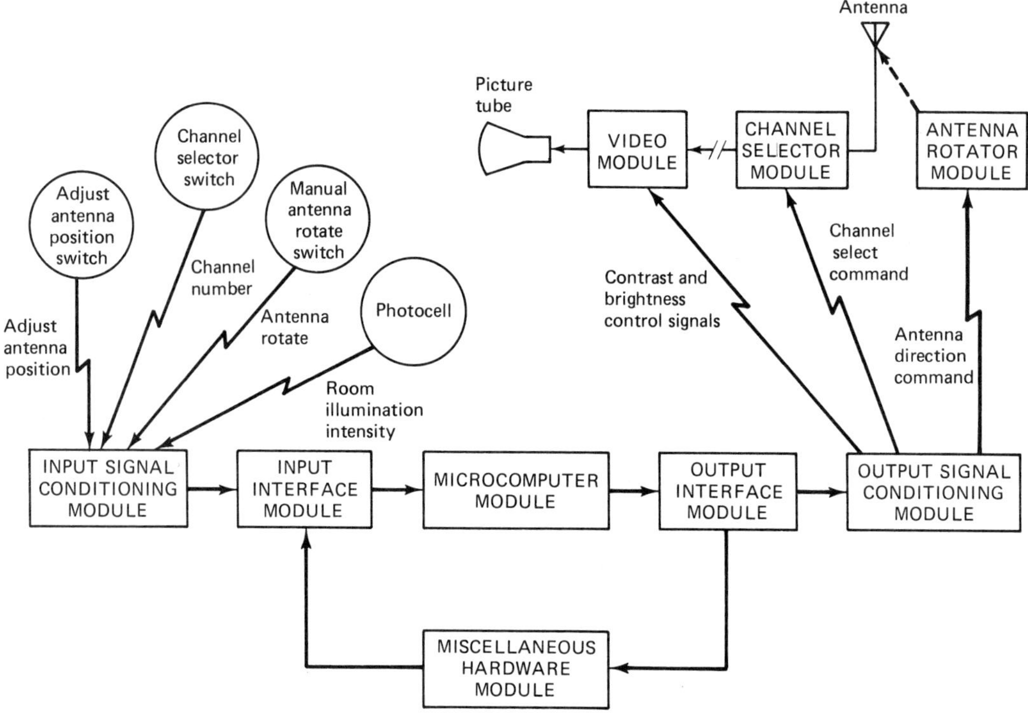

Figure 8-2. Partial hardware modularization for a microcomputerized TV set.

tion of a software system; that is, all of the functions provided by a module should be related.

For the television set example, the contrast and brightness of the picture, the movement of the antenna rotator, and the actuation of the channel selector mechanism in the CHANNEL SELECTOR module are all controlled by the microcomputer. To control these functions, the microcomputer has access to four inputs: the room illumination intensity (from the photocell), the antenna rotate command (from the manual antenna rotate switch), the channel number (from the channel selector switch), and the setting of the adjust antenna position switch. The microcomputer either examines these inputs regularly or it responds to interrupts generated as they change; in either case, if a change is detected, suitable software procedures are executed to respond to the changes. In operation, if the photocell output indicates that the room illumination has changed, the contrast and brightness control signals are adjusted and sent to the VIDEO module to compensate for the change. If the channel selector switch is moved to a new position, a suitable channel select command is generated and sent to the CHANNEL SELECTOR module to cause a new channel to be selected. Whenever a new television channel is selected, the antenna rotator is automatically adjusted to the position best suited for viewing the selected channel.

Let us consider how the information needed to adjust the antenna rotator is put into the television set initially.

When the television set is first installed, or when a new television station starts broadcasting, the antenna position is adjusted in the following manner: The adjust antenna position switch is turned on and the antenna position is adjusted by varying the manual antenna rotate switch. Once the optimum position for the antenna is found for the selected channel, the adjust antenna position switch is turned off. The microcomputer then saves the antenna control information for the selected channel in an ANTENNA CONTROL data structure. This process is repeated for each channel that needs to be initialized. The information in the ANTENNA CONTROL data structure is used to adjust the antenna each time the television set is tuned to a new channel.

In a software modularization, the *connectivity* between modules is shown in the procedures using *calls* and input and output parameters, and by the procedure calling tree. In a hardware modularization, it is necessary to show the connectivity between the modules in a diagram such as the one shown in Figure 8-2 for the example. Thus, for a complex system, the diagram showing the complete hardware modularization may be very large. As a result, it is sometimes desirable to divide a hardware design into subsystems in much the same way that the software part of the design is divided into subsystems. Thus, there are many parallels between software design and hardware design, as we have indicated previously.

We now restrict our description of the hardware to the hardware modules that comprise the microcomputer part of the system and its interfaces. As part of this discussion, we consider some low-level software issues that are closely related to hardware/software tradeoffs.

MICROCOMPUTER MODULE

When the microcomputer was first introduced, it was necessary to purchase a set of integrated circuit chips and to connect them together into a microcomputer system. Unfortunately, very little software or test equipment was available at that time to enable the completed microcomputer to be tested, to help design and construct the applications software, or to validate the operation of the completed system. The introduction of the microcomputer development system helped overcome both software and hardware difficulties; the introduction of completely tested modules and microcomputer and logic analyzers helped overcome the hardware difficulties. We examined the use of the microcomputer development system in Chapter 7. The use of microcomputer and logic analyzers is described in Chapter 9. In this chapter we restrict ourselves to examining the integrated circuit chips and modules from which the hardware portion of a microcomputer-based system can be built.

Most microcomputer component manufacturers provide a range of products which vary from integrated circuit chips through fully assembled and tested modules available in the form of printed-circuit boards or completely assembled systems. For developing a breadboard evaluation model of a system or for building low-volume products, the printed-circuit board modules or assembled systems are cost-effective. For building high-volume products, it is often more cost-effective to purchase the integrated circuit chips and assemble and test the modules in-house. This approach is especially cost-effective if a large part of the microcomputer system, such as the input or output interface, is highly customized and you must assemble and test it in-house in either case.

A functional block diagram for the Intel iSBC 80/05 single-board microcomputer module is shown in Figure 8-3. Other printed-circuit boards are available which contain integrated circuit chips to increase the number of available memory locations or the number of available input and output ports, to increase the capability of the interrupt system, or to provide DMA block transfer capability. A complete microcomputer system can thereby be assembled using several interconnected printed-circuit boards, a power supply, and some controls, such as a reset switch. It is straightforward to design the hardware part of a system containing a microcomputer when complete modules, which are available as off-the-shelf assemblies, are used. But let us also consider how to construct microcomputer hardware modules directly from integrated circuit chips to learn what functions are available and how they can be connected together into a system.

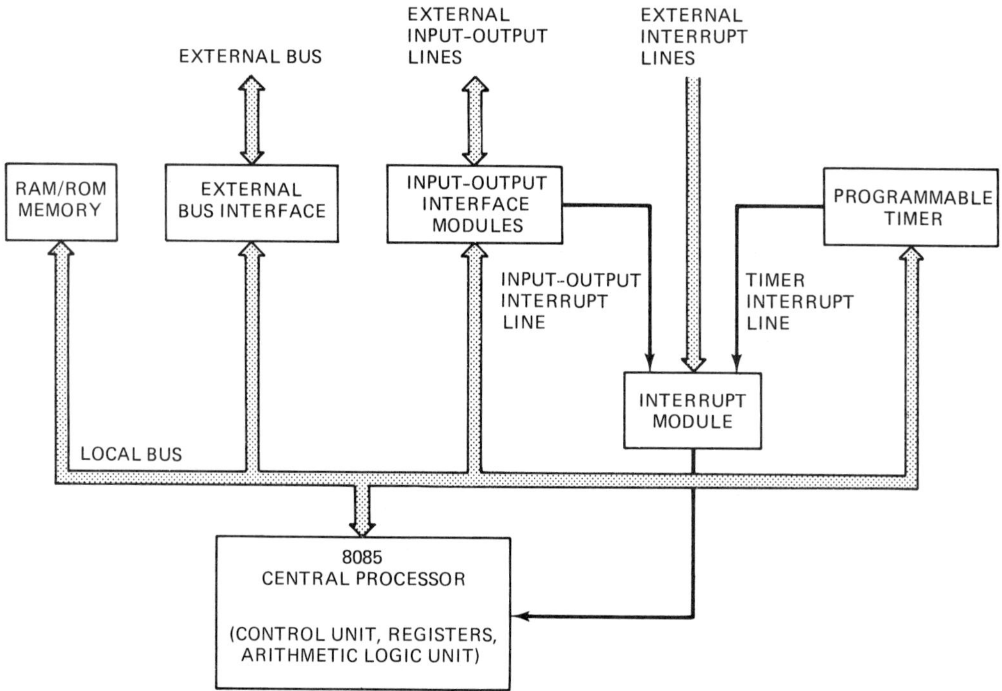

Figure 8-3. Intel iSBC 80/05 single board microcomputer.

MICROCOMPUTER CHIPS

The integrated circuit chips that can be used to build a microcomputer fall broadly into the following three categories: central processor, memory, and input-output. However, there are many chips that contain functions from more than one category. In fact, a single-chip microcomputer, such as the Intel 8048, contains an adequate number of functions from all three categories so that, for some applications, no other chips are needed for the microcomputer hardware part of the system. For many applications, however, several chips from each category are needed in order for the hardware to function as a microcomputer system. Let us consider each of the three categories of integrated circuit chips as well as how the chips are interconnected.

CENTRAL PROCESSOR

The central processor of a microcomputer system consists of a control unit, an arithmetic logic unit, one or more registers, and some limited interface capability. The latter capability provides for connecting memory and input/output integrated circuit chips to the central processor. We described the functional characteristics of the Intel 8085 microcomputer in Chapter 6, and in Figure 8-3 we showed how it is functionally connected to other integrated circuit chips to form a single-board microcomputer system. We now consider the specific signals that must be routed from one integrated circuit chip to another to make the microcomputer work. These signals with their abbreviated names are shown diagrammatically in Figure 8-4. We have grouped them according to functions: Bus Information, Bus Control, Interrupt Control, Serial I/O, Initialize Chip, and Clock Control. Figure 8-5 contains a brief description of each of the Intel 8085 microcomputer signals.

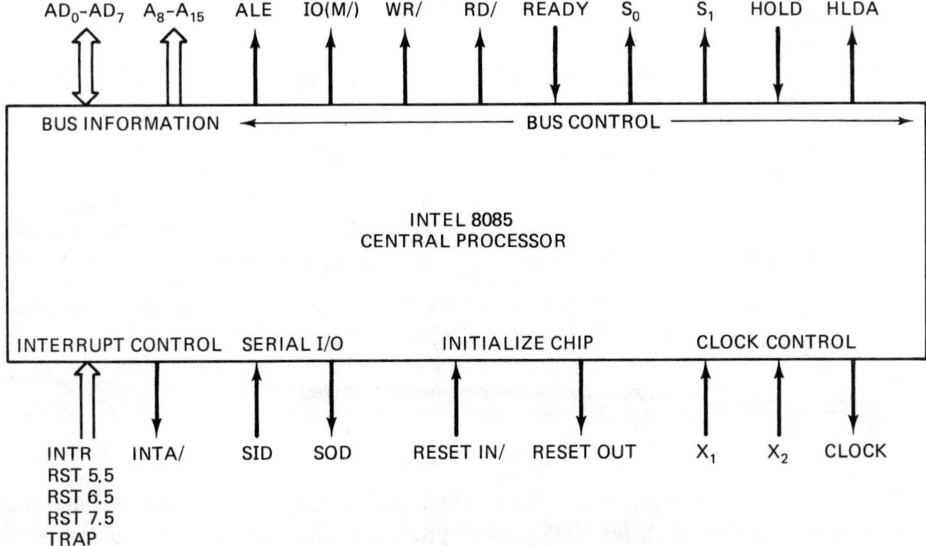

Figure 8-4. Intel 8085 integrated circuit chip signals.

Intel designation	Signal description	
AD_0	Address-Data 0	Least-significant bit of address bus or data bus
⋮	⋮	⋮
AD_7	Address-Data 7	Bit 7 of address bus or most-significant bit of data bus
A_8	Address 8	
⋮	⋮	⋮
A_{15}	Address 15	Most-significant bit of address bus
ALE	Address-data bus contains valid address to be latched by memory or peripheral device (Address latch enable)	
IO(M/)	Address bus contains an I/O port address if IO(M/) is high or a memory address if IO(M/) is low	
WR/	Write data into memory or send data to an I/O port	
RD/	Read data from memory or from an I/O port	
READY	Memory or I/O port is ready to send data to central processor; memory or I/O port has received data from central processor	
S_0, S_1	Central processor status bits	
HOLD	External device is requesting bus	
HLDA	Bus is relinquished to external device by central processor	
INTR RST 5.5 RST 6.5 RST 7.5 TRAP	Interrupt control signals described in Chapter 6	
INTA/	Central processor has acknowledged request on INTR interrupt signal	
SID	Serial input data (used with RIM instruction)	
SOD	Serial output data (used with SIM instruction)	
RESET IN/	Resets address of next instruction to zero (equivalent to JMP 0). Also resets the bus and interrupt control systems and the central processor registers.	
RESET OUT	Turned on when the central processor is being reset.	
X_1, X_2	Connection for control components for central processor internal clock generator or input for external clock generator signal.	
CLOCK	Central processor internal clock generator output from which other integrated circuit chip clock signals may be derived.	

Figure 8-5. The Intel 8085 central processor signals.

Figure 8-6 illustrates how integrated circuit memory and peripheral chips are connected to the Intel 8085 central processor chip. The figure illustrates only those bus signals needed when a *simple* microcomputer is built. Since the bus provides

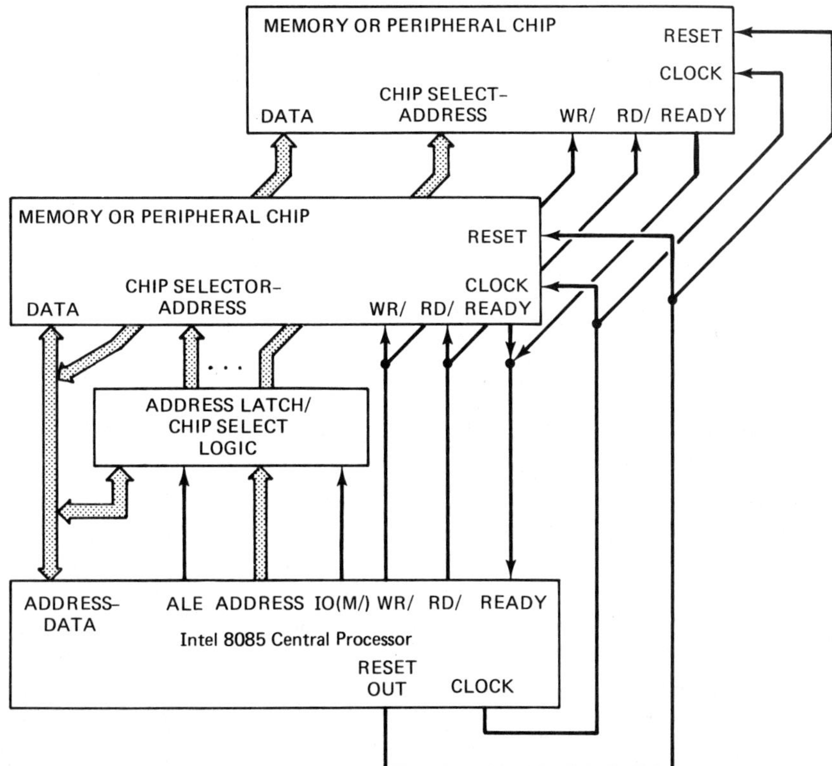

Figure 8-6. Connecting memory and peripheral chips to the Intel 8085 central processor.

the primary interface between the components of the microcomputer, let us use it as the starting point in our description of the Intel 8085 hardware. For uniformity in our description of the hardware, we use the convention that a signal is either *on* or *off* to represent that it is *active* or *inactive*, respectively. For an *active high* signal which is represented by a name without a slash after it, *on* is equivalent to the high or logical ONE state and *off* to the low or logical ZERO state. For an *active low* signal which is represented by a name with a slash after it, *on* is equivalent to the low or logical ZERO state and *off* to the high or logical ONE state.

In Chapter 6 we described the Intel 8085 data and address buses as if they were separate buses. Although they are functionally separate, the eight least-significant address bus lines are physically shared and thereby used as the data bus lines as well. The physical sharing of bus lines is done to restrict the number of connections between the Intel 8085 central processor chip and its environment since only forty pins are available for that purpose. In operation, a 16-bit address is placed on the address bus (AD_0 through AD_7 and A_8 through A_{15}) and the ALE (Address latch enable) signal is turned on. The ADDRESS LATCH/CHIP SELECT LOGIC sends the least-significant eight bits of the address (AD_0 through AD_7) to an Intel 8212 latch chip, as illustrated in Figure 8-7. The latch chip *latches* or saves this information until new information is sent at a later time. If the data in the memory location whose address was just provided is to be read into the central processor, the RD/ signal is turned on. The memory chip containing the addressed memory location then places the data from the addressed memory location onto the data bus (AD_0 through AD_7) to be copied into the central processor. Figure 8-8 shows the time relationships between these operations for the execution of the assembly language instruction LDA VALUE. Recall from Chapter 6 that, during the execution of this instruction, the data stored in the memory location whose address is represented symbolically by VALUE is moved into the ACCUMULATOR REGISTER. Note that the most-significant part of the address remains on the A_8 through A_{15} portion of the address bus during the time that the RD/ signal is on and so does not have to be saved in a latch. The decoder in the ADDRESS LATCH/CHIP SELECT LOGIC provides a suitable chip select signal for each memory chip. The chip select signals ensure that each memory chip responds only when it is correctly addressed. Since many addresses are contained on a single memory chip, the decoder maps all of the addresses assigned to a particular chip onto the chip select signal for that chip. Note that the IO(M/) signal must be low for a memory chip to be selected.

If data is to be moved from the central processor and stored into a memory location, the WR/ signal is turned on in place of the RD/ signal. The data is then placed on the data bus by the central processor and copied into the addressed memory location.

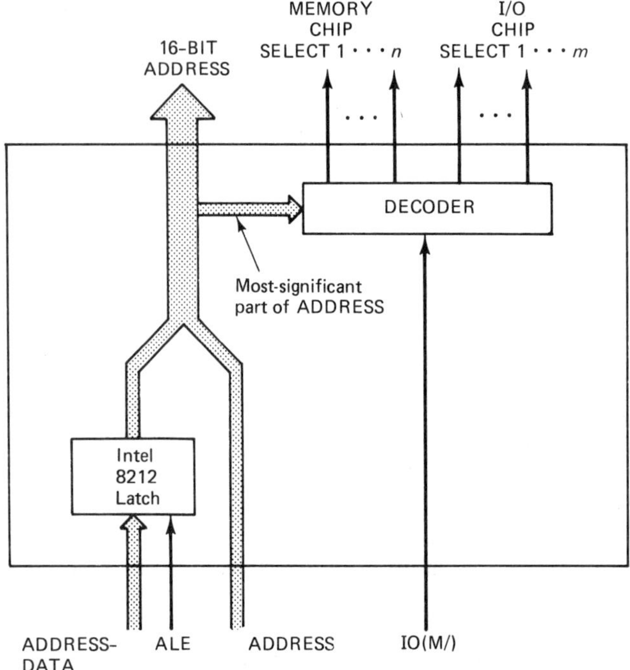

Figure 8-7. ADDRESS LATCH/CHIP SELECT logic.

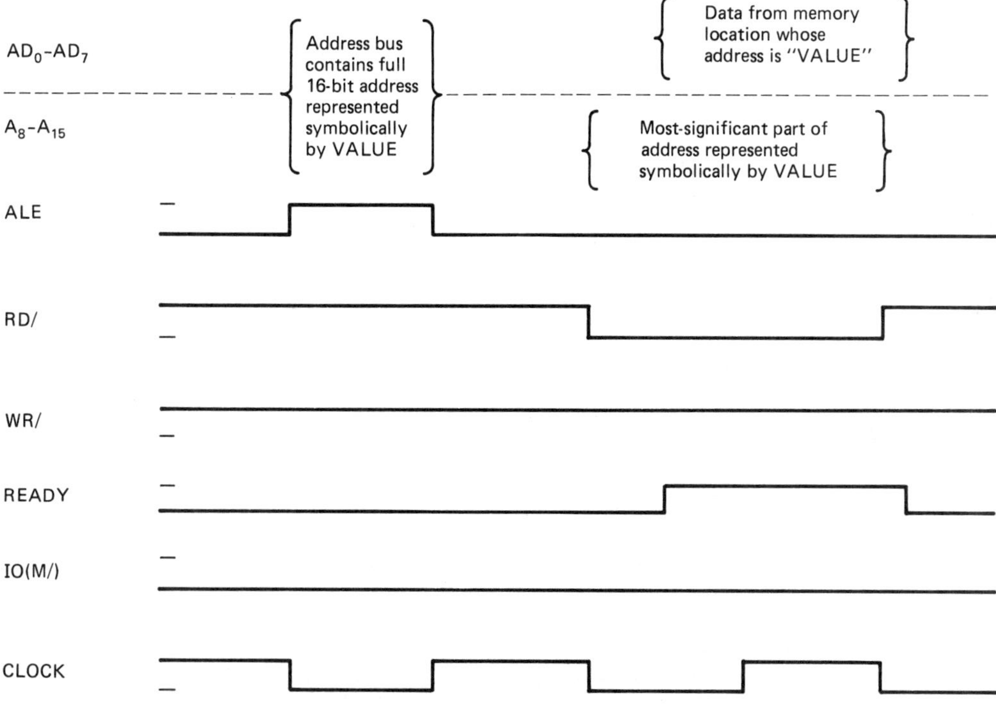

Figure 8-8. Time relationships between the bus operations during the execution of the instruction LDA VALUE.

If data is to be sent to or received from an I/O port rather than a memory location, the IO(M/) signal is made high during the operation, as shown in Figure 8-9 for the OUT 1 instruction. Note that an input or output port address is an 8-bit number instead of a 16-bit number. Thus, for consistency, it is placed on both parts of the address bus during the time that the ALE signal is on. However, during the time that the RD/ or WR/ signal is on, the address remains on the A_8 through A_{15} part of the address bus while the data is placed on the data bus. The decoder uses the 8-bit port address along with the state of the IO(M/) signal to generate a suitable chip select signal for each peripheral chip. Note that more than one port address can be assigned to a single peripheral chip; the decoder maps all of the port addresses assigned to a particular chip onto the chip select signal(s) for that chip.

The READY signal is used to make the central processor wait until the memory or an input or output port has completed placing data onto or removing data from the bus. It ensures that synchronization is maintained if a memory chip, for example, cannot operate sufficiently rapidly to keep up with the central processor. It permits the use of slow-speed memory or peripheral chips for applications where a lower speed of operation is acceptable or higher speed components are not available. READY also allows for the synchronization required when communicating between the Intel 8085 bus and the system bus which we discuss in a later section.

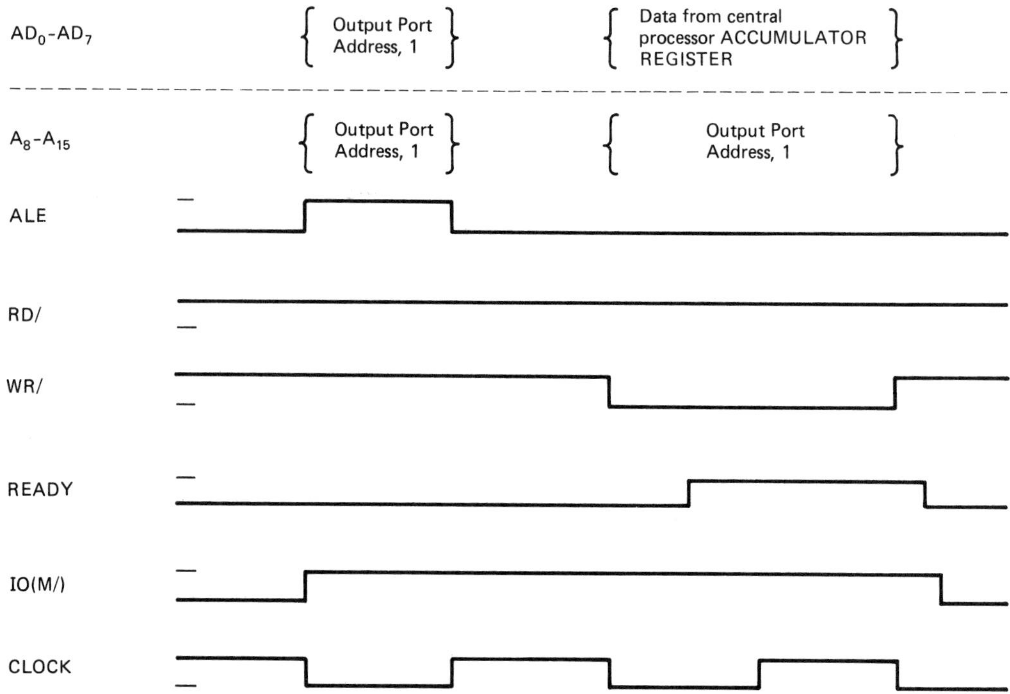

Figure 8-9. Time relationships between the bus operations during the execution of the instruction OUT 1.

The other bus signals are S_0 and S_1, HOLD and HLDA. S_0 and S_1 are status bits which indicate the status of the central processor. The four states of the central processor represented by the status bits are:

	S_1	S_0
HALT	0	0
WRITE	0	1
READ	1	0
FETCH	1	1

The HALT state indicates that the central processor is not using the bus. The WRITE state corresponds to *write to peripheral device*, as in the example for OUT 1 shown in Figure 8-9, and to *write to memory*. The READ state corresponds to *read from peripheral device*, as in the example for LDA VALUE, shown in Figure 8-8, and to *read from memory*. The FETCH state is similar to the READ state illustrated in Figure 8-8 except that the address supplied by the central processor is the address of a memory location that contains an instruction byte instead of a data byte. When a FETCH state is completed, the instruction byte received from the memory through the data bus is stored in the CONTROL UNIT part of the central processor, as described in Chapter 6. Depending on the instruction, up to three FETCH states may occur in sequence without an intervening READ or WRITE state. Similarly, two READ or two WRITE states may occur in an unbroken sequence if 16-bit data is being manipulated.

The HOLD signal is used when an external device must obtain control of the bus in order to communicate with the memory or with an input or output port. The external device turns HOLD on to request that the central processor stop using the bus. When the central processor completes its current operation, it stops using the bus and indicates that the bus is available by turning on the HLDA signal. The central processor then continues to operate for as long as it can without the use of the bus. It must then wait until the HOLD signal is turned off by the external device before it can again use the bus. After HOLD is turned off, the central processor turns off HLDA and proceeds to use the bus in the normal manner.

We have now completed our description of the Intel 8085 bus and how it operates. Since the operation of the memory and the operation of the input and output interfaces are intimately tied to the operation of the bus, we next consider some of the memory chips and input-output interface chips available for use in a microcomputer system. After we complete our description of these two topics, we will describe the use of the remainder of the central processor signals introduced in Figure 8-5.

MEMORY CHIPS

Thus far we have assumed that every location in the memory is used both for storing information and for retrieving stored information. This mode of operation is necessary for that part of the memory used to manipulate data structures that contain alterable data or parameters or used as a stack. A memory chip used in this manner is called a *read-write memory*. However, for historical reasons, read-write memory chips are called RAM chips using the acronym for *Random Access Memory*. Although *read-write* and *random access* are not synonymous terms, we nevertheless use the acronym RAM to mean read-write memory in order to maintain what has become standard terminology.

Two types of RAM chips are available: the *static* RAM and the *dynamic* RAM. One difference between the two types is that the dynamic RAM may contain more bits per chip than the static RAM. The other difference is that the information stored in the dynamic RAM must be regenerated or *refreshed* periodically. The design of the hardware must therefore provide a periodic refresh signal for this purpose.

The other type of memory is called a *read-only memory*, or ROM. Once information is stored in a ROM chip, either it cannot be altered at all or it can only be altered with substantial effort. Thus, ROM chips are used to store data structures containing invariant data or the instructions comprising the software part of the system. Instructions are normally put into ROM chips only after the software has been integrated and its correct operation verified. Invariant data and instructions do not normally change during system operation; by storing this information in a read-only memory, we need not worry about losing it should a power failure occur or should the central processor fail in a transient manner and erroneously attempt to store data into a memory location that contains such information.

In order to use both RAM and ROM chips in the memory of a system, we must be able to segregate the allocated memory into two parts: the part of the memory which stores instructions and invariant data structures and the part of the memory which stores data structures whose values may change during operation. Most compilers and assemblers, and their associated linkers and locaters, automatically make provision for this purpose. In our discussion of PL/M in Chapter 5 we described the use of the DATA attribute in a data declaration to initialize a PL/M variable, array, or structure. The use of this attribute ensures that the variable, array, or structure is assigned to an invariant part of the memory along with the instructions. ROM chips can then be used to implement this part of the memory. Variables, arrays, and structures that are declared without the DATA attribute as well as that part of the memory that is reserved for the stack are assigned to a part of the memory that is not invariant. RAM chips can then be used to implement the latter part of the memory.

Several types of ROM chips are available. A ROM chip is classified by how information is *programmed* or written into it in the first place and by how difficult it is to change the information once the ROM is progammed. The *mask programmable* ROM is manufactured using customer specified information without regard to whether data or instructions are specified. This ROM cannot be altered once it is manufactured. For high-volume production, the factory programmable ROM is very economical; after an initial set-up charge, the individual ROM chips are mass produced inexpensively.

Another type of ROM chip is the *fusible-link* ROM which can be programmed by the user. Once programmed, this ROM cannot be changed. A device called a *ROM programmer* is available for use with microcomputer development systems and allows the user to program fusible-link ROM chips. Thus, there is a manpower and time cost associated with programming each fusible-link ROM chip which makes it more expensive to use than the mask programmable ROM. The fusible-link ROM is nevertheless cost-effective for low-volume products. There is no initial set-up charge as in the case of the mask programmable ROM.

The third type of ROM is the *erasable-programmable* ROM, or EPROM. It can be programmed by the user in the same way that the fusible-link ROM is programmed. In fact, many ROM programmers can be used for both fusible-link ROM and EPROM chips. However, the information stored in an EPROM can be deleted or erased and the unit reprogrammed. Most types of EPROM chips are erased by illuminating them with ultraviolet light, a process which takes about ten minutes. The advantage of the EPROM over the fusible-link ROM is that if an error is discovered during system integration, it is not necessary to discard the EPROM, as would be the case if a fusible-link ROM were used. The EPROM can be erased and reprogrammed. The disadvantage of the EPROM is that it is not as reliable as the fusible-link ROM. It is possible for the programmed information in an EPROM to change with time, especially if the unit is not protected from light and radiation.

Note that the fusible-link ROM and the EPROM are often referred to as programmable ROMs or PROMs.

The fourth type of ROM is the *electrically-alterable* ROM, or EAROM. The EAROM is like a RAM since the information it contains can be changed during operation although much more slowly than with a RAM. However, information is not lost when power is turned off and, in that respect, the EAROM acts like a ROM.

This completes our description of the different types of memory chips available to the system designer. We next examine the types of chips available for use as input and output interfaces.

PERIPHERAL INTERFACE CHIPS

In the next sections we are going to describe some of the common peripheral interface chips used with the Intel 8085 microcomputer chip. Similar interface chips are available for use in other microcomputer systems and the latter chips can be connected to and used with the Intel 8085. In a similar manner, chips designed primarily for the Intel 8085 can also be used with other microcomputers. We describe a general-purpose parallel peripheral interface chip, a general-purpose communications interface chip, and a DMA block transfer controller chip.

PARALLEL PERIPHERAL INTERFACE CHIP

The Intel 8255 general-purpose parallel peripheral interface chip is a highly flexible device that can be *programmed* to operate in a variety of different modes. It is illustrated in Figure 8-10. It has three 8-bit ports that can be used for either input or out-

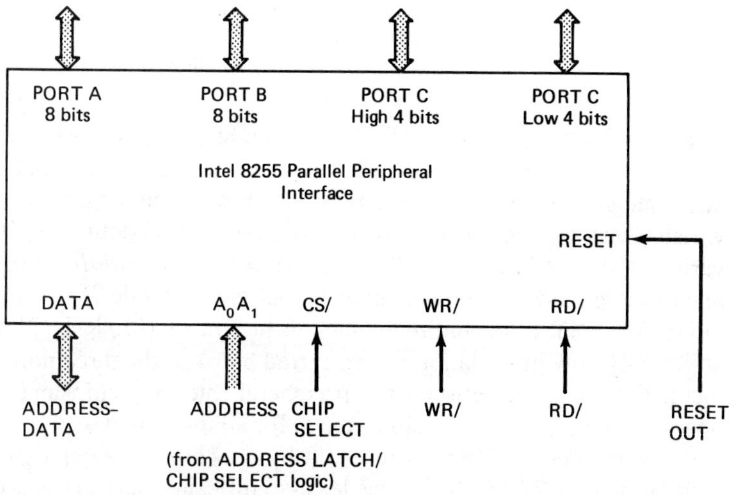

Figure 8-10. Intel 8255 general-purpose parallel peripheral interface chip.

put. Port C is further divided into two 4-bit ports that can be used either as input-output ports or for other purposes, as we shall see. The peripheral interface chip is connected to the Intel 8085 bus using the signals shown in Figure 8-10. Two address lines called A_1 and A_0 are needed in addition to the chip select signal obtained from the chip select logic. Let us examine how these three signals along with the RD/ and WR/ signals control the operation of the Intel 8255.

When the chip select signal, CS/, is off, the chip ignores the information on the other control lines. However, when CS/ is turned on, then, if RD/ is on and WR/ is off, it interprets the request from the central processor as an input operation. A byte is transferred to the data bus from port A, B, or C, depending on the logical states of the A_1 and A_0 signals, as shown below:

A_1	A_0	
0	0	Port A
0	1	Port B
1	0	Port C

As we shall see, all of these operations are not valid all of the time and they depend on how the chip is initialized. But when CS/ is on, if RD/ is off and WR/ is on, then the request from the central processor is interpreted as an output operation. The byte placed on the data bus by the central processor is either sent to port A, B, or C or is interpreted as *control information* by the chip, depending on the logical states of A_1 and A_0, as shown below:

A_1	A_0	
0	0	Port A
0	1	Port B
1	0	Port C
1	1	Control Information

Again, as for the input case, all of these operations are not valid all of the time.

The control information is used either to output a single data bit through port C or to change the mode of operation of the chip. In the former case, a single two-state variable may be controlled (turn a light on or off) without affecting any of the other variables. In the latter case, the Intel 8255 may be *initialized* so that it operates in one of three modes: the basic input-output mode (Mode 0), the strobed input-output mode (Mode 1), or the bidirectional interface mode (Mode 2). Note that these modes affect only how information is transferred between the three ports and their environment; the interface between the peripheral interface chip and the Intel 8085 bus operates in the manner described above for all three modes.

When a control byte is received by the chip, its most-significant bit is examined; if it is a ZERO, then the least-significant four bits are used for single-bit output, as illustrated in Figure 8-11. Three of these bits are used as an *address* to

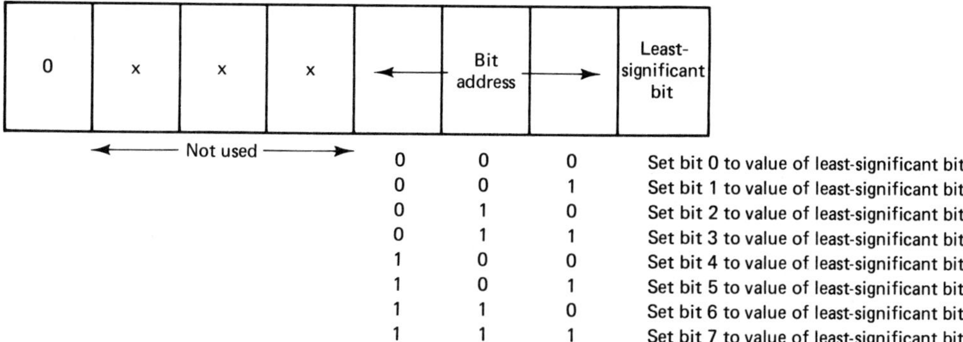

Figure 8-11. Control information used for single bit output.

determine which of the eight bits in port C is to be set; the last of these bits determines how to set the addressed bit. Thus, control byte 0XXX 0111 causes bit 3 of port C to be set to ONE whereas 0XXX 1010 causes bit 5 of port C to be set to ZERO. We use the letter X to designate a bit whose state is ignored when the control byte is interpreted. Once again, let us point out that all of these operations are not valid all of the time.

If the most-significant bit of the control byte is a ONE, the remaining bits are used to select the mode of operation of the chip, as illustrated in Figure 8-12. We illustrate mode selection with several examples and describe how the chip operates in these modes. The control byte 1001 0010 causes both port A and port B to be placed into the basic input mode and port C to be placed into the basic output mode. In the basic mode, a port can perform either input or output but not both. In this mode, outputs are *latched*, that is, the bits are held in their current state until they are changed by another output instruction. Inputs are not latched in the basic mode; the data transmitted to the central processor is determined by the state of the input lines when the input instruction is executed. Thus, for the above example, the only valid central processor instructions are the input instructions whose *address* references port A ($A_1 = 0$, $A_0 = 0$) or port B ($A_1 = 0$, $A_0 = 1$) and the output instruction whose address references port C ($A_1 = 1$, $A_0 = 0$). Note that it is possible in the

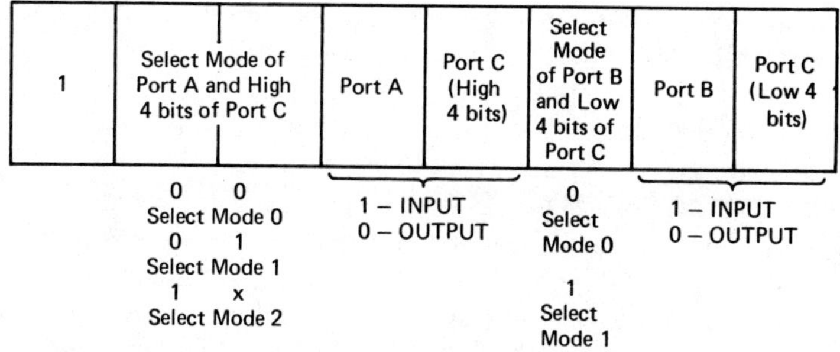

Figure 8-12. Control information used for mode selection.

basic mode to place four bits of port C into the input mode while the other four bits of port C are placed into the output mode. This is done, for example, by the control byte `1001 0011`. If port C is configured in this manner, the software designer or programmer must be aware that an output instruction to port C only affects the four bits in the output mode. Similarly, an input instruction which references port C causes only four valid bits to be transmitted to the central processor. The other four bits in the byte received by the central processor must be ignored by the software.

Another example of mode selection is given by the control byte `1011 0100`. This causes port A to be placed into the strobed input mode and port B to be placed into the strobed output mode. In the strobed mode, a port can also perform either input or output but not both. The bits of port C, however, are used as control signals to synchronize the operation of ports A and B with their environment; these signals are called *strobe* or *handshaking* signals. Both inputs and outputs are *latched* in this mode. Briefly, handshaking for the strobed input mode operates in the following manner. When an input device connected to a strobed input port is ready to send data to the Intel 8255 chip, it turns on the port C line which is designated as the *strobe input* signal for the input port. The chip responds by saving the input data in a buffer register (latching the data) and turning on the port C line designated as the *input buffer full* signal for the input port. A third port C line can be used as an *interrupt request* signal to the central processor to indicate that the input buffer contains valid data. The interrupt request signal can be *masked* by using a designated single-bit output command to port C which sets or resets the interrupt mask bit when the chip is operating in the strobed mode.

Handshaking for the strobed output mode operates as follows. When a byte of output data is sent to the Intel 8255 from the central processor, it is latched into an output buffer register. The chip then turns on the port C line which is designated as the *output buffer full* signal for the output port. When the output device connected to the strobed output port has accepted the data from the output port, it turns on the port C line designated as the *acknowledge* signal for the output port. A third port C line can be used as an *interrupt request* signal to the central processor to indicate that the output port is ready to accept new data. As before, the interrupt request signal can be masked to inhibit interrupt requests.

Ports A and B do not have to operate in the same mode simultaneously. For example, the control byte `1011 0000` puts port A into the strobed input mode and port B into the basic output mode.

The third mode is the bidirectional interface mode. It applies only to port A which then operates as a strobed fully latched bidirectional bus. An example of a control byte that places port A into the interface mode is given by `11XX X100`. This control byte also places port B into the strobed output mode. Since port A is used in a bidirectional bus mode, five port C lines are needed as control signals, as follows: input strobe, input buffer full, output buffer full, acknowledge, and interrupt request. The operation of port A in the bidirectional interface mode is similar to that described for the strobed mode except that input and output transfers can be interleaved in any sequence.

Finally, in the strobed and bidirectional interface modes, an input instruction can be executed to read *data* from port C. The *data* byte read into the central processor by this instruction contains *status* information which indicates the state of each of the handshaking signals, the interrupt request signals, and the interrupt masks. This completes our description of the Intel 8255 general-purpose parallel peripheral interface chip.

SERIAL COMMUNICATIONS INTERFACE CHIP

The peripheral interface chip described above is a parallel device; for the most part, information is transferred between the chip and a peripheral device eight bits at a time through one of the ports. Many peripheral devices, however, especially those used for communicating data over long distances, operate in a serial manner; information is transferred between these devices one bit at a time. The Intel 8085 can operate in a serial input-output mode in one of two ways: either SIM and RIM instructions can be executed or a communications interface chip such as the Intel 8251 can be used.

The SIM and RIM instructions introduced in Chapter 6 are used primarily for manipulating interrupt mask data. But, as we indicated in Chapter 6, these instructions can also be used for serial communications. The RIM instruction can be used to read a single bit of serial data into the most-significant bit of the ACCUMULATOR REGISTER (along with the interrupt status information). The serial data read by the RIM instruction is obtained from the SID, serial input data, line which is shown in Figure 8-4. Similarly, if the serial output enable bit is set in the ACCUMULATOR REGISTER when a SIM instruction is executed, a single bit of serial data is sent from the ACCUMULATOR REGISTER to the SOD, serial output data, line of the Intel 8085. The interpretation of these ACCUMULATOR REGISTER bits is shown in Figure 8-13. Using this serial input-output capability requires that software procedures be designed to manipulate the RIM and SIM instructions so that the critical bit-by-bit timing requirements of the serial interface are met. If, however, the Intel 8251 communications interface chip is used, information is transferred in parallel between the chip and the central processor; the serial timing requirements are then handled automatically by the communications interface chip.

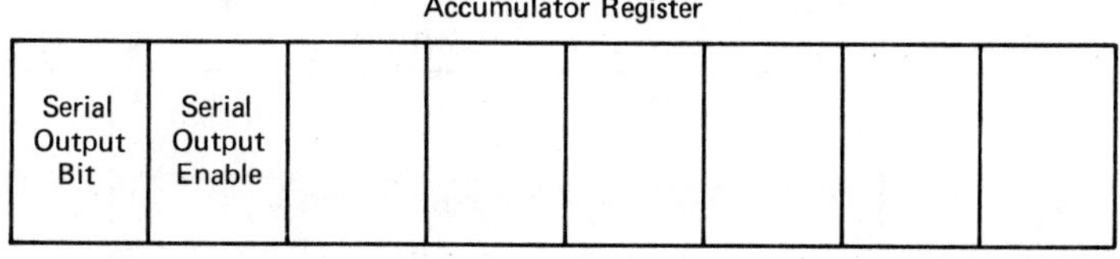

Figure 8-13. Interpretation of serial output bits in ACCUMULATOR REGISTER when SIM instruction is executed.

Because the Intel 8251 chip is often more cost-effective from a hardware/software tradeoff standpoint, we describe how it is used for serial communications rather than how the RIM and SIM instructions are used for that purpose.

Figure 8-14 illustrates the Intel 8251 general-purpose communications interface chip. It has a single set of serial output lines in the TRANSMIT section, a single set of serial input lines in the RECEIVE section, and a set of *modem control* signals which are used to simplify the interface between the communications chip and a *modem*. A *modem* is a device used to connect a digital system to a telephone line to permit digital information to be transmitted over long distances. The Intel 8251 chip is connected to the Intel 8085 bus as indicated in Figure 8-14. Only a single address line, called C(D/) for CONTROL-DATA, and the chip select signal which is obtained from the chip select logic are needed. These signals along with the RD/ and WR/ signals control the operation of the Intel 8251 chip.

As in the case of the peripheral interface chip, when the chip select signal, CS/, is off, the communications interface chip ignores the information on the bus control lines. When CS/ is turned on, if RD/ is on and WR/ is off, the chip interprets the request from the central processor as an input operation; a byte is transferred to the central processor via the data bus. The byte is a data byte that has been received from the RxD serial input if C(D/) is in the data state or low; it is status information if C(D/) is in the control state or high. If, when CS/ is on, RD/ is off and WR/ is on, the request is interpreted as an output operation by the central processor. The byte placed on the data bus by the central processor is treated as data

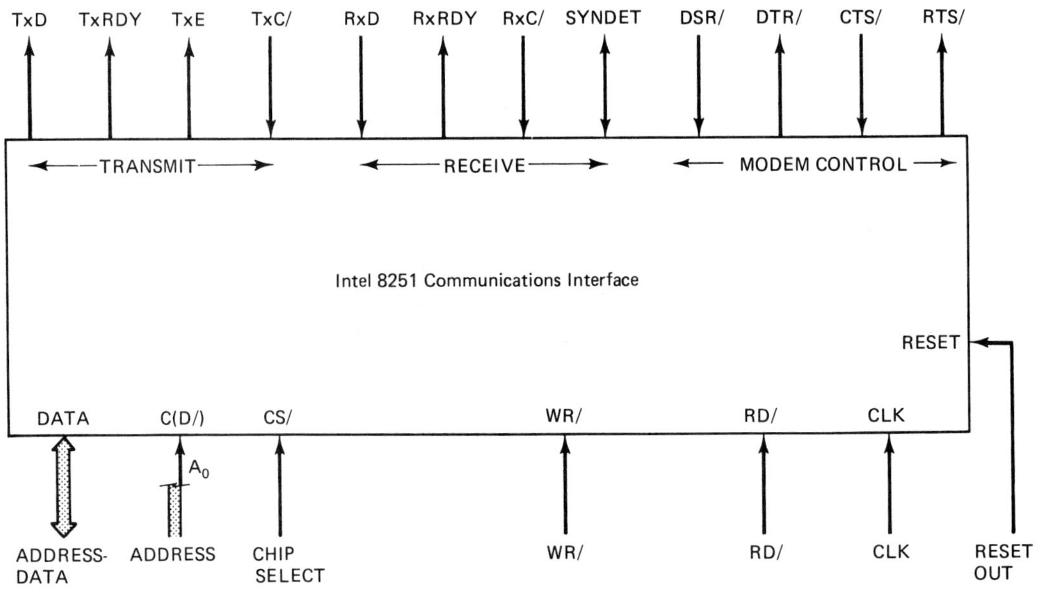

Figure 8-14. Intel 8251 general-purpose communications interface chip.

and sent to the TxD serial output if C(D/) is low or it is treated as control information if C(D/) is high.

The control information sent to the Intel 8251 chip is used for either mode control or for conveying command information to the chip. It must conform to a strict protocol to ensure that the device operates properly. The control byte following the occurrence of a RESET signal *must* contain mode control information to set the device into the desired operating mode. This mode control byte selects either synchronous or asynchronous operation, sets a multiplier factor which relates the TxC/ or RxC/ frequency to the serial information transmission rate or *baud* rate, the number of bits to be sent or received for each data byte, whether to check for even parity, odd parity, or neither, and so forth. If the synchronous mode is selected, then one or two *sync characters* must then be sent to the chip, depending on the specific characteristics selected for the synchronous mode. These sync characters are used to synchronize the chip with its environment since there is no other way to guarantee correct operation in the synchronous mode. Before data can be transferred, it is also necessary to send a control byte containing command information to the chip. The command byte is used to enable or disable the chip for transmitting or receiving serial data, to control the modem outputs, and so forth. After the initial command byte is sent to the chip, either data bytes or additional command bytes can be sent to the chip in any sequence.

When the status port of the Intel 8251 chip is read, the states of various control lines are sent to the central processor. In addition, if any of three types of potential error conditions occur, they are reported to the central processor. These error conditions are parity error, overrun error, and framing error. If parity error detection is selected, the received parity bit is checked against the received data bits and the *parity error flag* is set if an error is detected. If a received character is not read into the central processor before another character is received, the *overrun error flag* is set. Finally, if the chip is operating in the asynchronous mode and a valid stop bit signifying the end of a character is not received for each character, the *framing error flag* is set. Thus, the chip provides significant error detection capability to ensure that the data received is correct and valid.

A complete discussion of the interface between the Intel 8251 communications interface chip and a serial peripheral device or a modem is beyond the scope of this book. Nevertheless, let us briefly describe the signals used for this purpose. The RxC/, *receiver clock*, signal is an externally supplied clock signal whose rate must equal the baud rate of the serial information on the RxD, *receive data*, signal times the multiplier factor selected by the mode byte described earlier. Similarly, the TxC/, *transmitter clock*, signal is an externally supplied clock signal whose rate must equal the desired transmission rate of the serial information being sent on the TxD, *transmit data*, signal times the same multiplier factor. Thus, the transmit baud rate may differ from the receive baud rate although for most applications the two baud rates would be chosen to be equal. When operating in the synchronous mode, the SYNDET, *sync detect*, signal is used either to indicate that a valid sync character has been received during input or to detect that a transmitted sync character has been received by the peripheral device during output. The central processor selects how the SYNDET signal is to be used by setting the *external sync detect* bit in the mode byte to ONE for input or to ZERO for output.

When the chip is used with a modem, the four modem control signals are used with the signals described above. The modem control signals are as follows:

DSR/ - The *data set ready* signal is set by the modem to inform the chip that the telephone equipment connected to the modem is operational.

DTR/ - The *data terminal ready* signal is set by the chip to inform the modem that the microcomputer is operational.

CTS/ - The *clear to send* signal is set by the modem to request the chip to transmit data.

RTS/ - The *request to send* signal is set by the chip to request the modem to transmit data.

The TxRDY, *transmitter ready*, signal indicates that the chip is ready to accept a character from the central processor for output. The TxRDY signal can either be checked by the central processor directly or be used to generate an interrupt request. Similary, the RxRDY, *receiver ready*, signal indicates that a character has been received by the chip and that the chip is waiting to send the character to the central processor. As in the case of the TxRDY signal, the RxRDY signal can be checked directly or it can be used to generate an interrupt request. Finally, the TxE, *transmitter empty*, signal indicates that the chip has no character to transmit. In the synchronous mode, this signal indicates that sync characters are being sent out as *filler* characters. If the same line is used for both transmission and reception of information, that is, the chip is operating in the *half-duplex* mode, the TxE signal can be used to indicate the end of a transmission mode. The central processor can then send a command byte to place the chip into the receive mode.

The third of the peripheral interface chips we describe is the DMA block transfer controller chip.

DMA CONTROLLER CHIP

The Intel 8257 DMA controller chip is a flexible device that provides the necessary capability to perform DMA block transfers of data between memory and peripheral devices. The reader should refer to Figure 6-35 and its related discussion in Chapter 6 to see how a DMA controller operates from a functional viewpoint. Here we describe how a system containing a DMA controller is implemented with the Intel 8257 chip.

Four independent DMA channels are provided on a single Intel 8257 chip. As in the case of the other peripheral chips described above, the Intel 8257 chip can be *programmed* to operate in various modes. During operation, it can be addressed by the central processor as if it were an ordinary peripheral chip; this *slave* mode of operation is used to send commands and address information to the chip and to obtain status information from it. In the *master* mode of operation, the chip controls the operation of the system directly to perform the data transfer. In the latter mode, the chip must first request that the central processor stop using the bus. When this is done, it can command the memory to read (or write) data from (onto) the bus and simultaneously command a peripheral device to write (or read) data onto (from) the bus. Thus, information is transferred between the memory and a peripheral device without the intervention of the central processor. An Intel 8085 microcomputer system containing an Intel 8257 DMA controller chip is illustrated in Figure 8-15. We use this system to describe the differences between a system that contains a DMA controller chip and one that does not.

Since the DMA controller must simultaneously control reading and writing to the memory as well as to a peripheral device, it provides separate signals for this purpose. Thus, the IO(M/), WR/, and RD/ signals are replaced by the MEMW/, *memory write*, and MEMR/, *memory read*, signals for the memory, and by the IOW/, *I/O write*, and IOR/, *I/O read*, signals for the DMA controlled peripheral devices. The CONTROL LINE GENERATOR converts the central processor signals to the latter signals which are then routed to the memory and to the DMA controlled peripheral chips. The operation of the central processor is unchanged as a result of this modification.

The ADDRESS LATCH/CHIP SELECT LOGIC, which was shown in Figure 8-7, must be modified when an Intel 8257 DMA controller is used. The modified ADDRESS LATCH/CHIP SELECT LOGIC is shown in Figure 8-16. Two different address bus configurations are required when using the DMA controller: one for the *slave* mode and one for the *master* mode. When the DMA controller is operating in the slave mode, the most-significant eight bits of the address bus are obtained directly from the central processor A_8 through A_{15} lines. The least-significant eight bits are obtained from the central processor AD_0 through AD_7 lines and latched using the ALE (Address latch enable) control signal. These bits are enabled by a tri-state buffer when the DMA controller AEN (Address enable) signal is *off* since the AEN signal indicates that the DMA controller is operating in the slave mode when it is *off*. When the DMA controller is operating in the master mode, the most-significant eight bits of the address bus are obtained from the DMA controller D_0 through D_7 lines which are multiplexed onto the central processor AD_0 through AD_7 lines. They are latched using the ADSTB control signal and enabled by a tri-state buffer when the DMA controller AEN signal is *on*. The AEN signal indicates that the DMA controller is operating in the master mode when it is *on*. In the latter case, the least-significant eight bits of the address are obtained directly from the DMA controller A_0 through A_7 lines.

Before a DMA block transfer can take place, both the DMA channel and the peripheral device connected to that channel must be initialized. The initialization is performed by using programmed output transfers to send suitable information to the DMA controller chip and to the peripheral device. Figure 8-17 summarizes how the logical states of the A_0 through A_3 address lines are used to determine how the information sent to the chip is used. Since a memory address in the Intel 8085 central

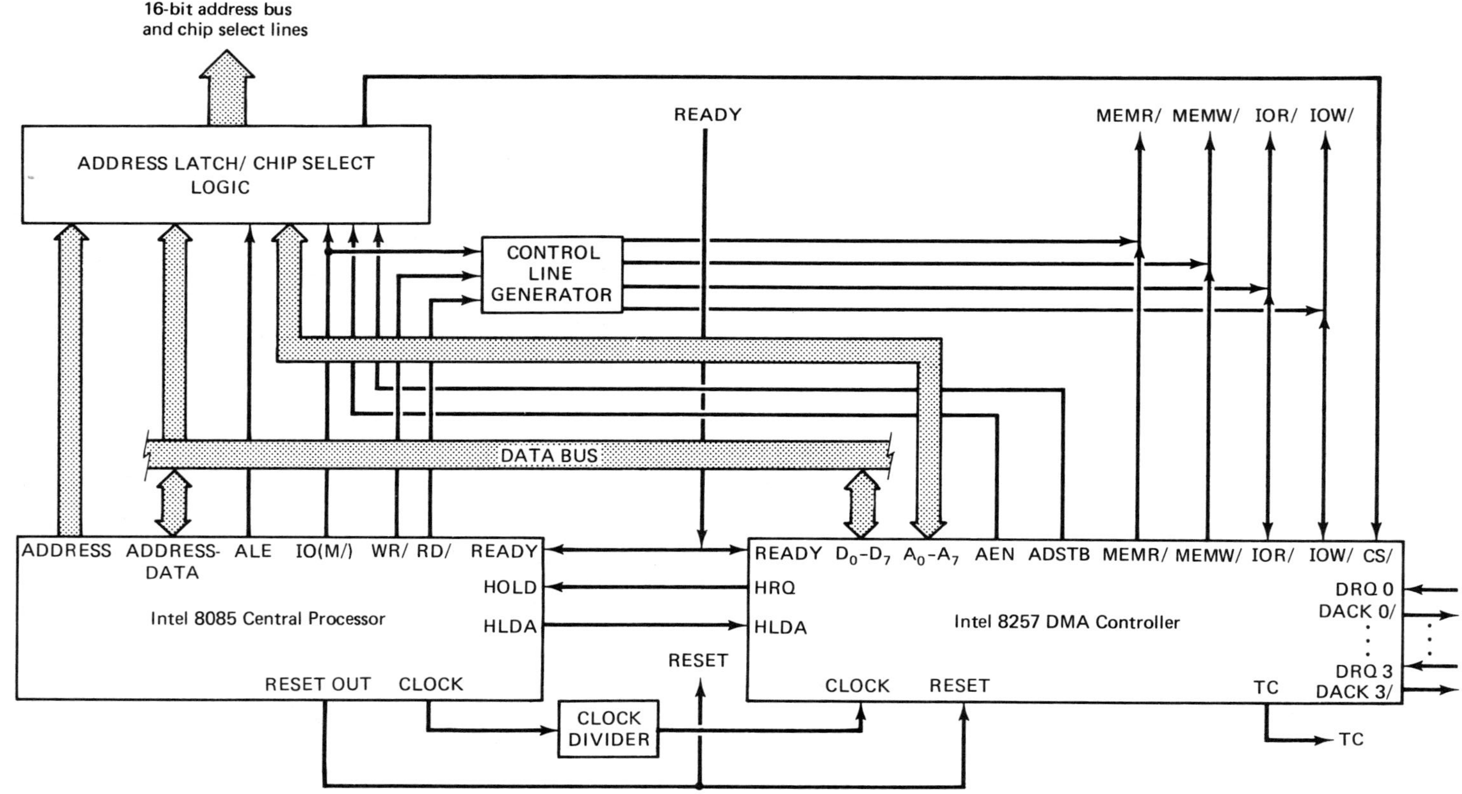

Figure 8-15. An Intel 8085 system which contains an Intel 8257 DMA controller.

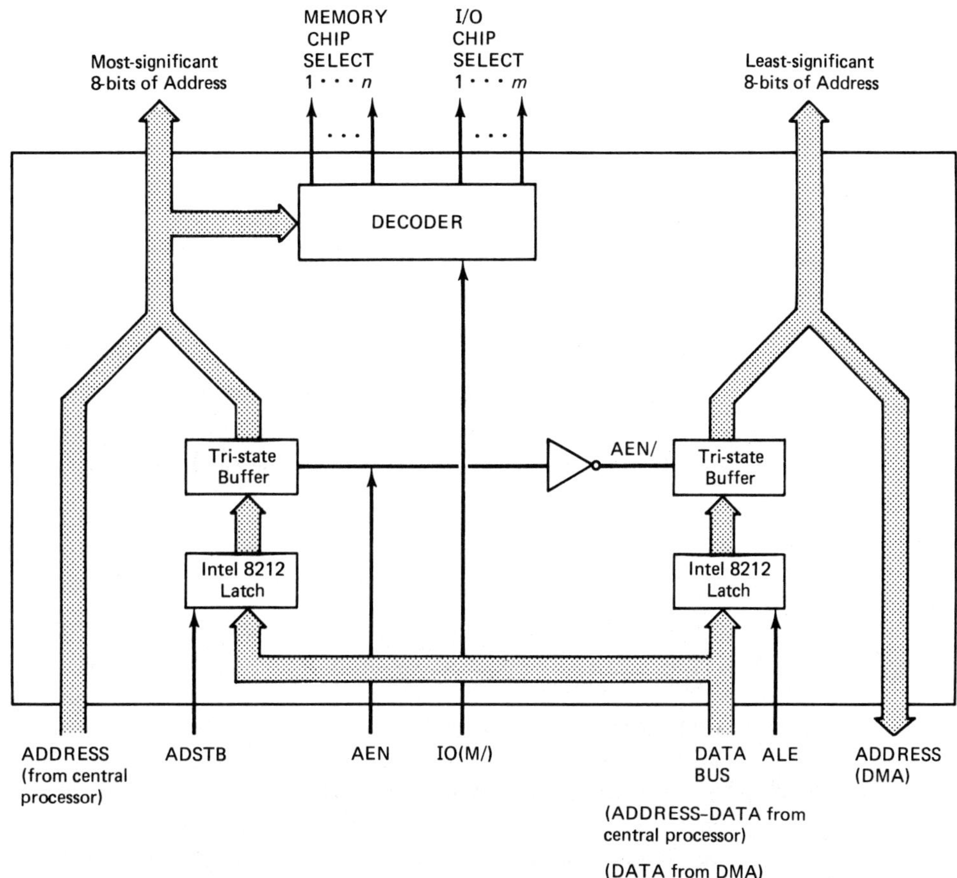

Figure 8-16. ADDRESS LATCH/CHIP SELECT logic for an Intel 8085 system which contains an Intel 8257 DMA controller.

processor is a 16-bit number, two transfers are needed to send a block memory address to the DMA controller chip. However, only one *chip select address* is provided for each initialization item for each channel. Therefore, *both* transfers are sent to the same *chip select address*. The first transfer sends the least-significant byte of the block memory address; the second sends the most-significant byte of the block memory address. To ensure that the chip maintains correct synchronization while the block memory address bytes are being sent, the two bytes should be sent in sequence. Moreover, the interrupt system should be disabled to prevent an intervening input or output transfer from taking place.

The block length/mode information consists of a 14-bit block length number and two mode bits. This information must be sent to the chip using a convention similar to that described for the block memory address information. When received by the chip, the least-significant fourteen bits are interpreted as the number $n - 1$

A_3	A_2	A_1	A_0	
0	0	0	0	Channel 0 block memory address
0	0	0	1	Channel 0 block length/mode
0	0	1	0	Channel 1 block memory address
0	0	1	1	Channel 1 block length/mode
0	1	0	0	Channel 2 block memory address
0	1	0	1	Channel 2 block length/mode
0	1	1	0	Channel 3 block memory address
0	1	1	1	Channel 3 block length/mode
1	0	0	0	{ Set mode (write) Status (read)

Figure 8-17. DMA controller initialization.

where n is the actual number of bytes to be transferred. The two mode bits, which are the most-significant two bits of the sixteen, are interpreted as follows:

0	1	Write
1	0	Read

When the DMA controller chip is placed into the write (or read) mode, an input (or output) block transfer between the memory and a peripheral device will take place.

If a programmed input transfer using one of the eight I/O port *addresses* described in connection with Figure 8-17 is executed by the central processor, data is read from the chip as follows. If the I/O port *address* that was used to initialize the block memory address for a channel is used, the memory address currently in use for the channel is sent to the central processor. If the *address* that was used to initialize the block length/mode information for a channel is used, the block length and mode information currently in use for the channel is sent to the central processor. Each of these input transfers requires that two consecutive input instructions using the same I/O port *address* be executed. As before, suitable precautions should be taken to ensure that no intervening input or output transfers take place.

After the DMA registers are initialized as described above, the operation of the DMA controller is enabled by a programmed output transfer to I/O port *address* 0001, which is the *set mode* operation shown in Figure 8-17. The byte sent to the chip by this operation contains information to enable or disable each of the four channels, or to enable or disable the four operating modes for the DMA controllers, as shown in Figure 8-18.

We now describe how the DMA controller performs a data transfer in the master mode after it has been initialized for a block transfer in the slave mode. Assume that channel 0 (the DMA channels are numbered from 0 to 3) is in the write mode, that is, the peripheral device connected to channel 0 is an input device, that the address of the first byte in the memory block and the block length have been sent to the chip and are stored in its internal registers, and that the channel has been enabled. When a byte is read by the peripheral device and is ready for transmission

Autoload Mode	TC Stop Mode	Extended Write Mode	Rotating Priority Mode	Channel 0	Channel 1	Channel 2	Channel 3

Figure 8-18. Set mode byte for enabling or disabling DMA modes and channels.

to the memory, the peripheral device turns on the DRQ 0, *DMA request 0*, signal. The DMA controller then requests control of the bus by turning on the HRQ, *hold request*, signal. When the central processor completes its current bus operation, it relinquishes control of the bus and turns on the HLDA, *hold acknowledge*, signal. Once the HLDA signal is received, the DMA controller turns on the DACK 0/, *DMA acknowledge 0*, signal which may be used as a chip select signal for the peripheral device controller chip. The DMA controller then sends the memory address to the ADDRESS LATCH/CHIP SELECT LOGIC, which operates as described earlier. To complete the process, the DMA controller turns on both the IOR/ and the MEMW/ signals.

The peripheral device responds to the IOR/ signal by placing a byte on the data bus. The selected memory chip responds by writing the data from the bus into the addressed memory location. When the transfer of the byte is complete, the IOR/ and MEMW/ signals are turned off, and if the block transfer is not complete, the memory address and the block length stored in the internal registers of the chip are incremented and decremented, respectively. The peripheral device then turns off DRQ 0, the DMA controller chip turns off DACK 0/ and HRQ, and the central processor turns off HLDA and again takes control of the bus. Note that if the DRQ 0 signal is not turned off, the DMA controller chip will not relinquish control of the bus and will perform another transfer immediately.

For output using channel 0, the peripheral device turns on the DRQ 0 signal when it is ready to read a byte from the memory. The sequence of events is similar to the input case, except that the IOW/ and MEMR/ signals are turned on to transfer the data from the memory to the peripheral device via the bus.

When the Intel 8257 DMA controller chip is used, an address is *not* needed to select a peripheral device. A peripheral device which turns on its DRQ signal responds automatically to the IOR/ or IOW/ signal from the DMA controller chip when it receives a DACK/ signal; the other peripheral devices connected to the DMA controller chip ignore these signals. Therefore, whenever a non-DMA peripheral device is used in a system containing a DMA controller, provision must be made to prevent the latter devices from being activated erroneously and causing an incorrect transfer to take place. One way to do this is to use the WR/ and RD/ signals for non-DMA devices. Another way is to use the AEN, *address enable*, signal, which is provided by the Intel 8257 chip to disable all non-DMA devices during a DMA controlled transfer.

If the byte being transferred is the last one in the block, then the TC, *terminal count*, signal, shown in Figure 8-16, is turned on. This signal can be used to inform the central processor to reinitialize the DMA channel for another block transfer. The TC signal can either be read by the central processor under the control of the software or it can be used as an interrupt signal.

If the *autoload* mode is enabled (see Figure 8-18), channel 2 can be used for repeated block transfers without requiring that the central processor reinitialize it at the completion of each block transfer. The block memory address, block length, and mode information for the next channel 2 block transfer can be sent to channel 3 while channel 2 is operating. Then, when the current channel 2 block transfer is complete, the channel is reinitialized automatically using the information contained in channel 3. If desired, the TC, *terminal count*, signal, which indicates that a block transfer has been completed, can be used to inform the central processor to reload channel 3 in preparation for another block transfer. The TC signal can either be read by the central processor or be used as an interrupt signal for this purpose. Note that channel 3 should not be used for any other purpose if the autoload mode is enabled.

If the *TC stop* mode is enabled, a channel is automatically disabled whenever a block transfer is completed. An exception occurs when the autoload mode is enabled simultaneously. In the latter case, channel 2 is not disabled at the end of a block transfer. The other channels, however, are unaffected by the autoload mode and are always disabled at the end of a block transfer if the TC stop mode is enabled.

The *extended write* mode can be used with some types of memory and peripheral devices to improve system operation. In this mode, the timing of the IOW/ and MEMW/ signals is altered to better match the requirements of the memory and peripheral devices. We do not pursue the details of this mode of operation further.

Finally, if the *rotating priority* mode is not activated, the DMA channels operate with fixed priority. Channel 0 has the highest priority and channel 3 has the lowest priority. Thus, if the DRQ signals for two or more peripheral devices are on when the DMA controller chip receives control of the bus, the DACK/ signal for the channel with the highest priority is turned on. A byte is then transferred between the device connected to that channel and the memory. Other devices are then serviced in turn according to priority. It is therefore possible in this mode for a single device to monopolize the DMA system. If the rotating priority mode is activated, the channel priorities change after each byte transfer, thereby preventing a single device from monopolizing the system. In this mode, after a channel is serviced, the next higher numbered channel is assigned the highest priority for the next byte transfer. The priorities of the remaining channels are then assigned in ascending numerical order. Note that channel 0 follows channel 3 in priority for this purpose.

In addition to being able to read the block address, block length, and mode information currently in use for each channel, status information can be read by executing a programmed input transfer using *address* 0001. The interpretation of the bits in the status byte obtained in this manner is shown in Figure 8-19. The four *TC status* bits indicate which channels generated a TC signal since status was last read. The *TC status* bits therefore indicate whether a block transfer has been completed during the latter time interval.

0	0	0	UPDATE FLAG	TC STATUS Channel 0	TC STATUS Channel 1	TC STATUS Channel 2	TC STATUS Channel 3

Figure 8-19. Interpretation of DMA status byte.

In the autoload mode the *update flag* is set when the TC signal is turned on and it remains set until the channel 2 registers are updated from the channel 3 registers. Thus, to prevent the information in the latter registers from being changed prematurely, the status byte should be read and the update flag tested before attempting to reload the channel 3 registers.

This completes our discussion of the peripheral interface devices. The reader who is interested in additional information, such as pin assignment and timing information, should refer to the Intel publications and other references listed in the bibliography. Let us now return to the Intel 8085 central processor and consider in more detail the signals introduced earlier in the chapter.

INTEL 8085 SIGNALS COMPLETED

The remainder of the Intel 8085 central processor signals described in Figure 8-5 are reproduced in Figure 8-20. They fall into four categories: the interrupt control signals, the serial data lines, the reset lines, and the clock lines.

Intel designation	Signal description
INTR, RST 5.5, RST 6.5, RST 7.5, TRAP	Interrupt control signals described in Chapter 6
INTA/	Central processor has acknowledged request on INTR interrupt signal
SID	Serial input data (used with RIM instruction)
SOD	Serial output data (used with SIM instruction)
RESET IN/	Resets address of next instruction to zero (equivalent to JMP 0). Also resets the bus and interrupt control systems and the central processor registers.
RESET OUT	Turned on when the central processor is being reset.
X_1, X_2	Connections for control components for central processor internal clock generator or input for external clock generator signal.
CLOCK	Central processor internal clock generator output from which other integrated circuit chip clock signals may be derived.

Figure 8-20. The Intel 8085 central processor signals.

The interrupt control signals, INTR, RST5.5, RST6.5, RST7.5, and TRAP, were described in Chapter 6. INTA/ is turned on by the central processor to acknowledge that an interrupt request on the INTR line has been recognized and that processing to service the interrupt has started. As we shall see, the INTA/ signal can be used by an interrupt controller chip to supply a RESTART or CALL instruction to the central processor. The need for the RESTART or CALL instruction and how it is used were described in Chapter 6. The Intel 8259 interrupt controller chip and how it is used to implement the operations of the INTERRUPT module are described in the next section.

The serial data lines, SID and SOD, and how they are used with the RIM and SIM instructions were described briefly in the communications interface section.

The reset lines are used for hardware initialization. RESET IN/ is an externally supplied signal that can be derived from a push button or from a simple time delay circuit which is activated when power is turned on. It resets the internal central processor states and the bus signals, disables the interrupt system, and sets to zero the contents of the central processor register containing the address of the next instruction to be executed. Thus, whenever the system is reset, the central processor immediately executes the instruction stored in memory location zero. RESET OUT is turned on whenever the central processor is being reset; it is usually sent to the other chips in the system so that they are reset at the same time. If a *jump* instruction to the EXECUTIVE procedure is stored in memory location zero, the EXECUTIVE procedure is executed whenever a reset occurs. In the burglar alarm system the stack pointer should be initialized *before* the INITIALIZE SYSTEM procedure is called; the latter procedure then calls the INITIALIZE HARDWARE and RESET SYSTEM procedures to complete the initialization of the system. Similar procedures should be called in other systems. As we have seen, the RESET SYSTEM procedure clears and initializes the software with the exception of the stack pointer. The INITIALIZE HARDWARE procedure sends out commands to *program* the interface chips. Thus, all hardware and software functions are completely initialized following a reset. Note that some of the hardware commands occur in sequences that must follow specific protocols. For this reason, the hardware and software initialization parts of the software are separated so that the INITIALIZE HARDWARE procedure is only executed whenever the system is reset externally.

Finally, the X_1 and X_2 lines are provided to permit external control components to be connected to the internal clock generator to establish the system clock frequency. Alternately, an external clock generator can be connected to the X_1 line to directly provide system clock signals. The CLOCK line provides a copy of the clock signal which can be sent to the other chips in the system to ensure that they are synchronized with each other and with the central processor.

INTERRUPT CONTROLLER

As we have seen, the Intel 8085 central processor chip has internal capability for five levels of interrupt. Therefore, for simple systems, no additional interrupt hardware is needed. In many systems, however, a great deal of concurrent processing is necessary and five interrupt levels are not sufficient. The Intel 8259 interrupt controller chip provides the hardware capability to permit up to eight interrupt request lines to be multiplexed onto the interrupt request signal. It also provides the control information needed to allow the central processor to respond directly to these external interrupts, as described in the section on multiple interrupts in Chapter 6. Moreover, the Intel 8259 chip is a flexible device and enables a variety of interrupt strategies to be implemented. For example, additional Intel 8259 chips can be added to a system to permit up to sixty-four vectored interrupt levels to be implemented in a relatively straightforward manner. An enhanced version of the interrupt controller, the Intel 8259A, supports both the Intel 8085 and the Intel 8086 central processors. In this section, however, we discuss how the Intel 8259 interrupt controller chip provides expanded interrupt capability for the Intel 8085 central processor and see how it is *programmed* during system initialization to provide the desired interrupt strategy.

Figure 8-21 illustrates how the Intel 8259 interrupt controller chip is connected to the Intel 8085 bus. The CS/ signal is provided by the chip select logic, A_0 is provided by the address bus, and WR/ and RD/ are provided either directly by the central processor or optionally by the CONTROL LINE GENERATOR (as IOW/ and IOR/) in a system containing a DMA controller. The INT (or INTR) and INTA/ signals are the interrupt request and interrupt acknowledge signals that interface the

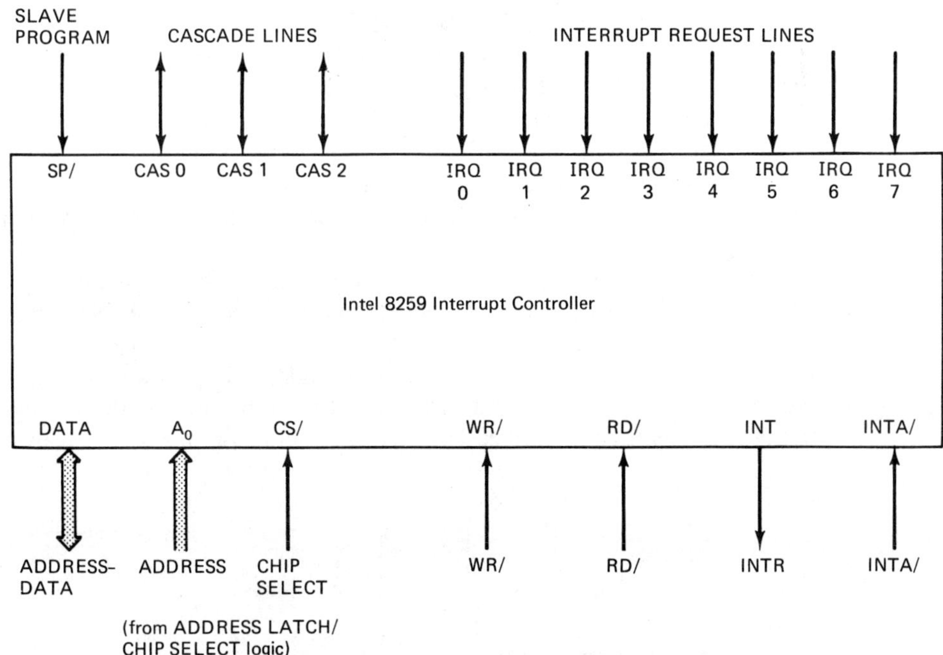

Figure 8-21. Intel 8259 interrupt controller chip.

interrupt module to the central processor. The IRQ_0 through IRQ_7 lines are the external interrupt request lines, the CAS_0 through CAS_2 lines are the *cascade lines* that permit additional interrupt controller chips to be added to the system to enable it to be expanded beyond eight interrupt levels, and SP/ is a *slave program* input that permits a *master-slave* hierarchy to be established among the chips to ensure correct system operation. We describe how to use the latter signals to expand the interrupt system later in this section. First, let us describe how a single Intel 8259 chip is used to provide control for up to eight external interrupt lines. For this purpose, the SP/ signal should be made high or ONE to indicate to the chip that it is operating as a master chip, that is, that it directly controls all of the interrupts connected to the INTR signal.

The Intel 8259 chip must be initialized before it can be used. Initialization is accomplished by sending two programmed output bytes to the chip. The address bit A_0 must be a ZERO when the first initialization byte is sent and bit 4 of the initialization byte must be a ONE. This protocol enables the initialization bytes to be distinguished from the command words used for *programming* the chip. The interpretation of the bits of the first initialization byte is shown in Figure 8-22. Bit 0 and bit 3 are ZERO, bit 1 is the *single chip indicator*, bit 2 is the *call address interval*, and bits 5 through 7 contain bits A_5 through A_7 of the address of the *interrupt vector block*. Since there is only one interrupt controller chip in the system, the single chip indicator must be set to ONE to indicate this to the chip. The call address interval selects whether the call instruction addresses supplied by the chip for the eight interrupt levels should be spaced four bytes apart (if bit 2 is a ONE) or eight bytes apart (if bit 2 is a ZERO). The address bit A_0 must be a ONE when the second initialization byte is sent out. The second initialization byte contains bits A_8 through A_{15} of the address of the interrupt vector block. By using the address information supplied in the two initialization bytes, the call address interval, and the interrupt level number, a different address can be generated for each interrupt request line, as shown in Figure 8-23, for both the four-byte spacing option and the eight-byte spacing option.

The Intel 8259 interrupt controller chip operates in the following manner after it is initialized. When an interrupt request line is turned on, the INT signal to the central processor is turned on by the chip. When the central processor responds by turning on the INTA/ signal, the interrupt controller chip puts a *call* instruction on the address-data bus. The central processor then turns off the INTA/ signal and examines this instruction. Since the *call* instruction requires a two-byte direct

Bit 7	Bit 6	Bit 5	Bit 4	Bit 3	Bit 2	Bit 1	Bit 0
A_7	A_6	A_5	1	0	Call Address Interval	Single Chip Indicator	0

Figure 8-22. Interpretation of first initialization byte (with $A_0 = 0$).

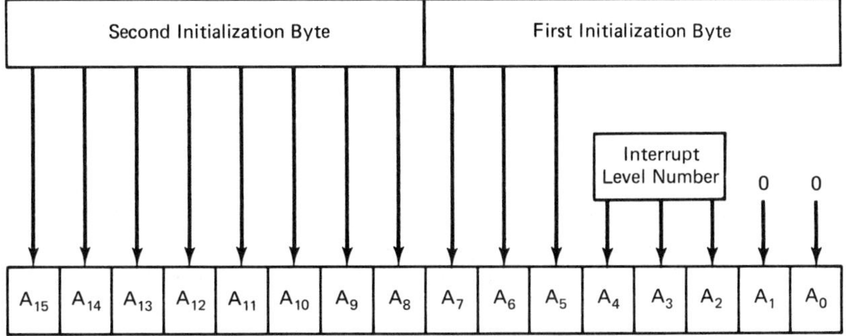

Figure 8-23(a). Interrupt vector address generation for four byte spacing option.

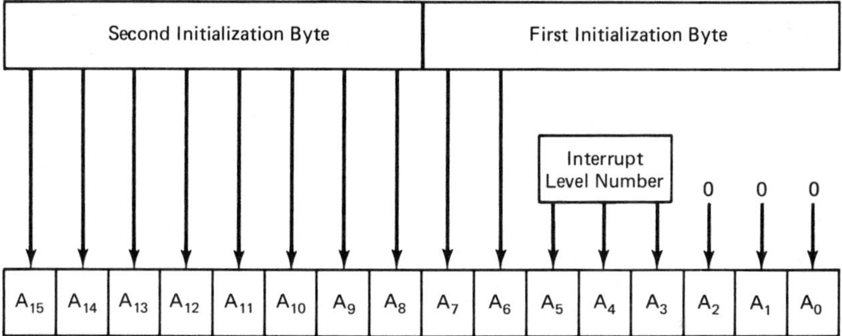

Figure 8-23(b). Interrupt vector address generation for eight byte spacing option.

address, INTA/ is turned on two more times by the central processor; each time INTA/ is turned on, a byte of the interrupt vector address, derived as shown in Figure 8-23, is put on the address-data bus by the interrupt controller chip to complete the sequence.

If the chip is not sent any command words after it is initialized, no interrupts are masked. Then, if two or more interrupt request lines are turned on together, the lowest numbered interrupt line is recognized and used to produce the first interrupt. Also, when an interrupt is recognized, all lower level interrupts are automatically inhibited until an *end of interrupt* command is issued to the chip by the central processor. Command words can be used to *program* the interrupt controller chip and thereby change its operating mode at any time. We illustrate the use of command words with several examples. If a byte is sent to the chip with the address bit A_0 set to ONE, and if the chip is not expecting an initialization byte, the byte is treated as the *first* command word of a sequence of up to three command words. This command word sets or resets each interrupt mask bit if the corresponding bit in the command word is a ONE or a ZERO, respectively. We described the concept of interrupt masking in Chapter 6. If an interrupt mask bit is set, the effect of turning on the corresponding interrupt request line is delayed until the mask is reset.

Additional command words can be sent to the chip to permit it to operate in either of the following modes: an *automatic* mode in which an interrupt level automatically becomes the lowest priority interrupt level after it has been serviced or a *special mask* mode which allows the interrupt controller to be used in a *polled mode* and which prepares the chip to send certain status information to the central processor. The additional command words can also be used to obtain status information from the chip and to send end of interrupt commands to the chip as mentioned above. We will not discuss the details of how the command words are used for these functions. The reader can refer to the Intel manuals in the bibliography for this purpose.

Up to now, we assumed that fewer than eight external interrupt lines are in use and that a single interrupt controller chip is used in a system. Figure 8-24 illustrates how several 8259 chips can be cascaded to provide additional interrupt levels. The SP/ signal for the particular chip used as a *master* is made high (ONE) as in the simple case; the SP/ signals for the remaining 8259 chips are made low (ZERO) to make them behave as *slave* chips. The INT signal from each slave chip is then connected to one of the IRQ inputs on the master chip. Finally, the cascade lines, CAS_0, CAS_1, and CAS_2, are connected together as if they were a *bus*, as shown in Figure 8-24. Note that the cascade lines cause information to be sent from the master chip to the slave chips. The state of the SP/ signal for each chip therefore determines whether the cascade lines for that chip are used to send or to receive information.

The configuration in Figure 8-24 contains three Intel 8259 interrupt controller chips; up to twenty-two distinct interrupt levels are possible with this configuration. The maximum configuration possible in a system uses nine 8259 chips. In the maximum configuration, an INT signal from a slave chip is connected to each of the IRQ inputs of the master chip and up to sixty-four distinct interrupt levels are possible.

When the interrupt controller chips are cascaded, it is necessary to initialize *each* of the chips so that they operate correctly. The initialization is done in the following manner. A sequence of *three* initialization bytes (rather than the two needed when a single chip is used) is sent to each of the chips. The single chip indicator, bit 1, of the first initialization byte must be ZERO in each case. The remaining bits of the first and second initialization bytes establish the call address interval and the addresses of the interrupt vector blocks. Note that a different interrupt vector block must be established for each chip. The single chip indicator in the first initialization byte indicates that the chips are cascaded and that a third initialization byte is therefore needed for each chip. When the third initialization byte is sent to a chip, the address bit, A_0, must be a ONE. The third initialization byte sent to the master chip contains a bit for each of its IRQ lines. If the bit is a ONE, this indicates that the corresponding IRQ line is connected to the INT signal from a slave chip; if the bit is a ZERO, then the IRQ line is either unused or connected directly to an external interrupt request signal. For the system shown in Figure 8-24, the third initialization byte for the master chip should be 1100 0000 to indicate that IRQ_6 and IRQ_7 are connected to slave chips. The third initialization byte sent to each slave chip contains an identification number in the three least-significant bits of the byte. This

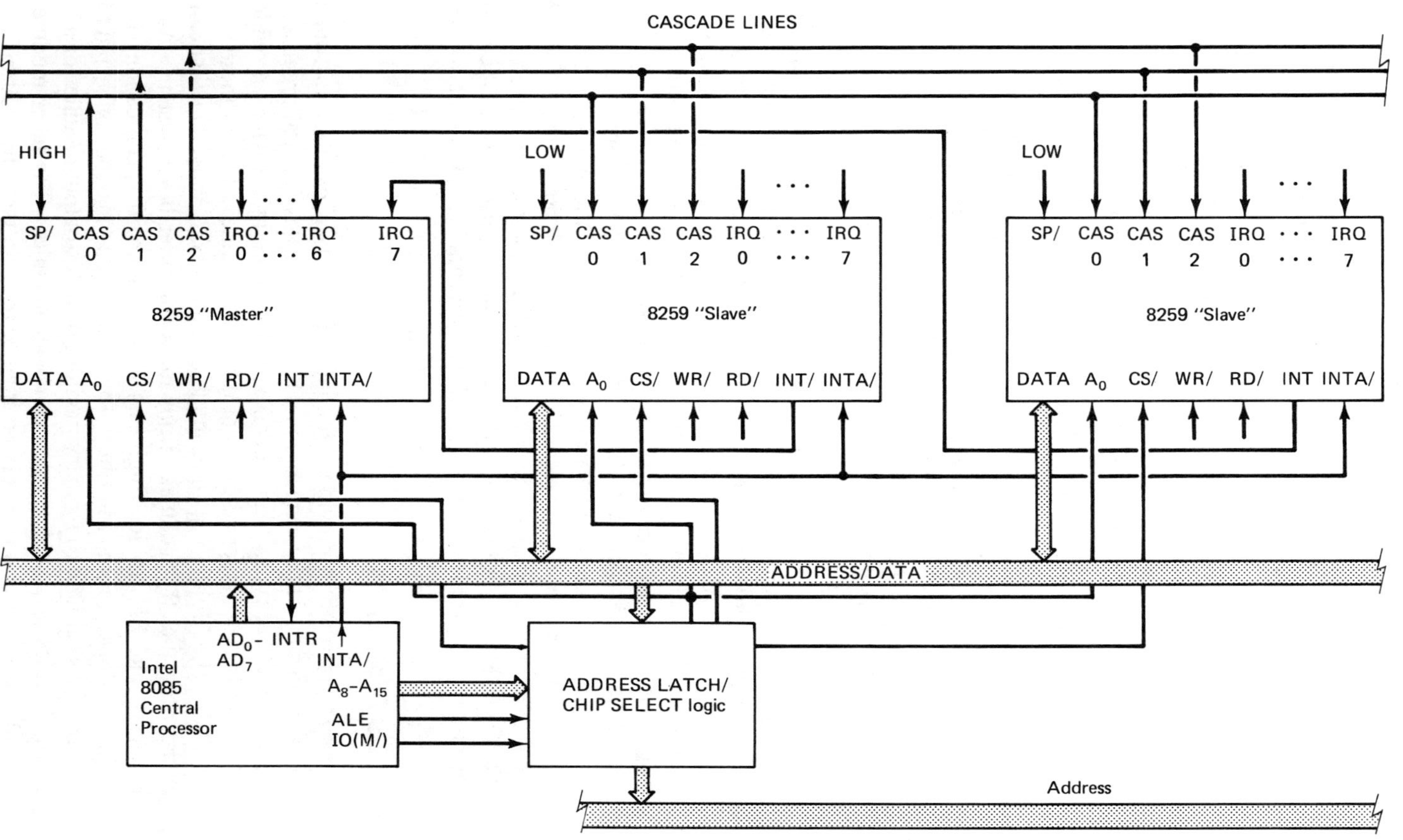

Figure 8-24. Cascading the 8259 interrupt controller chips.

identification number indicates to the slave chip which master interrupt request line it is connected to. Thus, the third initialization bytes for the two slave chips in our example should be 0000 0110 and 0000 0111. Let us now examine how a cascaded interrupt system operates.

If one of the external interrupt lines directly connected to the master chip (IRQ_0 through IRQ_5 in the example) is turned on, then the sequence of events that takes place is identical to what we described earlier for the single chip system. If, however, one of the interrupt request lines connected to a slave chip is turned on, the slave turns on its INT signal. The master then turns on its INT signal in the usual manner and, when INTA/ is turned on by the central processor, the master chip sends a *call* instruction to the central processor. However, when the INTA/ signal is turned on for the second and third times, the master chip commands the slave chip whose request is being passed on to send an interrupt vector address to the central processor. It does this by putting the identification number of the slave chip onto the cascade lines, thereby commanding the slave chip to respond directly to the INTA/ signal. If two or more interrupt request lines are turned on simultaneously, then priority is resolved by both the master and the slave chips. The master chip first resolves priorities among the slave chips and its own direct interrupt request lines; the selected slave chip then resolves priorities among its interrupt request lines. Note that when operating in this manner, each interrupt controller chip must be sent its command words separately. As a result, the chips can be made to operate in different modes. Also, two *end of interrupt* command words must be sent to complete each interrupt processing cycle: one to the master chip and one to the slave chip whose interrupt request is being serviced.

This completes our description of the Intel 8259 interrupt controller chip. In the description of this chip, of the memory chips, and of the input-output interface chips, we did not consider the subject of integrated circuit technology. The reader should refer to the bibliography for references that describe the different technologies (NMOS, CMOS, HMOS, TTL, I^2L, ECL, and so forth) used in the manufacture of integrated circuit chips and that describe how technology affects performance.

SYSTEM BUS CONCEPTS

The bus described in previous sections is an *internal bus* used to connect together the component parts of a microcomputer system whose central processor is an Intel 8085 chip. Other types of microcomputer buses are in use which provide communication between the internal buses of different modules. One of these is the the Intel Multibus. The Multibus is an example of a *universal system bus* that can be used to connect together the modules of *any* microcomputer-based system. An Institute of Electrical and Electronics Engineers (IEEE) standard specification, IEEE-796, is being developed for the Multibus. The modules that may be connected to the Multibus may be as simple as memory modules or input-output modules or as complex as DMA modules or complete microcomputer modules. The latter modules may contain different central processors or architectures. In fact, the Multibus permits 8-bit and 16-bit microcomputers to be connected together to form a *multiprocessor* or multiple microcomputer system. A simple convention used by the Intel Corporation is that the components contained on a single-board microcomputer such as the iSBC 80/05 are interconnected via an internal bus; they are connected to other boards via the Multibus. In addition to single-board microcomputers, Multibus compatible boards are available that contain memory modules, input-output modules for communicating with external digital devices, input-output modules with on-board analog-to-digital and digital-to-analog converters for communicating with external analog devices, communication controller modules, special-purpose input-output controller modules containing DMA controllers or disc controllers, and so forth.

Figure 8-25 illustrates how a Multibus is used to connect a multiprocessor system together. The figure shows *m* microcomputers, each of which may have its own memory, input-output controllers, and interrupt controller. Also shown are *n* DMA-based controllers which include the special-purpose input-output controllers such as the disc controller, *p* memory modules, and *s* input-output interfaces which include both digital and analog interfaces and communication controllers. A microcomputer or DMA-based controller module can act as bus master and thereby control the transfer of data on the Multibus or it can act as a bus slave and send and receive data over the bus under the control of one of the other modules acting as bus master. A memory or input-output module can only act as a bus slave. The *Multibus arbitration logic* shown in Figure 8-25 serves to resolve conflicts caused when several master subsystems request the use of the Multibus at the same time.

The Multibus has a 16-bit data bus. Information can be transmitted either as 8-bit bytes using only one-half of the data bus lines or as 16-bit words using the full 16-bit bus. It has a 20-bit address bus. An 8-bit master, such as an Intel 8085 micro-

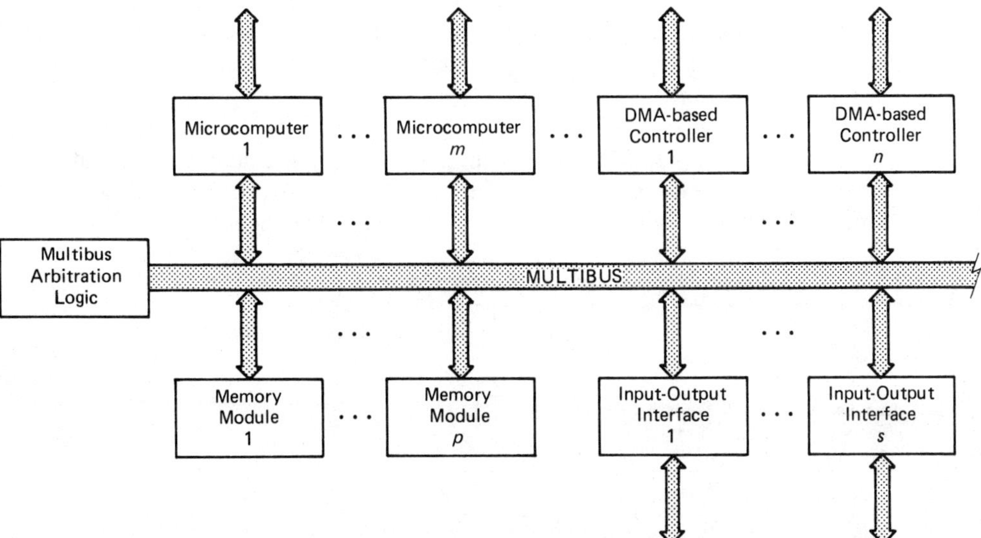

Figure 8-25. The Intel Multibus.

computer, uses sixteen address lines to communicate with a memory module and eight address lines to communicate with a port in an input-output interface module. A 16-bit master, such as the Intel 8086, uses all twenty address lines to communicate with a memory module and up to sixteen address lines to communicate with a port in an input-output interface module. The Multibus also provides eight interrupt lines. Therefore, modules connected to the bus can interrupt a bus master through the bus interrupt lines rather than directly. Thus, an additional hierarchy of interrupt levels is provided through the Multibus.

We will not describe how the Multibus operates in detail. Instead, let us examine how it operates from a functional viewpoint. In order for a microcomputer module to communicate with a slave module, it either executes a memory reference instruction or a programmed input or output instruction. If the memory address or the port address of the instruction does not reference one of the modules on the same board, the *Multibus interface* shown in Figure 8-26 *assumes* that it references a module on another board. It then automatically requests the use of the Multibus. If several bus requests are made at the same time, the Multibus arbitration logic resolves the conflict according to a preset priority. When the use of the bus is obtained by a requesting Multibus interface, it completes the memory reference instruction or programmed input-output instruction by communicating with the addressed module through the Multibus. If the addressed memory location is in the memory of another microcomputer, it is accessed through a *dual port memory interface* that permits the memory on a board to be accessed from either the internal bus or the Multibus. Thus, the dual port memory interface permits a microcomputer module to act as a slave device when its memory is accessed by another module; the Multibus interface permits it to act as a master device in order to access off-board memory or an input-output device. A DMA-based module acts as a slave device when programmed input or output instructions are *addressed* to it. This permits a microcomputer to send initialization data to a DMA module and to receive status information from it.

Another type of universal system bus is used for connecting microcomputer systems to input-output devices such as printers. An example of the latter type of bus is the Hewlett-Packard HP-IB bus which conforms to the IEEE-488 specification and permits digital instruments to be connected together into a system. Since

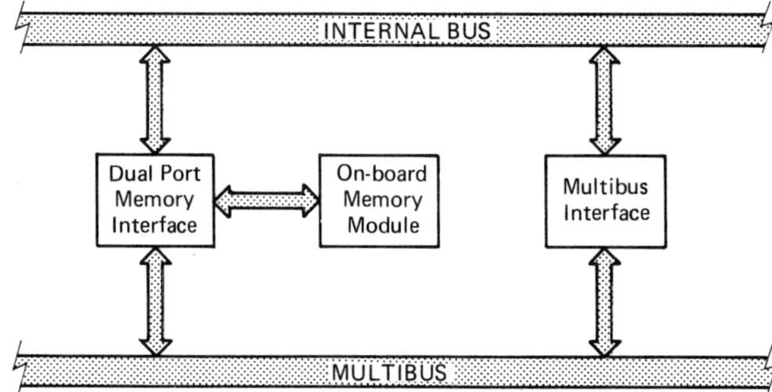

Figure 8-26. The microcomputer-Multibus interface.

many instruments now contain microcomputers, the HP-IB bus is a true microcomputer universal bus. The S/100 bus which conforms to the IEEE-696 specification is a highly flexible bus similar to the Multibus. It is finding great popularity in the personal microcomputer field.

ECONOMICS OF HARDWARE/SOFTWARE TRADEOFFS

In the section on the communications interface we discussed this hardware/software tradeoff: Should an Intel 8251 communications interface chip be used for serial communications or should software procedures that use the RIM and SIM instructions be designed instead? We described the use of the Intel 8251 chip since it is often the more cost-effective approach from the hardware/software tradeoff standpoint; however, we did not consider all of the economic implications of this decision. Let us do so now.

The economic implications of a hardware/software tradeoff encompass the following areas:

- Cost of hardware
- Cost of hardware development
- Production volume
- Cost of software development
- Product life
- Development time and schedule
- Value added
- Effect of tradeoff on system performance

When a decision is made to substitute a software procedure for a hardware chip, or vice versa, we must consider each of the above factors. As an example, let us assume that the following estimates apply to a system:

Per unit chip cost	\$ 5	Includes per unit cost of adding the chip to the system.
Cost of hardware development	\$4000	Differential cost between hardware needed with and without chip. Cost of integration is also included.
Production volume	1000	Units per year.
Cost of software development	\$8000	Differential cost between software needed with and without chip. Cost of integration is also included.
Product life	4	Years.
Development time	1	Month for hardware.
	2	Months for software.
Impact on schedule	½	Month longer, overall, for software.

Thus, for the hardware implementation, the added hardware costs per year of production are given by:

$$\text{Per unit chip cost} \times \text{Production volume} + \frac{\text{Cost of hardware development}}{\text{Product life}}$$

$$= \$5 \times 1000 + \frac{\$4000}{4}$$

$$= \$6000$$

For the software implementation, the added software costs per year of production are given by

$$\frac{\text{Cost of software development}}{\text{Product life}} = \frac{\$8000}{4} = \$2000$$

Therefore, the costs indicate that the software approach is more cost-effective in this example. The reader can verify that for lower production volumes, the hardware implementation is more cost-effective and that for higher production volumes, the software implementation is even more cost-effective. Note that we have assumed that the per unit cost of a chip is independent of production volume; this is not the case and must be taken into consideration to make the cost estimates valid.

In addition to considering costs, we must also take the other factors listed above into consideration. Although there is a one-month versus a two-month tradeoff in development times, the overall impact on the schedule is only one-half month since certain integration tasks can be overlapped; we also assumed that personnel are available to take advantage of an overlapped schedule. In this case, the impact on the schedule can be ignored. If the delay in the schedule were several months, consideration might have to be given to the potential loss of sales that could result from a later introduction date for the product.

Value added can be important in either of two ways depending on competition. If competition is not a problem, the selling price can reflect the added costs and a profit can be made from the extra value added. In this case, it may be advantageous to build the system in the most expeditious manner and to ignore the cost differential. If competition is a problem and cost must be kept low to compete, no profit can be made from the extra value added. The lowest cost solution should then be considered.

Finally, the effects of a hardware/software tradeoff on performance should be evaluated. For example, using the software approach for communications may slow down the overall operating speed of the system. It may then be necessary to replace the central processor with a higher speed unit or to use the hardware approach for communications, depending on which is preferred or more cost-effective. Moreover, using software instead of hardware may increase memory requirements, thereby trading one hardware cost for another.

Thus, the evaluation of a hardware/software tradeoff becomes a multidimensional problem and should be given careful consideration before the design is completed. Our modular approach to microcomputer system design does permit the substitution of a hardware module for a software module, and vice versa, even at a fairly late stage of the design cycle. However, every effort should be made to evaluate the tradeoffs carefully early in the system design cycle and thereby make decisions that do not have to be changed later.

Before we leave the subject of hardware design, let us look at the fifth documentation level, the hardware documentation level.

FIFTH DOCUMENTATION LEVEL

In the fifth documentation level we need both functional descriptions for the hardware as well as schematic and mechanical layout drawings illustrating how the chips and modules are laid out and interconnected. The functional descriptions are similar in nature to a functional specification and consist largely of text. As such, they may be produced and maintained in the same manner as the system and software documentation is produced and maintained. The schematic diagrams and mechanical layout drawings should be produced and maintained using standard engineering drawing techniques. If available, a computer-aided drawing system can be used to automate the production and maintenance of the drawings for this documentation level.

EXERCISES

8-1. For the microcomputer input-output interfaces for the computerized television set of Exercises 3-2 and 3-3, consider whether a parallel peripheral interface or a DMA controller would be preferred for the system. State the reasons for your choice.

8-2. Consider the input-output requirements for the computerized traffic light controller of Exercises 3-4 and 3-5. Would a parallel peripheral interface or a serial communications interface be preferred? Why?

8-3. Which type of microcomputer input-output interface is preferred for the computerized sports scoreboard of Exercises 3-6 and 3-7? What are the reasons for your choice?

8-4. Consider the input-output interface between the microcomputer and the keyboard and display devices in the computerized point-of-sale terminal of Exercises 3-8 and 3-9. Which type of interface do you prefer? Why?

Chapter 9

Hardware Check Out and Integration

In Chapter 7 we discussed how to check out and integrate the software modules and described the tools used for this purpose. In Chapter 8 we discussed the design of the various hardware modules that make up a system. We are now ready to discuss how to check out and integrate the hardware modules and describe the tools that can be used to assist in this task.

During the system design cycle for a microcomputer-based system it is preferable for the hardware to be both operational and as *bug*-free as possible before we proceed to integrate the software into the hardware. In many systems, hardware modules are built and ready for check out before the software modules are completed. It is especially important from a project schedule standpoint to eliminate as many *bugs* as possible from the hardware before system integration is started. If more problems are detected and corrected during the hardware integration phase, more time will be available for other purposes during system integration.

In this chapter we discuss the basic approaches to hardware check out, present guidelines on how to prepare a *hardware check-out plan*, discuss both *static* and *dynamic* hardware testing, present an example showing how to use low-level software input-output modules to check out the microcomputer hardware interface modules, and, finally, describe the tools available for hardware development and check out.

HARDWARE CHECK-OUT APPROACHES

Every microcomputer-based system is unique with respect to its specific hardware configuration. Thus, we should use a systematic approach for hardware check out so that we can deal with a variety of hardware configurations without starting over each time. In this section we discuss the basic approaches used to check out hardware modules prior to system integration.

A generalized hardware module diagram for a microcomputer-based system is shown in Figure 9-1. We use this diagram to discuss how to check out each of the hardware modules shown in the figure. In order to determine which check-out approach to use for a particular module, we must consider how the module interacts with the software.

Hardware modules that consist of *pure hardware*, that is, modules that have little or no interaction with the software, are amenable to conventional hardware check-out approaches. Hardware modules that interact a great deal with the software require a combined software/hardware approach to check out. For the modules shown in Figure 9-1, the MICROCOMPUTER module, the MEMORY modules, and the STANDARD INPUT/OUTPUT modules tend to be heavily software-driven. The CUSTOM INPUT/OUTPUT modules and the OTHER BUS MASTER modules interact less with the software and often contain a large amount of *pure hardware*.

We first discuss how to check out the pure hardware modules. This class of hardware modules has the advantage that check out can begin immediately after construction and does not require coordination with the software schedule. The best approach is to first check the module by using static, standalone check-out techniques to ensure that the module operates in a correct functional manner as designed. After the module is checked out statically, it should be operated dynamically to verify that its timing characteristics are correct. We discuss static and dynamic check out in more detail in the following sections. After the module is operating correctly in a standalone dynamic mode, it should then be integrated with the other hardware modules to ensure that its dynamic operation is correct when it is

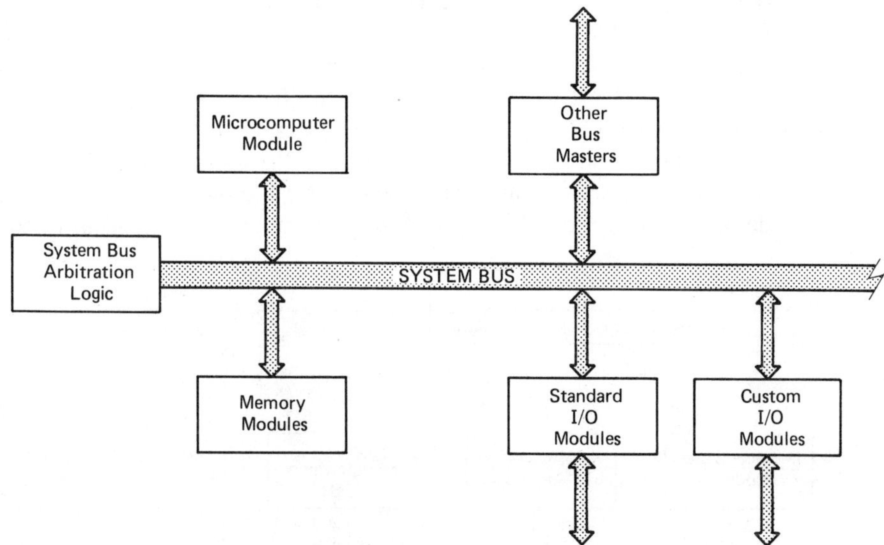

Figure 9-1. Generalized hardware module diagram.

driven by the rest of the system. The systematic progression from static check out to standalone dynamic check out to integrated dynamic check out provides an efficient way to detect, isolate, and correct both design and construction errors in the hardware. It is easier to correct obvious problems and to verify the functional operation of a module under static conditions than when the module is operating dynamically. Similarly, timing problems are more easily corrected when each module is operating dynamically by itself than when the whole system is operating together. Problems that occur when a complete system is operating dynamically are the most difficult to detect and isolate. Thus, identifying and correcting as many of these problems as possible before operating the modules as a system is highly cost-effective.

Check out of the software-driven hardware modules can be done in a similar manner. The major difference is that software is needed to completely check out these hardware modules. As before, we begin with static check out to verify that the module operates in a correct functional manner. Then, the MICROCOMPUTER module and MEMORY modules along with appropriate test software are used to provide a dynamic environment for the software-driven hardware modules. Figure 9-2 shows the module configuration used for this test. Because the software-driven hardware modules interact highly with the software, the same low-level software procedures which have been designed for use in the completed system should be used to drive the hardware during dynamic testing. For this reason, the MICRO-COMPUTER and MEMORY modules should be constructed and tested early in the design cycle so that they are available when needed to test the software-driven hardware modules. To provide the desired sequencing for a dynamic test, a TEST EXECUTIVE procedure is designed to call the existing low-level software procedures in a suitable order. The TEST EXECUTIVE procedure should first call an initialization procedure; it should also contain a DO FOREVER . . . END loop to call the low-level procedures to exercise the hardware repeatedly. After the test software has been checked out and is operating correctly, the hardware check-out process can begin; it can be carried out as though a standalone dynamic test of a pure hardware module were being performed. After the bugs in each hardware module are detected and corrected, it is necessary to integrate together all of the hardware

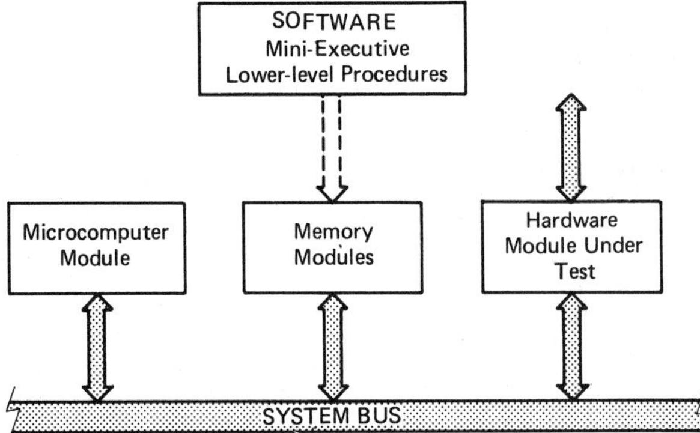

Figure 9-2. Configuration for software-driven dynamic check out.

modules in the system which interact with one another. However, for those modules which only interact with the MICROCOMPUTER and MEMORY modules, dynamic check out and integration are completed together.

A hardware module may contain both hardware that can be tested without the use of software and hardware that must be tested in a software-driven environment. In this case, integration consists of a combination of the pure hardware and the software-driven approaches. Figure 9-3 summarizes the hardware check-out and integration approaches we have just described. In the following sections we discuss static and dynamic check out in more detail and present an example to illustrate software-driven hardware check out.

STANDALONE STATIC CHECK OUT

In this section we discuss the hardware functions that can be checked out statically. We also introduce the tools that are best suited to performing static check out. As mentioned earlier, standalone static check out is used to verify that a module operates in a correct functional manner as designed. The various functions tested during static check out include power supply voltage levels, chip select logic, bus driver and direction control logic, clock generator logic, and any other logic whose inputs can be driven and whose outputs can be observed statically. The tools used to

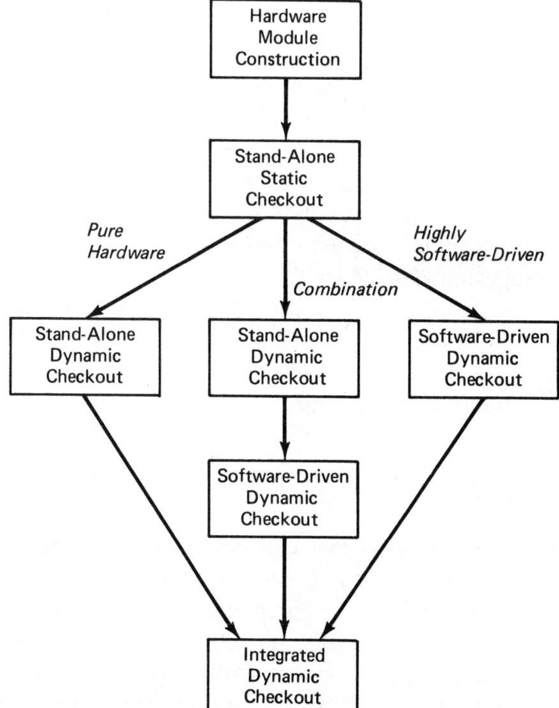

Figure 9-3. Hardware check out and integration approaches.

check each of these functions are listed in Figure 9-4. The tools themselves are discussed in more detail later.

Function to be checked	Digital voltmeter	Oscilloscope	Switch/display box	Logic analyzer
Bus and IC power supplies	X	X		
Bus direction control			X	X
Bus drivers	X		X	X
Clock generators		X		
Chip select logic			X	X
Other logic	X		X	X

Figure 9-4. Tools for checking static functions.

It is important to begin the static check out of a module by examining the power supply voltage levels both at the power supply distribution points and at each integrated circuit chip in the module. If the power supply voltage is not within specified limits or is connected incorrectly, the module either will not operate or will operate in an unreliable manner.

The drivers for the address, data, and control lines for each bus and the associated bus driver direction control logic should be checked out next. Taking the time to verify that the driver for each bit of a bus interface passes information in the correct direction under different static operating conditions is time well spent.

If a hardware module contains a clock generator, then verifying that the frequency, risetime, and amplitude characteristics are correct should also be done during static check out prior to starting dynamic check out.

Other logic that can be checked out at this time includes the chip select logic that decodes the address and control bus information and provides the chip select signals needed during system operation. It is important to verify that a chip is correctly selected when its address is placed on a bus so that chip selection problems are minimized during dynamic hardware check out.

STANDALONE DYNAMIC CHECK OUT

Let us now discuss the hardware functions that can be checked out dynamically. Dynamic check out is performed on those functions of each hardware module that can be made to operate at the speed at which the completed system will operate. The tests performed during standalone dynamic check out verify that the timing and the signal characteristics of these functions are correct. Problems caused by incorrect timing or by the presence of noise are very difficult to detect. Thus, it is more cost-effective to correct these problems at the module level than to do so during system integration.

The hardware functions that can be checked out dynamically include bus handshake and bus priority logic, memory access time, signal characteristics of bus signals, and other clocked sequential logic functions. The tools used to check each of these functions are shown in Figure 9-5. Note that during dynamic check out the switch/display box, signal generator, oscilloscope, and logic analyzer are used for checking all functions. This was not the case during static check out because the various functions being checked required different tool configurations. During dynamic check out, the switch/display box and signal generator supply module inputs and the oscilloscope and logic analyzer are used to observe module outputs.

Function to be checked	Switch/display box	Signal/pulse generator	Oscilloscope	Logic analyzer
Bus signals	X	X	X	X
Bus handshake logic	X	X	X	X
Memory access time	X	X	X	X
Bus priority logic	X	X	X	X
Clocked sequential logic	X	X	X	X

Figure 9-5. Tools for checking dynamic functions.

Dynamic check out is started by exercising and observing the signal characteristics of all address bus, data bus, and control signals. The risetimes and voltage levels for all of these signals should lie within the tolerances permitted by the specifications for each of the integrated circuit chips used in the system. If too many loads are connected to a bus driver, the risetimes or voltage levels may be degraded. If necessary, additional bus drivers should be added to the system to handle the load. Bus signals may also be degraded by noise when routed over relatively long distances. Thus, it is good engineering practice to use bus drivers and receivers at *both* ends of each bus to minimize the effects of noise and to help ensure that data is transferred reliably over the bus.

If a module contains bus handshake logic for memory or input-output transfers, it should be checked for correct timing. Most system buses use a handshaking protocol to provide positive confirmation for each data transfer. If the bus handshake logic is not operating correctly in every module that uses the system bus, transfers between the modules either may be delayed or may not be completed at all.

If the access time of a memory module is a critical factor for correct operation of the system, it can be measured and verified during standalone dynamic check out. By using the switch box to supply valid memory addresses and the signal/pulse generator to supply control signals, memory access times can then be measured with the oscilloscope or logic analyzer.

The modules that communicate with the SYSTEM BUS ARBITRATION module should be checked dynamically to verify that they correctly send information to and receive information from the SYSTEM BUS ARBITRATION module. If these functions are not implemented correctly, the system may lock up when a faulty module operates concurrently with other hardware modules in the system.

Finally, other clocked sequential logic in the module under test should also be checked and correct operation verified. Again, the timing and the signal characteristics should be observed and verified to be within specifications as described above.

SOFTWARE-DRIVEN DYNAMIC CHECK OUT

In this section we discuss the dynamic check out of hardware modules that interact highly with the software. After the static testing of the module is completed, the low-level software procedures which are designed for use in the completed system are used to drive the hardware for dynamic testing. Specific examples of hardware modules that should be software-driven during dynamic check out include analog input-output modules, parallel and serial digital input-output modules, programmable interval timers, programmable direct memory access (DMA) controllers, programmable interrupt controllers, and other software-driven peripherals.

The tools used for software-driven dynamic check out include those used during static and dynamic check out along with tools such as the microcomputer analyzer and the in-circuit emulator which permit the simultaneous observation of both software and hardware events. These tools allow us to operate each hardware module using test software and to simultaneously observe the execution of the software and its effect on the hardware in real-time. The microcomputer analyzer and the in-circuit emulator can also supply software-synchronized trigger signals to an oscilloscope. This capability permits us to examine the dynamic characteristics of a software-driven signal.

Let us now discuss software-driven dynamic check out using as an example the check out of a serial communications interface module. The module uses the Intel 8251 communications interface chip discussed in Chapter 8 to provide an interface between the system bus and a serial input-output port whose specifications conform to the Electronics Industries Association (EIA) RS-232-C standard. An Intel 8253 Programmable Interval Timer is used as a clock generator to provide the desired baud rate. A block diagram of the module is shown in Figure 9-6.

The check-out configuration for this module is shown in Figure 9-7. A standard RS-232-C compatible terminal is connected to the module to display the characters output by the module and to permit characters to be input to the module. The microcomputer analyzer or the in-circuit emulator is connected to the MICROCOMPUTER module both to control software-synchronized events and to display them. A logic analyzer or oscilloscope can be used to monitor and verify the operation of the hardware functions within the module.

As mentioned earlier, a TEST EXECUTIVE procedure is designed to call the existing low-level software procedures in the correct order. The TEST EXECUTIVE procedure should call an INITIALIZE HARDWARE procedure and contain a DO

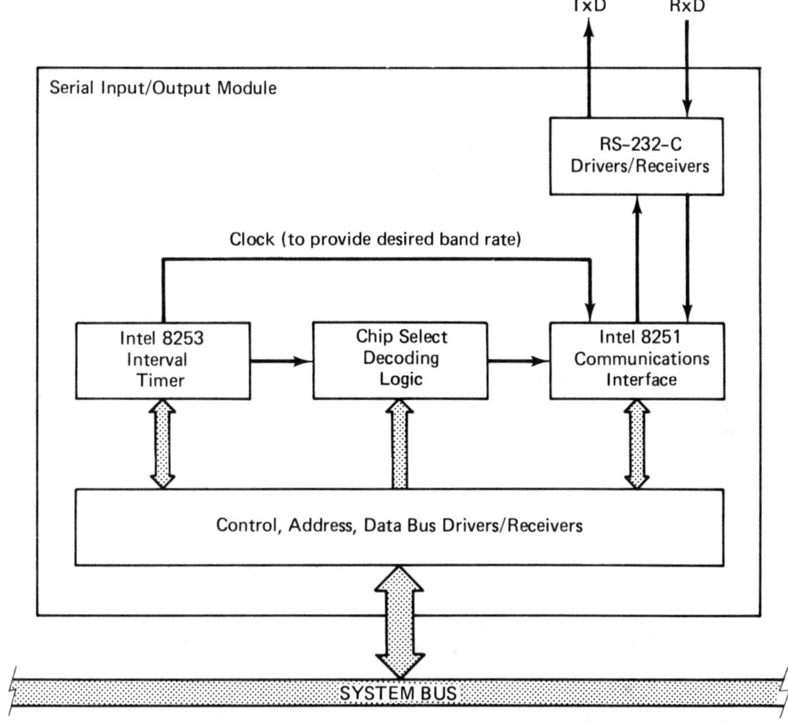

Figure 9-6. Serial communications module block diagram.

FOREVER . . . END loop to call the low-level procedures repeatedly. The design of suitable procedures for use during check out are shown in Figures 9-8 through 9-11. The same procedures are shown in Figures 9-12 through 9-15 after the design

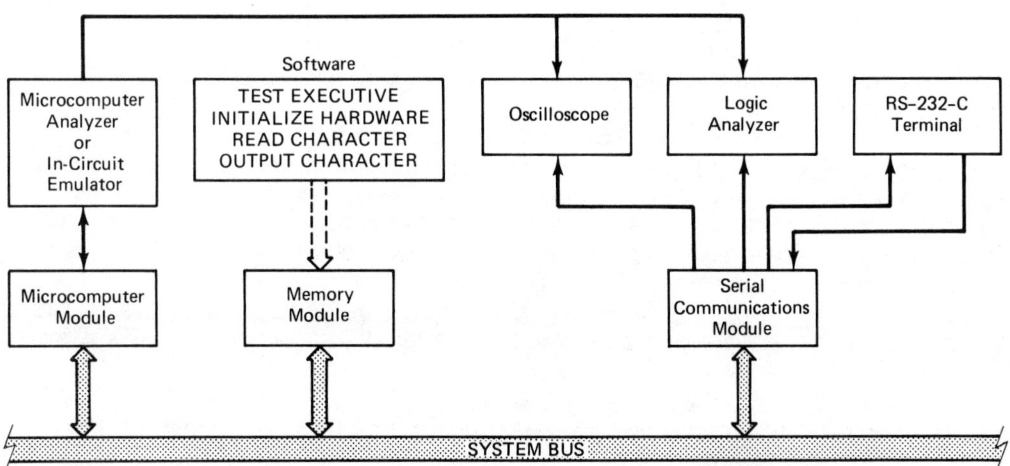

Figure 9-7. Serial communications check out configuration diagram.

language is converted into Intel 8085 assembly language; the listings produced by the Intel 8085 assembler are shown since they include the instruction addresses in the listings. Before discussing the specific check-out steps, let us walk through these test procedures.

```
PROCEDURE: TEST EXECUTIVE (;)
**************************************************************************
DESIGNED BY:    L. B. EVANS                      01-26-81
LOCAL PARAMETER:   CHARACTER
**************************************************************************
BEGIN PROCEDURE
  CALL: INITIALIZE HARDWARE (;)
  DO FOREVER
    CALL: READ CHARACTER (;CHARACTER)
    CALL: OUTPUT CHARACTER (CHARACTER;)
  END
END PROCEDURE
**************************************************************************
```

Figure 9-8. The TEST EXECUTIVE procedure.

The TEST EXECUTIVE procedure first calls INITIALIZE HARDWARE and then repeatedly calls READ CHARACTER and OUTPUT CHARACTER. Each character received from READ CHARACTER as an output parameter is immediately sent to OUTPUT CHARACTER as an input parameter. This repeated read-output sequence provides a dynamic environment to facilitate the check out of the serial communications interface module.

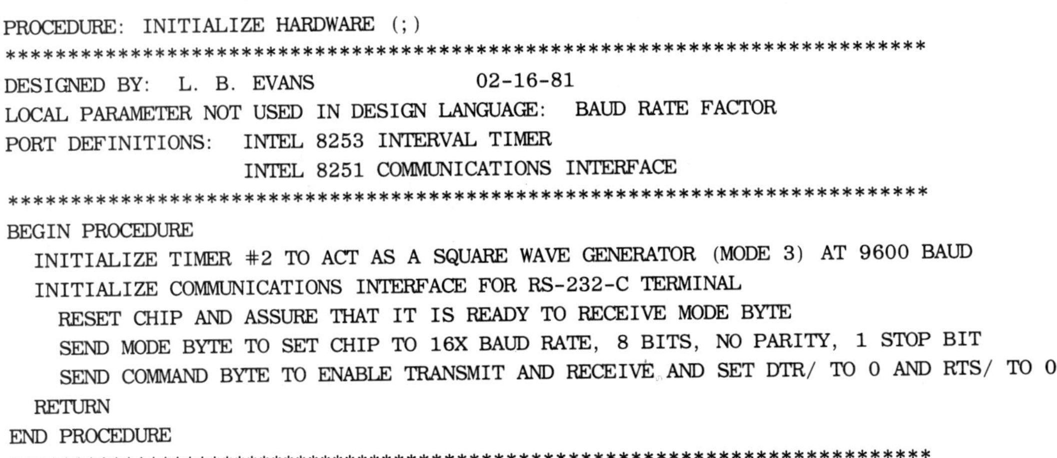

```
PROCEDURE: INITIALIZE HARDWARE (;)
**************************************************************************
DESIGNED BY:  L. B. EVANS              02-16-81
LOCAL PARAMETER NOT USED IN DESIGN LANGUAGE:  BAUD RATE FACTOR
PORT DEFINITIONS:   INTEL 8253 INTERVAL TIMER
                    INTEL 8251 COMMUNICATIONS INTERFACE
**************************************************************************
BEGIN PROCEDURE
  INITIALIZE TIMER #2 TO ACT AS A SQUARE WAVE GENERATOR (MODE 3) AT 9600 BAUD
  INITIALIZE COMMUNICATIONS INTERFACE FOR RS-232-C TERMINAL
    RESET CHIP AND ASSURE THAT IT IS READY TO RECEIVE MODE BYTE
    SEND MODE BYTE TO SET CHIP TO 16X BAUD RATE, 8 BITS, NO PARITY, 1 STOP BIT
    SEND COMMAND BYTE TO ENABLE TRANSMIT AND RECEIVE AND SET DTR/ TO 0 AND RTS/ TO 0
  RETURN
END PROCEDURE
**************************************************************************
```

Figure 9-9. The INITIALIZE HARDWARE procedure.

The INITIALIZE HARDWARE procedure performs the functions required to put both the Intel 8251 communications interface and the Intel 8253 interval timer into the operational mode required by the application. The first part of this procedure initializes the interval timer so that it acts as a square-wave signal generator to provide the desired RxC/ and TxC/ clock signals for the communications interface chip. The mode in which we use the communications interface chip requires a multiplier factor of sixteen; that is, the clock signals must be sixteen times the desired baud rate. The required clock signals are generated by the interval timer by dividing the system bus clock by an appropriate integer. Figure 9-16 lists the divisors required for various clock signal rates (it is assumed that the system bus clock operates at a frequency of 921.6 kilohertz). The instructions in memory locations 0010 H through 0013 H (the H stands for hexadecimal) in Figure 9-13 cause a mode byte to be sent to the interval timer chip to configure timer number 2 (there are three timers on the chip) to act as a square-wave generator. The mode byte also prepares the chip to use the next two bytes received as a 16-bit divisor. The least-significant byte of the divisor is then sent first followed by the most-significant byte as implemented by the instructions in memory locations 0014 H through 001B H shown in Figure 9-13. In the example, we chose a transmission rate of 9600 baud for use during check out so that the hardware is stimulated at the rate at which it is intended to be used. Slower rates are obtained by modifying the INITIALIZE HARDWARE procedure if desired.

Baud rate	Clock frequency (kHz)	Divisor
9600	153.6	6
4800	76.8	12
2400	38.4	24
1200	19.2	48
300	4.8	192

Figure 9-16. Clock signal divisors for the interval timer chip.

The second part of the INITIALIZE HARDWARE procedure initializes the communications interface chip. The three steps required to initialize the chip are as follows:

1. Ensure that the chip is in the reset state so that it is ready to receive a mode byte.
2. Send a mode byte to the chip.
3. Send a command byte to the chip.

To ensure that the chip is reset before sending out a mode byte, we first send out a software reset sequence consisting of four bytes. The four-byte sequence ensures that the chip is interpreting the bytes sent to it as command bytes and then sending a

```
PROCEDURE: READ CHARACTER (;CHARACTER)
**************************************************************************
DESIGNED BY:  L. B. EVANS            01-26-81
OUTPUT PARAMETER:  CHARACTER
**************************************************************************
BEGIN PROCEDURE
  WAIT UNTIL CHARACTER IS AVAILABLE AT INPUT PORT
  SET CHARACTER TO CHARACTER CODE READ FROM INPUT PORT
  RETURN
END PROCEDURE
**************************************************************************
```

Figure 9-10. The READ CHARACTER procedure.

```
PROCEDURE: OUTPUT CHARACTER (CHARACTER;)
**************************************************************************
DESIGNED BY:  L. B. EVANS          01-26-81
INPUT PARAMETER: CHARACTER
**************************************************************************
BEGIN PROCEDURE
  WAIT FOR OUTPUT PORT TO COMPLETE PREVIOUS CHARACTER TRANSMISSION
  SET OUTPUT PORT TO CHARACTER CODE TO BE TRANSMITTED
  RETURN
END PROCEDURE
**************************************************************************
```

Figure 9-11. The OUTPUT CHARACTER procedure.

```
:F1:ASM80 EXEC.ASM PRINT (EXEC.LST) DEBUG
ISIS-II 8080/8085 MACRO ASSEMBLER, V3.0
  LOC  OBJ         LINE        SOURCE STATEMENT
                        ;                       PROCEDURE: TEST EXECUTIVE (;)
                        ;                       ******************************************************************
                        ;                       DESIGNED BY: L. B. EVANS          01-26-81
                        ;                       LOCAL PARAMETER: CHARACTER
                                   DSEG
  0000                    CHAR:    DS    1
                        ;                       ******************************************************************
                        ;                       BEGIN PROCEDURE
                          EXEC:
                        ;                         CALL: INITIALIZE HARDWARE (;)
                                   CSEG
  0000 CD0100     D                CALL  INIT
                        ;                         DO FOREVER
                          LOOP:
                        ;                           CALL: READ CHARACTER (;CHARACTER)
  0003 CD0200     D                CALL  READ
  0006 320000     D                STA   CHAR
                        ;                           CALL: OUTPUT CHARACTER (CHARACTER;)
  0009 210000     D                LXI   H,CHAR
  000C 4E                          MOV   C,M
                        ;                         END
  000D C30300     C                JMP   LOOP
                        ;                       END PROCEDURE
                        ;                       ******************************************************************
```

Figure 9-12. Assembly language listing for the TEST EXECUTIVE procedure.

```
  OBJ   LINE        SOURCE STATEMENT

              ;                            PROCEDURE: INITIALIZE HARDWARE (;)
              ;                            **************************************************************************
              ;                            DESIGNED BY: L. B. EVANS       02-16-81
              ;                            LOCAL PARAMETER NOT USED IN DESIGN LANGUAGE:  BAUD RATE FACTOR
                           DSEG
06              BR9600  EQU  0006H
              ;                            PORT DEFINITIONS: INTEL 8253 INTERVAL TIMER
33              TIMCTL  EQU  33H
32              TIMER2  EQU  32H
              ;                                          INTEL 8251 COMMUNICATIONS INTERFACE
21              SERCTL  EQU  21H
20              DATUM   EQU  20H
              ;                            **************************************************************************
              ;                            BEGIN PROCEDURE
                INIT:
              ;                              INITIALIZE TIMER #2 TO ACT AS A SQUARE WAVE GENERATOR (MODE 3) AT 9600 BAUD
                        CSEG
10 3EB6                 MVI   A,0B6H
12 D333                 OUT   TIMCTL
14 3E06                 MVI   A,LOW (BR9600)
16 D332                 OUT   TIMER2
18 3E00                 MVI   A,HIGH (BR9600)
1A D332                 OUT   TIMER2
              ;                              INITIALIZE COMMUNICATIONS INTERFACE FOR RS-232-C TERMINAL
              ;                                RESET CHIP AND ASSURE THAT IT IS READY TO RECEIVE MODE BYTE
1C 3E00                 MVI   A,00H
1E D321                 OUT   SERCTL
20 D321                 OUT   SERCTL
22 D321                 OUT   SERCTL
24 3E40                 MVI   A,40H
26 D321                 OUT   SERCTL
              ;                                SEND MODE BYTE TO SET CHIP TO 16X BAUD RATE, 8 BITS, NO PARITY, 1 STOP BIT
28 3E4E                 MVI   A,4EH
2A D321                 OUT   SERCTL
              ;                                SEND COMMAND BYTE TO ENABLE TRANSMIT AND RECEIVE AND SET DTR/ TO 0 and RTS/ TO 0
2C 3E27                 MVI   A,27H
2E D321                 OUT   SERCTL
              ;                              RETURN
30 C9                   RET
              ;                            END PROCEDURE
              ;                            **************************************************************************
```

Figure 9-13. Assembly language listing for the INITIALIZE HARDWARE procedure.

```
LOC  OBJ              SOURCE STATEMENT

                   ;                       PROCEDURE: READ CHARACTER (;CHARACTER)
                   ;                       ********************************************************************
                   ;                       DESIGNED BY: L. B. EVANS       01-26-81
                   ;                       OUTPUT PARAMETER: CHARACTER
                           DSEG
0001                 CHAR1: DS    1
                   ;                       ********************************************************************
                   ;                       BEGIN PROCEDURE
                     READ:
                   ;                         WAIT UNTIL CHARACTER IS AVAILABLE AT INPUT PORT
                           CSEG
0031 DB21            WAIT1: IN    SERCTL
0033 FE02                   CPI   02H
0035 CA3100    C            JZ    WAIT1
                   ;                         SET CHARACTER TO CHARACTER CODE READ FROM INPUT PORT
0038 DB20                   IN    DATUM
003A E67F                   ANI   7FH
003C 320100    D            STA   CHAR1
                   ;                         RETURN
003F C9                     RET
                   ;                       END PROCEDURE
                   ;                       ********************************************************************
```

Figure 9-14. Assembly language listing for the READ CHARACTER procedure.

```
LOC  OBJ              SOURCE STATEMENT

                   ;                       PROCEDURE: OUTPUT CHARACTER (CHARACTER;)
                   ;                       ********************************************************************
                   ;                       DESIGNED BY: L. B. EVANS       01-26-81
                   ;                       INPUT PARAMETER: CHARACTER
                           DSEG
0002                 CHAR2: DS    1
                   ;                       ********************************************************************
                   ;                       BEGIN PROCEDURE
                           CSEG
                   ; OUTPUT:
0040 210200    D            LXI   H,CHAR2
0043 71                     MOV   M,C
                   ;                         WAIT FOR OUTPUT PORT TO COMPLETE PREVIOUS CHARACTER TRANSMISSION
0044 DB21            WAIT2: IN    SERCTL
0046 FE01                   CPI   01H
0048 CA4400    C            JZ    WAIT2
                   ;                         SET OUTPUT PORT TO CHARACTER CODE TO BE TRANSMITTED
004B 3A0200    D            LDA   CHAR2
004E D320                   OUT   DATUM
                   ;                         RETURN
0050 C9                     RET
                   ;                       END PROCEDURE
                   ;                       ********************************************************************
                   ;                       END MODULE
                   ;       END
```

Figure 9-15. Assembly language listing for the OUTPUT CHARACTER procedure.

command byte which is interpreted as a software reset command. The instructions in memory locations 001C H through 0027 H in Figure 9-13 cause this software reset sequence to be sent to the chip. The three zero bytes ensure that the chip is ready to receive the software reset command byte, 40 H.

As we saw in Chapter 8, the communications interface chip expects the byte received following a hardware or software reset to be a mode byte. Thus, the next byte sent to the chip will be interpreted as a mode byte. The mode byte is sent to the chip by the instructions in memory locations 0028 H through 002B H; it sets the chip into the asynchronous communications mode, sets the transmission rate multiplier factor to sixteen, and sets the number of bits per data byte to eight bits with no parity, one start bit, and one stop bit. The next byte sent to the chip is interpreted as a command byte and is sent by the instructions in memory locations 002C H through 002F H. It enables the chip so that it can transmit and receive serial data and it activates the data terminal ready (DTR/) and the ready to send (RTS/) signals. This concludes the initialization of the Intel 8253 interval timer chip and the Intel 8251 communications interface chip for the test system.

The READ CHARACTER procedure waits for a character to be received by the communications interface chip, reads the character into the central processor chip from the input port connected to the communications interface chip, stores the character in memory location CHAR1, and returns the character to the TEST EXECUTIVE as an output parameter. The loop in memory locations 0031 H through 0037 H reads a status byte from the communications interface chip and tests the second least-significant bit in the status byte to determine if a character has been received. When this bit indicates that a character is received, the loop is terminated and an input instruction is executed to read the character into the central processor chip; this step also prepares the communications interface chip to receive the next character.

The OUTPUT CHARACTER procedure receives a character from TEST EXECUTIVE as an input parameter, saves the character in memory location CHAR2, waits until the transmission of the previous character that was sent to the output port connected to the communications interface chip is completed, and sends the new character to the output port for transmission. A loop similar to that described for the READ CHARACTER procedure is used to read a status byte from the chip to determine if it is ready to accept new output data. When the status byte indicates that the transmitter is available, the character is sent to the output port connected to the communications interface chip by the instructions in memory locations 004B H through 004F H shown in Figure 9-15.

Now that we have described the check-out configuration of the communications interface module and the software that exercises the module, let us discuss the steps used during check out. Overall, we must verify that the module is properly initialized and that serial digital data is being received and transmitted according to the specifications for the module. During check out, the microcomputer analyzer or the in-circuit emulator is used to control the software and to display the results obtained during the execution of the software. The addresses of the memory locations containing the instructions shown in Figures 9-12 through 9-15 are used to supply information to the check-out tools which indicate where to start execution (starting points) and where to stop execution (breakpoints). Outputs supplied by the microcomputer analyzer and the in-circuit emulator can be used to synchronize or trigger an oscilloscope or a logic analyzer connected to the module. This configuration permits the display of the internal signals in the module to be synchronized with the execution of the software.

The software-driven dynamic check out of the communications interface chip includes the following steps:

1. Determine that the TEST EXECUTIVE procedure calls the INITIALIZE HARDWARE procedure.
2. Verify that the INITIALIZE HARDWARE procedure sends the correct sequence of bytes to the output ports.
3. Using an oscilloscope, determine that correct clock signals are generated by the interval timer chip after it is initialized.
4. Verify that the READ CHARACTER procedure is called and that the microcomputer repeatedly reads status bytes from the communications interface chip and checks the bit in the status byte which indicates whether a character has been received by the chip.
5. Depress a key on the terminal or other RS-232-C compatible input device and verify that the bit being checked indicates that a character has been received and that the ASCII character code corresponding to the pressed key is read into the central processor and stored in memory location CHAR in the EXECUTIVE procedure.
6. Verify that the OUTPUT CHARACTER procedure is called and that its input parameter is the same ASCII character code as was received in step 5.
7. Verify that the status byte that is read from the communications interface chip indicates that the chip is ready to accept a character before the character is sent to the chip. Also verify that the correct ASCII character code is sent to the output port. The character corresponding to the key depressed in step 5 should now appear on the terminal display screen.
8. Repeat steps 4 through 7 to verify operation for other characters.

In this section we used a communications interface chip as an example to demonstrate how to conduct the software-driven dynamic check out of a hardware module. The check-out configuration we presented and the software procedures used to exercise the hardware are typical of those used to check out a variety of similar modules. It is especially important to perform software-driven dynamic check out when the design contains intelligent peripheral devices. As stated earlier, problems detected during module check out are corrected more cost effectively than those detected during system integration.

HARDWARE DEVELOPMENT AND CHECK-OUT TOOLS

We now consider the development and check-out tools that are used during the standalone static, standalone dynamic, and software-driven dynamic hardware check out phases. Because of the higher complexity of microcomputer-based systems, more powerful check-out tools are required than are used during the check out of more conventional electronic hardware. The increased complexity of the tools is necessary, in part, because microcomputer-based systems are bus oriented. As we have seen, bus signal lines are often time-shared; that is, different types of information are sent on the same signal lines at different times. Thus, the tools used for check out must provide the capability to examine the information on a bus in a very selective manner.

The following subsections present the most important attributes of eight tools used during hardware check out and describe how they are used. These tools are the digital voltmeter, oscilloscope, static switch/display box, signal/pulse generator, logic analyzer, programmable logic analyzer, microcomputer logic analyzer, and in-circuit emulator.

Digital voltmeter. The digital voltmeter is used during static check out to check power supply voltage levels and to measure the DC signal characteristics of logic signals. The voltmeter is the best tool to use to determine that a given signal is within allowable tolerances when it is in either the logic ONE or the logic ZERO state. Note that a bus signal may legitimately be at a voltage level that corresponds to an *indeterminate* logic level if it is driven by *tri-state* buffers which are all in the inactive state simultaneously. The indeterminate logic level may persist until one of the tri-state drivers on the bus forces the signal either to a logic ZERO state or to a logic ONE state. However, an indeterminate logic level may also indicate that a faulty condition exists; it may occur if a signal driver is excessively loaded or if a signal line is undriven. In the latter case, the voltmeter indicates the bias voltage of a floating input line. Most digital voltmeters are also capable of measuring resistance and current. Thus, the voltmeter can be used to perform continuity checks and to measure the current drawn from the power supply by part of a module.

Oscilloscope. The oscilloscope is a valuable tool during dynamic check out. It is most useful for measuring the AC characteristics of logic signals. It can be used as a standalone tool to observe the free-running clock signals within a module to verify that their risetime, falltime, and frequency are correct. Its usefulness is enhanced during the other phases of dynamic check out if an intelligent trigger signal is provided by another tool to synchronize the oscilloscope with the software.

As we indicated earlier, during dynamic check out it is necessary to observe bus signals during specific time intervals that correspond to a particular function being checked out. In order to isolate and display the activity on the bus only during the desired time interval, a logic analyzer or in-circuit emulator is used to provide an intelligent trigger signal for the oscilloscope. In operation, the logic analyzer or in-circuit emulator waits until it detects that the desired event has occurred and then produces a pulse to trigger the oscilloscope so that only the signals of interest are displayed. For an event that has a short duration or occurs infrequently, an analog or digital *storage* oscilloscope may be needed to view the signal properly. If the event under observation is software-driven, then a DO FOREVER . . . END loop can be created that contains the software required to stimulate the event. Then, when the loop is executed, the event is retraced sufficiently often to enable the signals to be viewed on a standard oscilloscope.

Static switch/display box. The static switch/display box is a useful tool during both static and dynamic check out. It provides test inputs to a module which will be supplied by another module in the completed system. A schematic diagram of a switch/display box is illustrated in Figure 9-17. In use, the switch/display box is connected to the address/control lines and data lines of the module under test. Note that, if the module is connected to a bus, it may be necessary to supply thirty-two or more inputs to the module. The switch/display box also contains a set of discrete LEDs which display the state of each bit being switched. It uses tri-state drivers as shown in the figure so that it can be connected to output lines conveniently. The switch/display box is also used to supply static inputs to a module during dynamic check out.

Signal/pulse generator. A signal or pulse generator is used during standalone dynamic check out to provide clock and control signals supplied by another module in the completed system. The signal or pulse generator allows the module to be operated dynamically in a standalone configuration to verify timing. If a standard audio signal generator is used to supply the input to a module, it is good practice to connect it through a gate of the same type used in the final design to provide correct impedance matching.

Logic analyzer. A logic analyzer is an intelligent digital data acquisition device and is a powerful tool for checking out hardware modules during both static and dynamic check out. Logic analyzers are available containing a variety of capabilities and in many packaged forms. A logic analyzer may be purchased as a plug-in accessory for an oscilloscope, as a standalone device using a CRT or LED display, or as an option to an in-circuit emulator that is part of a microcomputer development system. Although we discuss only briefly the capabilities of the logic analyzer and how it is used, we emphasize that it is an extremely useful tool for checking out the hardware modules of a microcomputer-based system. In use, the logic analyzer is connected to a set of up to thirty-two digital signals in the hardware module and it then displays the states of these signals relative to the occurrence of a specified trigger condition. The trigger condition usually requires that a subset of these signals be in specified states. Once the trigger condition occurs, the display is started and the states of the signals are displayed for each subsequent clock period. For synchronization, a clock signal from the hardware module under test is supplied to the

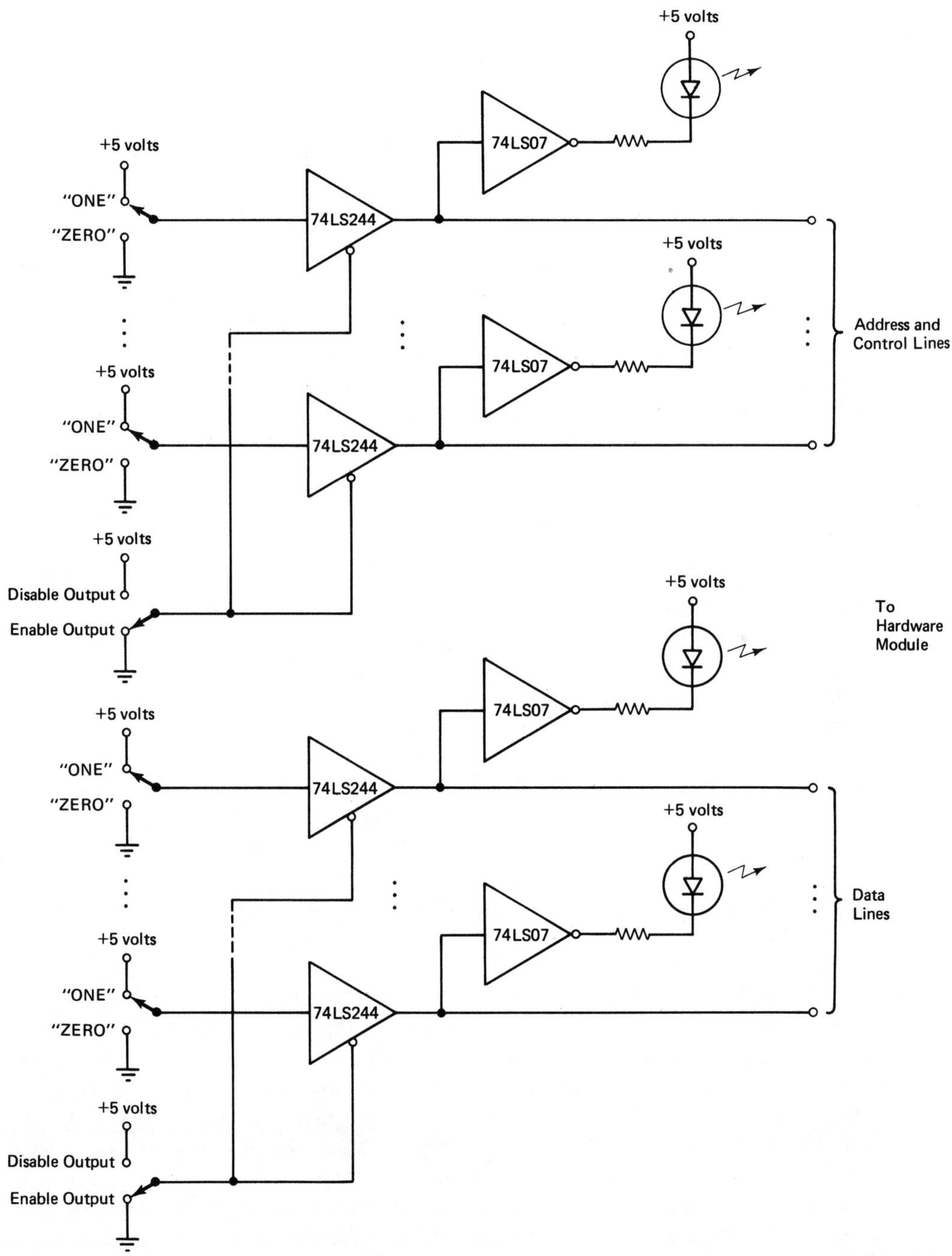

Figure 9-17. Static switch/display box schematic diagram.

logic analyzer to enable it to operate in a sampled-data mode. Some logic analyzers allow the user to specify that only certain signal states should be displayed once the trigger condition occurs. Many can also measure and display the absolute time between two displayed states. The latter feature is useful during dynamic check out since it permits timing to be verified. The logic analyzer is the best tool for examining signals on a bus. Since it has the ability to start its display when a particular event occurs, it allows specific information to be extracted from the continuous information flow on the bus.

Programmable logic analyzer. The programmable logic analyzer provides the basic functions discussed above. It differs from the standard logic analyzer since the specifications for trigger conditions and display modes may be automatically loaded into the logic analyzer from a computer instead of from a keyboard. This capability is useful if a test that has a relatively complex specification is to be repeated many times. Also, if the same test specification is to be used for a large number of modules, a programmable logic analyzer ensures that the same test is performed on each module.

Microcomputer logic analyzer. The microcomputer logic analyzer acquires data through direct connection to a microcomputer central processor. In use, it is configured for use with a specific central processor, such as the Intel 8085, through the use of a *personality* module. Because the characteristics of the central processor to which the microcomputer logic analyzer is connected are known, it can provide an intelligent display of the signals that are monitored. It converts these signals into machine language instructions and displays them in assembly language form. This format enables us to track the software as it is executed by the central processor. The display of the *disassembled* software is useful during software-driven dynamic check out since it permits us to observe simultaneous events in both the hardware and the software.

The microcomputer logic analyzer may contain an auxiliary probe that can be connected to a set of internal signals in the hardware module. The states of these hardware signals are then displayed adjacent to the disassembled central processor instructions. A suitable trigger condition for the microcomputer logic analyzer may be specified as an address on the central processor address bus, as data on the central processor data bus, or as a combination of states of the auxiliary probe signals. This flexibility allows the user to activate the microcomputer logic analyzer display on *either* software or hardware events. Today, the microcomputer logic analyzer is probably the most cost-effective tool for hardware integration for a wide variety of applications. As microcomputers become more powerful, however, it becomes more difficult to build an instrument that can perform the disassembly operation automatically and still be priced reasonably. Thus, as this is being written, microcomputer logic analyzers are readily available to work with most 8-bit microcomputers but are not yet available to work with 16-bit microcomputers. The in-circuit emulator we discuss next is therefore a good alternative to use when checking out a 16-bit microcomputer-based system.

In-circuit emulator. The in-circuit emulator was introduced in Chapter 7 and it is discussed again in Chapter 10 to illustrate how it is used during system integration. In this chapter we discuss its application to hardware check out and integration. The in-circuit emulator performs many of the functions that the microcomputer logic analyzer does during software-driven dynamic check out. It provides the user with a tool to start and stop the execution of the software, to examine data values before and after the execution of a program segment, to examine data values which are read from input ports or written to output ports, and to display the assembly language instructions corresponding to the machine language instructions being executed. Some in-circuit emulators also provide a data probe that can be used for the acquisition of digital data during the execution of the software. However, most in-circuit emulators do not provide the flexible, general-purpose capability provided by the logic analyzer. If the in-circuit emulator does not provide adequate data acquisition capability, an external logic analyzer can be used with the in-circuit emulator. The in-circuit emulator then controls the execution of the software and displays the instructions being executed and the logic analyzer displays the states of the desired internal hardware signals. In this mode of operation, the logic analyzer is synchronized either directly or indirectly with the in-circuit emulator. For direct synchronization, a trigger signal is provided to the logic analyzer by the in-circuit emulator to enable it to begin to acquire and display data. For indirect synchronization, the logic analyzer can be triggered by an event which is be detected in the hardware and which is directly related to the execution of the software. For example, if a chip select line is used to trigger the logic analyzer, the display is synchronized with the execution of an instruction that causes information to be sent to or read from the selected chip. Once the point of synchronization is reached, subsequent instructions are displayed by the in-circuit emulator and the corresponding signal states are displayed by the logic analyzer. Since both of the displays are referenced to the same starting point, they may be compared and analyzed in a straightforward manner.

SIXTH DOCUMENTATION LEVEL

The sixth documentation level contains the hardware integration and check-out plan. As in every other stage of the system design cycle, the work being performed must be properly documented. For hardware check out, a systematic check-out plan should be developed that can be followed by the design team members during the initial prototype system check out and also by the personnel whose job it is to check out production systems and to perform product maintenance and repair after delivery.

The check-out plan for each module should be written by the person responsible for the check out of that module. There are five components to a good check-out plan. We discuss each of them below.

Module functions to be checked. This section of the check-out plan describes the module functions that are tested before system integration. For the most part, these tests are performed in a standalone manner. However, it is possible that some functions are best checked out with other hardware modules and therefore should be done during hardware integration. Highly interactive module functions usually fall into this category.

Check-out approach and configuration diagram. This section describes the overall test approach and should include a top-level block diagram of the check-out configuration for each module. The diagram shows how the test equipment and hardware modules that are being checked out concurrently or have previously been tested are connected to the module under test.

Required test equipment. This part of the check-out plan consists of a list of the test equipment required during the check out of each module. This list is important for scheduling equipment when several modules are being tested at the same time. It can also be used early in the project schedule to determine if additional test equipment should be purchased or leased.

Required software. This section includes a list of the software modules required during hardware check out. These modules consist of procedures that are part of the software design as well as procedures designed specifically for hardware check out. As discussed earlier, a TEST EXECUTIVE procedure should be provided to call these procedures in a repetitive manner to exercise the hardware functions being checked out.

Detailed test sequence. This section describes each test sequence in a step-by-step manner. Each step should include sufficient detail so that an engineer and technician can conduct the test without needing additional information.

We have now completed our discussion of hardware check out and integration. In Chapter 10 we describe how the hardware and software modules that have been checked out independently are brought together during system integration.

EXERCISES

9-1. Design a hardware integration plan for the computerized television set (see the Exercises in Chapters 2 through 5).

9-2. Design a hardware integration plan for the computerized traffic light controller (see the Exercises in Chapters 2 through 5).

9-3. Design a hardware integration plan for the computerized sports scoreboard (see the Exercises in Chapters 2 through 5).

9-4. Design a hardware integration plan for the computerized point-of-sale terminal (see the Exercises in Chapters 2 through 5).

Chapter 10

System Integration and Evaluation

We have seen how to design, construct, and integrate both software and hardware modules and subsystems. The modules are now operational and the hardware modules are integrated together, as are most of the software modules. What remains is to install the software in the hardware and to integrate the two parts into a completely operational system. The evaluation of the completed system to verify that it meets the user requirements and functional specification completes the task of building a microcomputer-based system.

INTEGRATION OF SOFTWARE INTO HARDWARE

In Chapter 7 we described the integration plan and concentrated on the software integration phases. The hardware integration phases were covered in Chapter 9 along with the hardware check-out plan. We now consider the remainder of the integration plan that contains the system integration phases and includes the following:

- The installation of the software in the hardware and the verification that the software executes correctly in the hardware. In the earlier software integration phases, the facilities of the microcomputer development system in-circuit emulator were used to verify the functional operation of the software since the hardware was not yet checked out and available.
- The integration of the software modules that require that the INPUT, OUTPUT, and INTERRUPT hardware modules be operational.

Installation of the software in the hardware can be done in either of two ways. The first method utilizes the facilities of the in-circuit emulator to install the software in the hardware one module at a time, checking each module as it is installed. In the second method, all of the software is installed in the hardware at the same time; its operation is then verified by using the facilities of the common stub and the other tools, such as the microcomputer analyzer. In either case, once the software has been installed in the hardware, check out of the INPUT, OUTPUT, and INTERRUPT modules can begin.

The INPUT module is checked by using the low-level procedures that interface with the hardware to provide specific input values and by examining the values of the internal system parameters that depend on these inputs. These low-level modules are already operational since they were used during hardware check out. The OUTPUT module is checked by providing inputs to make the system operate in a controlled manner so that the output data is predictable. Then either the outputs are examined directly or the performance of the actuators controlled by the outputs is observed.

The INTERRUPT module is checked by executing the software that is not interrupt driven and by inducing hardware interrupts to occur. When the interrupt system has been verified in this way, the interrupts can then be permitted to occur naturally for final verification of the operation of the INTERRUPT module.

IN-CIRCUIT EMULATOR

The in-circuit emulator was introduced in Chapter 7 because it can provide symbolic memory addressing capability during software integration. But the in-circuit emulator has other capabilities that can be used during system integration to systematically install the software in the hardware system under development. By using the in-circuit emulator, the software is moved from the microcomputer development system into the hardware system under development one or two modules at a time, and the performance of the modules is verified as they are moved. Let us describe how this is done.

Figure 10-1 illustrates how the in-circuit emulator is connected during system integration. The microprocessor integrated circuit chip is removed from its socket in the hardware system under development and is replaced by the plug at the end of the cable from the in-circuit emulator. Initially, there are no programmable read-only memory (PROM) chips in the hardware and the memory sockets are empty. The software is loaded into the microcomputer development system memory and executed by the microprocessor in the in-circuit emulator using the hardware facilities that are accessible through the plug on the in-circuit emulator cable. Then, after verification of correct operation, one or two of the software modules is burned into PROMs by the PROM programmer and the PROMs are plugged into the memory sockets reserved for them. The in-circuit emulator software in the microcomputer development system is then reconfigured so that the installed software modules are executed from the hardware PROMs while the remaining software modules continue to be executed from the microcomputer development system memory. This operation is possible because the PROMs in the hardware are accessible to the microprocessor in the in-circuit emulator through the plug on the in-circuit emulator cable. Thus, the in-circuit emulator can selectively access the memory in either system. Since software integration has been completed, it is a relatively straightforward task

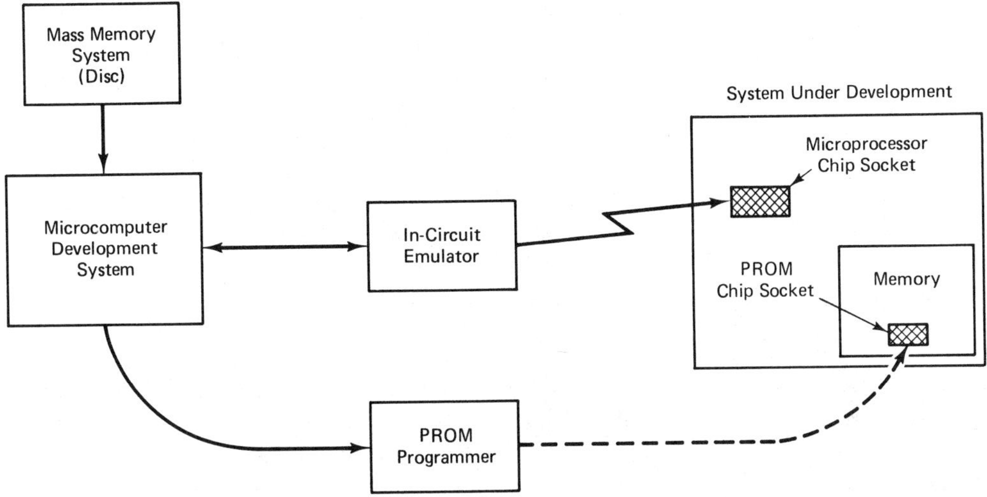

Figure 10-1. Use of the in-circuit emulator during system integration.

to burn the PROMs and thereby move the software into the hardware and verify its correct operation. It is equally straightforward to discontinue the use of the read-write memory in the microcomputer development system and use the read-write memory (RAM) chips in the system hardware.

One advantage of using the in-circuit emulator to move the software one module at a time into the system hardware is that it minimizes the iterations needed when burning the PROMs during check out. Despite this advantage, if an in-circuit emulator is not available, the software can be moved in a single step. All of the PROMs are burned at one time and the common stub, monitor, and microcomputer analyzer are then used to verify the operation of the software in the hardware.

Once the software that was checked out during software integration is functioning in the hardware, we can check out and integrate the INPUT, OUTPUT, and INTERRUPT software. In the next section we consider how to distribute the software among the PROM chips to minimize reburning the PROMs when correcting errors found in the latter stages of system integration.

INSTALLATION OF SOFTWARE IN HARDWARE

The use of programmable read-only memory chips provides a way of installing the software in the hardware during system integration. One or two at a time, the modules are burned into the PROMs, the PROM chips are installed in the hardware, and performance is verified using the facilities of the in-circuit emulator. Then, when all of the PROMs are burned, the software will be physically in place and operating in the hardware without the assistance of the microcomputer development system. The final system integration phases can then be started.

As stated repeatedly, errors in design or programming may occur at any point in the integration process. When an error is detected, it must be corrected. This requires that one or more procedures be corrected or redesigned, that the corrected procedures be recompiled, and that the software be linked and located. When a procedure is corrected, there is a high probability that some procedures will no longer be located in the same memory locations when the software is linked and located. The PROMs containing the relocated procedures must then be reburned. Moreover, if a module that has been burned into a PROM calls a procedure that has been moved, that PROM becomes unusable and must also be reburned. Burning PROMs is time-consuming. Therefore, let us consider an approach that minimizes the need to reburn existing PROMs when software is corrected.

If a *transfer vector* is used to complete the linking process for each procedure called by a procedure in another module, then the need to reburn PROMs during integration is minimized. Figure 10-2 illustrates both the commonly used calling linkage and the transfer vector calling linkage. The transfer vector calling linkage

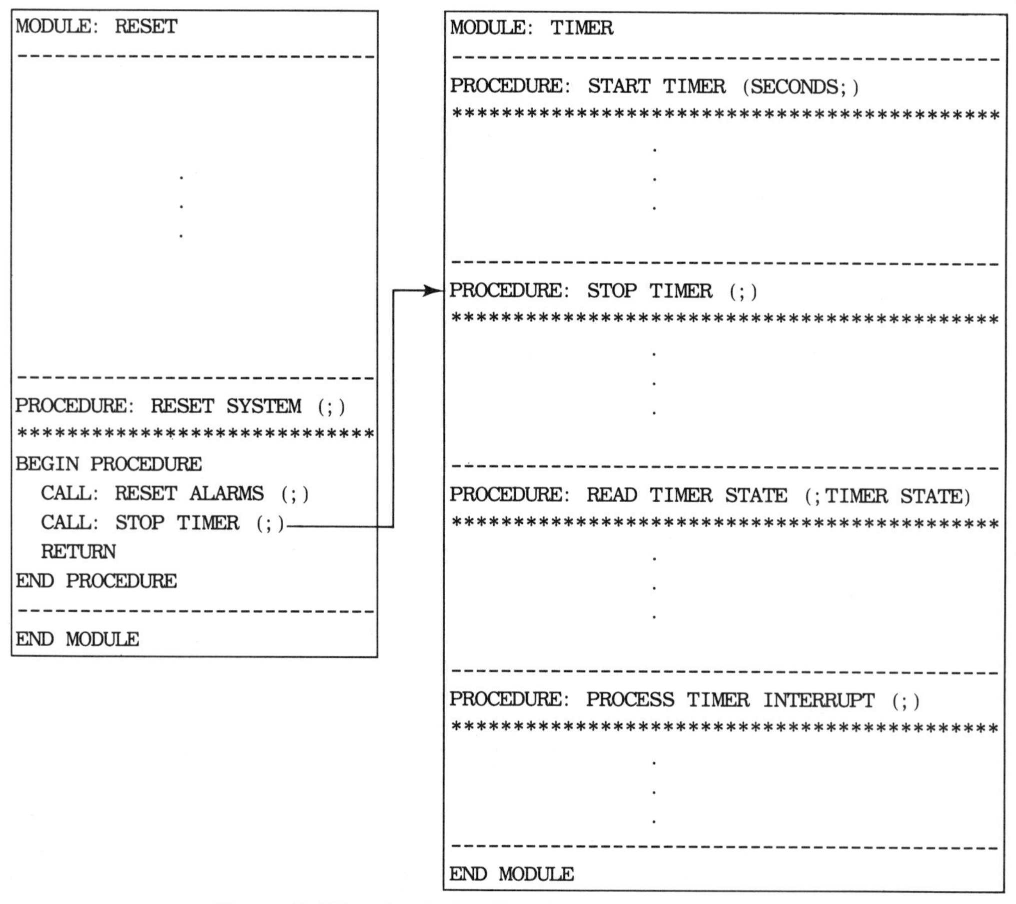
MODULE: RESET
PROCEDURE: RESET SYSTEM (;)
BEGIN PROCEDURE
CALL: RESET ALARMS (;)
CALL: STOP TIMER (;)
RETURN
END PROCEDURE
END MODULE
MODULE: TIMER
PROCEDURE: START TIMER (SECONDS;)
PROCEDURE: STOP TIMER (;)
PROCEDURE: READ TIMER STATE (;TIMER STATE)
PROCEDURE: PROCESS TIMER INTERRUPT (;)
END MODULE

Figure 10-2(a). Standard calling linkage for microcomputer software.

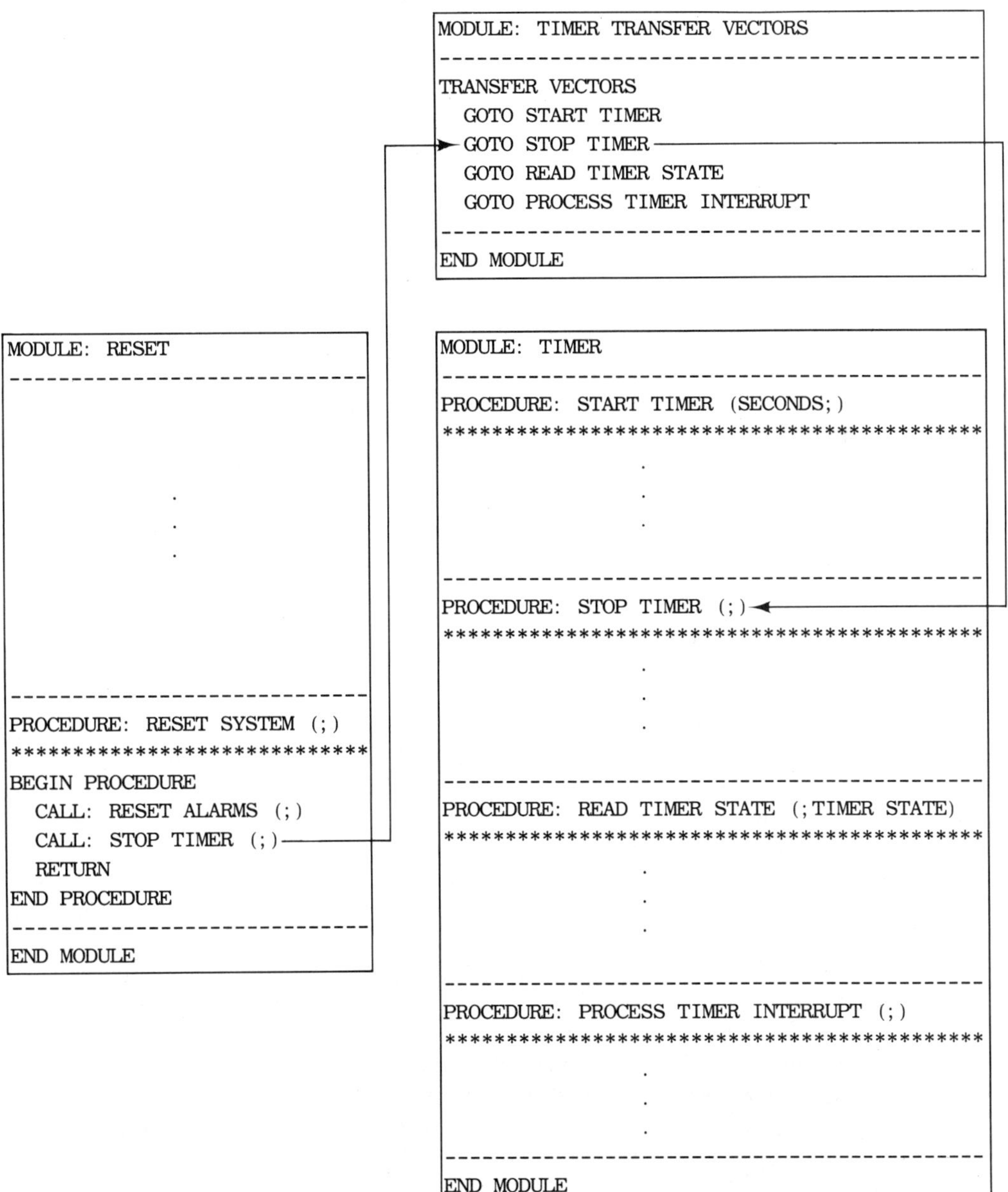
MODULE: TIMER TRANSFER VECTORS
TRANSFER VECTORS
GOTO START TIMER
GOTO STOP TIMER
GOTO READ TIMER STATE
GOTO PROCESS TIMER INTERRUPT
END MODULE
MODULE: RESET
PROCEDURE: RESET SYSTEM (;)
BEGIN PROCEDURE
CALL: RESET ALARMS (;)
CALL: STOP TIMER (;)
RETURN
END PROCEDURE
END MODULE
MODULE: TIMER
PROCEDURE: START TIMER (SECONDS;)
PROCEDURE: STOP TIMER (;)
PROCEDURE: READ TIMER STATE (;TIMER STATE)
PROCEDURE: PROCESS TIMER INTERRUPT (;)
END MODULE

Figure 10-2(b). Transfer vector calling linkage for microcomputer software.

requires that an additional operation be used to complete each call. Instead of calling a procedure directly, a *transfer vector procedure* is called; the transfer vector procedure is implemented as a single operation, such as a PL/M GOTO operation or assembly language *jump* instruction. This operation causes the actual procedure to be executed as if it were called directly. The transfer vectors are placed into a separate module called a *transfer vector module* so that, when the design is converted into a programming language, the transfer vector procedures remain grouped together. Then, if the name of the transfer vector module precedes the name of the procedure module in the link command, it ensures that the transfer vectors are located in the low-address locations of the PROM or group of PROMs when the linked modules are located. As a result, regardless of how the procedures themselves are modified, the linkage between calls from other modules and the transfer vectors will not change. Once the modules are linked and located in the PROMs, they must be linked together with the other modules in the system to connect all of the intermodule calls to their respective transfer vector procedures. Finally, after this last step has been carried out, each combined transfer vector and procedure module can be burned into the PROMs assigned to it.

Although the transfer vector linkage was used extensively for linking software in the fifties and sixties, it is no longer common, and microcomputer linkers do not provide this capability. However, many microcomputer high-level languages permit the transfer vector linkage to be implemented by the user or it can be implemented in assembly language, if necessary. In Figure 10-3 we illustrate how to implement the transfer vector linkage in Intel 8085 PL/M for the TIMER module. The PL/M GOTO operation that is equivalent to the assembly language unconditional *jump* instruction is used along with a procedure declaration to implement each transfer vector procedure. Note that the procedure names are assigned to the transfer vector procedures and a set of secondary names are assigned to the procedures themselves. The secondary names are declared as *external labels* in the transfer vector module since PL/M does not permit a GOTO operation to reference a procedure name. The steps in the calling sequence for the STOP TIMER procedure are illustrated with arrows in the figures.

If input or output parameters are passed to or returned from a PL/M procedure designed for the Intel 8085, they should not be declared in the transfer vector procedure declarations. Instead, they should be declared where they are used, namely, in the procedure declaration for the actual procedure. The PL/M compiler then causes these parameters to be moved between the calling procedure and the actual called procedure, as required. The transfer vector protocol for a procedure with a single byte input parameter is illustrated in Figure 10-3 by the START TIMER (TIMER 1) procedure; the protocol for a procedure that returns a single byte as an output parameter is illustrated in Figure 10-3 by the READ TIMER STATE (TIMER 3) procedure.

In the preceding description we assumed that each software module fits into an integral number of PROMs with a reasonable percentage of the memory left unused to provide for correcting errors. But the size of memory required for a module is rarely related to the size of the PROM in this manner. Thus, it may be necessary to combine modules, especially small modules, to ensure that large parts of the memory are not wasted. Transfer vector linkages can still be used when several modules are combined. To install these modules into a single PROM, the names of all of the transfer vector modules intended for the PROM must precede the names of the procedure modules in the link command. Then, when the transfer vector procedures for

```
/*MODULE: TIMER TRANSFER VECTORS                                          */
                                   TIMER$TRANSFER$VECTORS: DO;
/*----------------------------------------------------------------------- */
/*EXTERNAL DECLARATIONS                                                   */
                                    DECLARE (TIMER1,TIMER2,TIMER3,TIMER4) LABEL EXTERNAL;
/*----------------------------------------------------------------------- */
/*TRANSFER VECTORS                                                        */
/*  GOTO START TIMER                                                      */
                                    START$TIMER: PROCEDURE PUBLIC;
                                      GOTO TIMER1;
                                    END START$TIMER;
/*  GOTO STOP TIMER                                                       */
                                    STOP$TIMER: PROCEDURE PUBLIC;
                                      GOTO TIMER2;
                                    END STOP$TIMER;
/*  GOTO READ TIMER STATE                                                 */
                                    READ$TIMER$STATE: PROCEDURE PUBLIC;
                                      GOTO TIMER3;
                                    END READ$TIMER$STATE;
/*  GOTO PROCESS TIMER INTERRUPT                                          */
                                    PROCESS$TIMER$INTERRUPT: PROCEDURE PUBLIC;
                                      GOTO TIMER4;
                                    END PROCESS$TIMER$INTERRUPT;
/*----------------------------------------------------------------------- */
/*END MODULE                                                              */
                                   END TIMER$TRANSFER$VECTORS
```

```
/*MODULE: TIMER                                                           */
                                   TIMER: DO;
/*----------------------------------------------------------------------- */
/*PROCEDURE: START TIMER (SECONDS;)                                       */
                                   TIMER1: PROCEDURE (SECONDS) PUBLIC;
                                     DECLARE SECONDS BYTE;
/************************************************************************ */
/*                .                                                       */
/*                .                                                       */
/*                .                                                       */
/*----------------------------------------------------------------------- */
/*PROCEDURE: STOP TIMER (;)                                               */
                                   TIMER2: PROCEDURE PUBLIC;
/************************************************************************ */
/*                .                                                       */
/*                .                                                       */
/*                .                                                       */
/*----------------------------------------------------------------------- */
/*PROCEDURE: READ TIMER STATE (;TIMER STATE)                              */
                                   TIMER3: PROCEDURE BYTE PUBLIC;
                                     DECLARE TIMER$STATE BYTE;
/************************************************************************ */
/*                .                                                       */
/*                .                                                       */
/*                .                                                       */
/*----------------------------------------------------------------------- */
/*PROCEDURE: PROCESS TIMER INTERRUPT (;)                                  */
                                   TIMER4: PROCEDURE PUBLIC;
/************************************************************************ */
/*                .                                                       */
/*                .                                                       */
/*                .                                                       */
/*----------------------------------------------------------------------- */
/*END MODULE                                                              */
                                   END TIMER;
```

Figure 10-3. PL/M implementation of the transfer vector calling linkage.

the combined modules are located, they will be contiguous in the PROM, as required.

The Intel 8086 linker and locater provide examples of tools that work in a different manner than the corresponding tools we described for the Intel 8085. For the Intel 8086, all of the modules are linked together in a single operation and the linked software is then located in a single step. In order to divide the modules into separate PROMs, the locater is provided a starting PROM memory location for each module or group of modules. When transfer vector modules are used, the names of the modules in the link command must appear in the order described for the Intel 8085 linker. Note that the transfer vector modules, in this case, must be converted into assembly language since Intel 8086 PL/M does not permit the transfer vector linkage to be implemented directly.

ALTERNATE INTEGRATION APPROACH

Up to now, we assumed that most of the software is integrated together, installed in the hardware, and, along with the remainder of the software, integrated into the hardware. In many microcomputer-based systems, however, there is much interaction between the software and the hardware. In the latter system, a combined approach to software and system integration is often preferable.

If the combined software and system integration approach is selected, some of the hardware facilities must be operational earlier in the system design cycle. The remaining hardware facilities can then be added as they are needed during integration. The integration plan must specify which hardware and which software modules should be available at the beginning of each integration phase and which should be complete at the end of each phase.

The first two or three integration phases involve only software integration and may often be completed using only the facilities available in a microcomputer development system. When these initial integration phases are complete, an in-circuit emulator is used to connect the microcomputer development system to the hardware. Software modules that interface with corresponding hardware modules are then checked out and integrated. The integrated software modules are burned into PROMs and installed into the hardware. Then the performance of the integrated modules is verified in the hardware. During the remaining integration phases, these integrated modules can be utilized directly without the need to simulate their performance. Although not mentioned above, the common stub module can be integrated with the system at an early stage in the integration process and used along with the other check-out tools throughout integration.

An example of a system that can benefit from the combined software and system integration approach is the point-of-sale system. Much of the software in the point-of-sale system responds directly in some manner to the actuation of the function keys or the numeric keys. Thus, there is a distinct advantage to having the keyboard interface modules operational during as much of the system integration process as possible. Check out then consists of depressing various sequences of keys and noting if the system responds correctly. Since most of the feedback to the operator is through an alphanumeric display device, it is also useful if the display interface modules are also made operational during an early integration phase. Check out of the system can then be carried out in a very natural way. Moreover, the behavior of the system from a human factors viewpoint can be evaluated early during integration, thus permitting changes to the interface modules to be made more easily if it should become necessary to do so.

Both during integration and when the system is complete, it is necessary to evaluate performance to ensure that both the user requirements and the functional specification are satisfied. Let us now examine how to evaluate system performance.

SYSTEM EVALUATION

Throughout the system design cycle our goal is to build a microcomputer-based system that meets the user requirements and the functional specification. We have shown how to systematically design and construct both software and hardware modules and how to integrate these modules into a working system. We have also shown how to use software development tools to save time and effort and to assure that the system is adequately documented when it is complete. We now consider how to evaluate the performance of the completed system to ensure that it meets the user requirements.

If the system is built for a specific customer, it may be necessary to subject it to a set of *acceptance tests* which are specified by the customer. During the course of the acceptance tests, the *customer* determines whether the system performs in a manner that satisfies his or her requirements. If the system passes these acceptance tests, the customer accepts delivery of the system and installs it expecting that it will perform in an error-free manner. Thus, when we evaluate the performance of a system, we must be sufficiently thorough to ensure that it will pass the customer's acceptance tests regardless of how stringent they may be.

Although the final evaluation of a system takes place after the system has been built and is operating, we prepare for it throughout the system design cycle. When a review of the user requirements involves customer participation, system evaluation and acceptance testing has begun. Then, when we conduct reviews of the functional specification and the top-level design, the evaluation process continues. During check out and integration, we keep records that indicate that the modules are operating correctly both individually and when connected together. Thus, when the system is complete, much of the evaluation is also complete. What remains is to expose the system to both simulated and actual operating conditions to verify that it operates correctly under these conditions.

One of the problems that often shows up toward the end of the system design cycle is that the system may not operate at the required rate of speed even though it operates correctly functionally. One reason that this problem is likely to occur in our case is that the design language approach stresses clarity and accuracy instead of operating speed. In most real-time systems, however, only a small part of the software is critical with respect to achieving a high operating speed. It is therefore necessary to identify and isolate the critical modules. Then, these modules can either be redesigned or implemented with more efficient programming language operations or with assembly language instructions, if necessary, to increase their operating speed. In an extreme case, the microcomputer itself may be replaced with one that operates at a higher speed. Our use of design language and a high-level programming language, such as PL/M, makes it comparatively easy to substitute one microcomputer for another with minimum effort.

CONTINUING SUPPORT

Throughout the system design cycle we strive to design and build a system that contains no software or hardware *bugs* when it is delivered to the customer. But just as a hardware component may fail, software may also fail in service. The reasons for the two types of failure are different. Hardware fails because the physical or electrical characteristics of a component change with time, thereby causing its performance to deteriorate. Software fails if it is poorly designed or constructed or if it is not adequately checked out. All of these issues are addressed in this book. The inherent complexity of some systems prevents us from checking out software under all conceivable operating conditions. Thus, there is a need to provide continuing customer support after delivery.

When a software problem is discovered, it is first necessary to isolate the source of the problem. Good documentation is invaluable when trying to find and correct a software problem in an otherwise operational system. The self-documentation techniques we described permit a *software repairman* who was not involved during the system design cycle to *repair* the system. The common stub capability can help track down and localize a problem to a specific procedure or module. Once the faulty procedure or module is identified, software design or programming language operations can be changed to correct the problem. The system must then be rechecked sufficiently to ensure that it now operates correctly and that the changes have not created new problems.

Once the *bug* is corrected and the performance of the *repaired* system is verified, new ROMs must be prepared and installed in every system that has been built and delivered. The technique we described earlier for minimizing the burning of PROMs during system development also minimizes the number of ROM chips that must be discarded and replaced when a software *bug* is repaired in the field.

Thus, the systematic design methodology we presented has a profound influence on every phase of the development and continuing support of a microcomputer-based system. It simplifies the design, construction, documentation, and repair of the system. We have now reached the end of the *road map* of the book that was introduced in Chapter 1. Let us now examine several other applications of microcomputers to illustrate its broad potential.

EXERCISES

10-1. Design a set of acceptance tests for the computerized television set (see the Exercises in Chapters 2 through 5).

10-2. Design a set of acceptance tests for the computerized traffic light controller (see the Exercises in Chapters 2 through 5).

10-3. Design a set of acceptance tests for the computerized sports scoreboard (see the Exercises in Chapters 2 through 5).

10-4. Design a set of acceptance tests for the computerized point-of-sale terminal (see the Exercises in Chapters 2 through 5).

Chapter 11

Applications

We have seen that the microcomputer is a flexible component when used in a burglar alarm system or in a point-of-sale system. The microcomputer component can be used in many other applications such as indicated by the exercises; several other applications for which it is particularly suitable are:

- Games
- *Intelligent* terminals
- Automotive engine control systems
- White goods

In this chapter we discuss these applications to further illustrate the broad potential of the microcomputer and to introduce a variety of concepts to the reader. The reader is encouraged to design portions of the described applications; use the exercise presented at the end of this chapter as an example of how to design a simplified version of an actual system.

GAMES

The TV game started out as a fad and, as often happens for fads, interest waned rapidly after the initial excitement. Microcomputer-based games, however, have greatly increased flexibility over hard-wired games and have therefore sustained consumer interest in the TV game and moved it out of the fad category. The microcomputer-based games which use a TV or CRT display are now commonly called arcade games. Moreover, a number of microcomputer-based games, such as the microcomputer chess game, which do not use a TV or CRT display have been developed. In this section we concern ourselves only with a simple microcomputer-based TV game.

A block diagram of a *general-purpose* microcomputer-based TV game is illustrated in Figure 11-1. Functionally, the software for a particular game is either read

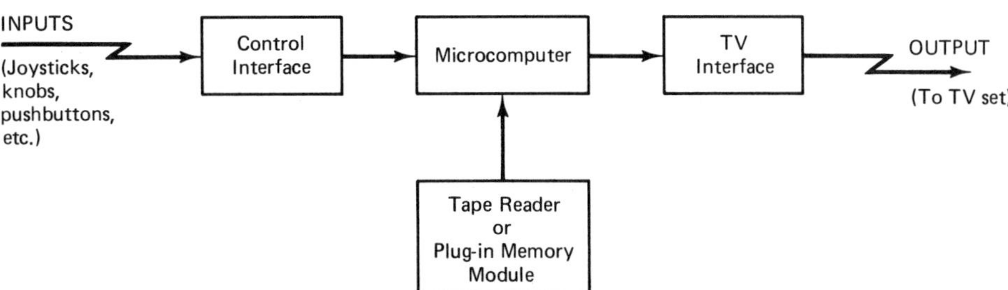

Figure 11-1. Microcomputer-based TV game.

into the microcomputer memory from a magnetic tape cassette through the tape reader or is obtained from a plug-in memory module. The system then displays the *playing field* on the TV display and waits for the START button to be actuated indicating that the players are ready to begin the game (see Figure 11-2). When the START button is pressed, the game is set into motion. A *ball* is *served* and moved across the TV screen and the players attempt to move their *paddles* to *hit* or intercept the ball as it moves toward their side of the *court*. The system keeps score and displays the score digitally on the TV screen, as shown in Figure 11-2. The RESET button permits the game to be stopped and restarted at any time. The additional inputs shown in Figure 11-2 permit varying the speed of the ball or the other game parameters to prevent the game from becoming boring. Although other games which can be read from tape or which are available through the plug-in memory modules may differ significantly, they all require that moving images be produced on the TV display. Let us examine how this is accomplished by the microcomputer using the *ball and paddle* game as an example.

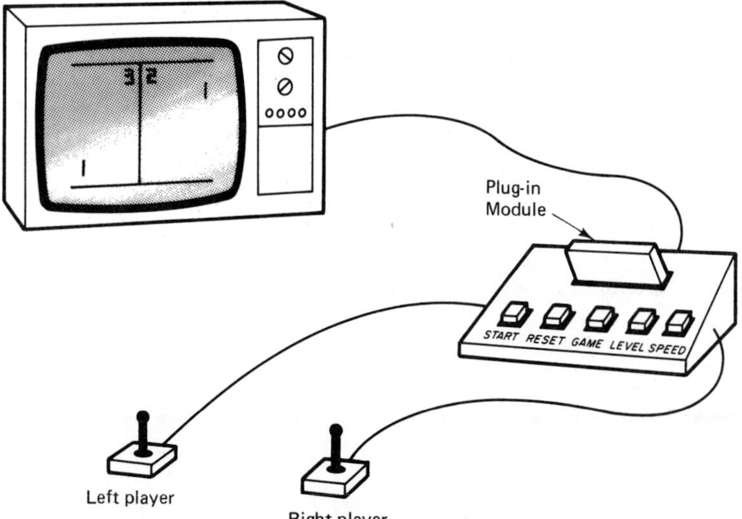

Figure 11-2. Illustration of a control panel and TV display for a TV game.

Figure 11-3 illustrates the portion of the system that includes the microcomputer and the TV interface. The TV screen is divided into a pattern of small squares, and a single bit in the display memory is assigned to each square on the display as shown in Figure 11-4 for four picture elements. Since a great deal of detail is not needed, the number of picture elements used is usually about ninety-six by eighty. Thus, for this example, a complete row of picture elements on the TV display requires ninety-six bits or twelve bytes of storage in the display memory. In addition, each *row* of twelve bytes is used six times so that six consecutive scan lines on the screen are produced for each *row*. The eighty *rows* therefore cause 480 scan lines to be generated, which is sufficient to completely cover a standard TV display screen. The scan converter operates in a continuous DMA block transfer mode. It retrieves each byte from the display memory as the TV scan line nears the portion of the screen to which the byte corresponds. The signal to the TV display is then modulated so that a square on the display is illuminated if the corresponding bit in the display memory is a ONE or remains dark if the bit is a ZERO. Figure 11-5 illustrates this concept for a small illuminated rectangle.

As the microcomputer modifies the information in the display memory, the illuminated part of the display changes its location and appears to move. Let us illustrate this concept by using the rectangle of Figure 11-5. Assume that the rectangle corresponds to a moving object that is to be moved horizontally to the right for a distance corresponding to 60 squares or five-eighths of the width of the screen. Also, assume that the rectangle is to move through this distance in one second. Thus, for each one-sixtieth of a second (16.7 milliseconds), the rectangle must be moved a distance of one square to the right. The microcomputer accomplishes this motion by enabling a clock interrupt which is timed to occur at intervals of one-sixtieth of a second. Then, at the occurrence of each interrupt, the bits corresponding to the rectangle are shifted to the *right* in the display memory by one bit position. For the example of Figure 11-5, this motion is accomplished by shifting the bits for each row of the rectangle, as shown on page 269. The example illustrates four successive interrupts.

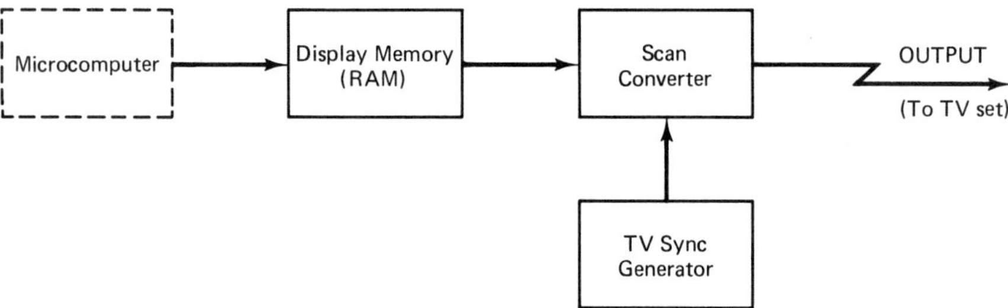

Figure 11-3. TV interface.

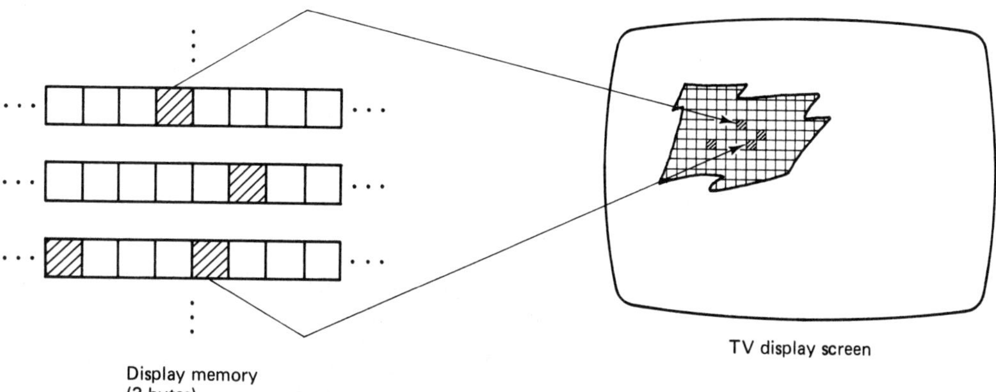

Figure 11-4. Correspondence between four bits in the display memory and four elements on the TV display screen.

... 00111100 00000000 ...	Initial pattern
... 00011110 00000000 ...	After first interrupt
... 00001111 00000000 ...	After second interrupt
... 00000111 10000000 ...	After third interrupt
... 00000011 11000000 ...	After fourth interrupt

Motion in an arbitrary direction is accomplished by treating the horizontal and vertical directions independently, shifting the bits as shown above for horizontal motion, and shifting the bits from *row to row* for vertical motion. Synchronization between the microcomputer and the display is not needed; the occasional distortion that results when the display memory is altered while it is being read by the scan converter is not noticeable, thanks to the persistence of human vision.

In an actual system, several objects such as a *ball* and two *paddles* may be in motion simultaneously, and a moving object may *hit* a stationary object or another moving object. The objects must be treated as separate entities to prevent a moving object from merging with another object and the two objects thereby becoming inseparable in the memory. Thus, information about each moving object should be stored and manipulated separately in the microcomputer memory. Then it can be superimposed with other objects before being stored in the display memory. Many strategies can be devised for this purpose; we do not pursue this aspect of the TV game further.

The playing strategy behind the game must be built into the software; it is a function of the rules of the game. If, however, a ball strikes a fixed boundary, such as a *wall*, the ball should rebound in a direction determined by the laws of physics, as shown in Figure 11-6. In the example shown, trigonometric calculations are unnecessary. The horizontal component of motion of the ball is reversed on impact while the vertical component of motion remains unchanged. Thus, the ball continues

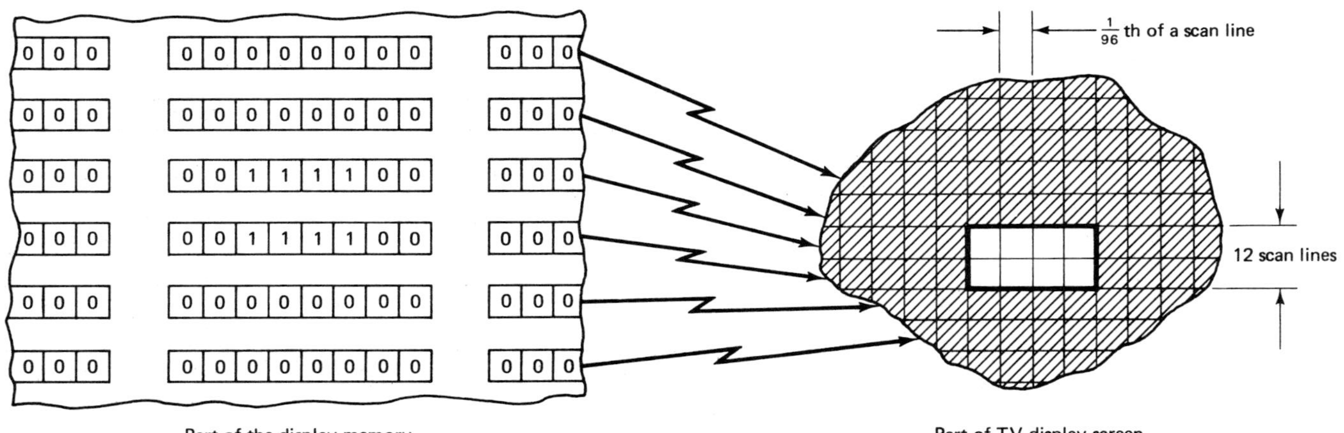

Figure 11-5. Example of an illuminated rectangular area as displayed on the TV screen.

to move at the same rate after its impact with the wall except that the horizontal component of motion is in the opposite direction. Similar rules apply to the other walls. If the ball strikes a paddle, the new direction of motion may depend on whether the paddle is stationary or in motion at the instant of impact. If the paddle is stationary, the ball reacts as if it hit a wall. If the paddle is in motion, the velocity of the ball is altered in the vertical direction as well. For example, if the ball and the paddle are both moving in a downward direction at the instant of impact, the vertical component of motion of the ball is increased after impact. This causes the direction of motion of the ball to change, as shown in Figure 11-7. The figure also illustrates the rebound strategy for upward motion of the paddle, in which case the vertical component of motion of the ball is decreased. In the particular case in which the vertical component of motion of the ball is small before impact and the paddle is moving rapidly in the opposite direction, the vertical component of motion of the ball can be reversed, as shown in Figure 11-8. As stated above, other strategies are also possible. Note that interesting strategies do not necessarily require complex software algorithms. In fact, in a good design, *complex* strategies are implemented with simple algorithms.

Before leaving the TV game, let us briefly examine several related concepts. To heighten interest, a sound can be generated each time the ball makes an impact. A simple *beep* is easily produced through the TV interface under microcomputer control. The game becomes even more interesting if tones of different pitch are produced. Then, a different beep can be selected by the microcomputer for each impact. A strategy can be developed to select which beep is used for any given condition. For example, a low-pitched beep may be used if the ball hits the paddle when there is almost no vertical component of paddle motion. For increasingly higher vertical components of paddle motion, increasingly higher-pitched tones are produced on impact. Similar strategies may be employed when the ball hits a wall; here the angle and speed of impact can be used to determine the pitch of the beep.

We assumed that six consecutive scan lines are produced by each *row* of bytes in the display memory. However, commercial television sets have an interlaced scan; the odd-numbered lines are displayed during one vertical scan and the even-numbered lines are displayed during the next vertical scan. Thus, each *row* of bytes

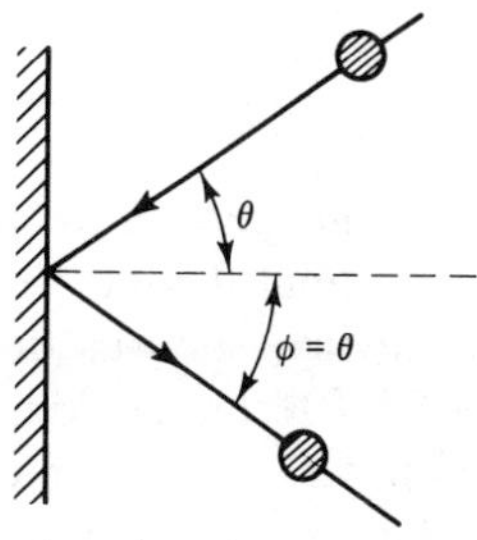

Figure 11-6. Rebound strategy for a TV game.

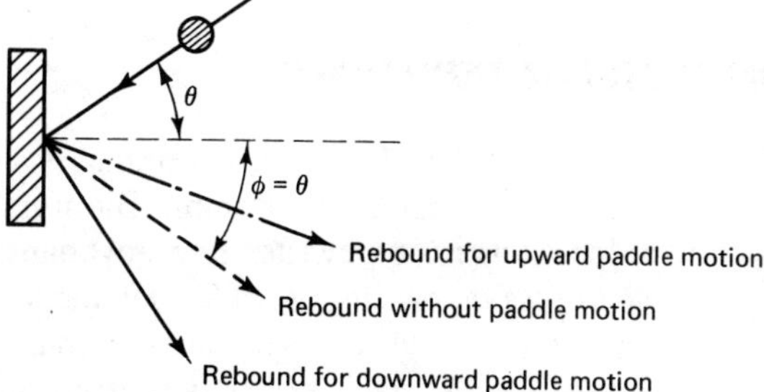

Figure 11-7. Rebound strategies for moving paddle.

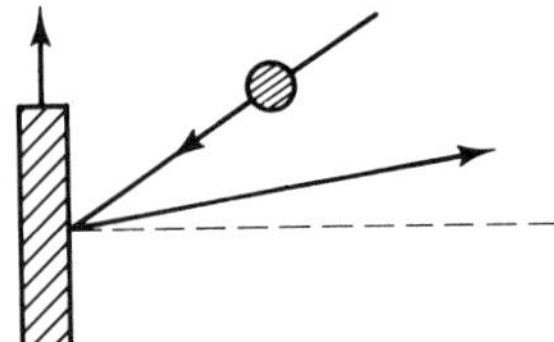

Figure 11-8. Rebound for rapid upward paddle motion.

in the display memory is used for only three successive scan lines. The interlace circuitry of the TV display then causes six consecutive lines on the TV display screen to correspond to each *row* in the display memory.

Another way to increase the excitement created by a TV game is to use color. For example, the *playing field* can be displayed in one color, the background in a second color, and the ball and paddles in other colors. To display color, additional bits are needed in the display memory for each picture element. If we assume that an additional bit is provided for each picture element, the size of the display memory is doubled and the number of colors that can be displayed is increased to four. Although having only four colors may appear to be restrictive, it is often sufficient; several items can be displayed in the same color without visual confusion. For example, the same color can be used for the ball and to display the score since the ball and score are separated on the display. In a color system, the scan converter must modulate the TV color carrier in response to a multibit code for each picture element. The circuitry needed to achieve this is relatively straightforward and does not add substantially to the cost of the game.

The flexibility of the microcomputer permits a virtually unlimited variety of games to be designed for and played on a TV game. We are limited only by the complexity of the software algorithms needed to implement a particular game strategy. It is even possible to provide a *development system* that allows the user to develop his or her own games. What is needed for this system is a set of software procedures that can provide a large variety of functions for the user. The user then *specifies* the game rules and the development system combines the procedures into a game that can be executed on the microcomputer. This *programming* requires a sophisticated development system that permits an unsophisticated user to *program* the system. We do not pursue this aspect of *system design* further.

INTELLIGENT TERMINALS

As we saw in Chapter 7, a terminal is a device that permits an operator to communicate with a computer system. The terminal consists of an input device, such as an alphanumeric typewriter-like keyboard, and an output device, such as the printer part of a typewriter or a TV-like display in the case of a CRT terminal. Many terminals are relatively simple and communicate with the computer system one character at a time. As each key is depressed on the keyboard, the corresponding character code is sent to the computer; whenever a character code is received from the computer by the terminal, it is immediately typed or displayed.

However, by adding a microcomputer to a CRT terminal, the latter can be made *intelligent*. As keys are depressed, the corresponding character codes are stored in the microcomputer memory and displayed on the screen. Errors are then corrected using facilities provided by the microcomputer in the terminal. When the text displayed on the screen is correct and complete, the operator can press a button to command the microcomputer to transmit the text to the computer in a single *block transfer*. The intelligent terminal has the advantage that typographical errors can be corrected in the terminal before transmission to the computer.

After a microcomputer is designed into a CRT terminal, many other functions can then be added inexpensively. For example, the terminal can be configured to communicate with a computer that uses any of a number of available *communication protocols*. Thus, the terminal can be used interchangeably with many different computers without modification. Although a treatment of the subject of digital communications is beyond the scope of this book, let us provide two examples to illustrate the concepts involved.

The communication protocol we describe requires that a *conversation* be carried on between the computer and the terminal using *control codes* to determine when data should be transmitted. For example, when the computer is ready to receive data from the terminal, it requests that the terminal send a block of data by sending a *request* control code to the terminal. The terminal responds by sending a block of data, followed by a *terminator* control code, to the computer. This protocol is illustrated in Figure 11-9.

A more sophisticated *handshaking* communication protocol is illustrated in Figure 11-10. In this example the request by the computer may be made before the computer is ready to receive data. The request must then be acknowledged by the terminal, which does so by sending a *ready* control code to the computer. After the computer receives the *ready* control code and when it is ready to receive data, it requests that the data be transmitted by sending a *start transmission* control code to the terminal. The terminal then responds by sending a block of data, followed by a *terminator* control code, to the computer. The microcomputer provides the flexibility needed to enable a variety of such protocols to be implemented inexpensively in a single terminal.

Control codes for *request* and *ready* are provided along with the alphanumeric character codes in the ASCII character code set which is described in Appendix B. However, insufficient standard control codes are available to specify all of the desired commands needed by an *intelligent* terminal. Therefore, code sequences

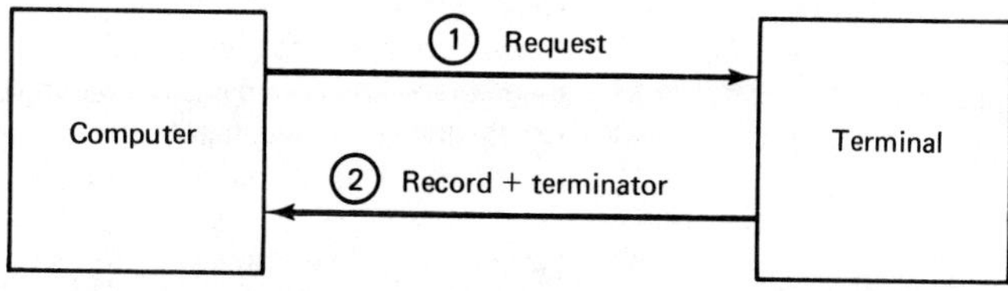

Figure 11-9. A simple communications protocol.

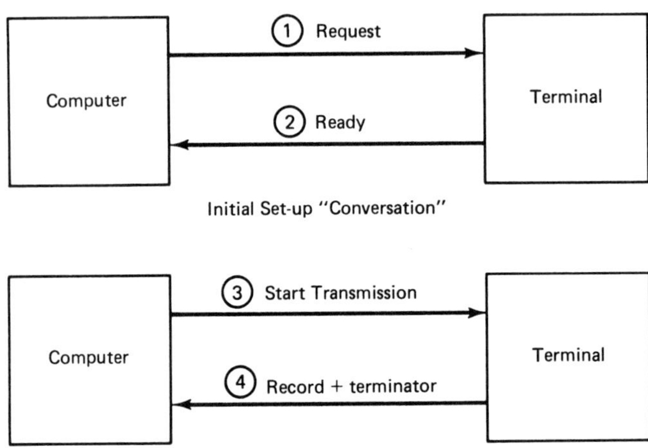

Figure 11-10. A handshaking communications protocol.

such as the so-called *escape* sequences are commonly used. In this case, whenever an *escape* control code is sent to the terminal, the alphanumeric character codes that immediately follow are interpreted as commands instead of character data. A single alphanumeric character code following the *escape* code is often sufficient. For complex commands, additional character codes may be transmitted; the exact number of additional character codes needed depends on the character code that immediately follows the *escape* control code but it may depend on the subsequent codes as well. Several *escape* sequences used in Hewlett-Packard 264x series terminals are shown in Figure 11-11. For terminals used to display graphic or pictorial data, *escape* sequences are used to cause lines to be drawn on the display screen. Examples of graphic escape sequences used in Hewlett-Packard 264x series graphics terminals are shown in Figure 11-12. Figure 11-13 illustrates how graphic *escape* sequences are used to draw a simple geometric figure on the screen of a Hewlett-Packard 264x series graphics terminal.

Escape A	Move cursor up one line
Escape B	Move cursor down one line
Escape C	Move cursor right one column
Escape D	Move cursor left one column
Escape H	Move cursor home (first column, first line)
Escape J	Clear screen
Escape K	Erase from cursor to end of line
Escape L	Insert blank line above line containing cursor
Escape M	Delete line containing cursor
Escape P	Delete character at cursor position
Escape S	Roll text up one line
Escape T	Roll text down one line

Figure 11-11. Examples of escape sequences.

*Escape**pA	Lift "pen" (to make next vector invisible)
*Escape**pB	Lower "pen" (to make next vector visible)
*Escape**pa300,200Z	Lift "pen" and draw invisible vector to location (300,200) on screen
*Escape**pb550,150Z	Lower "pen" and draw visible vector from current location to location (550,150) on screen.

Note 1. Upper and lower case characters have same interpretation but upper case character terminates graphic escape sequence.

Note 2. Z is used only as a terminator character and has no interpretation.

Figure 11-12. Examples of graphic escape sequences.

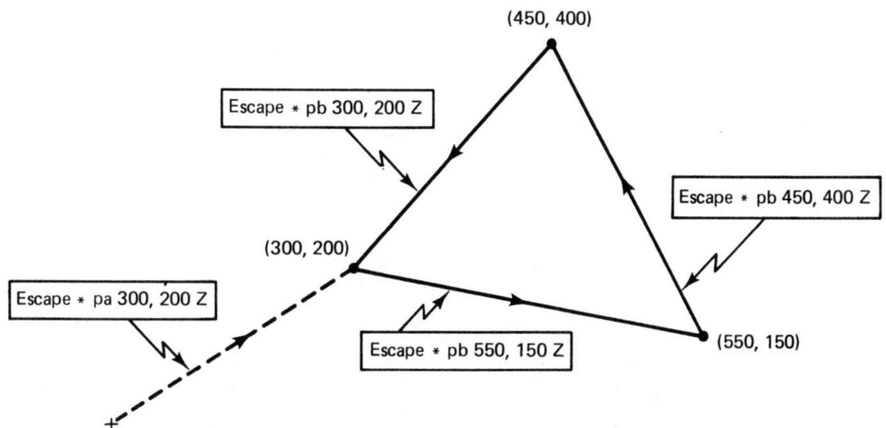

Figure 11-13. Use of graphic escape sequences.

AUTOMOTIVE ENGINE CONTROL SYSTEMS

With decreasing hardware cost and rapidly increasing capability, it was only a matter of time before the microcomputer found its way under the hood of an automobile. Real-time control of vehicles and automotive engines was hastened by societal and governmental pressures to reduce the air pollutants produced by the automobile and to decrease its fuel consumption. These goals can only be met if the fuel-air mixture fed to the internal combustion engine and the ignition timing are regulated more precisely than can be done with a mechanical carburetor and distributor. However, to perform the fuel management and ignition timing tasks, the microcomputer must be able to assimilate a great deal of real-time information about its environment and to take into account the characteristics of the particular engine being controlled. As a result, a description of a complete engine control system is beyond the scope of this discussion; instead, we present a simplified description to illustrate the concepts involved.

A block diagram of a microcomputer-based engine control system is illustrated in Figure 11-14. The input and output signal conditioning modules for this system and the engine control schedules are unique to this type of system and deserve spe-

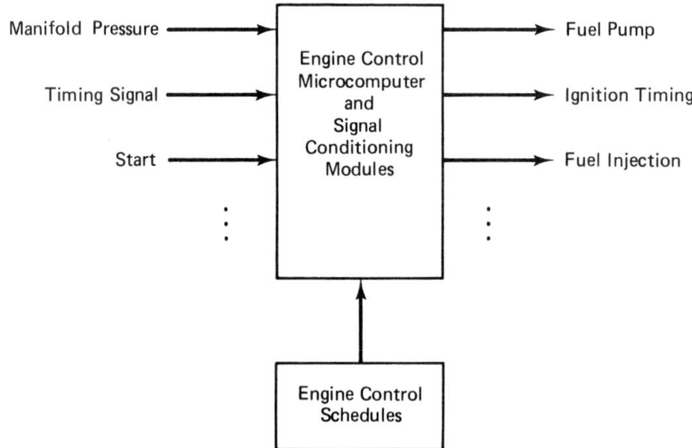

Figure 11-14. A microcomputer control system for an internal combustion engine.

cial attention. A standard analog-digital converter can be used for the manifold pressure sensor and other similar analog input signals. However, a different type of input signal converter is needed for the timing signal which consists of a series of timing pulses whose rate is proportional to engine speed. This input signal converter must measure the time interval between successive pairs of timing pulses and provide a digital number proportional to each time interval. The engine speed corresponding to each time interval can then be calculated in the microcomputer by multiplying the reciprocal of each digital number obtained from the input signal converter by a suitable calibration factor. The third type of input signal provides an indication of the state of an on-off condition and can be represented as a single-bit binary variable. The start signal, for example, indicates when the engine is being cranked by the starter motor.

The output signal conditioning module must be able to produce a variety of actuator signals. The fuel pump signal is a two-state signal that turns the fuel pump on before the engine is cranked by the starter motor and turns it off when the ignition switch is turned off. The ignition timing signal consists of a sequence of pulses whose precise timing is controlled by the microcomputer to assure optimum spark advance for the existing engine and environmental conditions. The fuel injection signal is a pulse whose timing and duration are both controlled by the microcomputer.

The engine control schedules are a set of tables containing the multidimensional functional relationships needed to control the actuator signals using information supplied by the input signals. These schedules must be relatively compact to keep the cost of the control system reasonable. Thus, they cannot store the necessary control information for all possible combinations of input signals. The microcomputer must then interpolate between the stored values to optimize the utilization of the control information in the engine control schedules. Moreover, the microcomputer must update some of the actuators at a very rapid rate when the engine is running at high speed. Thus, the architecture of a microcomputer for an internal combustion engine control system must be chosen so that it can rapidly perform the calculations needed for the interpolations. A sophisticated general-purpose microcomputer can easily perform the required interpolations at high speed but it may be too expensive for this application. As a result, it may be more cost-effective to design a special-purpose integrated circuit chip that contains both the microcomputer and the signal conditioning modules for the internal combustion engine control system. The principles presented in this book can be used to design a system containing a special-purpose microcomputer. The design of the hardware is then reduced in scope since much of the hardware is connected together on the integrated circuit chip. Also, since a high-level programming language is unlikely to be available, the design language may have to be converted directly into assembly language. Apart from these differences, our design methodologies apply directly to the design of a system containing a special-purpose microcomputer.

WHITE GOODS

The term *white goods* refers to the group of electrically operated consumer appliances which include refrigerators, stoves, ovens, washing machines, and dryers. In recent years, white goods manufacturers have begun to replace electromechanical timers and controllers with microcomputer-based units. The latter are capable of providing a great deal of flexibility for the consumer with many additional functions being made available at low incremental cost.

The microwave oven is an example of an appliance that can be controlled effectively by a microcomputer. Since microwave cooking requires shorter timing cycles than conventional cooking, the increased accuracy and user convenience afforded by a digital timer and controller are desirable. In addition, the increased flexibility that can be obtained through the use of a microcomputer can be fully utilized in this application.

Two variables must be controlled in a microwave oven: cooking time and power level. The microcomputer permits operating the oven through precise combinations of power levels and cooking times during the preparation of a single food item. For example, if the food to be cooked is frozen, it should first be defrosted at a medium power level for a specified period of time and then cooked at a higher power level for a second period of time. Finally, it can be kept warm at a very low power level until it is removed from the oven and served.

The power levels and times are easily set by using an array of push buttons and a digital display. An example of a microwave oven control panel is shown in Figure 11-15. A typical set-up sequence proceeds as shown on page 278.

Each box in the sequence represents the push of a button. The function buttons, such as the DEFROST button, light up when pushed; the numeric and time-related buttons cause the digital display to be updated as they are pushed. In the example the oven is set to turn on at 4:00 P.M. It defrosts for eight minutes at power level 5, cooks for ten minutes at power level 7, and keeps the cooked food warm for

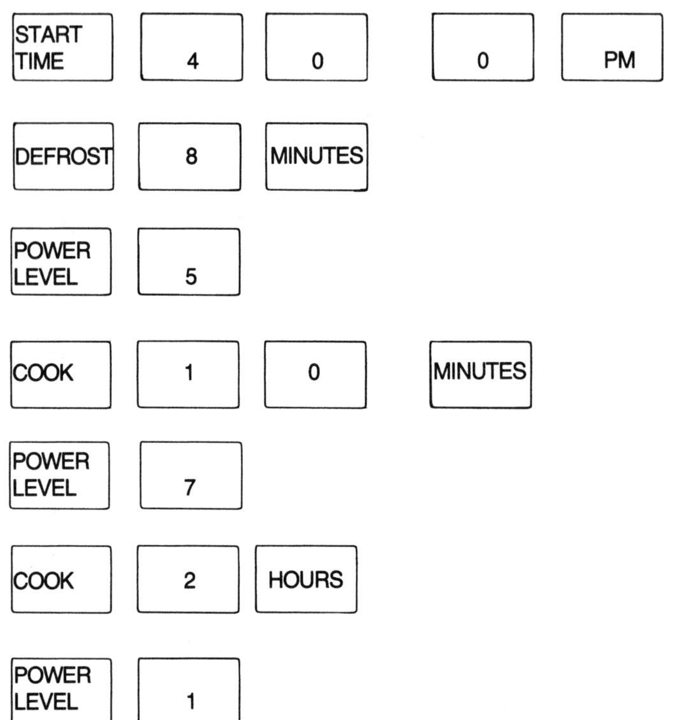

two hours at power level 1. To arm the oven so that it starts its cycle at 4:00 P.M., the START CYCLE button must be pushed. A cycle may be stopped at any time by pressing the CANCEL button.

Whenever the display is not being used to set up a cooking cycle, it displays the current time of day. To set the time of day, the SET CLOCK button is first pushed; then the HOURS button is used to set the correct time in hours, the MINUTES button is used to set the minutes, and the AM or PM button is used to set morning or evening. The SET CLOCK button is pushed a second time to restore the system to its normal state.

A FINAL WORD

The applications and the exercise presented in this chapter are intended to stimulate the reader into thinking about other ways to use microcomputers. There is virtually no limit to the variety of applications that can be implemented using a microcomputer as a component. To do so cost effectively and with a minimum of difficulty, however, requires that the work be done systematically so that complexity is reduced. The design concepts presented in this book can help the reader achieve this goal in a straightforward manner.

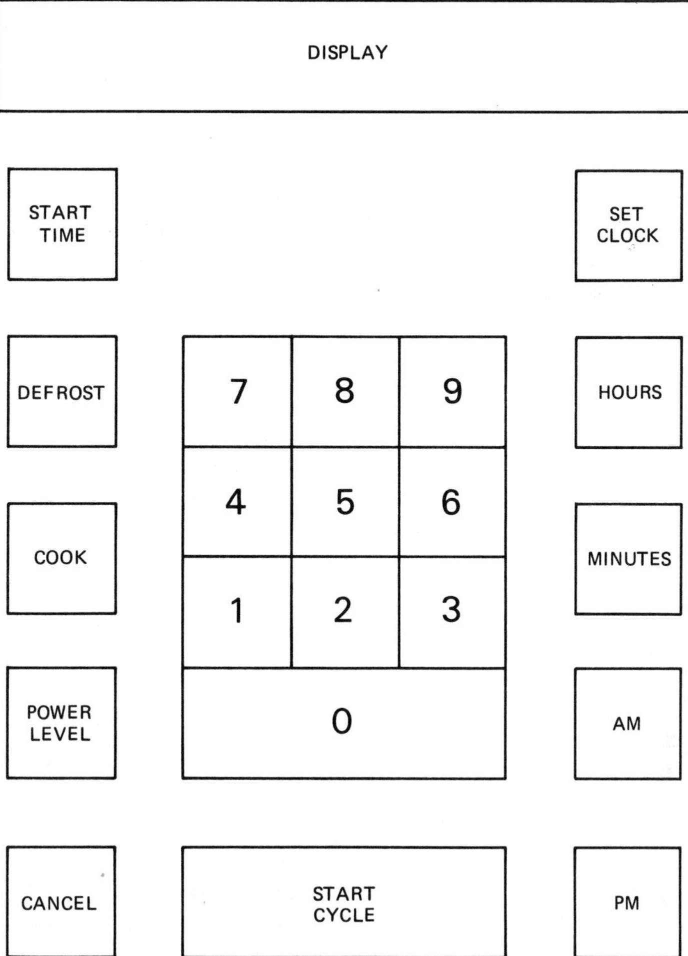

EXERCISE

The systems described in Chapter 11 are more complex than those used for exercises in earlier chapters. Thus, for the student to completely design one of these systems in a classroom environment would be difficult. But simplified versions of these systems can be defined which are suitable as problems for classroom solution. An example of a simplified TV game is provided below to illustrate.

11-1. Design the procedures for a TV game with the following characteristics:

(a) The game has two paddles, one for each player, which can be moved up or down.

(b) A goal is provided at each wall.

(c) The game is started by pressing a START button.

(d) Once started, the ball moves at a constant rate and at a forty-five-degree angle until it hits a goal. The score is then updated and the system waits until the START button is pressed.

(e) When the ball hits a wall or a paddle, it rebounds and continues to move at the same rate and at a forty-five-degree angle.

(f) The game ends after one player has scored fifteen points. Pressing a RESET button resets the score and prepares for a new game. The RESET button can also be pressed after a goal is scored regardless of the score.

Appendix A

Number Systems

A *number system* represents numeric information. The most common number system is the *decimal* number system. It consists of a set of ten symbols, as illustrated in Figure A-1, and a *decimal point* represented by a period. In the decimal number system a number is represented by a sequence of these symbols. The value of each symbol in a sequence depends on its position relative to the decimal point. If the decimal point is omitted, it is assumed to lie to the immediate right of the right-hand symbol of the sequence. Each symbol differs from its neighbors by a power of ten.

Name of symbol	Symbol
zero	0
one	1
two	2
three	3
four	4
five	5
six	6
seven	7
eight	8
nine	9

Figure A-1. The symbols of the decimal number system.

Thus, the sequence 325 represents the number whose value is given by

$$3 \times 10^2 + 2 \times 10^1 + 5 \times 10^0$$

or three hundred and twenty-five. Similarly, the sequence 25.2 represents the number whose value is given by

$$2 \times 10^1 + 5 \times 10^0 + 2 \times 10^{-1}$$

or twenty-five and two-tenths.

The number ten on which the decimal number system is based is called the *base* of the number system. In digital computing systems the *binary* number system, the *octal* number system, and the *hexadecimal* number system are also used. The bases for these number systems are 2, 8, and 16, respectively.

As we have seen, information is stored and manipulated in a microcomputer as *bits* or as groups of bits. A bit, or *binary digit*, is a variable that takes on a value of zero or one, the two symbols in the binary number system. A sequence of bits that represents numeric information can be converted into a decimal number by multiplying each bit by its corresponding power of *two*. For example, the bit sequence 0010 1101 represents the decimal number 45, as shown below.

$$\begin{aligned} 0010\ 1101 &= 0 \times 2^7 + 0 \times 2^6 + 1 \times 2^5 + 0 \times 2^4 \\ &\quad + 1 \times 2^3 + 1 \times 2^2 + 0 \times 2^1 + 1 \times 2^0 \\ &= 32 + 4 + 8 + 1 \\ &= 45 \end{aligned}$$

Binary numbers containing fractional parts can be converted to decimal in a similar manner. Note that a *binary point* is used to separate the integer and fractional parts of a binary number in the same way that a decimal point separates the two parts of a decimal number.

In microcomputer systems the octal (base eight) and the hexadecimal (base sixteen) number systems are used primarily to improve the readability of binary information. A simple relationship exists between these two number systems and the binary number system. Each symbol in the octal number system corresponds to three bits of the corresponding binary number; each symbol in the hexadecimal number system corresponds to four bits of the corresponding binary number. These relationships are illustrated in Figures A-2 and A-3. Thus, for example, 0010 1101 is equivalent to 055 (00 101 101) in the octal number system and 2D in the hexadecimal number system. To determine the value of an octal or hexadecimal number, a

Name of symbol	Symbol	Corresponding binary number
zero	0	000
one	1	001
two	2	010
three	3	011
four	4	100
five	5	101
six	6	110
seven	7	111

Figure A-2. The symbols of the octal number system.

Name of symbol	Symbol	Corresponding binary number
zero	0	0000
one	1	0001
two	2	0010
three	3	0011
four	4	0100
five	5	0101
six	6	0110
seven	7	0111
eight	8	1000
nine	9	1001
ten	A	1010
eleven	B	1011
twelve	C	1100
thirteen	D	1101
fourteen	E	1110
fifteen	F	1111

Figure A-3. The symbols of the hexadecimal number system.

rule similar to the one described for decimal and binary numbers is used. Therefore, the octal number 055 represents the decimal number 45, as follows:

$$\begin{aligned} 055 &= 0 \times 8^2 + 5 \times 8^1 + 5 \times 8^0 \\ &= 40 + 5 \\ &= 45 \end{aligned}$$

Similarly, the hexadecimal number 2D also represents the decimal number 45, as shown below:

$$\begin{aligned} 2D &= 2 \times 16^1 + 13 \times 16^0 \\ &= 32 + 13 \\ &= 45 \end{aligned}$$

As we saw in Chapter 6, hexadecimal representation is used to facilitate dealing with machine language instructions. It is easier to work with sequences of hexadecimal symbols than with sequences of bits. Thus, the machine language code for the Intel 8085 assembly language instruction ADC is written as 8E rather than 1000 1110, which is how it is represented in the microcomputer. No numeric value is associated with this machine language code which has meaning to the microcomputer in a non-numeric way. However, part of an instruction may represent a numeric value. For example, in the Intel 8085 machine language instruction DE 23, the DE represents the assembly language instruction SBI and the 23 is a hexadecimal number that represents the operand whose decimal value is 35. Thus, the machine language instruction represented by the hexadecimal sequence DE 23 is equivalent to the complete assembly language instruction SBI 35. In a similar manner, when a sequence of bits or hexadecimal symbols is used to represent a character code, its numeric value is not significant. Character codes are discussed in Appendix B.

Appendix B

Symbolic Data

In Chapter 5 we introduced the concept of numeric character codes. In Chapter 6 we showed how numeric character codes can be manipulated. In this appendix we describe the more general concept of symbolic data, that is, the representation and manipulation of information that consists of alphabetic and numeric characters as well as other symbols, such as commas, periods, question marks, et cetera. As before, we use the ASCII or American Standard Code for Information Interchange representation which is almost universally used for microcomputer systems.

Figure B-1 contains the standard ASCII representation. Each code is shown both in binary and in hexadecimal. In the figure the leftmost or *parity bit* of each code is set to zero; this convention is called *ZERO parity*. There are four common parity bit protocols, as follows:

1. The parity bit is always ZERO (ZERO parity).
2. The parity bit is always ONE (ONE parity).
3. The parity bit is set to ZERO if there is an even number of ONE bits in the code (even parity).
4. The parity bit is set to ZERO if there is an odd number of ONE bits in the code (odd parity).

The latter two protocols can be used to detect if one of the bits in a character code is erroneously altered during transmission over a communication line. When used locally in a microcomputer system, such as for communicating between a local terminal and a microcomputer, error checking is rarely implemented. In this case, ZERO parity or ONE parity is usually used.

Character representation	ASCII code representation		Character representation	ASCII code representation	
	Binary	Hexadecimal		Binary	Hexadecimal
NUL	0000 0000	00	@	0100 0000	40
SOH	0000 0001	01	A	0100 0001	41
STX	0000 0010	02	B	0100 0010	42
ETX	0000 0011	03	C	0100 0011	43
EOT	0000 0100	04	D	0100 0100	44
ENQ	0000 0101	05	E	0100 0101	45
ACK	0000 0110	06	F	0100 0110	46
BEL	0000 0111	07	G	0100 0111	47
BS	0000 1000	08	H	0100 1000	48
HT	0000 1001	09	I	0100 1001	49
LF	0000 1010	0A	J	0100 1010	4A
VT	0000 1011	0B	K	0100 1011	4B
FF	0000 1100	0C	L	0100 1100	4C
CR	0000 1101	0D	M	0100 1101	4D
SO	0000 1110	0E	N	0100 1110	4E
SI	0000 1111	0F	O	0100 1111	4F
DLE	0001 0000	10	P	0101 0000	50
DC1	0001 0001	11	Q	0101 0001	51
DC2	0001 0010	12	R	0101 0010	52
DC3	0001 0011	13	S	0101 0011	53
DC4	0001 0100	14	T	0101 0100	54
NAK	0001 0101	15	U	0101 0101	55
SYN	0001 0110	16	V	0101 0110	56
ETB	0001 0111	17	W	0101 0111	57
CAN	0001 1000	18	X	0101 1000	58
EM	0001 1001	19	Y	0101 1001	59
SUB	0001 1010	1A	Z	0101 1010	5A
ESC	0001 1011	1B	[	0101 1011	5B
FS	0001 1100	1C	\	0101 1100	5C
GS	0001 1101	1D	]	0101 1101	5D
RS	0001 1110	1E	^	0101 1110	5E
US	0001 1111	1F	_	0101 1111	5F
space	0010 0000	20	`	0110 0000	60
!	0010 0001	21	a	0110 0001	61
"	0010 0010	22	b	0110 0010	62
#	0010 0011	23	c	0110 0011	63
$	0010 0100	24	d	0110 0100	64
%	0010 0101	25	e	0110 0101	65
&	0010 0110	26	f	0110 0110	66
'	0010 0111	27	g	0110 0111	67
(	0010 1000	28	h	0110 1000	68
)	0010 1001	29	i	0110 1001	69
*	0010 1010	2A	j	0110 1010	6A
+	0010 1011	2B	k	0110 1011	6B
,	0010 1100	2C	l	0110 1100	6C
-	0010 1101	2D	m	0110 1101	6D
.	0010 1110	2E	n	0110 1110	6E
/	0010 1111	2F	o	0110 1111	6F
0	0011 0000	30	p	0111 0000	70

Figure B-1. The standard ASCII representation.

Character representation	ASCII code representation		Character representation	ASCII code representation	
	Binary	Hexadecimal		Binary	Hexadecimal
1	0011 0001	31	q	0111 0001	71
2	0011 0010	32	r	0111 0010	72
3	0011 0011	33	s	0111 0011	73
4	0011 0100	34	t	0111 0100	74
5	0011 0101	35	u	0111 0101	75
6	0011 0110	36	v	0111 0110	76
7	0011 0111	37	w	0111 0111	77
8	0011 1000	38	x	0111 1000	78
9	0011 1001	39	y	0111 1001	79
:	0011 1010	3A	z	0111 1010	7A
;	0011 1011	3B	{	0111 1011	7B
<	0011 1100	3C	|	0111 1100	7C
=	0011 1101	3D	}	0111 1101	7D
>	0011 1110	3E	~	0111 1110	7E
?	0011 1111	3F	delete	0111 1111	7F

Control code summary

NUL	Null	DLE	Data link escape
SOH	Start of heading	DC1	Device control 1 (X-ON)
STX	Start of text	DC2	Device control 2
ETX	End of text	DC3	Device control 3 (X-OFF)
EOT	End of transmission	DC4	Device control 4
ENQ	Enquiry	NAK	Negative acknowledge
ACK	Acknowledge	SYN	Synchronous idle
BEL	Bell	ETB	End of transmission block
BS	Backspace	CAN	Cancel
HT	Horizontal tab	EM	End of medium
LF	Line feed	SUB	Substitute
VT	Vertical tab	ESC	Escape
FF	Form feed	FS	File separator
CR	Carriage return	GS	Group separator
SO	Shift out	RS	Record separator
SI	Shift in	US	Unit separator

Figure B-1. (Continued).

As we have seen, to designate that an alphanumeric character code is to be used in PL/M, apostrophes are placed around the character. Then, when the PL/M compiler translates a statement, such as

```
IF CHARACTER >= '0' AND CHARACTER <= '9'
```

it replaces '0' with the ASCII code 0011 0000 and '9' with the ASCII code 0011 1001. When the microcomputer is executing the corresponding instructions, it treats the codes as numeric quantities. Since the numeric ASCII codes are in sequence, the test correctly determines whether the character code designated by CHARACTER lies between the codes for '0' and '9' and is therefore itself a numeric code.

A similar relationship exists for the alphabetic character codes. That is, the ASCII code for the letter 'A' has the lowest numerical value and the ASCII code for the letter 'Z' has the highest. Thus, when the PL/M statement.

```
IF CHARACTER >= 'C' AND CHARACTER <= 'Q'
```

is translated by the PL/M compiler and the corresponding instructions executed, the character code designed by CHARACTER is tested to determine if it represents a letter between 'C' and 'Q'.

As Figure B-1 illustrates, the ASCII representation provides codes for the upper-case and lower-case alphabetic characters, for the numeric characters, for symbols such as !, ", #, $, et cetera, and for control characters. The first three code types, along with the space, line feed, and carriage return codes, allow ordinary text to be represented, manipulated, and transmitted digitally. The control codes were initially included to facilitate using the ASCII representation to transmit information digitally over long distances via telegraph lines. In microcomputer systems, however, they are used both for communications and to extend the control capability of the microcomputer. Examples illustrating the use of the control codes for communication between a terminal and a microcomputer and to control a graphics terminal were provided in Chapter 11.

Appendix C

Summary of PL/M

This appendix contains a summary of examples that illustrate the conversion of design language constructs into PL/M.

Module declarations.

```
/*  MODULE: MAINTAIN INPUT RECORD                                           */
                                        MAINTAIN$INPUT$RECORD: DO;
                                           .
                                           .
                                           .
/*  END MODULE                                                              */
                                        END MAINTAIN$INPUT$RECORD;
```

Data declarations.

```
/*  OUTPUT PARAMETER: STATUS                                                */
/*                                                                          */
/*  NAME                SIZE    TYPE    CONTENTS              NOTES         */
/*  ----                ----    ----    --------              -----         */
/*  STATUS                 1    BYTE    FLAG                                */
                                        DECLARE STATUS BYTE;


/*  MODULAR DATA STRUCTURE: INPUT RECORD                                    */
/*                                                                          */
/*  NAME                SIZE    TYPE    CONTENTS              NOTES         */
/*  ----                ----    ----    --------              -----         */
/*  INPUT RECORD          10    BYTE    NUMERIC CODES                       */
                                        DECLARE INPUT$RECORD (10) BYTE;
```

```
/*  MODULAR DATA STRUCTURE: FILE                                                 */
/*                                                                               */
/*  NAME               SIZE    TYPE    CONTENTS              NOTES               */
/*  ----               ----    ----    --------              -----               */
/*  FILE                                                       1                 */
/*    RECORD                                                                     */
/*      SERIAL NUMBER   10     BYTE    NUMERIC CODES                             */
/*      NAME            20     BYTE    ALPHABETIC CODES                          */
/*      STREET ADDRESS  20     BYTE    ALPHABETIC CODES                          */
/*                                                                               */
/*  NOTE 1: FILE CONSISTS OF 256 RECORDS.                                        */
/*                                                                               */
                   DECLARE FILE (256) STRUCTURE (SERIAL$NUMBER ADDRESS, NAME (20) BYTE,
                                                 STREET$ADDRESS (20) BYTE);
```

Data declarations with initialization.

```
/*  MODULAR DATA STRUCTURE: CONTROL SCHEDULE                                     */
/*                                                                               */
/*  NAME               SIZE    TYPE    CONTENTS              NOTES               */
/*  ----               ----    ----    --------              -----               */
/*  CONTROL SCHEDULE    10     BYTE    NUMERIC VALUES                            */
          DECLARE CONTROL$SCHEDULE (10) BYTE DATA (10,15,25,40,60,76,88,98,106,110);
```

Procedure declarations.

```
/*  PROCEDURE:  CLEAR INPUT RECORD (;)                                           */
                                       CLEAR$INPUT$RECORD: PROCEDURE;
                                         .
                                         .
                                         .
/*  END PROCEDURE                                                                */
                                       END CLEAR$INPUT$RECORD;


/*  PROCEDURE:  BEEP (;)                                                         */
                                       BEEP: PROCEDURE PUBLIC;
                                         .
                                         .
                                         .
/*  END PROCEDURE                                                                */
                                       END BEEP;
```

Procedure declarations with input parameters.

```
/*  PROCEDURE: ADD TO INPUT RECORD (CHARACTER;)                                  */
                                       ADD$TO$INPUT$RECORD: PROCEDURE (CHARACTER);
                                         .
                                         .
                                         .
/*  END PROCEDURE                                                                */
                                       END ADD$TO$INPUT$RECORD;
```

Procedure declarations with output parameter.

```
/*  PROCEDURE:  TEST IF INPUT RECORD FULL  (;STATUS)                          */
                                          TEST$IF$INPUT$RECORD$FULL:  PROCEDURE BYTE;
                                            .
                                            .
                                            .
                                            RETURN STATUS;
                                            .
                                            .
                                            .
/*  END PROCEDURE                                                             */
                                          END TEST$IF$INPUT$RECORD$FULL;
```

Procedure declarations with data structures as input parameters.

```
/*  PROCEDURE:  PRINT  (RECORD;)                                          */
                                       PRINT:  PROCEDURE  (RECORD$POINTER)  PUBLIC;
/*  ***********************************************************************   */
/*    LOCAL PARAMETER:  RECORD POINTER                                     */
/*                                                                         */
/*    NAME              SIZE    TYPE       CONTENTS           NOTES        */
/*    ----              ----    ----       --------           -----        */
/*    RECORD POINTER      1     ADDRESS    STRUCTURE POINTER               */
                                          DECLARE RECORD$POINTER ADDRESS;
/*    INPUT PARAMETER:  RECORD                                             */
/*                                                                         */
/*    NAME              SIZE    TYPE       CONTENTS           NOTES        */
/*    ----              ----    ----       --------           -----        */
/*    RECORD                                                    1          */
/*      SERIAL NUMBER     1     ADDRESS    NUMBER                          */
/*      NAME             20     BYTE       ALPHABETIC CODES                */
/*      STREET ADDRESS   20     BYTE       ALPHANUMERIC CODES              */
/*                                                                         */
/*    NOTE 1:  RECORD IS BASED AT RECORD POINTER                           */
/*                                                                         */
                                          DECLARE  (RECORD BASED RECORD$POINTER)  STRUCTURE
                                                  (SERIAL$NUMBER ADDRESS,  NAME(20)  BYTE,  STREET$ADDRESS  (20)  BYTE);
                                          .
                                          .
                                          .
/*  END PROCEDURE                                                          */
                                       END PRINT;
```

Procedure declarations with data structures as output parameters.

```
/*  PROCEDURE:  SEARCH  (SEARCH KEY;RECORD)                                   */
                                          SEARCH:  PROCEDURE  (SEARCH$KEY)  ADDRESS PUBLIC;
/*  ***********************************************************************  */
                                            .
                                            .
                                            .
```

```
/*    OUTPUT PARAMETER: RECORD                                              */
/*                                                                          */
/*    NAME                SIZE    TYPE       CONTENTS               NOTES   */
/*    ----                ----    ----       --------               -----   */
/*    RECORD                                                                */
/*      SERIAL NUMBER      1      ADDRESS    NUMBER                         */
/*      NAME              20      BYTE       ALPHABETIC CODES               */
/*      STREET ADDRESS    20      BYTE       ALPHANUMERIC CODES             */
                                   DECLARE RECORD STRUCTURE (SERIAL$NUMBER ADDRESS, NAME (20) BYTE,
                                                              STREET$ADDRESS (20) BYTE);
/*    LOCAL PARAMETER: RECORD POINTER                                       */
/*                                                                          */
/*    NAME                SIZE    TYPE       CONTENTS               NOTES   */
/*    ----                ----    ----       --------               -----   */
/*    RECORD POINTER       1      ADDRESS    POINTER                        */
                                   DECLARE RECORD$POINTER ADDRESS;
/* ********************************************************************** */
                                   .
                                   .
                                   .
/*        SET RECORD TO SELECTED RECORD                                     */
                                   .
                                   .
                                   .
/*        RETURN                                                            */
                                          RECORD$POINTER = .RECORD;
                                          RETURN RECORD$POINTER;
                                   .
                                   .
                                   .
```

Control constructs.

```
/*  CALL: STOP TIMER (;)                                        */
                                               CALL STOP$TIMER;

/*  CALL: ADD TO INPUT RECORD (CHARACTER;)                      */
                                               CALL ADD$TO$INPUT$RECORD (CHARACTER);

/*  CALL: TEST IF INPUT RECORD FULL (;STATUS)                   */
                                               STATUS = TEST$IF$INPUT$RECORD$FULL;

/*  RETURN                                                      */
                                               RETURN;
```

(RETURN construct for procedure with output parameter STATUS)

```
/*  RETURN                                                      */
                                               RETURN STATUS;
```

Assignment constructs.

```
/*  SET STATUS TO FULL                                              */
                                                     STATUS = 1;

/*  SET STATUS TO NOT FULL                                          */
                                                     STATUS = 0;

/*  SET CONTINUOUS                                                  */
                                                     CONTINUOUS = 1;

/*  RESET CONTINUOUS                                                */
                                                     CONTINUOUS = 0;

/*  SET TIME TO SECONDS                                             */
                                                     TIME = 3600 * HOURS + 60 * MINUTES + SECONDS;
```

Loop constructs.

```
/*  DO                                                              */
                                                     DO;
                                                       :
/*  END                                                             */
                                                     END;

/*  DO WHILE KEYSWITCH IS ARMED                                     */
                                                     DO WHILE KEYSWITCH <> 0;
                                                       :
/*  END                                                             */
                                                     END;

/*  DO WHILE KEYSWITCH IS RESET                                     */
                                                     DO WHILE KEYSWITCH = 0;
                                                       :
/*  END                                                             */
                                                     END;

/*  DO FOR EACH SWITCH                                              */
                                                     DO INDEX = 1 TO 5;
                                                       :
/*  END                                                             */
                                                     END;

/*  DO FOREVER                                                      */
                                                     DO WHILE 1 = 1;
                                                       :
/*  END                                                             */
                                                     END;
```

Test constructs.

```
/*  IF KEYSWITCH IS ARMED                                          */
IF KEYSWITCH <> 0
/*    THEN  RETURN                                                 */
  THEN  RETURN;


/*  IF KEYSWITCH IS RESET                                          */
IF KEYSWITCH = 0
/*    THEN  RETURN                                                 */
  THEN RETURN;


/*  IF KEYSWITCH IS ARMED AND TIMER STATE IS EXPIRED               */
IF KEYSWITCH <> 0 AND TIMER$STATE = 0
/*    THEN  RETURN                                                 */
  THEN  RETURN;


/*  IF FULL INDICATOR SHOWS THAT INPUT RECORD IS FULL              */
IF FULL$INDICATOR = 10
/*    THEN  SET STATUS TO FULL                                     */
  THEN  STATUS = 1;
/*    ELSE  SET STATUS TO NOT FULL                                 */
  ELSE  STATUS = 0;


/*  IF CHARACTER CONTAINS A NUMERIC KEY CODE                       */
IF CHARACTER >= '0' AND CHARACTER <= '9'
/*    THEN  DO                                                     */
  THEN  DO;
/*            IF STATUS INDICATES INPUT RECORD IS NOT FULL         */
          IF STATUS = 0
/*              THEN  CALL: ADD TO INPUT RECORD (CHARACTER;)       */
           THEN  CALL ADD$TO$INPUT$RECORD (CHARACTER);
/*              ELSE  CALL: BEEP(;)                                */
           ELSE  CALL BEEP;
/*          END                                                    */
        END;
```

Appendix D

Other High-Level Microcomputer Languages

This appendix contains examples that illustrate the conversion of design language constructs into BASIC, FORTRAN, and PASCAL. Although all three languages are used in microcomputer systems, BASIC is popular in personal microcomputer systems, FORTRAN is a widely used scientific and engineering problem-solving language on all types of computing systems, and PASCAL is becoming popular as a problem-solving language for microcomputers.

BASIC

BASIC comments are designated if the word REMARK appears as the first word on a line. Since only the first three characters are significant, the letters REM are sufficient to designate a comment or REMARK. Each line in a BASIC program, including each comment line, must be preceded by a line number. As described in Chapter 7, this permits the text of a program to be created and modified easily. If a line is typed without a line number, it is treated as a command. For example, the command RUN causes the program to be executed immediately.

Many BASIC systems restrict the number of characters in a symbol or name to six or sometimes fewer characters. In such a system, many names must be replaced by short mnemonics. For example, the data structure name, CONTROL MATRIX, which we use as an example below, could be shortened to CNTRLM or even to CM.

Module declarations. BASIC is not a modular language. Most versions of BASIC do permit software to be broken into procedures, called *subroutines*. But many of the BASIC systems that permit subroutines require that all of the subroutines be manipulated together to enable information to flow more easily between the subroutines. Thus, the software consists of a single *module* and all data is *modular* data by default. Thus, a module declaration is not needed.

Data declarations. Many versions of BASIC do not require an explicit declaration for data variables. Every data variable in a program is assumed to be capable of representing a numeric value which consists of both an integer part and a fractional part, such as the number 25.478. An exception is the *string* variable which represents a sequence of alphanumeric character codes. String variables are denoted by using a dollar sign following the last character of the variable name. For example, the BASIC variable FILE would contain a numeric value which could represent a file number, whereas the BASIC string variable FILE$ would contain a string of character codes which could represent the name of the file. FILE and FILE$ then represent different variables and both may be used in the same BASIC program. In some versions of BASIC other data types can be manipulated. In that case, a data declaration is needed.

Arrays *must* be declared in BASIC.

```
10 REM - DATA STRUCTURE:  SERIAL NUMBER
20 REM
30 REM - NAME              SIZE    TYPE       CONTENTS    NOTES
40 REM - ----              ----    ----       --------    -----
50 REM - SERIAL NUMBER      20     INTEGER    NUMBER
60                                                  DIM SERNO (20)
```

DIM is short for DIMENSION, the BASIC construct that declares that SERNO is an array of twenty serial numbers. Depending on the version of BASIC being used, the index that specifies a particular element in an array can take on values in the range from either zero or one up to the number needed to achieve the size specified in the data declaration. Thus, in the example, the twenty elements in the array are specified by either SERNO(0), . . . , SERNO(19) or SERNO(1), . . . , SERNO(20), depending on the system in use.

In many versions of BASIC, arrays can be two- or even three-dimensional so that information can be stored and manipulated in matrix form.

```
10 REM - DATA STRUCTURE:  CONTROL MATRIX
20 REM
30 REM - NAME              SIZE    TYPE       CONTENTS                 NOTES
40 REM - ----              ----    ----       --------                 -----
50 REM - CONTROL MATRIX    10x2    INTEGER    ENGINE PARAMETERS
60                                                  DIM CNTRLM (10,2)
```

Data declarations with initialization. Initialization of a data structure is done using a loop containing a READ statement and providing values to be *read* in one or more DATA statements. The loop construct in BASIC is described in more detail shortly.

```
 10 REM - DATA STRUCTURE:   SERIAL NUMBER
 20 REM
 30 REM - NAME              SIZE    TYPE       CONTENTS    NOTES
 40 REM - ----              ----    ----       --------    -----
 50 REM - SERIAL NUMBER      20     INTEGER    NUMBER
 60                                                  DIM SERNO (20)
 70                                                  FOR INDEX = 1 TO 20
 80                                                    READ SERNO (INDEX)
 90                                                  NEXT I
 10                                                  DATA 110,115,125,140,160,176,188,198,206,210
110                                                  DATA 217,222,234,238,251,263,271,284,289,295
```

Procedure declarations. Two types of procedures called *subroutines* are used in BASIC. The more common subroutine does not permit input or output parameters to be passed between the calling procedure and the called procedure. The beginning of this subroutine is identified only by line number; no procedure declaration is needed and a RETURN statement identifies the end of the subroutine.

```
1000 REM - PROCEDURE:  BEEP (;)
1010 REM - BEGIN PROCEDURE
1020 REM -    (first line of procedure)
1030                                    (first statement of subroutine)
  .
  .
  .
1080 REM -    RETURN
1090                                    RETURN
1110 REM - END PROCEDURE
```

The other type of BASIC subroutine optionally permits parameters to be passed between the calling procedure and the called procedure. The example below illustrates its use when no parameters are passed.

```
2000 REM - PROCEDURE:  BEEP (;)
2010                                    SUB BEEP
  .
  .
  .
2080 REM - END PROCEDURE
2090                                    SUBEND
```

Procedure declarations with input or output parameters.

```
3000 REM - PROCEDURE:  SEARCH (SEARCH KEY;MATCH)
3010                                    SUB SEARCH (SRCHKY,MATCH)
  .
  .
  .
3130 REM - END PROCEDURE
3140                                    SUBEND
```

When the SUB procedure SEARCH is called in BASIC, pointers to the variables specified in the calling procedure are sent to the called procedure. These pointers equate the variables, SRCHKY and MATCH, to the variables specified in the calling procedure. Therefore, by varying MATCH, the related data in the calling procedure is varied. In this manner, information contained in output parameters is returned to a calling procedure in BASIC. Note that if the value of an input parameter is changed in the called procedure, the related information in the calling procedure is also changed. Thus, if the value of an input parameter is to be manipulated in the called procedure, it should first be copied into a local parameter to avoid a potential error condition.

Procedure declarations with data structures as input or output parameters.

```
4000 REM - PROCEDURE:  PRINT (INPUT RECORD;)
4010                                        SUB PRINT (INREC () )
  .
  .
  .
4080 REM - END PROCEDURE
4090                                        SUBEND
```

The empty brackets after INREC indicate that a one-dimensional array is being passed into the procedure PRINT as an input parameter. Parentheses with commas, such as, (,) and (,,), indicate that a two-dimensional or three-dimensional array is being passed into the procedure. The size of the array need not be specified in the procedure declaration. Since BASIC does not distinguish between input and output parameters, output parameters that are arrays are treated in the same manner.

Control constructs. For the first type of procedure, the BASIC GOSUB construct is used to call the procedure. As indicated in the section on procedure declarations, a RETURN construct is required. For the second type of procedure, the BASIC CALL construct is used to call the procedure. As indicated in the section on procedure declarations, a RETURN construct is not required, being replaced by the SUBEND construct which both indicates the end of the procedure and causes the execution of the procedure to be terminated.

```
200 REM - CALL:  BEEP (;)
210                                     GOSUB 1000

300 REM - CALL:  BEEP (;)
310                                     CALL BEEP

400 REM - CALL:  SEARCH (SEARCH KEY;MATCH)
410                                     CALL SEARCH (SRCHKY,MATCH)
```

```
500 REM - CALL:  FIND (SERIAL NUMBER;MATCH)
510                                    CALL FIND (SERNO (),MATCH)

1080 REM - RETURN
1090                                   RETURN
1110 REM - END PROCEDURE

1180 REM - END PROCEDURE
1190                                   SUBEND
```

Assignment constructs. The use of the word LET in the assignment construct in BASIC is optional, as illustrated by the first two examples below.

```
310 REM - SET STATUS TO FULL
320                          LET STATUS = 1

310 REM - SET STATUS TO FULL
320                          STATUS = 1

370 REM - SET STATUS TO NOT FULL
380                          LET STATUS = 0

510 REM - SET CONTINUOUS
520                          LET CONTS = 1

570 REM - RESET CONTINUOUS
580                          LET CONTS = 0

800 REM - SET TIME TO SECONDS
810                          LET TIME = 3600 * HOURS + 60 * MINUTS + SECNDS
```

Loop constructs. There are no DO . . . END or DO WHILE . . . END constructs in BASIC. To provide the equivalent of the DO . . . END construct for use in a test construct, some versions of BASIC permit the constructs within the DO . . . END to be typed on a single line. Since this is not always possible, we recommend that *jump* or GOTO instructions be used in a manner similar to what was illustrated in Chapter 6 for converting design language into an assembly language. The DO WHILE . . . END construct can be simulated using a test construct with a *jump* or GOTO instruction. Examples of these constructs are provided in the section on test constructs. The DO FOR EACH . . . END and the DO FOREVER . . . END constructs are shown on page 300.

```
900 REM - DO FOR EACH SWITCH
910                                   FOR INDEX = 1 TO 5
  .
  .
  .
980 REM - END
990                                   NEXT INDEX
```

As illustrated, the NEXT . . . phrase is used to designate the end of a DO FOR EACH . . . END loop in BASIC.

```
1000 REM - DO FOREVER
  .
  .
  .
1070 REM - END
1080                                  GOTO 1000
```

Note that the label used in a BASIC GOTO statement can reference a line containing a comment; during operation the comment is ignored and the next BASIC statement is executed.

Test constructs.

```
1100 REM - IF KEYSWITCH IS ARMED
1110 REM -   THEN  SET STATUS
1120                            IF KEYSW <> 0 THEN LET STATUS = 1

1200 REM - IF KEYSWITCH IS RESET
1210 REM -   THEN  RESET STATUS
1220                            IF KEYSW = 0 THEN LET STATUS = 0

1300 REM - IF KEYSWITCH IS ARMED AND TIMER STATE IS EXPIRED
1310 REM -   THEN  SET STATUS
1320                            IF KEYSW <> 0 AND TIMST = 0 THEN LET STATUS = 1

1400 REM - IF FULL INDICATOR SHOWS THAT INPUT RECORD IS FULL
1410 REM -   THEN  SET STATUS TO FULL
1420 REM -   ELSE  SET STATUS TO NOT FULL
1430                            IF FINDR = 0 THEN STATUS = 1 ELSE STATUS = 0
```

Some versions of BASIC do not permit the use of the ELSE part of the test construct. The use of *jump* or GOTO instructions must then be used to permit the complete IF . . . THEN . . . ELSE . . . construct to be implemented, as shown on page 301.

```
1500 REM - IF FULL INDICATOR SHOWS THAT INPUT RECORD IS FULL
1510                                               IF FINDR = 10 THEN GOTO 1530
1520                                                 GOTO 1560
1530 REM -    THEN  SET STATUS TO FULL
1540                                                 STATUS = 1
1550                                                 GOTO 1580
1560 REM -    ELSE  SET STATUS TO NOT FULL
1570                                                 STATUS = 0
1580 (NEXT LINE OF PROCEDURE)
```

The example below illustrates the use of the GOTO to implement both the ELSE phrase and the DO . . . END construct.

```
1600 REM - IF CHARACTER CONTAINS A NUMERIC KEY CODE
1610                                               IF CHAR$ >= "0" OR CHAR$ <= "9" THEN GOTO 1630
1620                                                 GOTO 1720
1630 REM -    THEN  DO
1640 REM -             IF STATUS INDICATES INPUT RECORD IS NOT FULL
1650                                               IF STATUS = 0 THEN GOTO 1670
1660                                                 GOTO 1700
1670 REM -               THEN  CALL:  ADD TO INPUT RECORD (CHARACTER;)
1680                                                 CALL ADDREC (CHAR$)
1690                                                 GOTO 1720
1700 REM -               ELSE  CALL:  BEEP (;)
1710                                                 CALL BEEP
1720 REM -          END
1730 (NEXT LINE OF PROCEDURE)
```

The simulating of the DO WHILE . . . END construct using the test construct is illustrated by the examples below.

```
1800 REM - DO WHILE KEYSWITCH IS ARMED
1810                                               IF KEYSW <> 0 THEN GOTO 1830
1820                                                 GOTO 1890
1830 (FIRST LINE OF BLOCK)
  .
  .
  .
1870 REM - END
1880                                                 GOTO 1810
1890 (NEXT LINE OF PROCEDURE)
```

```
2000 REM - DO WHILE KEYSWITCH IS RESET
2010                                               IF KEYSW = 0 THEN GOTO 2030
2020                                                 GOTO 2090
2030 (FIRST LINE OF BLOCK)
  .
  .
  .
2070 REM - END
2080                                               GOTO 2010
2090 (NEXT LINE OF PROCEDURE)
```

In this section we discuss the newest version of FORTRAN known formally as FORTRAN 77. The reader should note that older versions of FORTRAN (FORTRAN II and FORTRAN IV) are not usually distinguished from FORTRAN 77; the generic term FORTRAN is used for all three.

FORTRAN comments are designated if the letter C appears as the first character on a line. Characters 1 through 5 of each line that is not a comment may be used as a label which consists of a number from 1 through 99999. The use of labels in FORTRAN will be illustrated shortly. Character 6 of each line is normally left blank. If, however, a FORTRAN statement contains more characters than can fit onto a single line, then part of the statement can be placed on the next line. To indicate that two or more lines are to be interpreted as a single statement, character 6 of the second and each subsequent line should be a nonblank character.

Many FORTRAN compilers restrict the number of characters in a symbol or name to six or fewer characters. In such a system, many names must be replaced by short mnemonics. Thus, the data structure name CONTROL MATRIX that we use as an example below could be shortened to CNTRLM. If longer names and symbols are permitted, an underscore character is often used to separate the words in a name or symbol, such as in the example CONTROL_MATRIX. We use both conventions in the examples of this section.

Module declarations. FORTRAN is not a modular language in the usual sense that a module consists of a set of procedures that has access to modular data structures. It does permit software to be broken into procedures which are called *subroutines*. The programmer can organize groups of these procedures into modules for design and documentation purposes, but the language itself does not support modularity. Therefore, a modular declaration is not needed.

Data declarations. Many versions of FORTRAN do not require an explicit declaration for data variables. If a variable begins with one of the letters I through N, it is treated as a positive or negative INTEGER. The number of bits used to represent the integer depends on the specific computer and the FORTRAN compiler. A variable beginning with any other letter is treated as a positive or negative REAL number, that is, one which consists of both an integer part and a fractional part, such as the REAL number 25.478. If a FORTRAN compiler allows a data variable to be declared as a *type* other than INTEGER or REAL, then a data declaration is needed.

```
C- OUTPUT PARAMETER:   STATUS
C-
C- NAME              SIZE   TYPE        CONTENTS            NOTES
C- ----              ----   ----        --------            -----
C- STATUS              1    BYTE        FLAG
                                              BYTE STATUS
```

Arrays *must* be declared in FORTRAN.

```
C- DATA STRUCTURE:   RECORD
C-
C- NAME              SIZE   TYPE        CONTENTS            NOTES
C- ----              ----   ----        --------            -----
C- RECORD             10    CHARACTER   NUMERIC CODES
                                              CHARACTER RECORD (10)
```

This declaration defines an array of ten bytes which can only be used for storing character codes. In FORTRAN the index used to specify an element in an array usually ranges from one up to the array size specified in the data declaration. Other sets of index limits can be specified in FORTRAN, but we shall not pursue how to specify them here. Thus, in the example, the elements of the array RECORD are specified by RECORD (1), . . . , RECORD (10).

Another declaration that can be used to define a ten-byte array in some versions of FORTRAN is given by:

```
BYTE RECORD (10)
```

In the latter case, the information stored is not restricted to character codes; any 8-bit value can be stored.

FORTRAN arrays can be two- or three-dimensional so that they can store information in matrix form.

```
C- DATA STRUCTURE:   CONTROL MATRIX
C-
C- NAME              SIZE   TYPE        CONTENTS            NOTES
C- ----              ----   ----        --------            -----
C- CONTROL MATRIX    10x2   INTEGER     ENGINE PARAMETERS
                                              INTEGER CONTROL_MATRIX (10,2)
```

Data declarations with initialization.

```
C- DATA STRUCTURE:   CONTROL MATRIX
C-
C- NAME              SIZE   TYPE        CONTENTS            NOTES
C- ----              ----   ----        --------            -----
C- CONTROL MATRIX    10x2   INTEGER     ENGINE PARAMETERS
                          INTEGER CONTROL_MATRIX (10,2)
                          DATA CONTROL_MATRIX /110,115,125,140,160,176,188,198,206,210,
2                               217,222,234,238,251,263,271,284,289,295/
```

Note that the number 2 (bottom, left in the previous program) is the sixth character of the second line of the DATA statement in the above example. It indicates that the two lines comprise a single FORTRAN statement, as described earlier.

Procedure declarations.

```
C- PROCEDURE:   BEEP (;)
                                                        SUBROUTINE BEEP
                    .
                    .
                    .
C- END PROCEDURE
                                                        END
```

Procedure declarations with input parameters.

```
C- PROCEDURE:   ADD TO INPUT RECORD (CHARACTER;)
                                                        SUBROUTINE ADDREC (CHR)
                    .
                    .
                    .
C- END PROCEDURE
                                                        END
```

Procedure declarations with output parameters. A procedure with a single output parameter can be implemented using the FUNCTION procedure in FORTRAN, as shown in the example below.

```
C- PROCEDURE:   TEST IF INPUT RECORD FULL (;STATUS)
                                                        FUNCTION TSTFUL
                                                        INTEGER TSTFUL
        .                                                   .
        .                                                   .
        .                                                   .
                                                        TSTFUL = STATUS
                                                        RETURN
                                                            .
                                                            .
                                                            .
C- END PROCEDURE
                                                        END
```

In a FUNCTION procedure, the name of the procedure must be declared as a FORTRAN variable. This variable must also be set to the desired output parameter value before the execution of the procedure is terminated. The data declaration for the output parameter, STATUS, which is an internal parameter in a FORTRAN FUNCTION procedure, is not shown. We have shown how STATUS is used to set the variable TSTFUL.

FORTRAN does not differentiate between input and output parameters in a SUBROUTINE procedure. Thus, a procedure with more than one output parameter can be implemented using the SUBROUTINE declaration, as shown below.

```
C- PROCEDURE:  INPUT OUTPUT EXAMPLE (INPUT;OUTPUT1,OUTPUT2)
                                              SUBROUTINE INOUTX (INPUT,OUTPT1,OUTPT2)
C- **********************************************************************
C- INPUT PARAMETER:  INPUT
C-
C- NAME               SIZE   TYPE        CONTENTS          NOTES
C- ----               ----   ----        --------          -----
C- INPUT               1     CHARACTER   NUMERIC CODES
                                                CHARACTER INPUT
C-
C- OUTPUT PARAMETERS:  OUTPUT1,OUTPUT2
C-
C- NAME               SIZE   TYPE        CONTENTS          NOTES
C- ----               ----   ----        --------          -----
C- OUTPUT1             1     CHARACTER   NUMERIC CODES
C- OUTPUT2             1     INTEGER     NUMERIC VALUE
                                                CHARACTER OUTPT1
                                                INTEGER OUTPT2
```

When the SUBROUTINE procedure INOUTX is called in FORTRAN, pointers to the variables specified in the calling procedure are sent to the called procedure. These pointers equate the variables, INPUT, OUTPT1, and OUTPT2, to the variables specified in the calling procedure. Therefore, by varying OUTPT1 and OUTPT2, the related data in the calling procedure is varied. Thus, information contained in more than one output parameter can be returned to a calling procedure in FORTRAN. Note that if the value of an input parameter is changed in the called procedure, the related information in the calling procedure is also changed. Thus, if the value of an input parameter is to be manipulated in the called procedure, it should first be copied into a local parameter to prevent a potential error condition.

Procedure declarations with data structures as input or output parameters. FORTRAN permits an array to be passed between two procedures as easily as a single input or output parameter. For consistency, the array must be declared both in the calling procedure and in the called procedure. The example below illustrates a procedure declaration for passing an array into a procedure as an input parameter. Since the FORTRAN calling convention for a SUBROUTINE procedure does not distinguish between input and output parameters, output parameters that are arrays are treated in the same manner.

```
C- PROCEDURE:  PRINT (RECORD;)
                                    SUBROUTINE PRINT (RECORD)
```

In FORTRAN, information in a data structure which is defined in one procedure can be made available to other procedures without passing it as a parameter. This can be done by using a COMMON declaration in addition to the data declaration. This technique permits a data structure to be manipulated as if it were a modular data structure. But since FORTRAN does not support modularity, the programmer, rather than the compiler, is responsible for restricting access to a data structure when using the FORTRAN COMMON declaration. The design language modular data structure definition helps the programmer to control access to a *modular* data structure when using FORTRAN.

```
C- PROCEDURE:  CLEAR INPUT RECORD (;)
C- ****************************************************************************
C- MODULAR DATA STRUCTURE:  INPUT RECORD
C-
C- NAME                SIZE    TYPE        CONTENTS            NOTES
C- ----                ----    ----        --------            -----
C- INPUT RECORD         10     BYTE        NUMERIC CODES
                                                 BYTE INPUT_RECORD (10)
C-   FULL INDICATOR      1     BYTE        COUNTER
                                                 BYTE FULL_INDICATOR
                                                 COMMON /INPUT_RECORD/ INPUT_RECORD,FULL_INDICATOR
C- ****************************************************************************
C- BEGIN PROCEDURE
C-   DO FOR EACH ELEMENT IN INPUT RECORD
C-     SET ELEMENT TO 'ZERO' CODE
                                                 INPUT_RECORD (INDEX) = '0'
C-   END
C-   SET FULL INDICATOR TO EMPTY
                                                 FULL_INDICATOR = 0
C-   RETURN
C- END PROCEDURE


C- PROCEDURE:  TEST IF INPUT RECORD FULL (;STATUS)
C- ****************************************************************************
C- MODULAR DATA STRUCTURE:  INPUT RECORD
C-
C- NAME                SIZE    TYPE        CONTENTS            NOTES
C- ----                ----    ----        --------            -----
C- INPUT RECORD         10     BYTE        NUMERIC CODES
                                                 BYTE INPUT_RECORD (10)
C-   FULL INDICATOR      1     BYTE        COUNTER
                                                 BYTE FULL_INDICATOR
                                                 COMMON /INPUT_RECORD/ INPUT_RECORD,FULL_INDICATOR
                              .
                              .
                              .
```

Control constructs.

```
C-      CALL:  STOP TIMER (;)
                                                  CALL STOP_TIMER

C-      CALL:  ADD TO INPUT RECORD (CHARACTER;)
                                                  CALL ADDREC (CHR)

C-      CALL:  TEST IF INPUT RECORD FULL (;STATUS)
                                                  STATUS = TSTFUL

C-      CALL  INPUT OUTPUT EXAMPLE (INPUT;OUTPUT1,OUTPUT2)
                                                  CALL INOUTX (INPUT,OUTPT1,OUTPT2)

C-      RETURN
                                                  RETURN
```

Assignment constructs.

```
C-      SET STATUS TO FULL
                                                  STATUS = 1

C-      SET STATUS TO NOT FULL
                                                  STATUS = 0

C-      SET CONTINUOUS
                                                  CONTINUOUS = 1

C-      RESET CONTINUOUS

C-      SET TIME TO SECONDS
                                                  TIME = 3600*HOURS + 60*MINUTES + SECONDS
```

Loop constructs. There are no DO . . . END or DO WHILE . . . END type constructs in FORTRAN. The equivalent of the DO . . . END construct in a test construct is provided by the THEN and ELSE constructs along with an ENDIF construct. The DO WHILE . . . END construct can be simulated using a test construct with a *jump* or GOTO instruction. Examples of these two constructs are provided in the section on test constructs. The DO FOR EACH . . . END and the DO FOREVER . . . END constructs are shown on page 308.

```
C- DO FOR EACH SWITCH
                                          DO 100 INDEX = 1,5
         .
         .
         .
C- END
100                                       CONTINUE
```

As illustrated, a label (100 in the example) is used to designate the end of a DO FOR EACH. . . END loop in FORTRAN. The FORTRAN CONTINUE construct causes no action to be taken; it is used with a label to designate a specific location in a procedure.

```
C- DO FOREVER
200                                       CONTINUE
         .
         .
         .
C- END
                                          GOTO 200
```

Test constructs. The relational and logical operators used in the test constructs in FORTRAN are listed in the table below.

Operator	Interpretation
.EQ.	is equal to
.LT.	is less than
.GT.	is greater than
.LE.	is less than or equal to
.GE.	is greater than or equal to
.NE.	is not equal to
.NOT.	not
.AND.	and
.OR.	or

```
C-   IF KEYSWITCH IS ARMED
                                          IF (KEYSW.NE.0) THEN
C-      THEN  SET STATUS
                                              STATUS = 1
                                            ENDIF

C-   IF KEYSWITCH IS RESET
                                          IF (KEYSW.EQ.0) THEN
C-      THEN  DO
C-               RESET STATUS
                                              STATUS = 0
C-               RETURN
                                              RETURN
C-            END
                                            ENDIF
```

Since FORTRAN has no DO . . . END construct, the THEN and ENDIF define a set of *brackets* which perform the DO . . . END function for the IF . . . THEN test construct. When the IF . . . THEN . . . construct is used in FORTRAN, an ENDIF construct is needed even if only a single operation follows the THEN, as shown in the first example above. An alternate FORTRAN construct can be used to implement an IF . . . THEN test construct in which a single operation follows the THEN, as shown in the first example below.

```
C-    IF KEYSWITCH IS ARMED
C-      THEN  SET STATUS
                                                   IF (KEYSW.NE.0) STATUS = 1


C-    IF FULL INDICATOR SHOWS THAT INPUT RECORD IS FULL
                                                   IF (FINDR.EQ.10) THEN
C-      THEN  SET STATUS TO FULL
                                                       STATUS = 1
C-      ELSE  SET STATUS TO NOT FULL
                                                     ELSE
                                                       STATUS = 0
                                                     ENDIF
```

In the IF . . . THEN . . . ELSE . . . test construct, the THEN and ELSE define a set of *brackets* for the THEN part of the test construct and the ELSE and ENDIF define a set of *brackets* for the ELSE part of the test construct. The THEN, ELSE, ENDIF *brackets* are necessary even if DO . . . END *brackets* are not used in design language as illustrated in the example above.

```
C-    IF CHARACTER CONTAINS A NUMERIC KEY CODE
C-      THEN  DO
                                                   IF (CHR.GE.'0'.AND.CHR.LE.'9') THEN
C-                IF STATUS INDICATES INPUT RECORD IS NOT FULL
                                                       IF (STATUS.EQ.0) THEN
C-                  THEN  CALL: ADD TO INPUT RECORD (CHARACTER;)
                                                         CALL ADDREC (CHR)
C-                  ELSE  CALL: BEEP (;)
                                                       ELSE
                                                         CALL BEEP
                                                       ENDIF
C-            END
                                                     ENDIF
```

The simulation of the DO WHILE . . . END construct using the test construct is illustrated by the following examples.

```
C-    DO WHILE KEYSWITCH IS ARMED
300                                    IF (KEYSW.NE.0) GOTO 320
310                                      GOTO 400
320 (FIRST LINE OF BLOCK)
          .
          .
          .
C-    END
                                         GOTO 300
400                                      CONTINUE


C-    DO WHILE KEYSWITCH IS RESET
500                                    IF (KEYSW.EQ.0) GOTO 520
510                                      GOTO 600
520 (FIRST LINE OF BLOCK)
          .
          .
          .
C-    END
                                         GOTO 500
600                                      CONTINUE
```

PASCAL

PASCAL comments are designated by the use of the curly brackets { and }. Although there are usually no restrictions on the number of characters in a symbol or name, only the first eight characters are significant in some versions of PASCAL and should therefore be made unique. Although PASCAL compilers do not differentiate between upper- and lower-case characters, some *standards* have been adopted by PASCAL users. For uniformity, we shall use upper-case characters for design language constructs and for most PASCAL keywords, such as the PASCAL keyword PROCEDURE. For PASCAL names, we shall use lower-case characters except for the first character in each word of the name. Thus, the design language name, MAINTAIN INPUT RECORD, is converted into the PASCAL name MaintainInputRecord. Symbols are treated in the same manner as names, except that the first character is a lower-case character. For example, the design language symbol, INPUT RECORD, is converted into the PASCAL symbol, inputRecord.

In PL/M, a semicolon is needed to *terminate* each construct. In PASCAL, the semicolon is used as needed to *separate* constructs rather than to terminate them. Thus, when the design language test construct

```
IF
  THEN  DO


        END
  ELSE
```

is converted into PASCAL, it is incorrect to place a semicolon after the PASCAL construct corresponding to the END in design language. A semicolon at that point would cause the ELSE part to be considered a separate construct by the compiler and may not make sense. It should be noted that, in some cases, the presence of a semicolon is optional and causes no difficulty for the compiler. In our examples, semicolons are inserted only where they are required or where there is a high likelihood that they will be required by context. Otherwise, they are omitted. The reader should refer to one of the PASCAL texts or manuals listed in the bibliography for a description of the syntax of PASCAL and a detailed explanation of the use of semicolons in a PASCAL program.

Module declarations.

```
{MODULE: EXECUTIVE                                          }
                                     PROGRAM Executive;
       .
       .
       .
{END MODULE                                                 }
                                     END.
```

Note that the END associated with a module must be followed by a period.

In standard PASCAL only a single module or PASCAL PROGRAM is possible. However, PASCAL-80 for the Intel 8085 microcomputer permits separate modules to be designed and compiled and the resulting object modules to be linked together into a software system. Furthermore, the Intel system permits PASCAL, PL/M, and FORTRAN object modules to be linked together since the same calling conventions are used for each language by the Intel compilers. To distinguish it from the single module PROGRAM, the module declaration for the EXECUTIVE module for a multiple module system takes the form shown below.

```
{MODULE: EXECUTIVE                                          }
                                     PARTITIONED PROGRAM Executive;
       .
       .
       .
{END MODULE                                                 }
                                     END.
```

The module declarations for the remaining modules then take the form:

```
{MODULE:  MAINTAIN INPUT RECORD                                        }
                                          COMPONENT MaintainInputRecord;
            .
            .
            .
{END MODULE                                                            }
                                          END.
```

Data declarations.

```
{OUTPUT PARAMETER:  STATUS                                             }
{                                                                      }
{NAME              SIZE    TYPE        CONTENTS              NOTES     }
{----              ----    ----        --------              -----     }
{STATUS              1     INTEGER     FLAG                            }
                                          VAR status:  integer;
```

```
{MODULAR DATA STRUCTURE:  INPUT RECORD                                 }
{                                                                      }
{NAME              SIZE    TYPE        CONTENTS              NOTES     }
{----              ----    ----        --------              -----     }
{INPUT RECORD       10     CHARACTER   NUMERIC CODES                   }
                                          VAR inputRecord:  ARRAY [1..10] OF char;
```

The specification [1. .10] in the example indicates that the index used to specify the elements of the array ranges from one to ten. Any range can be specified in a PASCAL declaration. Thus,

```
VAR inputRecord:  ARRAY [−5..5] OF char;
```

declares that inputRecord contains eleven character codes and that the elements of the data structure in the latter example are specified by inputRecord (−5), . . . , inputRecord (0), . . . , inputRecord (5).

PASCAL arrays can be multidimensional so that information can be stored in matrix form.

```
{DATA STRUCTURE:  CONTROL MATRIX                                       }
{                                                                      }
{NAME              SIZE    TYPE        CONTENTS              NOTES     }
{----              ----    ----        --------              -----     }
{CONTROL MATRIX    10x2    INTEGER     ENGINE PARAMETERS               }
                              VAR controlMatrix:  ARRAY [1..10,1..2] OF integer;
```

Data declarations with initialization. PASCAL does not provide a simple way to initialize a complete data structure. A separate assignment construct must be used to initialize each element of an array, as shown on page 313.

```
{DATA STRUCTURE:  CONTROL MATRIX                                               }
{                                                                              }
{NAME                SIZE    TYPE          CONTENTS                  NOTES     }
{----                ----    ----          --------                  -----     }
{CONTROL MATRIX      10x2    INTEGER       ENGINE PARAMETERS                   }
                                        VAR controlMatrix: ARRAY [1..10,1..2] OF integer;
                                            .
                                            .
                                            .
                                        BEGIN
                                               controlMatrix [1,1] := 5;
                                               controlMatrix [1,2] := 3;
                                               controlMatrix [2,1] := 7;
                                               controlMatrix [10,2] := 4;
                                            .
                                            .
                                            .
```

Procedure declarations.

```
{PROCEDURE:  CLEAR INPUT RECORD (;)                                            }
                                                 PROCEDURE ClearInputRecord;
{******************************************************************************}
{BEGIN PROCEDURE                                                               }
                                                 BEGIN
        .
        .
        .
{END PROCEDURE                                                                 }
                                                 END;
```

Procedure declarations with input parameters.

```
{PROCEDURE:  ADD TO INPUT RECORD (CHARACTER;)                                  }
{******************************************************************************}
{INPUT PARAMETER:  CHARACTER                                                   }
{                                                                              }
{NAME                SIZE    TYPE          CONTENTS                  NOTES     }
{----                ----    ----          --------                  -----     }
{CHARACTER             1     CHARACTER     NUMERIC CODES                       }
                                        PROCEDURE AddToInputRecord (character: char);
{******************************************************************************}
{BEGIN PROCEDURE                                                               }
                                        BEGIN
        .
        .
        .
{END PROCEDURE                                                                 }
                                        END;
```

In PASCAL the data declaration for an input parameter to a procedure is combined with the procedure declaration for that procedure, as illustrated above. A separate declaration for the input parameter, CHARACTER, is not needed.

Procedure declarations with output parameters. A procedure with a single output parameter can be implemented using the FUNCTION procedure in PASCAL, as shown in the example below.

```
{PROCEDURE: TEST IF INPUT RECORD FULL (;STATUS)                    }
                                         FUNCTION TestIfInputRecordFull: integer;
{******************************************************************}
{BEGIN PROCEDURE                                                   }
                                         BEGIN
                                            .
                                            .
                                            .
                                            TestIfInputRecordFull := status;
                                            .
                                            .
                                            .
{END PROCEDURE                                                     }
                                         END;
```

For a FUNCTION procedure, the name of the procedure is automatically declared as a PASCAL variable (an integer in the above example) by the procedure declaration. This variable must be set to the desired output parameter value before the execution of the procedure is terminated. The data declaration for the output parameter, STATUS, which is a local parameter in PASCAL, is not shown. We have shown how STATUS is used to set the PASCAL variable TestIfInputRecordFull.

An example of a PASCAL FUNCTION procedure with an input parameter is shown below.

```
{PROCEDURE: SEARCH (SEARCH KEY; MATCH)                             }
{******************************************************************}
{INPUT PARAMETER: SEARCH KEY                                       }
{                                                                  }
{NAME            SIZE   TYPE       CONTENTS              NOTES     }
{----            ----   ----       --------              -----     }
{SEARCH KEY        1    INTEGER    NUMERIC KEY                     }
                                   FUNCTION Search (searchKey: integer): integer;
{******************************************************************}
{BEGIN PROCEDURE                                                   }
                                   BEGIN
                                      .
                                      .
                                      .
                                   Search := match;
          .                           .
          .                           .
          .                           .
{END PROCEDURE                                                     }
                                   END;
```

As in the previous example, we have omitted the data declaration for the output parameter, MATCH, which is a local parameter in PASCAL. We have shown how MATCH is used to set the PASCAL variable Search.

A procedure with more than one output parameter can be implemented using the PROCEDURE declaration and declaring the output parameters with the construct VAR, as shown below.

```
{PROCEDURE: INPUT OUTPUT EXAMPLE (INPUT;OUTPUT1,OUTPUT2)              }
{*********************************************************************}
{INPUT PARAMETER: INPUT                                               }
{                                                                     }
{NAME              SIZE   TYPE        CONTENTS              NOTES    }
{----              ----   ----        --------              -----    }
{INPUT               1    CHARACTER   NUMERIC CODES                   }
{                                                                     }
{OUTPUT PARAMETERS: OUTPUT1,OUTPUT2                                   }
{                                                                     }
{NAME              SIZE   TYPE        CONTENTS              NOTES    }
{----              ----   ----        --------              -----    }
{OUTPUT1             1    CHARACTER   NUMERIC CODES                   }
{OUTPUT2             1    INTEGER     NUMERIC CODES                   }
                        PROCEDURE InputOutputExample (input: char; VAR output1: char;
                                                       VAR output2: integer);
```

In the example, when the procedure InputOutputExample is called, the value of the input parameter is copied from the specified variable in the calling procedures to the variable, input, in the called procedure. Modifying the variable, input, within the called procedure therefore does not affect the value of the variable in the calling procedure. Since the construct VAR is used for the two output parameters, pointers to the variables specified in the calling procedure are sent to the called procedure. These pointers equate the variables, output1 and output2, to the variables specified in the calling procedure. Therefore, by varying output1 and output2, the related data in the calling procedure is varied. Thus, information contained in more than one output parameter can be returned to a calling procedure in PASCAL.

Procedure declarations with data structures as input or output parameters.

```
{PROCEDURE: PRINT (INPUT RECORD;)                                     }
{*********************************************************************}
{INPUT PARAMETER: INPUT RECORD                                        }
{                                                                     }
{NAME              SIZE   TYPE        CONTENTS              NOTES    }
{----              ----   ----        --------              -----    }
{INPUT RECORD       10    CHARACTER   NUMERIC CODES                   }
                        PROCEDURE Print (VAR inputRecord: ARRAY [1..10] OF char);
```

The example illustrates passing an array into a procedure as an input parameter. Since the calling convention for a PASCAL PROCEDURE using the VAR data declaration does not distinguish between input parameters and output parameters, output parameters that are arrays can be treated in the same manner.

Procedure declarations for a multiple module system. In a system composed of multiple modules the procedure declarations for the procedures in the COMPONENT modules called by procedures in other modules take the following form:

```
{PROCEDURE: CLEAR INPUT RECORD (;)                              }
                                   SEGMENT PROCEDURE ClearInputRecord;
```

An external procedure declaration is also needed for each SEGMENT PROCEDURE in every module containing a procedure that calls that SEGMENT PROCEDURE. The PASCAL-80 external procedure declaration takes the form shown below.

```
                                   SEGMENT PROCEDURE ClearInputRecord;
                                   SEPARATE;
```

Control constructs.

```
{CALL: STOP TIMER (;)                                      }
                                        StopTimer;

{CALL: ADD TO INPUT RECORD (CHARACTER;)                    }
                                        AddToInputRecord (character);

{CALL: TEST IF INPUT RECORD FULL (;STATUS)                 }
                                        status := TestIfInputRecordFull;
```

There is no RETURN construct in PASCAL. The execution of a procedure terminates when the END construct corresponding to END PROCEDURE is reached. Thus, it is necessary to ensure that all paths in a procedure terminate at the end of the procedure. The GOTO construct can be used for this purpose, as illustrated below in the WAIT FOR KEYSWITCH ARMED procedure. In the example we have converted only the pertinent design language constructs into PASCAL.

```
{PROCEDURE: WAIT FOR KEYSWITCH ARMED (;)                         }
{BEGIN PROCEDURE                                                 }
{  DO FOREVER                                                    }
{    CALL: READ KEYSWITCH (;KEYSWITCH)                           }
{    IF KEYSWITCH IS ARMED                                       }
{      THEN  RETURN                                              }
                                              THEN  GOTO 100;
{  END                                                           }
                                              END;
{END PROCEDURE                                                   }
                                         100: END
```

Note that a label is a number which ranges from 1 to 9999 in PASCAL. It must be declared *before* it is used just as variables and data structures are declared in data declarations. The declaration for a PASCAL label takes the form:

```
LABEL 100;
```

As an alternative to the GOTO construct, procedures may be designed so that all paths lead directly to the end of the procedure. As an example of the latter approach, the alternate version of the WAIT FOR KEYSWITCH ARMED procedure of Figure 4-11 is shown below in design language. Since the RETURN construct immediately precedes the END PROCEDURE construct, it does not have to be converted into a PASCAL construct for the procedure to execute correctly. Converting this procedure into PASCAL is then straightforward; it is left as an exercise for the reader to do later since we have not yet described how to convert loop and test constructs.

```
PROCEDURE: WAIT FOR KEYSWITCH ARMED (;)
BEGIN PROCEDURE
  CALL: READ KEYSWITCH (;KEYSWITCH)
  DO WHILE KEYSWITCH IS RESET
    CALL: READ KEYSWITCH (;KEYSWITCH)
  END
  RETURN
END PROCEDURE
```

Assignment constructs.

```
{SET STATUS TO FULL                                         }
                                       status := 1;


{SET STATUS TO NOT FULL                                     }
                                       status := 0;


{SET CONTINUOUS                                             }
                                       continuous := 1;


{RESET CONTINUOUS                                           }
                                       continuous := 0;


{SET TIME TO SECONDS                                        }
                                       time := 3600 * hours + 60 * minutes + seconds;
```

Loop constructs.

```
{DO                                                              }
                                            BEGIN
        .
        .
        .
{END                                                             }
                                            END;


{DO WHILE KEYSWITCH IS ARMED                                     }
                                            WHILE keyswitch <> 0 DO
                                              BEGIN
        .
        .
        .
{END                                                             }
                                              END;
```

If a single construct is contained within the DO WHILE . . . END construct, the PASCAL BEGIN . . . END construct may be omitted, as illustrated below.

```
{DO WHILE KEYSWITCH IS RESET                                     }
                                            WHILE keyswitch = 0 DO
{  CALL: READ KEYSWITCH (;KEYSWITCH)                             }
                                              keyswitch := ReadKeyswitch
{END                                                             }


{DO FOR EACH SWITCH                                              }
                                            FOR index := 1 TO 5 DO
                                              BEGIN
        .
        .
        .
{END                                                             }
                                              END;
```

As in the above example, if a single construct is contained within the DO FOR EACH . . . END construct, the BEGIN . . . END construct may be omitted.

```
{DO FOREVER                                                        }
                                              WHILE 1 = 1 DO
                                                BEGIN
  .
  .
  .
{END                                                               }
                                                END;
```

In PASCAL, the DO FOREVER . . . END construct can always be used in an EXECUTIVE procedure which has no RETURN construct. It can be used in other procedures if a GOTO construct is used as illustrated earlier in this section. If the use of the GOTO construct is undesirable, then the DO FOREVER . . . END construct should be replaced by alternate constructs such as the DO WHILE . . . END construct.

Test constructs.

```
{IF KEYSWITCH IS ARMED                                                }
                                         IF keyswitch <> 0
{  THEN  SET STATUS                                                   }
                                           THEN  status := 1;


{IF KEYSWITCH IS RESET                                                }
                                         IF keyswitch = 0
{  THEN  RESET STATUS                                                 }
                                           THEN  status := 0;


{IF KEYSWITCH IS ARMED AND TIMER STATE IS EXPIRED                     }
                                         IF (keyswitch <> 0) AND (timerState = 0)
{  THEN  SET STATUS                                                   }
                                           THEN  status := 1;


{IF FULL INDICATOR SHOWS THAT INPUT RECORD IS FULL                    }
                                         IF fullIndicator = 10
{  THEN  SET STATUS TO FULL                                           }
                                           THEN  status := 1;
{  ELSE  SET STATUS TO NOT FULL                                       }
                                           ELSE  status := 0;
```

```
{IF CHARACTER CONTAINS A NUMERIC KEY CODE                         }
                                    IF (character >= '0') AND (character <= '9')
{  THEN  DO                                                       }
                                      THEN  BEGIN
{          IF STATUS INDICATES INPUT RECORD IS NOT FULL           }
                                               IF status = 0
{            THEN  CALL: ADD TO INPUT RECORD CHARACTER;)          }
                                                 THEN  AddToInputRecord (character)
{            ELSE  CALL: BEEP(;)                                  }
                                                 ELSE  Beep;
{         END                                                     }
                                           END;
```

Note that the semicolon following ELSE Beep is optional and may be omitted.

Bibliography

This bibliography contains a selected list of books and manuals for further reading.

MICROPROCESSORS/MICROCOMPUTERS—GENERAL

AUMIAUX, M. *The Use of Microprocessors.* New York: John Wiley, 1980.

BARNA, A., AND D. I. PORAT. *Introduction to Microcomputers and Microprocessors.* New York: John Wiley, 1976.

COOPER, J. A. *Microprocessor Background for Management Personnel.* Englewood Cliffs, N.J.: Prentice-Hall, 1981.

GARLAND, H. *Introduction to Microprocessor System Design.* New York: McGraw-Hill, 1979.

GIBSON, G. A., AND Y. C. LIU. *Microcomputers for Engineers and Scientists.* Englewood Cliffs, N.J.: Prentice-Hall, 1980.

GIVONE, D. D., AND R. P. ROESSER. *Microprocessors/Microcomputers—An Introduction.* New York: McGraw-Hill, 1980.

GREENFIELD, J. D., AND W. C. WRAY. *Using Microprocessors and Microcomputers: The 6800 Family.* New York: John Wiley, 1981.

GRILLO, J. P., AND J. D. ROBERTSON. *Microcomputer Systems—an applications approach.* Dubuque, Iowa: Wm. C. Brown, 1979.

KLINGMAN, E. E. *Microprocessor Systems Design.* Englewood Cliffs, N.J.: Prentice-Hall, 1977.

KORN, G. A. *Microprocessors and Small Digital Computer Systems for Engineers and Scientists.* New York: McGraw-Hill, 1977.

LEE, S. C., ed. *Microcomputer Design and Applications.* New York: Academic Press, 1977.

LENK, J. D. *Handbook of Microprocessors, Microcomputers, and Minicomputers.* Englewood Cliffs, N.J.: Prentice-Hall, 1979.

OGDIN, C. A. *Microcomputer Management and Programming.* Englewood Cliffs, N.J.: Prentice-Hall, 1980.

OLESKY, J. E., AND G. B. RUTKOWSKI. *Microprocessor and Digital Computer Technology.* Englewood Cliffs, N.J.: Prentice-Hall, 1981.

PEATMAN, J. B. *Microcomputer-based Design.* New York: McGraw-Hill, 1977.

SHORT, K. L. *Microprocessors and Programmed Logic.* Englewood Cliffs, N.J.: Prentice-Hall, 1980.

SIPPL, C. J. *Microcomputer Handbook.* New York: Petrocelli/Charter, 1977.

STREITMATTER, G. A., AND V. FIORE. *Microprocessors—Theory and Applications.* Reston, Va.: Reston, 1979.

TOCCI, R. J., AND L. P. LASKOWSKI. *Microprocessors and Microcomputers: Hardware and Software*, 2nd ed. Englewood Cliffs, N.J.: Prentice-Hall, 1982.

WAKERLY, J. F. *Microcomputer Architecture and Programming.* New York: John Wiley, 1981.

REFERENCE DICTIONARY

SIPPL, C. J., AND D. A. KIDD. *Microcomputer Dictionary and Guide.* Champaign, Ill.: Matrix Publishers, 1976.

IMPACT OF COMPUTERS ON SOCIETY

KEMENY, J. G. *Man and the Computer.* New York: Scribner's, 1972.

MONTAGU, A., AND S. S. SNYDER. *Man and the Computer.* Philadelphia, Pa.: Auerbach Publishers, 1972.

WISE, K. D., K. CHEN, AND R. E. YOKELY. *Microcomputers: A Technology Forecast and Assessment to the Year 2000.* New York: John Wiley, 1980.

HUMAN FACTORS

MEADOWS, C. T. *Man–Machine Communication.* New York: John Wiley, 1970.

COMPUTER SCIENCE

KATZAN, H., JR. *Introduction to Computer Science*. New York: Petrocelli/Charter, 1975.

SOFTWARE ENGINEERING

BUCKLE, J. K. *Managing Software Projects*. New York: American Elsevier, 1977.

BROOKS, F. P. *The Mythical Man-Month: Essays on Software Engineering*. Reading, Mass.: Addison-Wesley, 1975.

GOOS, G., AND J. HARTMANIS, eds. *Software Engineering—An Advanced Course*. New York: Springer-Verlag, 1975.

GUNTHER, R. C. *Management Methodology for Software Product Engineering*. New York: John Wiley, 1978.

HUGHES, J. K., AND J. I. MICHTOM. *A Structured Approach to Programming*. Englewood Cliffs, N.J.: Prentice-Hall, 1977.

JACKSON, M. A. *Principles of Program Design*. New York: Academic Press, 1975.

JENSEN, R. W., AND C. C. TONIES. *Software Engineering*. Englewood Cliffs, N.J.: Prentice-Hall, 1979.

LINGER, R. C., H. D. MILLS, AND B. I. WITT. *Structured Programming: Theory and Practice*. Reading, Mass.: Addison-Wesley, 1979.

MAYNARD, J. *Modular Programming*. Philadelphia, Pa.: Auerbach Publishers, 1972.

MCGOWAN, C. L., AND J. R. KELLY. *Top-Down Structured Programming Techniques*. New York: Petrocelli/Charter, 1975.

WIRTH, N. *Systematic Programming: An Introduction*. Englewood Cliffs, N.J.: Prentice-Hall, 1973.

YOURDON, E. *Structured Walkthroughs*, 2nd ed. Englewood Cliffs, N.J.: Prentice-Hall, 1980.

MICROCOMPUTER SOFTWARE

OGDIN, C. A. *Software Design for Microcomputers*. Englewood Cliffs, N.J.: Prentice-Hall, 1978.

PROGRAMMING—PL/M

INTEL CORPORATION. *PL/M Programming Manual*. Santa Clara, Calif.: Intel Corporation.

MCCRACKEN, D. D. *A Guide to PL/M Programming for Microcomputer Applications*. Reading, Mass.: Addison-Wesley, 1978.

COMPUTER ARCHITECTURE

BAER, J. L. *Computer Systems Architecture*. Potomac, Md.: Computer Science Press, 1980.

STONE, H. S., ed. *Introduction to Computer Architecture*, 2nd ed. Chicago: Science Research Associates, 1980.

MICROCOMPUTER ARCHITECTURE

DOTY, K. L. *Fundamental Principles of Microcomputer Architecture*. Beaverton, Oreg.: Matrix Publishers, 1979.

GREENFIELD, S. E. *The Architecture of Microcomputers*. Boston: Little, Brown, 1980.

LIPPIATT, A. G. *The Architecture of Small Computer Systems*. London: Prentice-Hall International, 1978.

PROGRAMMING—ASSEMBLY LANGUAGE

DUNCAN, F. G. *Microprocessor Programming and Software Development*. London: Prentice-Hall International, 1979.

MCGLYNN, D. R. *Modern Microprocessor System Design*. New York: John Wiley, 1980.

INTERFACING MICROCOMPUTERS

ARTWICK, B. *Microcomputer Interfacing*. Englewood Cliffs, N.J.: Prentice-Hall, 1980.

GARRETT, P. H. *Analog Systems for Microprocessors and Minicomputers*. Reston, Va.: Reston, 1978.

LIPOVSKI, G. J. *Microcomputer Interfacing: Principles and Practices*. Lexington, Mass.: Lexington Books, 1980.

OPERATING SYSTEMS

BARRON, D. W. *Computer Operating Systems*. London: Chapman and Hall, 1971.

MICROCOMPUTER OPERATING SYSTEMS

INTEL CORPORATION. *ISIS-II Systems User's Guide*. Santa Clara, Calif.: Intel Corporation.

INTEL CORPORATION. *PL/M-80 Compiler Operator's Manual*. Santa Clara, Calif.: Intel Corporation.

INTEGRATION AND DEBUGGING

BROWN, A. R., AND W. A. SAMPSON. *Program Debugging: The Prevention and Cure of Program Errors*. New York: American Elsevier, 1973.

BRUCE, R. *Software Debugging for Microcomputers*. Reston, Va.: Reston, 1980.

COFFRON, J. W. *Practical Troubleshooting Techniques for Microprocessor Systems*. Englewood Cliffs, N.J.: Prentice-Hall, 1981.

GHANI, N., AND E. FARRELL. *Microprocessor System Debugging*. New York: John Wiley, 1980.

MYERS, G. J. *The Art of Software Testing*. New York: John Wiley, 1979.

MICROCOMPUTER HARDWARE/LOGIC DESIGN

BISHOP, R. *Basic Microprocessors and the 6800*. Rochelle Park, N.J.: Hayden Book Co., 1979.

COFFRON, J. W. *Practical Hardware Details for 8080, 8085, Z80 and 6800 Microprocessor Systems*. Englewood Cliffs, N.J.: Prentice-Hall, 1981.

INTEL CORPORATION. *8085 Microcomputer Systems User's Manual*. Santa Clara, Calif.: Intel Corporation.

INTEL CORPORATION. *Component Data Catalog*. Santa Clara, Calif.: Intel Corporation.

INTEL CORPORATION. *Systems Data Catalog*. Santa Clara, Calif.: Intel Corporation.

KRAFT, G. D., AND W. N. TOY. *Mini/Microcomputer Hardware Design*. Englewood Cliffs, N.J.: Prentice-Hall, 1978.

MANO, M. M. *Digital Logic and Computer Design*. Englewood Cliffs, N.J.: Prentice-Hall, 1979.

PEATMAN, J. B. *Digital Hardware Design*. New York: McGraw-Hill, 1980.

STOUT, D. F., AND M. KAUFMAN. *Handbook of Microcircuit Design and Application*. New York: McGraw-Hill, 1980.

WINKEL, D., AND F. PROSSER. *The Art of Digital Design: An Introduction to Top-Down Design*. Englewood Cliffs, N.J.: Prentice-Hall, 1980.

PERSONAL COMPUTING

BUNNELL, D. *Personal Computing, A Beginner's Guide*. New York: Hawthorn Books, 1978.

FREIBERGER, S. J., AND P. CHEW, JR. *A Consumer's Guide to Personal Computing*. Rochelle Park, N.J.: Hayden Book Co., 1978.

KOFF, R. M. *Home Computers, A Manual of Possibilities*. New York: Harcourt Brace Jovanovich, Inc., 1979.

SOLOMON, L., AND S. VEIT. *Getting Involved with Your Own Computer, A Guide for Beginners*. Short Hills, N.J.: Ridley Enslow Publishers, 1977.

WELLS, B. *Personal Computers: What They Are and How to Use Them.* Englewood Cliffs, N.J.: Trafalgar House Publishers, 1978.

COMPUTERS FOR BUSINESS

SILVER, G. A. *Small Computer Systems for Business.* New York: McGraw-Hill, 1978.

PROGRAMMING—BASIC

ALBRECHT, R. L., L. FINKEL, AND J. R. BROWN. *BASIC*, 2nd ed. New York: John Wiley, 1978.

SASS, C. J. *A Structured Approach to BASIC Programming.* Newton, Mass.: Allyn and Bacon, 1980.

PROGRAMMING—FORTRAN

KATZAN, H., JR. *FORTRAN 77.* New York: Van Nostrand Reinhold, 1978.

PAGE, R., AND R. DIDDAY. *FORTRAN 77 for Humans.* St. Paul, Minn.: West Publishing Co., 1980.

PROGRAMMING—PASCAL

ATKINSON, L. *Pascal Programming.* New York: John Wiley, 1980.

BOWLES, K. L. *Microcomputer Problem Solving Using Pascal.* New York: Springer-Verlag, 1977.

GROGONO, P. *Programming in PASCAL.* Reading, Mass.: Addison-Wesley, 1978.

MOORE, L. *Foundations of Programming with Pascal.* New York: John Wiley, 1980.

WILSON, I. R., AND A. M. ADDYMAN. *A Practical Introduction to Pascal.* New York: Springer-Verlag, 1978.

Index

J

L

M

N

O